Books by Joseph C. Goulden

THE BENCHWARMERS (*1974*)
MEANY (*1972*)
THE SUPERLAWYERS (*1972*)
THE MONEY GIVERS (*1971*)
TRUTH IS THE FIRST CASUALTY (*1969*)
MONOPOLY (*1968*)
THE CURTIS CAPER (*1965*)

THE
Benchwarmers

The Private World of
the Powerful Federal Judges

by Joseph C. Goulden

BALLANTINE BOOKS • NEW YORK

FOR
The fastest curve in the Northeast—
an understanding (if non-judicial) forum.

Library of Congress Catalog Card Number: 74-82978

SBN 345-24852-X-195

This edition published by arrangement with
Weybright and Talley, Inc.

First Printing: February, 1976

Printed in the United States of America

BALLANTINE BOOKS
A Division of Random House, Inc.
201 East 50th Street, New York, N.Y. 10022
Simultaneously published by
Ballantine Books of Canada, Ltd., Toronto, Canada

Contents

THE BENCHWARMERS

Prologue

During the last months of 1973, as I completed work on this book, I maintained a rough log of some of the things United States district court judges were doing around the country:

- In Philadelphia, Judge John Fullam attempted to salvage the bankrupt Penn Central Company, lest its final, total collapse tilt the eastern United States into industrial chaos. Judge Fullam in effect served as the chief policy officer of what had been the nation's largest railroad, with assets of more than $4.5 billion.
- In Washington, Judge John J. Sirica patiently picked his way through the sordid congeries of scandal known as Watergate. Although his procedures brought frequent cries of foul play from civil libertarians, Judge Sirica more than any other single individual "broke" the Watergate case and in doing so brought the Nixon Administration to the brink of ruin.
- In Oklahoma City, Judge Sherman Christiansen entered a $352.5 million antitrust judgement against IBM for predatory marketing practices. Because the decision struck at the very heart of IBM's way of doing business, the company's stock nosedived. Within a few weeks Judge Christiansen reconsidered and lowered the award to $259.5 million. But for uncounted thousands of IBM investors, the damage was already done. A single order by a 68-year-old judge in the Southwest, a man virtually unknown outside his home state's legal community, had caused a four-day blip in the stock market that cleaved the value of IBM shares by an incredible $5.5 billion.
- In Richmond, Virginia, Judge Robert R. Merhige,

Jr., ruled that President Nixon engaged in a "flagrant abuse of executive discretion" by impounding $6 billion in water pollution control funds that had been voted by Congress. The suit was one of more than 30 during 1973 in which a United States District Court judge held that the President could not flout Congressional will on spending—whether an administration likes it or not, there is more to the United States government than the presidency alone.

- In Detroit, Judge Damon Keith held that Hamtramck, a small, mostly Polish-American city completely surrounded by Detroit, used urban renewal as "Negro removal." Keith, a black, directed Hamtramck and the Department of Housing and Urban Development to build low-cost housing in the city for Negroes displaced by urban renewal projects.

- In Pensacola, Florida, Judge Winston Arnow fined CBS Television News $500 because one of its artists sketched from memory four persons involved in a trial in his court. Arnow compared the artist's work with taking photographs through a window with a telephoto lens. CBS lawyers argued that ordering an artist to purge her memory of what she witnessed in court was as ridiculous as attempting to restrict a writer from describing what he saw. (Luckily for the causes of common sense and freedom of the press, the Fifth Circuit Court of Appeals reversed Arnow's capricious order: artists and journalists remain free to describe what they witness in a public court proceeding.)

Enough. The list could be extended nigh indefinitely. The point of it is that United States district judges do damnably important business in our nation. Their decisions affect how we make and spend our money, where our children attend school, our neighborhood living patterns, the quality of the environment around us, how the big national corporations conduct their affairs, how our society punishes its violent and its white-collar criminals.

Nonetheless the 480 district judges toil in virtual anonymity, even though in a practical sense each of them wields more direct power than any number of Congressmen or Senators—or, for that matter, the vice president of the United States. Because the United States Supreme Court speaks with finality (save in instances such as pornography, where it can't make up its collective mind what's dirty and what's permissible) the public tends to identify the federal judiciary with the learned justices of this court. The district courts are dismissed as the bush leagues of law, run by jurists whose decisions don't really matter because they can always be reversed. That this is so is a pity, for the district judges are the shock troops of the judiciary. As courts of first resort they have initial contact with the cases that so frequently evolve into momentous decisions by the Supreme Court.

So why is it that a district judge is seldom known outside his home district? That what local reputation he has is generally confined to lawyers? One episode is illustrative: early in research for this book I began asking trial lawyers and legal scholars to rank the five outstanding district judges in the country. After mulling the idea, few would attempt to do so, even though they knew judges in virtually every district. As a professor at a District of Columbia law school saw the situation: "A judge has a 'national' reputation only if he lucks into a well-publicized case, and doesn't flub it. He might put a gloss on his standing with the legal academics by writing for law reviews. But just what is a 'great' judge? The toughest cases, the ones that are the hardest to handle, could be on an obscure issue of patent law that no one gives a hang about. When you talk about 'great' the civil rights people will point to a guy like Frank Johnson in Alabama, who stood up to George Wallace when that was neither popular nor safe. The strict constructionists—that's a nice, polite Southern term for 'segregationist,' you know—they'll admire a judge like old Harold Cox of Mississippi, who just loves to give the Justice Department unmitigated hell in school and voting cases.

"Same thing in the business field. If a lawyer wins a case, he's going to think nice things about the judge. If he loses, wow, what a bum on the bench. What I'm saying, in a rather rambling way, is that judicial ability is in the eye of the beholder."

Said another man, a Chicago trial lawyer: "My impulse is to say that the most famous trial judge on the federal bench is Charles Wyzanski of Boston. But I'll bet you could stop a hundred people on Boston Common and not more than one or two would have heard of him. Except, of course, if you happened to hit a couple of lawyers."

A few months later I told this story to Chief Judge David N. Edelstein, of the Southern District of New York, easily the most prestigious district court in the country, both in terms of judicial caliber and in importance of cases. "Hell," Edelstein retorted, "we could run the same test right here with the same results." He gestured to the street outside the small Italian restaurant where we were eating lunch, a place hard by the soaring federal courthouse on Foley Square. "Go out there and stand in Foley Square and ask the first twenty people who David Edelstein is, and not one of them will know—*including* any lawyers you might stop. Yes, we do our work in a public vacuum."

The anonymity is largely of the judges' making, which is why I put Judge Winston Arnow's contempt action against the CBS artist on my what's-happening list at the start of this chapter. The Arnow episode by itself was a triviality, and one quickly set to rights by the Fifth Circuit Court of Appeals.* But the action of this jackanape Floridian does typify, if in somewhat gross form, an arrogance that is pervasive among far too many federal judges. A substantial number of the judges—a majority, I concluded after months of mingling with them—think the courts of our land are no one's business but their own, and they actively discourage snooping by outsiders. The judges foster the notion that they are a class apart from the rest of us, members of a brotherhood whose rites are too arcane to be discussed in public. "Judges are regarded by the public as the custodians of a special body of knowl-

---

* The eleven circuit courts are an intermediate appellate level between the district courts and the Supreme Court.

edge," remarks Simon Rifkind, a federal judge in New York for a decade, now in private practice again. "In a way they are viewed like the Egyptian priests who are believed to have held within their bosoms the secret of life." Judge John J. Biggs, Jr., of Wilmington, Delaware, relates that when he was appointed to the Third Circuit Court of Appeals in the 1930s his friend H. L. Mencken told him, "John, I want you to remember that a judge is a law student who corrects his own papers." Few judges heed such advice; they behave as if they were anointed, not appointed. Judge Biggs, who delights in telling the Mencken story, himself is endowed with a mammoth ego: one Philadelphia lawyer calls him "the biggest bore on the Eastern seaboard, and I include Congress."

Judicial arrogance derives from the fact that a federal judge is truly a powerful character. He towers above state judges in professional prestige, in salary in most instances (a district judge earns $40,000 a year; 32 states pay their trial judges less than $30,000 and eight of them a maximum of less than $23,000), and, with a few exceptions that shall be noted, in the importance of cases they hear. The federal judge is also generally assumed to give a fairer shake to persons in his court:

> The United States courts are further above mere local influence than the county courts; their judges can act wtih more independence; cannot be put under terror, as local judges can; their sympathies are not so nearly identified with those of the vicinage. . . . We believe we can trust our United States courts, and we propose to do so.

The words are those of a congressman of the 1870s, arguing that reconstruction statutes be enforceable in the federal courts, not the state courts. A century later, most lawyers are more comfortable when they can maneuver a case into one of the 92 district courts in the United States (which have from one judge in the state of Maine to 26 judges in the Southern District of New York, which covers Manhattan and 26 counties to the north and west of New York City). Statutory law severely limits the kinds of cases that can be put into a federal court. Civil actions, which in most instances must involve $10,000 or more, are of two types: diversity of citizenship (a Virginia motorist runs over a Maryland citizen in Delaware); or a dispute that "arises under the Constitution, laws, or treaties of the United States." * The monetary limit does not apply when the alleged wrong involves deprivation of personal liberty. Chief Justice Warren Burger, who would like to cleave federal jurisdiction drastically, tells time and again of a suit brought by a state prisoner who claimed a guard took seven packages of cigarettes from him without justification, and sued. The district judge, Burger says, "plaintively asked if he could dispose of the whole lawsuit by sending the prisoner $3 or seven packages of cigarettes." In the criminal area the federal courts deal with offenses covered by federal statutes ranging from bank robbery to interstate transport of a stolen auto. The federal judges *are* plagued with picayune issues; nonetheless, on any given day they deal with cases of more importance—and more national significance—than the state judges.

Further, the federal judge has lifetime tenure (barring impeachable conduct, and none has been so cashiered since 1936). The federal judge, unlike the president and the Congress, need not face a periodic rendezvous with the electorate. Aside from personal pride and peer pressure, no force on earth can compel a federal judge to work if he chooses to loaf. He can carouse, gamble, harangue people in his court, and chew tobacco on the bench. He can deal in real estate and stocks and bonds (but must disqualify himself if any cases in which he has a financial interest come before his court). He can spend as little time as he wishes in court. If a federal judge decides his court will operate from 11 A.M. to 2 P.M. daily, four weeks a year, so be it, and no posse exists that can compel him to labor an hour longer. Nor can the public determine the identity of the loafers other than by per-

---

* Admiralty cases are an exception; see Chapter Two, "When the System Works I: Watching Wall Street."

sonal observation of each of the 480 judges. The Administrative Office of the United States Court, the housekeeping agency for the federal judiciary, compiles monthly statistics of how many cases each judge handles. The purpose is to establish a national norm, so that the judges can impress Congress with their caseloads when they ask for appropriations each year. But work records of individual judges are among the most tightly guarded secrets in Washington.*

Because his position does command *ex officio* respect, a federal judge spends his time immersed in sycophants. Many of them are silly enough to listen to the flattery, or—worse—to believe it. Many times during work on *The Benchwarmers* I dined publicly with judges. In most instances they shook hands with a procession of glad-handing tablehoppers, chiefly lawyers who gave the judge the fawning attention a bond salesman devotes to a rich prospective client. At bar functions the adulation is downright embarrassing. At the American Bar Association's 1973 convention in Washington, to cite a prime example, Chief Judge Walter E. Craig, of Phoenix, Arizona,* held court in a stairwell of the Sheraton Park Hotel for a full hour. For the first twenty minutes I stood to the side and watched; he shook no fewer than 45 hands, and at one time more than a dozen persons waited their turn. When I wandered back later, Craig remained busy— and *very* pleased with the attention.

I asked a New York lawyer in the crowd why he bothered to stand in line for a ceremonial handshake and hello with a judge who presided 2,500 miles dis-

---

* The judges' secrecy in this instance is especially peculiar because many of them work far more hours than, say, the lawyers who practice in their courts. There is a judges' time-study in the public domain that was conducted for the Third Circuit Court of Appeals in 1971–72 by the Federal Judicial Center, the research and training arm of the judiciary. The study found that the judges worked an average of 2,300 hours annually, by conservative computation.

* The chief judge of a district is the senior man under age 70; he has administrative responsibility for the court in addition to his personal caseload.

tant from his office. "Oh," he replied, "common courtesy is one thing; Wally used to be ABA president. Again, you never know when you are going to be trying a case away from home."

Did he really think such a casual handshake would be favorably remembered by Craig if the lawyer in fact ever did appear in his court?

"Damned if I can answer that," the lawyer said. "But the first time I get into chambers with a judge for the pretrial conference, if we have met or have a common friend, I sure remind him of it."

The lawyer paused and looked at my newsman's badge. "You going to quote me on any of this by name? If not, I'll tell you something else."

"Go ahead," I replied, "I've never heard of you."

"Well, I look at it this way. After most men have been on the bench a few months, they think they *deserve* praise as one of the trappings of office, the same as having a robe and gavel. If you don't bow and scrape they feel you are putting them down, acting discourteous to them. Sure, it makes me uncomfortable, treating some second-rate political jerk as if he were Learned Hand or Brandeis. But it gets to be a habit. You go through a goddamned ceremony as if you are being received by the Emperor of China. You do everything but kow-tow.

"Take my home district, now. Ed Palmieri † is married to a Frenchwoman, and as a young man he lived abroad. Palmieri prides himself on his knowledge of French. Now it happens that I'm fluent in French, and I learned from someone or another that Palmieri loves the opportunity to show off his linguistics. So when I'd go into chambers for a pretrial I'd offer him a pleasantry in French, and he'd beam and respond in kind. This drove the opposing lawyers wild—to hear me and Palmieri chattering away in a foreign language, obviously very much at ease with one another. Now is that flattery or tactics?"

The lawyer admitted a lack of any concrete proof that the gimmick swayed Palmieri; nonetheless he felt

---

† Judge Edmund L. Palmieri, in senior status since 1973.

he "got a psychological leg up on the other side." He continued: "I'm giving you a trade secret, I suppose, but since Palmieri is no longer active, it's of no value to me."

The formal trappings of the judiciary remind the judge daily of his importance. The stage-setting of a federal courtroom is intended to give an aura of high dignity to whatever happens there. As a symbol of his prestige the judge wears a black robe, a hand-me-down from the English monarchy that American public opinion does not permit to be draped across the carcass of any political official. (Imagine, if you will—or can—the bulbous Senator Russell Long in a toga, or Vice President Ford in a powdered wig.) Custom alone dictates that a judge wear the robe; its sole practical function, aside from impressing awed laymen, is to conceal paunches and soup stains (reliable agents inform me that in Alabama and Louisiana the robe also encourages several judges to work in their undershirts on steamy days). But the judges regard the robe as a vital judicial folk custom. As Chief Justice William Howard Taft once proclaimed:

Judges should be clothed in robes, not only that those who witness the administration of justice should be properly advised that the function performed is one different from, and higher than that which a man discharges as a citizen in the ordinary walks of life, but also, in order to impress the judge himself with constant consciousness that he is a high-priest in the temple of justice.

Consider, too, the instructions that Judge Ruggero Aldisert of the Third Circuit Court of Appeals compiled for his law clerks—recent law graduates who are ostensibly hired to do research and other legal work for the judge:

The travelling law clerk is . . . my personal bailiff. He must see that I am in the robing room on time. . . . The travelling law clerk should ascertain, before I go on the bench, that the court crier has arranged my seat properly, that he has provided a good supply of sharp pencils, ice water and writing pads. He must insure that I have all briefs and appendices at my spot. He should ascertain from me, before I go on the bench, that I have my reading glasses and some candy in my pockets.

The judge's entrance into the courtroom—essentially a man arriving at his place of work—is marked by a set ceremony befitting the approach of a deity, or a southern lodge ritual. A nervous bailiff peeks through a door at the rear of the courtroom until he determines that the judge indeed is mobile, and en route, and then wallops the wall with his fist and bellows, "ALL RISE AND REMAIN SILENT!" So everyone must get up and gawk attentively towards the bench; the alternative, after all, is jail for contempt of court. No other branch of government, not even an unpopular presidency, relies upon the force of law to require citizens to render quasi-regal homage. Enter now the judge, face impassive. He pauses for the second stanza of the bailiff's chant: "Hear ye, hear ye, hear ye, the United States District Court for the Northern District of California [or wherever we are today] is now in session. Draw near that you may be heard. God save the United States and this honorable court. Please take your seats." Only then does the judge flop into his chair behind the bench (a fancy but time-honored name for what is actually an outsized desk), so elevated that when he is seated his eye level is some three feet above that of any other person in the court.

Thus do haberdashery, pomposity and carpentry make a superior fellow of the United States district judge.

Or do they? The thesis of *The Benchwarmers* is quite direct. Federal judges are of political origin, and when they ascend to the bench they remain humans, and are not magically transformed into omnipotent oracles. Who *are* the federal judges? How do they get their positions? What philosophical baggage do they carry with them? What extra-judicial forces affect their decisions? How do the judges behave, professionally and personally, when they gain power? What impact have the Nixon law-and-order appointees had upon the federal judiciary?

First, a word about the origins of the American judiciary. The founders of the nation had a long and bitter quarrel with the Crown about the position of judges in the colonies. The colonists wished them to hold office during "good behaviour" so as to avoid control by the King. When the crown refused, and demanded the surrender of the colonial charters, the colonists resisted by instituting suit in the English courts. Predictably, judges serving at the pleasure of the king ruled against them.

This experience was much on the mind of the framers of the Declaration of Independence when they complained that King George III "has made judges dependent on his will alone for the tenure of their office." During drafting of the Articles of Confederation, a faction headed by John Dickinson of Delaware moved to make the tenure of judges terminable by the President on demand of both houses of Congress, parallel to the British system. Countering, Edmond Randolph of Virginia proposed an independent judiciary to serve during "good behavior," and prevailed. The historian John Fiske called the federal judiciary "the most remarkable and original of all the creations of that wonderful convention." Fiske continued:

> To make a federal government immediately operative upon individual citizens, it must of course be armed with federal courts to try and federal officers to execute judgement in all cases in which individual citizens were amenable to the national law. But for this system of United States courts extended throughout the states and supreme within its own sphere, the federal constitution could never have been put into practical working order.

The judiciary's authority to interpret the federal Constitution, and laws passed by the Congress, "is the most distinctive feature in the government of the

United States," and a difference in the American and British systems more fundamental than the separation of the executive branches. As Fiske wrote: "In Great Britain the unwritten constitution is administered by the omnipotent House of Commons; whatever statute is enacted by Parliament must stand until some future Parliament may see fit to repeal it." Under the United States system, of course, an act passed by both houses of Congress and signed by the president, may still be set aside by the courts as unconstitutional.

And, further, the courts are obeyed. A Federal judge in North Carolina marvelled to me, "If I order the commander of the local military post to release a man from service because he was illegally inducted, the commander obeys—despite the fact that he has a division of troops and cannon against my one marshal." Which is not to say that obedience is reflexive. Southern diehards resisted the Supreme Court's 1954 edict on school integration for more than a decade before acquiescing to the law of the land. The important point is that the mass public eventually accepted the Court's rule. So, too, did a previously defiant President Nixon, who in October 1973 announced he would ignore a court order that he surrender tape recordings to the Watergate grand jury—and who performed a 180-degree turnaround with 48 hours when a "fire storm" of indignation swept the nation, and produced the subpenaed items.

The federal judiciary is the third branch of the American government, but one which is peculiarly exempt from outside scrutiny, insofar as its personalities and politics are concerned. This is bad, because godawful things happen regularly in the federal courts. Lawyers know about them, and talk about them at lunch and trade meetings, and cluck-cluck with disapproval about how horrible old Judge So-and-So is getting to be. Professor Harold Chase of the University of Minnesota, author of the leading academic study of the district judges, estimates that ten percent of them "are incapable of doing a first-rate job due to the disabilities of illness (including failing eyesight and defective hearing) and old age." Anyone who roams the federal courts quickly learns the identities of the aged and the infirm—of judges who literally have their courtrooms wired for sound, so that the amplified voices of lawyers and witnesses can be fed into their hearing aids, and who nod into sleep during testimony. These men can be pitied. So, too, can judges such as Chief Judge Oliver J. Carter of San Francisco, who developed such a block about making decisions in cases that he voluntarily underwent prolonged psychotherapy. But unless a judge goes absolutely bananas on the bench and starts throwing fits, or paper clips at witnesses, not even his colleagues will chastise him for offensive, incompetent or biased behavior.

Theodore Voorhees, the Washington–Philadelphia superlawyer long prominent in judicial matters for the American Bar Association, states:

A great many practicing lawyers have had the unhappy experience of appearing periodically before a federal judge with the knowledge that the outcome on a particular issue will depend upon the whim, the prejudice or the sobriety of the judge on the day of trial. Lawyers and clients alike are insulted or abused. Protest is likely to lead to sure defeat in the case. Helplessness and frustration are shared by the lawyers and their clients alike. The spectacle is one that reflects great discredit on our courts, but the conscientious well-behaved judges, though constituting a vast majority, are as unable to do anything to restrain the misbehaving judge as are the lawyers and litigants.

Affirms another Washington lawyer, an antitrust specialist: "Often the problem isn't so much meanness or drunkenness as it is outright incompetence. I remember well a pretrial conference before Judge Andrew Hauk in Los Angeles. He opened by telling me and the opposing lawyer his interpretation of what we were trying to prove in the case, and the issues that had to be decided. We exchanged knowing glances and nodded, and as soon as we left Hauk's court we settled. Why? Well, Hauk had completely misstated *both* sides of the case, and neither of us wished to risk our client's neck by putting any decisions before him at all.

"Another time, I had an intricate question before Judge Emett Choate of Miami. Both sides filed exhaustive briefs—ones we really worked on, that explored the issue from all sides—and we flew down to Florida for the hearing. We sat in Choate's court for two or three hours and watched him horse around with some other cases, and he finally got to our matter. His opening line was, 'Well, what brings you boys to Florida today?' He hadn't even looked at our briefs. He was ready to rule off the top of his head on a matter that had taken some damned good legal talent to study. There's another instance where we bailed out of a case in a hurry.

"Sure, the federal judiciary is good; I'll go federal rather than state any day. But so much of it is the luck of the draw. You get a lazy judge, or a dumb judge, and you'd be better off trying the case before a justice of the peace in rural Kentucky."

A prime example of a mean judge is Charles H. Carr of Los Angeles, who can charitably be described as misanthropic. Among the many features of the modern world actively disliked by Carr is long hair on men. When a particularly hirsute lawyer appeared in court a few years back Carr immediately got into a squabble with him over a trial date. "I am not here to play games," Carr announced.

"I am not here to play games either," the lawyer replied.

"Well, you look like it," Carr replied. "From your looks, I can't tell whether you are a girl or a boy. Are you a man?"

The lawyer said, "I think the moustache can be reflected. . . ."

Carr broke in. "I am talking about the long hair. I wasn't sure whether you were a man or a woman."

"I don't know what proof Your Honor requires, but I would say yes, I am," the lawyer said.

"You don't need to strip," Carr charitably advised the lawyer.

"Thank you, Your Honor," the lawyer said. Then

Carr let the proceeding move on to more serious business.*

Astute trial lawyers quickly learn to exploit philosophical leanings of judges, and there is an active, if underground exchange of insiders' intelligence. Justice Department trial lawyers, for instance, quake at the thought of taking a tax case before the irascible Judge Cale Holder of Indianapolis, who acts as if the Sixteenth Amendment is among the more daft acts ever committed by government. Similarly, the Labor Department has a tough time with wage-and-hour and industrial safety cases in the U.S. district court in Dallas. "Judge-shopping" was especially important to lawyers defending selective service cases during the height of the Vietnam War. A Los Angeles attorney told me: "I never wanted to take a draft violator before a Los Angeles jury, which tended to be white, middle-class, conservative, with midwestern attitudes about the military; they'll kill you. So would the L.A. judges. So if I had a guy who intended to refuse service, I'd have him go to the induction center in Oakland, across the bay from San Francisco, and do his number there. He'd be arrested by the FBI, indicted, and then throw himself upon the mercy of one of the San Francisco judges. Quite frankly, most of the San Francisco judges were as anti-war as Abbie Hoffman, and their sentences were far lighter than what you could expect in Los Angeles—a quarter or a third the jail time, if they sent them away at all. Sure, it's playing with a stacked deck, but why not? You'd be a fool not to take advantage of every loophole you find when you are saving a kid from going to a shitty war." Lawyers specializing in draft cases routinely exchanged such tips. The trial department of one Washington superfirm is more

---

* One of Carr's hard-line cronies on the Los Angeles bench, Judge Hauk, is struck by the hilarity of this anecdote, and he has told a slightly different version to public audiences. By Hauk's account, Carr's punch line was as follows: "I would have you take down your pants and resolve this question of gender once and for all. But judging from the way you look, I'd have to rule there was not sufficient evidence to render a decision." Carr claims he said no such thing.

formal. It maintains a "black book" with intelligence reports on perhaps one-fourth the trial judges in the federal judiciary: biographical data, hobbies, friends, procedural quirks of his courtroom, lists of "do's and don'ts," local lawyers with whom he is comfortable (for guidance in hiring local counsel if the case is to be tried away from Washington). The book is closely guarded, and, according to a partner in the firm, "damned candid." The lawyer said, "If you are going to Hartford to work against a judge who can be shoved, you sure want to know about it in advance."

Fitness questions of another sort are raised by judges such as Charles R. Richey, of the District of Columbia, who in the opinion of some lawyers can't forget the clients they served before going on the bench. Richey had a thriving corporate practice, with banks and other financial institutions as clients, before his appointment in 1969. And Richey can't shake his background. In 1973 three activist Washington lawyers tried to bring a class action suit requiring savings and loan associations to pay interest on escrow accounts maintained by the defendants with homeowners' money and drawn upon to pay property taxes and insurance. The savings and loan associations had free use of the sums—millions of dollars—for months before making the payments. In a class action any person in the same circumstances as the formal plaintiffs would be entitled to equal recovery. Judge Richey agonized over the case for months, finally ruling that the homeowners had a good case. But he said that the "interest of the community" dictated that he deny class action status to the suit. "A large class action recovery," opined Richey, "might well have a deleterious effect upon the area lending market at a time [of tight money] when the community can least afford it." The three individual plaintiffs eventually recovered interest on their escrow accounts, but not the scores of thousands of other homebuyers in the District of Columbia.

A lawyer familiar with Richey's handling of the case said at its conclusion: "A clear case of judicial bias. The only clear thing about his handling of the case was that he admitted publicly that he was worried about the consequences of justice."

In fairness, Judge Richey is by no means the only federal judge with built-in predilections. Chief Judge Carl A. Weinman, of Cincinnati, has an outspoken dislike for cases developed by the Federal Equal Employment Opportunities Commission (EEOC)— chiefly, suits by persons denied employment or promotion because of race, sex or age. If an indigent person brings such a case through the auspices of EEOC, federal law requires that the court appoint an attorney for him. But when a potential plaintiff comes into his court, Weinman says he tells him, "You pick your lawyer and have him call me because I want to tell him that if he doesn't win he will not be paid. If he wins he can get paid." Resultantly, Weinman boasts, "only about 50 percent of the cases" are ever filed. Judge Newell Edenfield, of Atlanta, once said flatly from his bench, "I am hereby serving notice that in my district I am not going to have any more of these class actions, except in the most extraordinary circumstances."

Such attitudes are explained away by the judges on grounds of "judicial efficiency." They are bad because they have the net effect of denying American citizens access to the courts. Contrast, if you will, the industrious zeal of an elderly Los Angeles judge named Peirson Hall.

Hall, now in his seventies, for years was chief judge of his district. He is now in senior status, and could live at his desert home in Palm Springs at full salary, and do no work whatsoever. Hall hasn't had an easy adult life. A protracted, bitter divorce fight in his middle-years cost him what wealth he had accumulated, and for a while he was so broke he lived in his chambers in the Los Angeles courthouse. But now that he could relax, Hall works at a pace matched by only a few of his younger colleagues around the country.

Hall's speciality is airline crash cases involving a multitude of defendants and plaintiffs, grotesquely complex affairs to try or settle because of the number of parties who could be held responsible, in whole or in part; the amount of insurance coverage available to be divided among the victims' families; and the varying value of the claims (the widow of an executive in his mid-40's with four children quite naturally is going to receive more money than the survivor of a childless old lady).

Hall has a reputation among airline lawyers of being "a real damned terror" in settling these cases (the words of a San Francisco practitioner). In a not untypical case, an airliner crashed into an ice cream parlor in 1971, causing 49 deaths. Hall settled 47 of the 49 claims in less than two years. "The first one I had, in the 1950s, it took me eight years," Hall told me. "But I've learned. And I tell you why I push these things. Many times the victims are family men who leave a widow and small children—you know how executives fly around these days. Now if she has to wait eight years for settlement, the time has long gone when she *really* needed the money, when little Johnny was in school, or Mary was going off to college.

"One reason I'm so sensitive is that my father dropped dead right after I was born. My mother had three small children, and all she could do was cook. So she cooked, and her three small children—including me, Pete Hall—spent our childhood in institutions.

"I know how grievous it is for a woman to be in that kind of situation. She takes her husband to the airport, and twenty minutes later she is a widow. I do a lot of innovating to get these cases moving. At first, the lawyers buck pretty hard. The plaintiff lawyers are the worst; they're always yelling for more money. The defense lawyers want to get rid of the cases rather than delay. The airlines must retain a contingent liability fund for everybody who is killed. When they go down to the banks to borrow money, and have to show this reserve, it doesn't look good; it cuts down their borrowing power."

So when Hall smells delay he gets downright mean. In 1972 a military jet collided with an Airwest liner. The government and Airwest privately agreed on a division of financial responsibility for settlement with the plaintiffs (80 percent for the government, the remainder for Airwest). Nonetheless, the government lawyers would not stipulate these terms into the record, despite prodding by Hall. "Finally I blew up. Sixteen or eighteen lawyers were spending unnecessary days on the case. The government was requiring them to take 25 or so depositions on the question of liability when agreement had already been reached among the defendants; regardless of the size of the judgements, the defendants knew who was going to pay what. Airwest was willing to skip the question of liability; the government was not.

"That did it. I called the government attorney's attention to a section of the United States Code [the federal law], one that is seldom used, that holds a lawyer financially responsible for unnecessary costs caused by frivolous delay. I told him, 'I'm going to invoke this section against you. I don't know how much these lawyers' time is worth, but you might find out if you are not careful!' The next day he entered the stipulation, and the case got moving again."

The day I visited Hall he wore a baby-blue knit jumpsuit with an orange vest and an ascot as he worked in his chambers. "These are not my normal judicial robes," he explained. "But I wanted to get away to the desert today, and what the hell, if you can get some work done in advance, you're so much to the better. Now this case I'm working on now, we have 74 plaintiffs, and many of these are young widow ladies who .. ."

As I left the judge's chambers hours later his secretary remarked, "He talks about going down to the desert today to rest, but the way he's going, I don't expect it. He'll be here tomorrow, too."

The Benchwarmers is concerned with the personalities and the politics of the federal trial bench—how a man is appointed to the judiciary, and how he behaves once he gets there. The first chapter explores the appointing process, and how the varying demands of the Senate, the White House, the political parties and the organized bar are brought into sometimes precarious balance. There are two chapters on how the judicial system looks when it is working as it should—in New York, under Chief Judge David N. Edelstein; and in Washington, under Chief Judge John J. Sirica, of Watergate fame. There are two chapters on how the system can become botched—through a single judge, as in Oklahoma City with the ferociously erratic Stephen S. Chandler; and through most of a district bench, as was true in Chicago, where a goodly number of the judges were incompetent to serve for one reason or another. There is a brief look at the role of the circuit courts of appeal, the intermediate bench between the district trial courts and the Supreme Court, from the perspective of the circuit court in the District of Columbia—the most controversial in the nation. And there is an exploration of judicial self-government— the velvet-gloved and oh-so-private techniques the judges use in an attempt to make their wayward brethren behave, or retire.

Early in work on this book I ran headlong into the core fact for the reason that federal judges have long enjoyed immunity from criticism. A lawyer who complains publicly about judicial foibles is inviting all sorts of nasty troubles. The judges form a mutual protection association as formidable as the Mafia, or a band of orange-bottomed Malaysian baboons. "You get crosswise with one judge," a Philadelphia lawyer lamented to me "and the whole pack will help him get even. Once I had a run-in with Judge Tom Clary here. I called him on a procedural matter; he was wrong, and I was right, and we had quite a hassle. I won the argument (Clary just wasn't thinking right) but I made a mistake. I embarrassed him before some other lawyers, and he had to back down. A few days later I made reference to the incident in a class I teach at the Penn law school, as an example of how a judge isn't always right, and how a lawyer should stand up for himself.

"Well, word of this [the law school reference] apparently got around town. A few months later I was up before Judge Al Luongo, who is a good fellow but who is also close to Clary, both of them being good Democratic politicians before going on the bench.

"Luongo looked down at me and said, 'Oh, yes, I

know Mr. ———— by reputation. I hear that he is teaching a how-to-do-it-yourself course in contempt of court out at the Penn law school. I just want him to understand that I'll give him something for his syllabus if he tries to test the patience of this court.'

"I smiled kind of weakly and didn't say a word. Luongo was cold and correct throughout, and he made me follow the book on some chicken things that a judge usually overlooks in pretrials for the sake of convenience. It was hazing. I knew it, and Luongo knew that I knew it, and neither of us said a word."

Many lawyers cite bar ethical codes to justify their silence, even in instances where a judge's conduct is nothing less than a scandal. Although the code recognizes that a lawyer, as a citizen, "has a right" to criticize judges publicly, it cautions that "he should be certain of the merit of his complaint, use appropriate language, and avoid petty criticisms, for unrestrained and intemperate statements tend to lessen public confidence in our legal system. Criticisms motivated by reasons other than a desire to improve the legal system are not justified." The code also limits the out-of-court statements a lawyer can make on a case, even when it is completed. Although bar disciplinary actions are rare, the code's language is sufficiently vague—and ominous to frighten most lawyers away from adverse public comments on judges.

The federal court for the Eastern District of Illinois —which is to say, Chicago—goes even a step further, with a court order that effectively declares inoperative the First Amendment to the United States Constitution. When I heard of this order by word of mouth I simply did not believe my informant, whereupon he procured a certified copy from the court clerk. The order, dated November 12, 1965, deserves quotation in full as the extreme to which federal judges will go to shield themselves from public discussion or criticism:

> The members of the bar of this court are reminded that they as well as the judges should, in accordance with the Canons of Judicial and Legal Ethics, refrain from commenting on and attempting to explain

through any source of news media, action taken or anticipated *in any pending litigation* [emphasis added].

Extra-judicial comments and out-of-court explanations or statements by the bar, notwithstanding their being an attempt to avoid criticism, frequently tend to create rather than resolve misconceptions and suspicions in the mind of the public.

Violations of this policy by any member of the bar of this court would be a subject of discipline pursuant to Rule Eight [disbarment proceedings].

In the words of Chicago law professor Melvin Lewis, the "policy statement," as the order is entitled, "was universally understood to mean that no lawyer was free to comment publicly on any matter of federal litigation, whether he was involved in the case or not." And the Chicago judges have enforced the rule with lynch-mob gusto.

Nonetheless a sizable number of attorneys, in Chicago and elsewhere, care enough about the American legal system to talk about the shortcomings of the judiciary. Rather than involve over one hundred lawyers in bar grievance proceedings (or worse) I have carefully shielded the identities of most of the informants quoted in this book. As a citizen (and a journalist) my basic credo is that anyone who wields power in America deserves critical outside examination, and that when anyone with power behaves furtively, there's usually something hidden off in the shadows that should be brought forth for closer inspection. Beginning, in this instance, with the way lawyers are transformed into federal judges.

CHAPTER ONE

Getting There: The Politics of Judicial Selection

In mid-1972 a lawyer from Nashville, Tennessee, addressed a letter to Richard Kleindienst, then the attorney general of the United States:

> To confirm our telephone conversation of yesterday afternoon, I would be very appreciative if I could be given consideration for appointment to fill the current vacancy on the United States District Court for the Middle District of Tennessee. Senator [Howard] Baker told me recently that the Justice Department intends to make its selection for this position in the near future. I surely won't want to sound self-serving or self-promoting but I sincerely feel I would be a "sound" man for this judgeship for many reasons.
>
> Since 1953 I have been engaged in a general corporation practice in my home city of Nashville. I have an "a" rating from Martindale & Hubbell [the legal directory] and so far as I know have a general community reputation for being a competent professional. Although my trial experience has been relatively limited the last ten years because of my senior status in my firm, I am certainly not a stranger to a courtroom. During one ten-month period, when my firm was counsel to——Insurance Company, I defended no less than 21 personal injury actions (winning "favorable" verdicts in all but two; a substantial majority of my verdicts were upheld on appeal). As you will see from the enclosed bio-

graphy, I have broad business and community experience as well. I have been a leading figure in the Nashville United Fund campaign, several hospital fund drives, and our major local youth organization. I am also a director of seven corporations, one "national," the remainder regional. Although I realize I would resign these directorships upon appointment to the bench, I cite them as evidence of the variety of my professional background. Here I think I am in accord with a view that President Nixon expressed to me privately here during his visit in 1967, when I was helping informally in his pre-campaign planning, that is, many of the court decisions that have so alarmed responsible members of the bar are attributable to the fact that they came from judges with "narrow, parochial" backgrounds who tended to decide cases on technical grounds rather than on the basis of informed common sense.

My political loyalty to the Republican Party is well-established. I worked for "the ticket" each year since 1952, and my contributions in cash have been commensurate with my rise in my profession. Both Senator Baker and his wife have been guests in our home. I have also been close to Governor Dunn and Maxey Jarman,* who I am sure you have met on your own visits to Tennessee. Although I have never held formal party office, I think that even a cursory check with local Republicans would document that I am one of the men responsible for the building of our present strong party in Tennessee. As the attached letter from B. B. Gullett, the president of our state bar association, will attest, I also enjoy wide support for this position among members of the bar.

Any consideration you would give to me for nomination to this vacancy would be greatly appreciated. If you feel a personal interview would be useful, I would be most happy to come to Washington on four hours' notice.

Cordially,

---

* A millionaire Nashville industrialist who has given generously to the Republicans.

The Tennessee lawyer's letter is quoted at length because it illustrates a fact that many men forget once they attain the bench: judges are of political, not divine, origin, and an attorney who is shy about promoting himself is unlikely ever to don judicial robes. (The Tennessee man failed, but for reasons other than enthusiasm: Senator Baker, months earlier, had promised the judgeship to another person.)

"What's the best way to become a federal judge?" The staff man of a Midwestern senator repeated my question. "Well, the oldest joke is that you should have the foresight to be the law school roommate of a future United States senator; or, that failing, to pick a future senator for your first law partner." When I asked another Senate man how many "applications" were generated for the average judicial vacancy, he pondered a minute before answering: "Do you want the figure by unit count or by weight? Way, way into the hundreds, and not just crank mail, either." He showed me what he called a "typical self-nominating dossier," a file folder fully four inches thick, containing letters from (in no particular order) four sitting United States district judges; a former lieutenant governor, five past presidents of local and state bar associations; more law-firm letterheads than I cared to count, most on heavy bond paper with fancily-scripted names running down the left margin and veritably harrumphing prestige and money; a law school dean and a respectable smattering of law professors (three of whom appeared to be classmates of the prospect); nineteen corporate and business executives; officers of half a dozen civic and service clubs, and the man's hometown congressman. The congressman's letter was written in such veiled, circuitous language that I wondered, idly, whether the representative was endorsing the man, or warning against him: "I am sure that you are aware of ————'s qualifications for the federal bench, and that you will give them full consideration in filling the current vacancy. Having known———for years, I commend his candidacy to your earnest attention." As a cover document the aspiring jurist had attached a hefty biographical background sheet listing every happening in his life of real or imagined significance that conceivably could make him an attractive candidate. (But why bother boasting of being treasurer of a men's Sunday School class, or of having served the Lions Club as parliamentarian, treasurer and recording secretary in addition to president?)

The Senate man let me prowl in the file and made sure I caught some of the more flagrant howlers. What does this all mean? Does such a presentation influence a senator's decision? The aide stared at me as if I had asked whether the earth was *really* round. "Christ, no," he said. "The only thing a lawyer will get out of a campaign like that is a place on the senator's Christmas card list. If a guy is so little known to the senator that he has to write a letter telling about himself, he isn't about to be put on the bench." The aide paused. "Maybe that's an overstatement. These campaigns help when the senator is trying to choose between a dozen or so different people. If you can demonstrate a hell of a lot of people are sincerely behind you, the senator is bound to listen. But a self-starting campaign, where some John Doe stirs up his friend—uh uh, he's wasting his paper."

The Constitution is vague on how district judges should be appointed, and totally silent on their qualifications. A district judge need not have reached a certain age. He is not required to be a United States citizen, nor to live in the district where he is to serve. Nor, for that matter, must he be a lawyer. The only reason presidents nominate judges is because George Washington did so, and no one disputed him, and his successors continued the practice. Not until 1948 did Congress provide explicitly that all circuit and district judges be appointed with the advice and consent of the Senate. Lacking constitutional guidelines, the appointive system has evolved through custom. And an essential element of our custom is that political connections are as important to a prospective judge as is his legal ability. The route to a judgeship can be as tenuous, and as trap-laden, as a presidential campaign; and hopefuls can be vetoed on grounds other than merit at several stages. There are a variety of basic equations—but each has the common factor of politics.

A lawyer who wishes to be a judge must be politically and personally acceptable to the senators from his home state, if their party controls the White House. Senators split the patronage under varying arrangements. If he wishes, the senior senator can control all the appointments. More often, the senators take turns. A good current example is the arrangement between Senators Jacob Javits and James Buckley for New York appointments. Although Buckley was elected as a Conservative, he got along better with the Nixon White House than did Javits, and hence received a share of the patronage.

If the president and the senators are from opposite parties, the White House makes the selections, through recommendations from its political allies in the state (including, on occasion, powerful members of the House of Representatives). Political expediency causes many exceptions to this rule. Because Senator James Eastland, as chairman of the Senate Judiciary Committee, can dynamite nominations (by delaying hearings on them) the White House doesn't displease him on any Mississippi appointments. "The judges they pick for Mississippi might be Republicans," says John Holloman, the judiciary committee staff director, "but they are Eastland Republicans." Senators Alan Cranston and John V. Tunney, both Democrats, convinced the Nixon Administration that California appointments should be split three Republicans to one Democrat. Their threat was to stall confirmation of undesirable Republicans, possible through the intricate political minuet known as senatorial courtesy. Their trade-off was to agree to hold their noses and vote yes regardless of what caliber of Republican judge Nixon put on the California bench.

"Nixon's appointments have not exactly enriched the federal judiciary in our poor state," opined one Los Angeles lawyer. And one hears quiet mutterings among California Democrats that the senators goofed, or worse. One outraged lawyer is Stephen Barnett, a law professor at the University of California at Berkeley. "They signed away their right to protest," laments Barnett. "They can't do anything to stop poor appointments. They should have reserved the right to 'advise and consent.' "

When the Senators are divided politically (one from one party, one from the other) they strike their own bargains. Patronage for the off-party senator relies upon such factors as his relations with the White House and how well he gets along with the other senator. Even under the Nixon Administration Senator Harrison J. Williams, a Democrat, gets one of four New Jersey appointees from his benign Republican colleague, Clifford Case. The situation is different for Michigan, with hyperpolitical senators who really don't care for one another: Robert P. Griffin, a Republican, takes all judicial patronage just as did Philip A. Hart, a Democrat, during the Kennedy-Johnson years. In Massachusetts, Senator Edward W. Brooke, a Republican, ignores Senator Edward M. Kennedy.

If a president is willing to take the risk, he can sometimes ignore both senators, regardless of their parties, and appoint whom he pleases. In 1968 President Johnson punished Senator George McGovern, who was supporting Robert Kennedy for the presidency, by permitting Senator Quentin Burdick (D., N.D.) to pick a judge for the Eighth Circuit Court of Appeals, even though it was South Dakota's turn to make the choice. Johnson also used judgeships—or, more accurately, the lack thereof—as a weapon against his longtime political adversary, Ralph Yarborough, a Texas senator from 1957–70. According to Yarborough, "Johnson and Ramsey Clark [a Texan in the Justice Department from 1961–68, lastly as attorney general] told lawyers in every little country courthouse in the state that 'if it wasn't for Ralph Yarborough, you would be a federal judge, he's blackballing you.' And these lawyers believed it, and held it against me. An outrageous lie, of course; I didn't blackball anyone. Lyndon and Ramsey used this to cut me off at the knees, though, to make people mad at me."

Administrations of both parties routinely promote United States attorneys to the federal bench after several years service (by one estimate, half of them eventually become judges). In the opinion of Washington law professor Arthur S. Miller, a ranking academic critic of the judiciary, the prosecutorial background "means that they carry [Justice] departmental preferences with them to the bench." Similarly, notes Miller, "a federal district judge aspiring to be an appeals judge not only starts out with the attitudes of a United States attorney but, more subtly and of more importance, knows that his elevation must be approved by the department. How much that knowledge might tip the scales of justice in favor of the government is unknown—but certainly it argues for taking the appointing function out of the department."

For the White House, judgeships serve the utilitarian function of prestigious dumping ground for persons who, for one reason or another, are no longer of use to an administration. In early 1973, for example, the Nixon Administration persuaded Joseph T. Sneed to resign as dean of the Duke University law school to become deputy to Attorney General Richard Kleindienst. Sneed was not eager to leave academia; he had been at Duke only since 1970 and was comfortable there. But he went on to Washington anyway. A few months later the Watergate scandal forced Kleindienst to resign, and Elliot Richardson took over the Justice Department. A cabinet officer is permitted to pick his deputy, and Richardson opted for William Ruckelshaus —not because he disliked Sneed, but because he wanted his own man. But what to do with Sneed? Duke, of course, by now had chosen a new law dean, so he could not return to North Carolina. The Justice Department felt a certain moral obligation to Sneed, in view of the fact it had persuaded him to leave a classy lifetime deanship for such a short-lived political appointment. So the Administration began job hunting for Sneed.

In late June 1973 a federal judge in Los Angeles interrupted our interview to take a call from Richard H. Chambers, chief judge of the Ninth Circuit Court of Appeals. When he finished, he said to me, "Hey, that was good news. Bob Kelleher [a federal district judge in Los Angeles] is going to get that vacancy on the ninth circuit. Chambers said the Justice Department approved him, and the nomination is going forward. A good man. He's Republican, and Nixon appointed him, and I'm Democratic as hell. But that's no matter. He's a fine judge." The judge mentioned a state trial judge who was to be Kelleher's replacement on the district bench. He called to his secretary, "Remind me to give Kelleher a ring and congratulate him."

Chambers' information proved premature. Just before the Kelleher nomination was publicized, someone at the Justice Department blinked and said, "Hey, wait a minute, this is where we can unload Joe Sneed. We don't owe anything to Kelleher. He's already had one appointment from us; let him wait for the next vacancy." So Kelleher was shunted aside and Sneed was sent to the West Coast to serve on the circuit appeals court.

Another example: in the winter of 1971 Richard McLaren, the assistant attorney general for antitrust matters, was restive and disgusted. In at least two instances corporation executives went over his head, both to the White House and within the Justice Department, to thwart what should have been major antitrust actions. Richard Kleindienst, then the deputy attorney general, refused to permit McLaren to sue to halt ITT's acquisition of the Canteen Corporation, the United States's largest producer of vending machines. After bickering with the White House, Kleindienst finally permitted a suit to be filed *after* the merger was consummated, a strategic goof. In another instance, Kleindienst refused to let McLaren sue to block the merger of Warner Lambert Pharmaceutical Company (1969 sales of $887.3 million) with Parke-Davis and Company ($273.5 million). (Mudge, Rose, Guthrie & Alexander, the former Wall Street law firm of both President Nixon and Attorney General Mitchell, represented Warner Lambert, whose board chairman, Elmer Bobst, was a close personal friend of Nixon's.) Kleindienst's handling of both cases was so peculiar that during 1970 and 1971 even Justice Department lawyers muttered about "political considerations" and "a fix."

Richard McLaren, a man who could have answered questions about the cases, wanted to be a federal judge;

by reliable account, only the promise of a judgeship persuaded him to remain in office as long as he did. But a confirmation hearing would have given critics of the Nixon Administration's antitrust policy a forum in which to pursue their suspicions. A highly critical report on antitrust activities issued by a Ralph Nader group in the summer of 1971 focused on the hapless McLaren. The press was revealing the first sketchy details of yet another matter: ITT's payment of $400,000 to underwrite the 1972 Republican national convention, a transaction in smelly chronological and political juxtaposition to settlement of yet another antitrust case on terms favorable to ITT. According to a transcript of a taped White House conversation that leaked from the House Judiciary Committee during the impeachment inquiry, Nixon exclaimed of McLaren: "Get the son of a bitch out of here."

So how could the Nixon Administration get McLaren onto the bench without subjecting him to embarrassing questions? The Justice Department hoked up what it thought to be a foolproof scenario. On December 2, 1971, the Justice Department suddenly notified the Senate Judiciary Committee that Judge Julius J. Hoffman intended to retire from the United States District Court in Chicago at the end of the year. Chicago courts were so awfully overburdened, Justice said, that a replacement must be approved immediately. Would it be possible for an appointment of McLaren to be handled expeditiously? After all, the same committee only three years earlier had cleared him for the assistant attorney general position without dissent. Charles Percy, Illinois' Republican senator, fell dutifully into line, and he called his Democratic colleague, Adlai Stevenson, and told him what a good fellow McLaren was and how badly he was needed on the bench. Stevenson, an unsuspecting chap who has the bad habit of believing what other politicians tell him, said he had no objection. So that afternoon, when the Senate convened, Richard W. McLaren received the fastest confirmation ever afforded a candidate for the federal bench. An assistant legislative clerk read the nomination from the White House and the presiding officer droned, "Without objection, the Senate will consider the nomination, and without objection, the nomination is confirmed." Senator Philip Hart (D., Mich.), who normally has a keen nose for mischief, exuded, "I am delighted. Mr. McLaren has served conscientiously as assistant attorney general in charge of antitrust for several years. Those of us who have had contact with him have come to respect and admire him. I compliment the President on the appointment." McLaren left immediately for a European vacation.

Several months later, when the politics of the ITT settlements became apparent, senators recognized they had let a key figure slip through their fingers. Stevenson especially felt hoodwinked; as he lamely told the Senate:

> I was told at the time that the district court in Chicago faced a backlog of cases—and that Judge Hoffman was requesting immediate senior status. The Congress, I was told, would soon recess for Christmas, and so immediate action on the nomination was necessary.
>
> I now find that there was no backlog of cases and that Judge Hoffman did not want immediate senior status. I do not know the real reason for McLaren's hasty departure from the Justice Department.*

On rare occasions, the scent of a political quid pro quo has been detected in the vicinity of an appointment. One such episode involved Judge Francis L. Van Dusen, an aloof Philadelphia patrician who was appointed to the district bench there in the 1950s and later promoted to the circuit court. The story began in 1952, when Pennsylvania industrialists, financiers and businessmen contributed heavily to the Eisenhower presidential campaign via the Pennsylvania Republican Finance Committee. Later some of the contributors

---

* In private Stevenson complained bitterly that Percy helped the Nixon Administration in the deception. However, aides to Percy denied complicity, saying, "We bought the same bill of goods." One Percy man said McLaren had been wanting the judgeship for at least two years.

came to the chairman, Philip Sharples, and asked a quid pro quo. They wanted a "sound man" put into a vacant federal judgeship, and they had found him in Van Dusen, a partner in the superfirm of Dechert, Price, Myers & Rhoads. But because of a complex internal fight in the state GOP, neither of Pennsylvania's Republican senators would endorse Van Dusen. Hence the contributors put the question directly to Sharples: Would he go over the senator's head to Attorney General Herbert Brownell, with whom he had worked closely during the Eisenhower campaign? (Brownell had been Ike's manager.) Sharples tried, but Brownell responded coolly, saying he did not want to usurp the senator's patronage rights. So Sharples got blunt. He wrote Brownell:

> . . . I think the time has come for me to say to those whom it concerns—and I am not quite sure who they are—that the policy of completely disregarding the Republicans who finance campaigns— after the campaign is over—must be changed or we shall have a seriously increased difficulty in securing finances the next time they are required. I am really afraid of a sit-down strike on the part of our better contributors if they are continually ignored. . . .
>
> Contributors to and workers for the Republican Finance Committee of Pennsylvania are very much interested in seeing Mr. Van Dusen made a federal judge. . . . It is my opinion that it would be a serious blow to the prestige and morale of the . . . committee if Mr. Van Dusen is not confirmed. . . .

Sharples concluded one of several letters to Brownell by asking whether the Republican hierarchy intended "to take any interest in the wishes of the people who put up the money" for campaigns.

Sharples made his point, for the Eisenhower Administration went ahead with the nomination even in the absence of senatorial support. When one of Van Dusen's Pennsylvania enemies leaked the Sharples letters during his confirmation hearing, Senator Joseph C. O'Mahoney (D., Wyo.) said they had the effect of "putting a price tag on the nomination." Van Dusen testified he had made no promises to supporters on how he would rule in taxation or other cases, and that his own political contributions had been "minimal." The internal GOP feud eventually subsided, and Van Dusen won confirmation.

Van Dusen's rulings on the district bench did not disappoint his supporters. He was known as a judge who listened sympathetically to requests for injunctions in labor disputes, and who seldom caused any discomfort for insurance company lawyers. A good example: An Eastern Air Lines jet crashed in Boston Harbor in 1960, killing 37 Philadelphia-area residents (plus 25 from elsewhere). Survivors of the victims wanted the case tried in Pennsylvania, which has no limits for wrongful deaths; the airline wanted it moved to Massachusetts, which has a $20,000 limit. (State limits are binding even though the cases are tried in federal court.) During protracted pretrial proceedings Van Dusen consistently sided with the airline, to the point where the plaintiffs' lawyers charged that he had lost his "impartiality." The circuit court of appeals finally had to order him out of the case.

Finally, a President may appoint a man to the bench simply because he likes him, or owes him a favor. Senator Bennett Clark (D., Mo.), son of former House Speaker Champ Clark, was a longtime political and personal friend of President Harry Truman—and, in fact, nominated Truman for vice-president at the 1944 Democratic convention. But as Truman told biographer Merle Miller, Clark "was drunk half the time and more. . . ." After being defeated for reelection Clark tried to practice law in Washington, but didn't do very well. So Truman appointed him to the Tenth Circuit Court of Appeals. "Why?" asked Miller. Truman replied, "I felt I owed him a favor, that's why, and I thought as a judge he couldn't do too much harm, and he didn't. . . . [H]e wasn't the worst court appointment I ever made. By no means the worst." Nonetheless, Truman said, "I'm none too proud of it." Another purely "presidential" appointment was that of Judge Wilfred Feinberg to the Second Circuit Court of Ap-

peals in New York in 1966. The connection was
through the judge's brother, Abraham Feinberg, a
Manhattan banker, businessman, and philanthropist
who has raised money for Democratic politicians since
the Truman days. When Lyndon Johnson asked Abraham what he could do to reciprocate his financial kindness, he supposedly replied, "Nothing for me. Now,
my brother Wilfred. . . ." Wilfred went on the court
soon thereafter.

*Mention the name of Judge Joseph Samuel Perry
to lawyers who try cases in the federal district court in
Chicago, and they'll sniff with disdain and begin telling
stories about his judicial blunders, and how frustrating
it is to appear before a jurist who one man called
"maybe the sorriest guy on the federal bench in the
Midwest." But Perry does have a redeeming quality:
he is one of the few judges in the Republic who has
admitted publicly how he went about scheming for
appointment, and the politics of his origin. In a speech
to the Chicago Bar Association soon after his appointment, Perry told of settling in suburban DuPage County
after graduation from the University of Chicago law
school, and his entry into Democratic politics. Here is
what Perry told the Chicago bar about his rise:*

"*I will be frank about it. At first I talked about
amongst the Republicans about doing some work—
there was no Democratic party out there—but the
Republicans didn't need me. . . . So I proceeded to
organize the Democratic party out there and to make
it tough for the Republicans. . . . Later, I landed in
the legislature and kept working along and served my
term there. Then I got out of politics and came back
and practiced law.*

"*And then I gambled. I saw a man—Paul Douglas—
who looked as though he might be elected to the United
States Senate. I backed him and as a result I had his
support. My political friendship with my good friend
Scott Lucas [then the other Illinois Senator], in the
meantime, had grown bit by bit and Scott was not mad
at me.*

"*Since we are talking confidentially I will be perfectly frank with you folks in admitting that I tried to obtain this appointment seven years ago and learned then that it requires not one but two senators. At that time I was out of politics and they did not need me. Therefore, I decided that this time if I wanted that appointment I had better get back into politics—which I did.*

"When I learned, as I soon did, that everyone shoots at the top man—that he is everyone's target—I went to each of the senators and said, 'Listen here, if you are going to back me, for heaven's sake don't make me number one. Be sure to back me and get me on the list but don't make me number one.'

"As it turned out that proved to be pretty good strategy because everyone else was shot off and, no use lying about it, I helped to shoot them off. The result of it was I landed on top. I have the job now and I am going to stick."

Sam Perry is a rarity, for most judges find mention of their political origins distasteful, as if purging their backgrounds would enhance their cherished aura of omnipotence. In ten successive interviews in California I asked judges, "How important was politics to your appointment?" Seven saw absolutely no connection whatsoever; an eighth said, "You know, I never really thought about that point." Judge Peirson Hall of Los Angeles struck me as more candid: "I worked hard for Franklin Roosevelt in the days when California had no Democratic Party to speak of. In 1939 I began running for the Senate, and the party convinced me it would be best if there wasn't a contest for the Democratic nomination. So I withdrew and campaigned for Sheridan Downey. They gave me this judgeship as sort of a consolation prize—and one, I might add, that I have enjoyed."

Judge Alfonso Zirpoli of San Francisco also takes unabashed pride in the three decades of politics that preceded his appointment. "How did I get on the bench? Well, after being co-chairman of San Francisco Citizens for Kennedy–Johnson in 1960, along with Paul Fay, Bobby Kennedy called me one day and. . . ." You get the idea. Yet another Pacific Coast judge—a man who had been a Republican country chairman—

told me unblinkingly, "I happen to believe in our institutions. So far as I know, politics had absolutely nothing, nothing at all, to do with my nomination. I worked hard as a lawyer and I like to think that I was selected on the basis of ability. Now I'd appreciate it if you would not use my name, for I don't want to sound boastful, but I'd be hard-pressed to give you the name of another lawyer in ——————— [his home town] who has better qualifications than I do for the bench."

Chief Judge Edward J. Devitt, of the United States District Court for Minnesota, feels his colleagues are deceiving themselves—but no one else—with their disclaimers of politics. Devitt, a regular speaker at the seminars the Federal Judicial Center stages for newly appointed district judges, delights in deflating the freshly-stuffed shirts in his audience. The thrust of Devitt's standard lecture is that federal judges shouldn't strut so pompously:

Some judges may become so impressed with their importance that they forget the practical facts of their judicial birth. . . . I doubt if federal judges ever will be appointed solely on the basis of merit. That would be the millennium. So long as the United States Senate has the constitutionally granted authority to "advise and consent" to such appointments, it is unlikely that some politics will not be involved in most of them.

The truth remains . . . that we were appointed to office because, personally or vicariously, we knew the United States senators; and that, I emphasize, is not a sinful thing at all.

The point is that it is distinctly unbecoming to claim later that we were chosen solely because of our outstanding ability as lawyers and leaders of the bar, and that we were reluctantly persuaded to give up our lucrative practice and were practically dragged up to the bench.

That would be taking ourselves too seriously.

Similarly, senators have an ambivalent position on their role in judicial appointments. The senators fiercely guard their rights when a vacancy occurs; only one in recent history—the late Robert F. Byrd, Sr., of Virginia —declined to select candidates (however, Byrd did not hesitate to veto people he didn't like, and his son and successor, Harry F. Byrd, Jr., plays the judicial game by the conventional rules). Yet one quickly detects a vague unease with the politics of the system among incumbent and former senators. Ralph W. Yarborough of Texas, for instance, found many practical drawbacks in judicial politics during his 13 years in the Senate. "Every appointment means you lose twenty to forty good campaigning friends," Yarborough told me. "The man you put on the bench can't work for you any longer, and the others who wanted the appointment get mad and quit. It's a mixed blessing—but a great thing when you are running." Under federal law a candidate cannot promise specific appointments to a supporter, a stricture easily bypassed with a wink and a quiet talk in the corner. As one former senator says, "Other than money, patronage is the best power a politician has going for him."

Many persons who have seen the judicial selection system from the vantage point of insiders feel politics are a malign influence. Soon after he resigned as attorney general in late 1973, Elliot L. Richardson said he was concerned "that existing practices diminish the quality of the federal judiciary by unduly restricting the pool of potential appointees." Richardson would have the Justice Department create its own staff and procedures to search for judicial prospects, and evaluate their qualifications for appointments. Richardson felt his idea would "help foster not only an improved judiciary but also an increased sense of confidence in the judicial branch." Richardson's successor, William Saxbe, the former Ohio senator, emphatically disagreed. At his confirmation hearing Saxbe told senators: "You and I are here through politics. If you remove politics from certain aspects of American life, you remove party responsibility. . . . When you start depoliticizing things, you depoliticize yourself." Given senatorial zeal for preservation of patronage, the reform suggested by Richardson is unlikely. Persons disgruntled with the system must settle for what solace they can find in that most hoary of political excuses, "Both parties do exactly the same thing."

Oh, indeed they do, and have for decades. Ben R. Miller, a Baton Rouge attorney who served on the American Bar Association's federal judiciary committee for nine years, kept a political log of appointees during the period. As Miller reported in the *ABA Journal:*

Appointments by Mr. Truman . . . include these:

One was the brother of a Democratic United States senator.

One was a son of a Democratic United States senator.

One had himself served an interim appointment as a Democratic United States senator.

Two were former Democratic attorneys general of their state.

One was a former Democratic governor.

One had managed a Democratic governor's successful campaign.

Two had been delegates to the Democratic National Convention.

Six had been Democratic members of their state legislature.

Two others had occupied responsible Democratic party positions in their state.

Similar appointments by Mr. Eisenhower included these:

One was a former Republican senator.

One was the law partner of a Republican senator.

One was the campaign manager of a Republican senator.

One was a former Republican governor.

Four were former Republican congressmen.

One was the law partner of a former chairman of the Republican National Committee.

One was, at the time of his nomination, Republican national committeeman.

One was a former member of the Republican National Committee.

Six were delegates to Republican national conventions.

Five were former Republican members of their state legislatures.

Three were campaign directors for, [and] appointees to special positions by, an unsuccessful Republican nominee for president.

One was an unsuccessful Republican candidate for Congress and later for state attorney general.

One is the husband of a Republican national committeewoman.

A more current example of bench politics is the Eastern District of Pennsylvania, which sits in Philadelphia. Judge Herbert Fogel, appointed in 1973, was a prominent Republican fund-raiser and practiced in the firm of Senator Hugh Scott (R., Pa.), the senate minority leader. Judge Clarence Newcomer had been a Republican district attorney in Lancaster County; James Gorbey, a Republican mayor of Chester; Daniel Huyett, a Scott worker in Reading, where he was county GOP chairman; C. William Kraft, a Republican district attorney in Delaware County; Edward Becker, a volatile partisan lawyer for the Republican City Committee in Philadelphia. There are two former lieutenant governors of Pennsylvania who could not find higher elective office and settled for bench appointments: John Morgan Davis, a Democrat, and Raymond Broderick, a Republican. The chief judge, Joseph Lord, in 1959 defended the late Representative William J. Green, Jr., the long-time Democratic chairman in Philadelphia, in a criminal bribery trial. Green was acquitted; shortly thereafter, Lord went on the federal bench. Charles Weiner was Democratic majority leader in the state senate, and a Philadelphia ward leader; Alfred P. Luongo, also a Democratic ward chairman, came to the judiciary from the Philadelphia City Council. Another Democratic judge, Thomas J. Clary, went on the bench after failing to win election as Philadelphia district attorney.

Judgeships can also be comfortable consolation prizes for losing candidates; indeed, they are often promised in advance by a state party organization (with the blessing of the administration and the senator) in order to entice men into doubtful races. For example, the Nixon Administration put three Republicans onto the bench after they lost races for governor: William Steger of Texas; Stanley Blair of Maryland; and Hugh Dillin of Indiana. The bench is also a refuge for Congressmen who fail to win re-election: Frank Wilson of Tennessee and John Fullam of Pennsylvania, both Democrats, and Rhodes Batcher of Kentucky and Charles Moye of Georgia, Republicans.

With raw politics dominant at the appointing level, what restraints other than conscience and public relations prevent senators and an administration from putting odious hacks on the bench? The best the system can offer is the American Bar Association, which in turn raises yet another set of disquieting problems. Foremost among these questions is that of ABA partiality towards monied, conservative lawyers, men dedicated to the preservation of a judicial milieu in which they have prospered.

We Deem Him Qualified
(to the tune of "Satisfied")

No doubt you've heard of our committee, friends,
It is the one which kills or recommends.
Before a candidate the bench ascends
He must have from us
This well-known chorus:

He's qualified, yes he's qualified,
Qualified to be judge.
Our Oh Kay is the open sesame
To whiten any smudge
Though he's not just what he ought to be,
We none the less think on the whole that he
Is still entitled now to our decree,
We deem him qualified.

Suppose a lawyer takes a little bribe,
Or to a padded payroll does subscribe.

You might expect from us a diatribe.
But we're not so mean.
We just wash him clean.

Some judges from a trifling incident
Fly into a wild spell of temp'rment.
They rave and swear and get quite violent.
But still their rage does cool,
When they hear us drool,
He's qualified, he's qualified.

A judge cannot stay always upon the bench;
He sometimes must adjourn, his thirst to quench.
To countenance such conduct gives a wrench
But while we deprecate,
We still asseverate,
He's qualified, he's qualified. . . .

—From the Chicago Bar Association's
annual Christmas show, circa 1935.

One of the pillars of the San Francisco financial district, physically as well as figuratively, is the massive Standard Oil Building, on Bush Street at the foot of Telegraph Hill. Here is headquartered one of the largest industrial corporations in the West. Standard permeates the political and economic life of California. It pumps vast quantities of oil from beneath California, and refines it and sells it from retail outlets in every hamlet in the state. The sheer size of Standard means it has an inordinate number of legal problems. It sometimes splashes oil where oil does not belong. It gets into fights with competitors and its franchised dealers. Its vehicles collide with other people's vehicles. Workers are injured in its refineries and seek recompense.

Tucked away on the upper floors of the Standard Oil Building is a law firm responsible for resolving as many of these legal problems as possible. Pillsbury, Madison & Sutro is itself a power in California. With 180 partners and associates, it is not only San Francisco's largest firm but also its best in the opinion of many West Coast lawyers. Prestige by association is a tenuous concept, but PMS (as Pillsbury Madison is known in lawyers' shorthand) is good enough to be counsel for Standard Oil and a host of other major California corporations (including Pacific Telephone and Telegraph Company) and seldom does a day pass that a PMS lawyer isn't in a state or federal court somewhere in California, representing one of its blue-chip clients.

PMS is an important law firm for yet another reason: a name partner, John Sutro, is chairman of the American Bar Association's standing committee on the federal judiciary. An *ex officio* title goes with the chairmanship, "The Judge Maker." The reason for The Judge Maker's clout in the United States legal establishment is quite direct. If a lawyer being considered for appointment as a federal district or circuit court judge is found not qualified under standards set by the ABA committee, the President will not nominate him for office.*

Such an absolute privilege is owned by no other pressure group in the United States, and has been granted by no previous United States president. Trade associations, corporate lawyer/lobbyists, big trade unions, consumer organizations and others assuredly are consulted on appointments to federal agencies affecting their well-being. Any administration, for instance, checks with the National Association of Broadcasters before filling a vacancy on the Federal Communications Commission, or with the AFL–CIO before ap-

---

* After the Haynsworth/Carswell debacles, the Nixon Administration no longer gave the ABA veto authority on Supreme Court appointments. In the fall of 1971, when the administration searched for nominees for two vacancies, Attorney General John N. Mitchell reportedly said at a White House meeting that Senator Robert C. Byrd (D., W. Va.) would have trouble getting ABA approval because of his night-law-school background and lack of experience as a practicing lawyer. "Fuck the ABA," the President is said to have responded. And in one of his last official acts before resigning in August 1974, President Nixon went against an ABA recommendation and nominated Governor Thomas J. Meskill of Connecticut for the Second Circuit Court of Appeals.

pointing a secretary of labor. But consultation does not equate with veto authority.

Only, the ABA doesn't like that word "veto." When Richard Kleindienst, then the attorney general, used it in a 1973 speech—one in which he spoke very favorably of the ABA's "partnership" with the Nixon Administration in selecting judges—the pained reaction of bar elders was revealing. Robert L. Trescher, a Philadelphia trial lawyer who preceded John Sutro as chairman of the ABA Federal Judiciary Committee, felt Kleindienst was "indiscreet," and at the ABA convention in Washington later that year he and other bar officials expended considerable energy disclaiming "veto" power. "There is no way legally for the ABA to have the power of veto," Trescher said. "I would not get excited if the president did not follow our views."

The denials, of course, are rank nonsense, for the ABA's power is real even if extra-constitutional. The ABA is chary of acknowledging its privilege because much of the general public (and many lawyers as well) still consider it a lodge of moss-backed old fogies who spend their time devising new and intricate ways to screw people. Put most simply, the ABA wants to exercise professional birth control over the judiciary, but not take full responsibility for doing so. If it did, the public might rise up and demand that a president make his own choice for judges—subject to the advice and consent of the Senate—without delegating a veto to outsiders. The ABA's predicament is delightful. On the one hand, it wants presidents to follow its guidance and put men of its . . . ah, *expectations* . . . on the bench. Concurrently, it does not dare claim too much credit within earshot of outsiders, lest the whole scheme collapse. Hence anything the ABA says publicly of its judicial screening role must be heard with the understanding that reality isn't always as advertised.

The chief defect in the ABA screening system is that the veto is not wielded by the 170,000-odd lawyers who are the ABA membership, but by a tight committee of twelve men, appointed by the ABA president. The ABA in the past decade has done much to shed its

reputation as a bastion of economic and political conservatism in America. Some 40 percent of its membership is now age 35 or younger, for instance, and the
ABA worries about things other than narrow professional issues. But modernization does not extend to the
Federal Judiciary Committee. There members seem to
have dropped from the same rigid mould: men in their
fifties and sixties who work in large firms and represent banks and insurance companies and other large
corporations. One searches the roster in vain for a
personal or domestic relations injury specialist, a criminal lawyer, a law professor, a black, a woman, or a
chicano.

One ABA officer (who spoke from anonymity) told
me these omissions are irrelevant, and he compared
the screening with the time-trials at the Indianapolis
Five Hundred race: "When a driver gets on the track
at Indy he wants to make sure he's racing with professionals, and that the place isn't cluttered up with
amateurs. Well, it's the same way with our process.
The Federal courts are the 'fast track' of the American
judiciary, and there must be a way of insuring that only
the best men available get on the bench. We can't
afford any accidents. Now these personal injury fellows,
these guys have a viewpoint. They represent a single
kind of client, the plaintiff, and that's all right, I don't
begrudge them that. But really, now, wouldn't it be
somewhat one-sided to put one of them in a position
where they could, uh, put one of their buddies on the
bench? Is that really fair?"

"Oh," I replied, "probably about the same as selecting a lawyer who spent his professional career *defending* personal injury cases on behalf of an insurance company."

"That really isn't relevant," the ABA officer said,
and changed the subject.

As of 1973–74, these were the lawyers who formed
the ABA's standing committee on the federal judiciary:

Chairman and member-at-large: John Sutro of San
Francisco, whom we met earlier, and to whom we shall
return in a moment.

First circuit: Gael Mahony, 48,* of the Boston firm of Hill & Barlow, a 39-lawyer firm which specializes in antitrust, corporate and real estate practice law. A Republican, Mahony was an assistant United States attorney in Massachusetts during the Eisenhower Administration and then a special assistant to former Massachusetts attorney general (now United States senator) Edward Brooke.

Second circuit: Albert R. Connelly, 64, of the Wall Street firm of Cravath, Swaine & Moore, one of the nation's leading corporate firms, with more than 100 lawyers. Republican.

Third circuit: Robert M. Landis, 54, of Dechert, Price & Rhodes, of Philadelphia. With 115 lawyers, it is the backbone of the Philadelphia insurance and banking bar, and very Main Linish.

Fourth circuit: Norman P. Ramsey, 52, of Semmes, Bowen & Semmes, Baltimore. Though smallish (38 lawyers) by super-firm standards, its clients include such corporations as Bethlehem Steel, Continental Can, Eastman Kodak, DuPont, General Electric, General Tire & Rubber, Xerox, Mobil, the Baltimore *Sunpapers,* the American Insurance Association, the Association of Aviation Underwriters, and ten other insurance companies and groups. Democrat, active bar politician.

Fifth circuit: Sherwood W. Wise, 64, of the Jackson, Mississippi, firm of Wise, Carter, Child, Steer & Caraway. Counsel for fifteen insurance companies and groups, ranging from American Fire & Casualty to Zurich Insurance Company. General counsel for Mississippi Power & Light, Mississippi counsel for State Farm Insurance and the Illinois Central Railroad. (For years one of Wise's specialties was defending railroads in personal injury cases.) Also does work for Commercial Credit Corporation and Philco Financial Corporation.

Sixth circuit: Joseph E. Stopher, 60, of Boehl, Stopher, Graves and Deindoerfer, Louisville, Kentucky. It is a 13-partner firm that represents 24 insurance companies and groups, plus such corporate clients as Ford

---

* Ages are as of the autumn of 1973.

Motor, Texas Eastern Transmission Company, Coca-Cola, and the Louisville Trust Company. Skilled trial lawyer.

Seventh circuit: Don H. Reuben, 46, of Kirkland & Ellis, the superfirm of Chicago, with 58 partners and 54 associates. Reuben is a close friend and sometime unofficial spokesman for former Chief Judge William J. Campbell of Chicago, and his clients include the *Chicago Tribune*. Reuben is powerful in Chicago and national bar affairs, and people who know him feel he has political ambitions. ABA president Chesterfield Smith, who appointed Reuben to the ABA Federal Judiciary Committee, volunteered to me in a conversation that Reuben's representation of the conservative *Tribune* "made me pause and think awhile before I put him on the committee." No complaints have been heard.

Eighth circuit: Richard E. Kyle, 69, of Briggs & Moran, St. Paul, Minnesota, a 35-lawyer general practice firm. Retired army colonel, heavy background in insurance trial work. Republican.

Ninth circuit: DeWitt Williams, 65, of Seattle, Washington. Phi Beta Kappa graduate of the University of Washington. His small (eight-partner) firm is heavy in insurance clients and also represents the Washington State Medical Association, General Motors, General Motors Acceptance Corporation, and Reynolds Metals. Long active in ABA politics.

Tenth circuit: John R. Couch, 58, of Pierce, Couch, Hendrickson, Gust & Short, Oklahoma City. An insurance trial lawyer, he is active in the insurance section of ABA and the International Association of Insurance Counsels; 15-member firm represents 26 insurance companies and groups, Armco Steel, the City National Bank & Trust Company of Oklahoma City, and Oklahoma Natural Gas Company.

District of Columbia: Charles A. Horsky, 64, of the Washington firm of Covington & Burling, the city's largest (140-odd lawyers) and most prestigious. Horsky specializes in fending off labor problems of client corporations. Brainy, Democratic, he was a White House adviser on District of Columbia affairs during the Kennedy-Johnson years.

Critics assert the one-sided nature of the committee means that members can block appointments of judges who might cause trouble for their corporate clients. Senator Philip Hart, the populist-leaning Democrat from Michigan, once complained of the imbalance when Bernard Segal, a past committee chairman, appeared before a Senate judiciary subcommittee: "It does not include anyone very much younger than I am and I regret to say that is not very young, and it certainly does not include anybody whose color is different from mine. It represents the men who have demonstrated excellence in the practice of what you and I were prepared for when we were in law school—when a course on poverty law would have sounded like something that was suggested by somebody just arriving from the moon."

So what sort of men has the organized bar sought to keep from the bench? One nominee who encountered extraordinary bar opposition because of his background in the labor movement was George C. Edwards, whom President Kennedy picked for the Sixth Circuit Court of Appeals in 1963. Edwards at the time was police commissioner of Detroit, a post he had reached by a most unlikely path. Edwards says his father, a Dallas lawyer, "was probably the best known socialist in the state of Texas for most of his life. I might add, this was not a post for which there was keen competition."

After studies at Harvard law school the young Edwards plunged into labor organizing work in the volatile 1930s. He worked as a field organizer for the League for Industrial Democracy. (An LID successor group, the American Student Union, fell into Communist hands after Edwards left it; he said it was "properly characterized" as Communist by the United States attorney general.) Edwards helped the United Auto Workers in its sit-down strikes in the auto industry. At the Yale & Towne Company, a group of strikers of which he was a part hurled lead weights at police from a factory roof, and picked up tear gas bombs and tossed them back at officers. Edwards and others in the group were fined $250 and sentenced to 30 days in jail by a judge who said: "The testimony in this case is overwhelming that these respondents contemptuously defied the order of the court to evacuate the plant. . . . This has ceased to be a labor controversy. It is not even a question of the legality of a sitdown strike . . . it has now become a question of whether we have a government of law and order or not." Later, while helping the LID organize coal miners in Fort Smith, Arkansas, Edwards and other union leaders were arrested for "barratry." (By Edwards' account, "we were leading a community sing-song when the police arrived." He scoffed at the barratry charge. "Somewhat impossible because . . . it is an offense which can be committed only by a lawyer, and none there were lawyers.")

In the early 1940s, however, Edwards settled into law and politics. He was elected president of the Detroit City Council, a city judge, and then ran for the Michigan Supreme Court and won the largest margin ever given a candidate for state office. He resigned in December 1961 to serve as Detroit police commissioner. But when his nomination for the circuit court came before the Senate Judiciary Committee for confirmation his foes could remember only the old labor strife.

The opposition centered in Tennessee, which is in the sixth circuit area. Most strident was Thomas Crutchfield, speaking for the Chattanooga Bar Association. Opined Crutchfield:

Rudyard Kipling wrote a story many years ago in which he concluded that a leopard does not change its spots. One might say that the Chattanooga bar's opinion in opposing George Edwards is based upon this conclusion. Here is a man who has violated court orders. Here is a man who was not just a member but was an *organizer* of a union. Let him be on the platform and not on the bench.

I cannot for the life of me believe that a person can be brought up to have the faith and the trust and the respect for his father that he states in the record . . . was the leader of the Socialist Party and not have a part brush off on him. . . . I think that this has something to do with our conclusion that a leopard does not change its spots.

Dick L. Lamsden, president of the Nashville Bar Association, opposed Edwards because of his "lack of respect for the orders of the court and his lack of respect for property rights." Senator Olin Johnston asked, "You are basing your opinion purely upon what he did back in the 1930s?" "That is correct," replied the unforgiving Mr. Lamsden.

The Michigan Bar Association, to its credit, stood up for Edwards (as did the ABA Federal Judiciary Committee). Nathan B. Goodnow, president of the Michigan bar, said his firm had represented Yale & Towne in the labor dispute in which Edwards had been arrested. He admitted there was a "bona fide contention that our client had been guilty of one or more unfair labor practices," and that Edwards, then 23 years old, was arrested along with 120 other men and women. Even as "a Republican, as a lawyer on the other side of the fence in that case, I cannot help but feel that it was a fine thing that he and others did in leading that cause."

The hearings dragged over two months but Edwards ultimately won overwhelming confirmation. In the succeeding decade he has acquired a reputation as one of the more erudite and scholarly judges in the federal system.

The ABA has answers for critics who complain that its screening committees are not balanced. As Bernard Segal once patiently explained to a Senate committee, members are chosen by circuit, and are not intended to be "representative" of any segment of the bar. "The committee is only a conduit . . . for the opinions expressed by the judges and the lawyers who know the nominee best in the community in which he practices," Segal protested. A few years later Robert Trescher, another past chairman, made much the same argument when we talked in his Philadelphia office.

"I've heard it said we ought to have blacks, women, labor union members, and what-all on the committee. I don't go along with that. We're not advocating a cause

—the cause of the blacks, the women's libbers, the labor unions, or any other cause. We are exercising an investigative and judicial function. We size people up for their competence to serve as a federal judge. We try to be open-minded and objective. We would be mistaken to stack the deck in any way. To put a woman on the committee just because she is a woman stacks the deck."

Segal concluded, "Nobody ever accused the committee of not being objective and thorough."

Which is not exactly accurate, and which is one reason I sought out John Sutro at the Pillsbury, Madison & Sutro office in the Standard Oil Building in San Francisco one bright July morning. A few days earlier, in another law office around the corner, an attorney had given me an angry speech about the "bastardly, incestuous situation" wherein one of Sutro's partners had been named a federal district judge.

The judge in question was Charles Renfrew. The lawyer didn't question Renfrew's competence ("He's a conservative, and I'm not, but he's intellectually honest and a good judge"), but the fact that his law partner was a part of the mechanism that got him onto the bench. The core of his complaint was that the Nixon Administration put forth Renfrew as a counterweight to "some real loser appointments, ones the ABA wouldn't have bought otherwise." He mentioned specifically Judge Spencer Williams, a frostily conservative veteran of the Ronald Reagan Administration.

"These ABA people will give you a lot of crap about objectivity of screening and the like," this man said. "Well, one way for the administration to keep ABA in line is to throw the ABA a bone every now and then. That way, it's hard for the ABA to turn down a real loser—hell, that wouldn't be gentlemanly."

Sutro proved to be a sparse, gregarious, cheerfully profane fellow who had practiced law (as he told me several times in our 90-minute chat) for 44 years, a past president of the California state bar and the San Francisco chamber of commerce; one of the few lawyers I've ever met who can use the professional trick of answering my question with his question and not being obnoxious about it.

Now that Renfrew appointment. *Reading from my notes, I told Sutro what the other lawyer had said. Fah, fah, fah, responsed Sutro, his arm swinging in an exasperated circle.* "Being on this goddamned committee is a handicap for me, in that respect. Because of it, I can't promote, endorse or recommend anyone for a judgeship. I specifically disqualified myself from anything to do with the Renfrew screening when his nomination came through. I wouldn't even read his personal data questionnaire. The same thing a few years earlier when another of our partners, Judge [Gerald S.] Levin,* was nominated."

I had to interrupt. "You mean two former Pillsbury, Madison & Sutro partners are on the bench in San Francisco?"

Sutro didn't pause. "Sure, and both top rank men, too, damned good trial judges. Now no one did Charlie Renfrew a favor by putting him on the bench. He earned pretty good money in this firm, more than he'll ever make as a judge, you can bet your life.† He de-

_____
* Now deceased.

† Sutro's remark about financial sacrifice was warranted, for big-city lawyers who accept federal judicial appointments almost invariably suffer a cut in annual income. Since 1969 a federal district judge's salary has been frozen at $40,000 (a chief judge gets $2,500 more). During 1973 Judge Thomas A. Masterson of Philadelphia and Chief Judge Sidney O. Smith, Jr., of Atlanta resigned because "of the inadequacy of their judicial salaries," and Judge Frederick B. Lacey of Newark announced his intention to do so for the same reason. According to a letter sent Congress in early 1974 by Rowland F. Kirks, director of the Administrative Office of the United States Courts, "It is reliably reported that 15 lawyers in one area [reportedly New York] have declined judicial appointments because of the inadequacy of judicial salaries." A relatively junior partner in a Washington, New York or Chicago superfirm earns $40,000 very early in his career. Judge Arnold Bauman of New York served only two years before resigning in the spring of 1974, writing President Nixon that inflation "has resulted in a substantial reduction in my real income and has constrained me to conclude that I can no longer continue. . . . [T]he future appears bleak and the problem, for me, is insoluble."

cided he could make a better contribution to the country, and accepted the appointment. He is a selfless man."

The ABA enters the judicial selection process after the White House, senators and other political figures decide on one or more prospects to fill a vacancy. The contact points between the Justice Department and the ABA are, respectively, the deputy attorney general and the chairman of the committee on the federal judiciary. "When I was chairman," said Philadelphia trial lawyer Robert Trescher, Sutro's predecessor, "we worked it very informally. When a name came up, the deputy AG would write or call me stating that X was under consideration for a judgeship. A letter also went to the circuit member and to the candidate himself. The candidate would be asked to fill out a personal data questionnaire we've developed [the PDQ, as everyone calls it] and send copies to the chairman, the circuit representative, and the Justice Department." The five-page questionnaire, with 29 questions, asks great detail about the prospect's personal and professional life (for instance, if he is divorced, he must reveal both the grounds and which spouse initiated the action). The PDQ attempts to pin down the lawyer on his actual trial experience:

> Describe not more than ten of the more significant litigated matters which you handled and give the citations, if the cases were reported. Please give a capsule summary of the substance of each case, and a succinct statement of what you believe to be the particular significance of the case. Please identify the party or parties you represented, describe in detail the nature of your participation . . . and the final disposition. . . . Please also state . . . (a) the dates of the trial period . . . (b) the name of the court and . . . judge and (c) the names and addresses of counsel for the other parties.

The prospect must list outside business activities and directorships, any violations of the law (other than traffic tickets up to $25), any past investigations for "possible violation of a criminal statute," whether he has ever been subject to a tax lien or other collection procedure, suits against him by clients, any other litigation in which he has been defendant, and any bar disciplinary actions (or complaints) of which he has been the target.

"The PDQ alone is enough to scare away most borderline cases," Trescher said. "Several times there's been the situation where a lawyer *thinks* he wants to be a judge, and then realizes he's going to have to lay out his career, and that he really doesn't stack up."

The circuit representative relies heavily upon the PDQ and personal contacts in his background check. He analyzes the cases cited in the PDQ to see if they are as described—"how important and complete they really are," as Trescher said—and talks with the judges and other lawyers involved. Concurrently, he is talking with his own network of sources in the legal community. According to Trescher, "The committee members usually know a large number of lawyers through the circuit; anyone who gets on the committee has been active in the bar, and you get around that way. When you do these interviews you stress carefully at the start that 'X is being considered' because at this point he is not a formal nominee, remember. I say something on this order: 'I will not disclose that I have talked to you nor that you talked to me. My report is only as good as the candor with which you speak to me. In my report I will not use your name if you so prefer. I would prefer to use your name, for it would make a difference in evaluating the person. But under no circumstances do names get outside this committee —not to the deputy attorney general, the senator, the president of the United States, or anyone else.'

"People usually open up right away, even if I don't know them personally. I am amazed that people who have no reason to know me would be so candid over the telephone. And often what they say is at variance with what the prospect might think. You'll find a situation where a lawyer wrote a letter of recommendation. He'll say, 'Yes, I wrote a letter for him, but . . .' and proceed to make comments that are . . . well, quite at odds with the letter. We place very little value on letters, especially solicited letters. And you can tell by the contents when they are solicited."

The number of interviews varies (Sutro told me he once did 95 on a borderline case). Trescher noted, "If you talk to ten or fifteen people, all of whom say he's a bum, you stop. If ten or fifteen all say he's good, you might also stop, there's no point in going on. But if you get a division, you usually keep going until you are certain you have him sized up accurately." If the prospect begins to look doubtful, the circuit representative will likely interview him personally. "It's a matter of fairness to the candidate, to give him an opportunity to respond to charges, to clear up any discrepancies. For example, if lawyers you interview say he has no trial experience of consequence, and the PDQ says otherwise, you would of course talk to him. It's delicate, to conduct these interviews without revealing the source of adverse comments. But they do give an insight into the man's propensity for truth. In his PDQ he might have listed some case as important, and you find he wasn't in court when it was tried. So in the interview, when he is asked specifically about it, he might say, 'Well, it was my *client*, but I actually had my partner try the case.' " Although Trescher did not say so directly, he indicated that such fuzziness well might keep a man off the bench.

The circuit representative's "first phase report" goes only to the committee chairman and the deputy attorney general; it is not circulated to other committee members. According to Trescher, "the chairman goes into as much detail as the deputy attorney general wants. If the case is clear-cut, he might be satisfied with a summary; if the report is adverse, we'll almost always give him the substance of the interviews. After all, he [the deputy attorney general] has to go back to the political force—the senator or the White House—and they are entitled to a good reason for turning a man down; he has to be armed. If a man is found not qualified at this stage, it usually ends then. It's a rarity for the political backers to pressure for that name; they usually have another one waiting."

By Trescher's estimate, about twenty percent of the prospects are found "not qualified" by the first-phase screening. The official ABA line is that the rejects vanish; that politicans supporting the prospect find another man. Well, this isn't exactly true. In 1971 Senator Jacob Javits (R., N.Y.) got crosswise of Brooklyn Republican leaders who wouldn't settle for anyone other than Mark Constantino for the federal district court in the Eastern District of New York. The ABA committee, however, rejected Constantino on the grounds of competence. Whereupon Javits made such a plaintive appeal to Albert R. Connelly, the ABA circuit representative, that the committee decided: oh, well, Javits usually gives us good nominees; let's bend the rules for him—just this once.

In addition to the first-phase screenings, the ABA committee on occasion runs a hyper-secret "preliminary unofficial" investigation when a judgeship is being considered for someone who is prominent but who has a quavery personal and/or professional background— two 1973 examples being a member of Congress who lost his seat and a state judge who aspired for the federal bench. According to Trescher, "Usually this person does not want to run the risk of even a preliminary check, even with the superconfidentiality of the report. He knows a large number of people would be contacted. Even though the report is not binding, he fears an adverse finding might impair his reputation. So this is a situation where the guy will ask his senator or the Justice Department, 'Can't you just get a preliminary line on what my chances are?' The deputy attorney general will call me and ask if I'll get in touch with three or four people. There are no letters, nothing at all in writing. Then I'll call the circuit representative and ask him to go to people who can be trusted. My report goes directly to the deputy attorney general, by phone. Quite a lot of these persons are found unqualified—most of them, in fact. When you add these names to the ones who come to us through regular channels, twenty-five percent of the people we screen are found unqualified."

If the first-phase report shows the person to be

qualified (by ABA standards) the deputy attorney general immediately makes a formal request for screening. The formal process is perfunctory; seldom does the circuit representative go beyond his first-phase interviews. There is one exception: "The rule is pretty firm that he must have an interview with the nominee. The only departure—and they are rare—is when the investigator is under a time pressure, and he already knows the person. You do these in a man's office. It is remarkable what you can learn by looking at a lawyer's office; if it's a rat's nest, you can tell a lot about his mental processes and habits." The PDQ is explored in detail, and a written report goes to all ABA committee members. They vote via letter to the chairman as to how the nominee should be ranked.

And it is at this point that the screening process vanishes into total secrecy: except for a general comment that "occasionally there are splits," neither Trescher nor Sutro would talk about the unanimity, or lack thereof, among the committee; or whether one or more members are prone to cast a blackball; or whether any philosophical or political biases are reflected in the votes. When the committee's recommendation is transmitted to the deputy attorney general no splits or minority opinions are reflected. If one accepted the printed record as fact, which is not my intention, every approval (or rejection) was by unanimous vote. The fact that the ABA can block appointments galls many lawyers; the secrecy heightens suspicions that professional bias—subliminal or avowed—sabotages any prospect who has offended corporations and insurance companies in the past. One Midwestern lawyer (who begged anonymity) told me: "Although I'm a Democrat, in 1970 I was supposed to be part of a three-judge package deal, with the White House putting in two people and Senator ———, my friend, nominating me. Well, they did the screening, and the senator called me, real pained. He said, 'What's the matter—are you a bankrobber in your spare time or something?' It turns out the ABA had thumbed me down, and the only reason the senator could come up with was that I was 'professionally erratic,' whatever the hell that means. I thought way back into memory and the only thing I could think of that might have offended———, who was our circuit representative, was that I beat the pants off his firm in a utilities rate case in the 'sixties. This is something I can never prove, but I'll believe until my dying day that he dropped a sandbag on me."

Harold W. Chase, in an academic study of judicial selection, turned up what he called "disquieting allegations" about two past members of the ABA committee. According to what lawyers told Chase, one of the circuit representatives summoned local attorneys to his hotel suite "and proceeded to hold court in a most imperious fashion, which they thought was insulting." The lawyers felt the circuit representative displayed an anti-Catholic bias. When discussing an investigatee who had attended a Catholic university law school, he reportedly asked, "What could he have learned in that Papist school?" Chase's other episode involved a United States attorney who had been avidly pursuing a judgeship. During a trial the prosecutor roughed up the opposing lawyer, a former member of the ABA committee. Later, in the corridor, the lawyer told the United States attorney: "I know what you want to be and believe me, I'm going to see to it you never get it." Notwithstanding the threat, the prosecutor did become a federal judge a few years later.

The ABA people insist that total secrecy is essential, that given lawyers' professional inhibitions about criticizing one another publicly, any "open" screening would turn the process into the collection of meaningless platitudes. Said one past member of the screening committee: "Any lawyer can find friends to write testimonials for him. But these same people, once they get off in a corner, will tell you they damned well don't want to try a case before him."

By Trescher's testimony one hypocrisy (not his word, but that's what he was talking about) of the screening is that senators and the White House use the committee to knock down unworthy candidates. "We don't mind being used; we don't like being abused," Trescher said. "We consider it part of our work to make it easier for political powers to say 'no.'

Senators, by and large, want well-qualified people for judgeships. But the fact remains that they are subjected to strong pressures from people who do not know what makes a good judge. It's not at all uncommon to get four to six names for one vacancy, and to spend long hours making calls, and to learn very early in the game that some of them are miserably qualified. But you know you are helping get them off the senator's back, and you do it cheerfully. Now I do get ruffled when you get six names and they come up, say, one exceptionally well-qualified, two qualified, and three non-qualified, and then the political powers join behind one of the qualifieds, rather than the top man. At that point we feel abused—but, of course, we recognize that it is not our responsibility to make the appointment."

When a state court judge was being considered for the federal district bench not so long ago, he confided to a lawyer friend, "I want the job for the money. There's no other reason. That's all there is to it." According to another lawyer, the state judge—let's call him M—was so unsure of himself on the bench that he would recess court and seek out another judge for advice before ruling.

M had another problem as well—or many lawyers in his community thought so, at any rate. Before becoming a state judge M got rousingly drunk at a public political event, and in the words of a lawyer present, "disgraced himself." Thereafter M carried the whispered reputation: "Heavy Drinker."

The question: Should this background, as revealed during the ABA's prenomination screening, disqualify M for appointment as a federal district judge?

The answer: No, for the ABA circuit representative doing the background investigation didn't stop with those bits of information. Checking further, he found that some of M's colleagues on the bench thought the better of him because he did ask questions when he didn't know the answers, rather than attempt to bluster his way through a trial. The colleagues called him a "hard worker" and a "learner" and said he "needed less help each month."

The circuit representative confirmed that the report of public drunkenness was true. However, he found that the episode had so frightened M that he cut back his drinking to near-abstinence level. No one was found who had first-hand information that M continued to be a problem drinker. The representative also concluded that given M's work record on the state bench, his remark about wanting the federal judgeship "for the money" was irrelevant, that indeed the job did pay more and that M considered it a promotion for a man of his age. The ABA committee evaluated M as "qualified" and he received the appointment.

How has he performed? I don't know, for the person who permitted me to read the ABA committee's background report deleted M's name and home state.

The ABA waited almost a full century for the unique status bestowed upon it by the Nixon Administration, for it has sought since its very creation to meddle in judicial selection. The leading brahmins of the New York corporate bar founded the ABA in 1878 in the exclusive spa of Saratoga Springs, New York. Judges were very much on the brahmins' minds, for they (and their clients) had problems. Although the robber baron era of American capitalism was at its zenith, and many of the great corporate buccaneering feats had yet to be performed, the first stirrings of the populist movement were felt in the land. Historically, the courts had protected American capitalism from any sweeping tides of public opinion. Now, however, the brahmins were no longer comfortable with popularly-elected politicians, nor with the courts, for that matter. True, in 1876 the United States Supreme Court held eight-hour-day laws unconstitutional. But the same year the Court ruled, of all things, that states could regulate public utilities—meaning that railroad magnates, among others, would have to answer to authorities more compelling than their own consciences.

According to an academic study by Joel B. Grossman on the ABA's influence in selection of federal judges, the bar leaders "saw the judiciary as the last bastion of defense against encroachments on the entrepreneurial prerogative, and intensified their efforts to assure the recruitment of judges who shared their own views of society." In public the ABA talked about such lofty aims as "judicial excellence" and "competence of the trial bench." The ABA's private aims were less lofty. In Grossman's view:

> An inevitable "confusion" between professional qualifications and ideological soundness marked the judicial-selection efforts of the ABA right through the New Deal period. . . . These efforts . . . were clear and frank attempts to gain a measure of control over the decision-making process. It was as much self-interest as public interest that provided the occasion and the impetus for the ABA's judicial selection efforts.

In its first decades the ABA paid little attention to the federal courts, which were considered "safe," for the most part because federal judges reflected ABA social and economic values. Exceptions occasionally arose. In 1916 the ABA decided Louis Brandeis was "not a fit person" for the Supreme Court, and William Howard Taft, a past president both of the United States and the ABA, and six other former ABA presidents, urged Woodrow Wilson not to appoint him. Wilson ignored the ABA. So, too, did the United States Senate in 1929 in rejecting the appointment of the reactionary antilabor jurist, John Parker, to the Supreme Court. The latter defeat so grieved the ABA that it created a special panel to "advise" the Senate Judiciary Committee on federal court appointments. But neither President Hoover nor President Roosevelt took the ABA seriously, and the committee vanished in 1934.

The ABA activities frantically revived in 1946 because of a Supreme Court decision holding that the insurance business was part of interstate commerce and thus subject to antitrust regulation. Many companies interpreted the ruling to mean they were not subject to state regulation, and behaved accordingly—which is to say, badly—until Congress passed a law saying the states in fact could regulate them. But the case had an unsettling impact on both the business community and

62 • THE BENCHWARMERS

the corporate bar, for, as Grossman states, "it came to
be regarded by some lawyers as symptomatic of the
disregard which the 'Roosevelt Court' was showing
toward traditional values and legal precedents." * So
once again the ABA decided to seek the privilege of
putting its stamp of approval on federal nominees.

The key debate was in a June 1946 meeting of the
House of Delegates, the ABA's permanent policy body.
William L. Ransom, a New York lawyer and onetime
ABA president, spelled out the problem: "Criticism
of the courts is a right and function of the bar . . .
[but] mere criticism and the expression of disrespect
fall short of what is expected of us." He urged creation
of a committee "to promote the appointment and confirmation of competent and qualified candidates and to
oppose . . . unfit candidates." Some in the association
wanted to go even further and support the candidacies
of specific lawyers for vacancies. John Buchanan of
Pittsburgh, a political realist, noted, "You cannot oppose very successfully a man with powerful political
backing, who has an unimpeachable family and church
record, and a modest practice in which he has been
guilty of no misconduct, unless you can support, in his
stead, the appointment of a real lawyer." Without such
support, Buchanan said, "real lawyers will stand little
chance against the men who have supported a party
ticket through thick and through thin, [and] who think
that they have reached the place in political service
which entitles them to recognition as judges of the
federal courts." But the ABA majority refused; the
ABA would comment on other people's candidates but
not put forth any of its own.

For the ABA, the new activist policy happily coin-
cided with the Republican capture of control of Congress for the first time since 1932. The Republican
leadership and the ABA quickly struck up a symbiotic
relationship. For the ABA, the benefit was a promise
that it would be heeded in the Senate. As Senator

* The ABA was also disturbed at internal dissension on the
court, chiefly a public feud between Justices Jackson and
Black.

Alexander Wiley (R., Wis.), chairman of the Senate Judiciary Committee, put it, "Full weight will be given to the recommendations of recognized legal groups which have not been accorded the weight and respect which are their just due." For the Republicans, the benefit was the ABA's usefulness as a tool with which they could attempt to thwart objectionable appointments by President Truman. Joel Grossman, among others, wonders whether the ABA would have been issued "the same invitation if the 80th Congress had remained in Democratic hands. As a constant critic of the actions and decisions of the post-1937 Supreme Court Justices [when FDR finally managed to break the deadhand grip of the Nine Old Men], the ABA was the perfect instrument through which Senate Republicans could attempt inroads on the nominations of a Democratic president." Although Senate Republicans were not consulted in advance on judicial appointments, even in their home states, they could use adverse ABA recommendations as a pretext to reject some nominations, and as a bargaining tool to force Truman to submit more acceptable candidates.

Truman didn't like the ABA role at all, and especially after the ABA teamed with the Senate Republicans to beat his appointment of Frieda Hennock, a member of the Federal Communications Commission, to the district court in the Southern District of New York. The grounds were supposed unethical conduct in a case more than a decade earlier, details of which were never revealed publicly. Truman stood behind Ms. Hennock to the end, and said he had appointed "plenty of good judges opposed by the bar associations," and that bar opposition did not disturb him. He welcomed bar endorsements, but said lack of bar support would not deter him from making any appointments. The Justice Department, with Truman's blessing, refused to consult with the ABA prior to nominations, despite pleas that it do so. And when the Democrats regained control of Congress in 1950 Senator Pat McCarran (D., Nev.), the new judiciary committee chairman, declared he was "firmly resolved that the bar associations shall not choose the judiciary of the country." During the Truman Administration the ABA opposed a total of ten nominations; four were rejected. One Truman appointee the bar supported was Judge Robert T. Tehan, of Milwaukee, who went on the bench in 1949. The appointment was political: Tehan was Wisconsin Democratic chairman, and helped win the state for Truman in 1948. Not until Tehan was confirmed was it discovered that he had not filed income tax returns from 1936 to 1944. Tehan claimed he was broke, and he finally settled with the tax people. His tenure was marked by frequent and bitter wrangles over his handling of bankruptcy cases, with opponents on two occasions asking the House Judiciary Committee to initiate impeachment proceedings. Tehan retained formal bar support throughout the controversies. He went into senior status in 1970.

To the ABA's dismay, the Eisenhower Administration also proved initially hostile—in practice if not in enunciated policy. Both Attorney General Herbert Brownell and his deputy (and later successor), William Rogers, said many nice things about the virtues of ABA involvement. At the same time, they used judgeships to reward campaign supporters and pay off various political debts. Ten of the appointments were in the face of adverse ABA recommendations. The Administration did not consult the ABA in naming Earl Warren as chief justice. But there is evidence the decision wasn't a presidential one. When Bernard Segal of Philadelphia became chairman of the ABA judicial committee in 1956 he met with Brownell and Rogers to ask that his panel be permitted to comment on Supreme Court justices in advance of appointment. As Segal tells the story, "Mr. Brownell and Mr. Rogers threw their hands up in horror and said, 'Oh, no. That has always been an exclusive prerogative of the president. It is rarely discussed even with the senators from the prospective appointee's home state. . . .' " At the very moment of this conversation, President Eisenhower was asked at a press conference what would have to be the qualifications of the successor to Justice Sherman Minton, who had retired. "I believe . . . that we must never appoint a man [to the Supreme Court] who doesn't have the recognition of the ABA," Ike replied. Segal recollects with glee, "By the time I got to the railroad station, this was in the evening newspapers in Washington. I could not wait to get to the telephone. Indeed, I missed my train trying to reach Mr. Brownell and Mr. Rogers."

With Brownell and Rogers gravely embarrassed, the Justice Department thereafter gave the ABA the names of judicial prospects for informal screening in advance of their nominations. The ABA devised a rating system for the candidates: unqualified, qualified, well-qualified, and exceptionally well-qualified.* During the remaining two years of the Eisenhower Administration the ABA commented on— but could not veto—judicial candidates. The important point is that the ABA had finally gotten its foot inside the door.

We must digress a moment to politics. In the late 1950s federal judges complained of overwork and asked for help. Learned studies confirmed that the nation, indeed, needed more judges. But the Democrats controlling Congress were not about to hand the lame-duck Eisenhower a basket of such rich patronage plums even when the administration, in either desperation or last-ditch pragmatism, offered to split the appointments 50–50. Bar leaders talked outragedly about "political irresponsibility" and Vice President Nixon egged them on, telling the 1959 ABA convention, "I believe it is essential . . . that the number of judges in our federal courts from each of the two major political parties should be approximately equal." The Democrats chuckled and held their ground. True, the federal trial bench *was* almost equally divided between Democratic and Republican appointees, but only because Eisenhower had continued the noble tradition of going to his own party for appointees, thereby balancing off two-score years in which Roosevelt and Truman did the same thing, which in turn balanced off a dozen years in which Harding, Coolidge and Hoover. . . . Anyway, you get the idea.

---

* The definitions of these ratings have changed over the years, in language if not in substance. The current criteria are listed in the Appendix.

The partisan percentages run this way: Harding, 95 percent; Coolidge, 92; Hoover, 82.7; Roosevelt, 95; Truman, 91; and Eisenhower, 92.5. The Democrats said, in effect, the game's been played this way by both teams most of the century, and phony piety by the Republicans and the bar leaders (most of whom were and are Republican anyway) is no reason to change. (Presidents Johnson and Nixon continued the partisan tradition: 94 percent of Johnson's nominees were Democrats; 92 percent of Nixon's first-term appointments were Republicans.)

Promptly upon Kennedy's election, Congress zipped through an omnibus judgeship bill giving the new president—and, of course, the politicians who helped elect him or whose friendship he now needed—an unprecedented store of judicial boodle to distribute. The act created 71 new judgeships. That wasn't all. Because of vacancies the Democratic Senate had not permitted Ike to fill, Kennedy during his first twenty months in office appointed 147 persons to the federal bench. By way of perspective, Harding, Coolidge and Hoover didn't have that many judgeships in their combined terms. In one slam-bang stretch of 47 days, from August 11 through September 27, 1961, 69 judges were nominated or appointed, an average of almost eleven per week.* By midsummer 1962 almost 40 percent of federal judges were Kennedy appointees.

The Kennedy Administration churned up many of the nominees through an informal "spotter" system of lawyers around the country coordinated by the deputy attorney general, Nicholas Katzenbach, and four assistant attorneys general: Louis Oberdorfer, Ramsey Clark, H. Jack Miller, and William Orrick. By the existing record, Attorney General Robert F. Kennedy tended to put more faith in this chain of contacts than he did in the ABA committee. Kennedy did agree to give the ABA an advance look at prospective nominees, although he did not bind himself to follow its findings.

---

* The Republicans had their turn with passage of another omnibus judgeship bill in 1970. Nixon nominated 74 judges between June 2 and December 22.

The ABA recognized Kennedy's political problems in trying to satisfy patronage demands after eight years of Republican rule. As Bernard Segal, then the chairman of the Federal Judiciary Committee, told the ABA convention in 1962, "We are fully aware that political pressures are great on any President, especially at the start of a new administration marked by a change from one party to another. . ."

A further complication, Segal said, was the "fact that many judges and lawyers so readily comply with the requests of even clearly unqualified candidates or their sponsors, by sending letters of endorsement or commendation in their behalf. Thus, they arm political supporters with what appear to be strong substantiation of claims that their candidates are men of the highest qualification when the contrary is the fact."

The Kennedys, for their part, were glad to make use of the ABA when they could. During the first 18 months of the administration, the Justice Department asked the ABA to report on 459 persons. Of the 158 found not qualified, 150 were not heard of again, even though, as Segal noted, "many had strong sponsorship and substantial political support." Without the ABA, he boasted, "there is no doubt that at least some of them, probably a substantial number, would have been appointed." (Of the eight not-qualifieds who *were* appointed, Segal and the ABA notwithstanding, more in a moment.) The ABA was also most pleased that the vast majority of the people it rated "exceptionally well-qualified" during the informal screening were appointed.

Which is not to suggest that relations were always smooth. The attorney general's inner circle did not entirely trust all the ABA people. As one former assistant attorney general has said, "When you deal with the ABA, you have to deal from knowledge. . . . I gave a name to the ABA. They sent it back saying the man wasn't qualified; he had lousy grades in law school. I told them he was Phi Beta Kappa and Order of the Coif; they must have been misinformed. It just so happened that someone on the ABA committee had another candidate whom he wanted appointed and planted a false story. Heads of ABA committees occasionally give false information when they have their own candidates. The Department of Justice must have the capability of knowing as much as the ABA, and this should all be done privately."

Stung by the ABA criticisms, the Justice Department occasionally reminded the bar that the president and the Senate—not the nation's lawyers—bore the responsibility for appointing federal judges. Speaking to the ABA House of Delegates in mid-1962, Deputy Attorney General Nicholas B. Katzenbach said he did not doubt that some judges selected by the administration would prove to be "unworthy and unqualified." But he felt its choices would be as good as any made by the ABA screening committee. Polite but sarcastic, Katzenbach said, "I would be very surprised if this committee were omniscient and infallible . . . and I do not think that they would claim that infallibility. I think that at least some of the judges found by this committee to be qualified will . . . prove to have been bad appointments."

The Justice Department often felt the ABA was too rigid, especially its criteria on age (no appointments of persons 60 years or over) and experience (ordinarily at least 15 years as a lawyer, including "a substantial amount of trial experience"). The latter, for all practical purposes, meant lawyers must be 40 or over to be considered for appointment to the bench —and Attorney General Kennedy was only 35 when the administration began. Hence the Justice Department was not as respectful of the age rule as the ABA would have liked, and about twenty percent of its nominees fell shy of the 15-year rule. The ABA, while claiming that it "approves the practice of appointing *some* [my emphasis] promising younger lawyers to the bench when they have had sufficient experience," harrumphed in the next breath that it really didn't feel that way at all. "Most of them," it said of the younger Kennedy appointees, "appeared to be able men on the threshold of promising careers as practicing lawyers, but they had not yet had very great exposure, nor an opportunity to demonstrate their mature capacities." In other words, spare us these kids.

Just to balance things, however, the Kennedy Justice Department went off the other end of the ABA age scale in selecting Sarah T. Hughes of Dallas, who was past the maximum age of 64. (How far? Mrs. Hughes stopped counting her birthdays publicly decades ago.) A state trial judge for 26 years, the petite Judge Hughes walked with a teenager's bounce and seldom missed a court day. In terms of energy, intellect and common sense she was the star of the Dallas trial bench. She was also fiercely Democratic. As a courts reporter for the *Dallas News* in 1960, I was startled one day to enter Judge Hughes' office and find her and a secretary clad in red, white and blue Kennedyette uniforms; they were ready for the candidate's motorcade. (Her campaigning done for the day, Judge Hughes slipped her black judicial robes over the JFK garb and went back to work.) In 1961 Vice President Johnson and House Speaker Sam Rayburn insisted that Judge Hughes receive a federal appointment. The ABA said no, that she was unqualified because of age. Attorney General Kennedy told Speaker Rayburn of the opposition and said he was inclined to agree; regardless of Judge Hughes' abilities, the administration did not want to break an age rule it had implicitly accepted. "Sonny boy," the venerable Rayburn replied, "in your eyes most folks look too old." Kennedy apparently decided he'd rather offend the ABA than the redoubtable Rayburn, so he called in Ramsey Clark, an assistant attorney general, and told him, "Ramsey, in three minutes I want you to give me some solid reasons why we should take Sarah Hughes as a judge." Clark, a Texan, was well aware of the political bind on his boss, and he didn't need three minutes. "There are three reasons," he said. "We need woman judges, and she has been a good one on the state court. Women live longer than men, so if you want to be scientific about it, give her the benefit of the doubt. Third, a gentleman never asks a lady her age." *

---

* The Hughes appointment was also caught up in intense bargaining between Vice President Johnson and Senator Yarborough over four Texas judiciary vacancies. Johnson tried to claim them all, citing an alleged precedent set by Vice Presi-

Thirteen years later Sarah T. Hughes runs as active a trial calendar as ever—even though she is in her late seventies—and is regarded as one of the top judges in the state.

From the ABA's viewpoint, the first Kennedy years were what one man called a "feeling-out period," with neither side entirely sure of the motives and good faith of the other. One committee member recollects, "Nick Katzenbach kept telling us they had a few 'must obligations.' Well, we sort of ducked and let some so-so appointments go by. Let me be frank. We were dealing with a new administration, and with people who were suspicious of the ABA. The Kennedy people weren't the corporate types; in a lot of areas we just didn't synchronize. I had the idea that if we turned down too many judges, Bob Kennedy and Katzenbach would have told us to go to hell. They could have done it, too, from the public relations standpoint that the 'Republican fat-cat lawyers' in the ABA were gunning for good liberal Democratic lawyers."

In picking judges, however, the Kennedys had far more trouble with the Senate than with the ABA. Senator James Eastland (D., Miss.) ran the Senate Judiciary Committee in those days, and the Kennedys decided early on to listen to him on appointments in the heart-of-Dixie Fifth Circuit, which includes Alabama, Georgia, Florida, Texas, Louisiana, and Mississippi. Of 20 appointments to district judgeships in the

---

dent John Nance Garner in the 1930s. Yarborough resisted, and Senator James Eastland (D., Miss.) backed him, and refused to clear any appointments through the judiciary committee until the Texas senator was satisfied. Johnson first agreed to make appointments in Houston and Dallas, while Yarborough would take vacancies in East and West Texas, where he had much political support. Then Johnson changed his mind, and Yarborough agreed to take Dallas and Houston. Hence he had final say on Judge Hughes' appointment. Yarborough is convinced Johnson's initial support of Judge Hughes was a gesture, since she was too old for approval. However, Yarborough had been friendly with Mrs. Hughes since they served in state government in the 1930s, and he says he insisted that the Justice Department go through with her appointment.

Fifth Circuit between 1961 and 1963, five went to men who were consistently hostile on civil rights issues both before and after going on the bench. As Victor Navasky wrote in his exhaustive study of the Justice Department in the Kennedy years,* "While there can be legitimate debate about their [the judges'] motives and fine distinctions may be made among them . . . there can be no denying that during the turbulent Kennedy years these men, along with others whose records are spottier, consistently decided civil rights cases against Negroes (and white civil rights proponents) who had clear law on their side, evidenced by the fact that their rulings were invariably overturned in the upper courts." The judges, all still active, are William Harold Cox of Mississippi, E. Gordon West of Louisiana, Robert Elliott of Georgia, and Clarence Allgood and Walter Gewin of Alabama. The worst of the lot has been Cox, Eastland's roommate in college and a man who actively pursued a judgeship from the moment the administration began. Robert Kennedy interviewed Cox at length before approving the nomination, and reported Cox has sworn to "uphold the Constitution." (Judge Elbert Tuttle, of the Fifth Circuit, is reliably reported to have said of the conversation: "The trouble . . . is that they were talking different languages. When Bobby asked him if he would uphold the law of the land, he was thinking about *Brown v. Board of Education* [the landmark 1954 school desegregation decision]. But when Cox said yes, he was thinking about lynching. When Cox said he believed Negroes should have the vote, he meant two Negroes." Once on the bench Cox referred to black litigants as "niggers" and was outspokenly hostile to civil rights cases. He once wrote John Doar, then the assistant attorney general in the Justice Department's Civil Rights Division, "I spend most of my time in fooling with lousy cases brought before me by your Department in the Civil Rights field and I do not intend to turn my docket over to your department for your political advancement." During a voter registration case he stormed, "Who is telling these people they

---

* *Kennedy Justice,* Atheneum, New York, 1971.

can get in line [to attempt to register] and push people around, acting like a bunch of chimpanzees?" (The ABA, for the record, rated Cox "extremely well-qualified" at his confirmation hearing.)

By reliable account the ABA bent its own guidelines a few times to let so-so candidates slip through. In one instance the Kennedy Administration wanted a Mexican-American judge for South Texas, in view of the large *latino* population there. (The decision was "right" for a practical matter as well: more than eighty percent of the Mexican–Americans voted Kennedy–Johnson.) The ABA objected to the first three names submitted, however, and the attorney general had committee chairman Segal in for a little chat. Whereupon Segal lobbied the committee into a "qualified" vote for Reynaldo B. Garza, who proved to be a competent if not brilliant jurist. But in the words of an ABA committee member of the period, "Regardless of the surface smoothness, there was a hell of a lot of pushing and shoving, with the bar trying to hold to the guidelines, and the administration trying to balance us with the politicians. I'm not going to put any names into this, but I'd guess there were ten, twelve cases where someone we found 'not qualified' the first time around was jiggled over the line when Justice griped."

According to this man, several persons on the committee in late 1961 decided to throw down the gauntlet. They would choose "a particularly smelly appointment" and make a major effort to block it in the Senate. "The idea was to put the administration on notice that, while we would bargain, we wouldn't flop over and play dead just to keep up the fiction that we had a real say in things. Now some of the people, Segal particularly, had the idea that there were tactical advantages to keeping quiet even when a lousy appointment came along, that we could have more influence in the long run if we didn't embarrass the administration publicly. I didn't buy that. Either screening was for real or it wasn't. So there was a real feeling we should look for a 'horrible example' appointment and fuss about it."

The "horrible example" came soon enough—in New York, which received eight new judgeships in the omnibus bill. Because both New York senators were Republicans, the Kennedys turned elsewhere for nominations. One person consulted was Representative Emanuel Celler, titular leader of the state's congressional delegation, and chairman of the House Judiciary Committee. Celler had only one name: Irving Ben Cooper. Celler seldom made patronage demands; Celler's committee was to handle civil rights legislation; and Celler was a man with whom the Kennedys must do business. Hence Cooper was tantamount to a "must" appointment.

On the surface Cooper looked attractive. As a young lawyer he worked on the famed Seabury probe of corruption among New York police, and served Mayor Fiorello La Guardia as a special counsel. Appointed to the Court of Special Sessions, a criminal trial bench, Cooper sat for more than twenty years before retiring. He was popular both with the Jewish community and the Democratic Party—a non-doctrinaire liberal who enjoyed a splendid public image.

But lawyers who practiced before Cooper and judges who sat with him knew another side of the man: a blustering, egotistical tyrant whose courtroom behavior was so erratic that (according to the affidavit of a Legal Aid Society lawyer) many lawyers jeeringly called him "Bellevue Ben." When the Justice Department asked the bar's informal opinion of Cooper in August 1961 the judiciary committee of the Association of the Bar of the City of New York (ABCNY) concluded he was unqualified. Undeterred, Kennedy waited until Congress adjourned, then nominated Cooper as an interim appointee, meaning he could sit until the Senate acted on him. The bar accepted the challenge. The ABCNY hired a special investigative counsel, Seymour M. Klein, who spent two months talking with people who knew Cooper. According to what Klein found, Cooper had been a judicial disgrace almost from the moment he became a state court judge. Some items in chronological order:

- Judge Matthew J. Troy, a retired justice of the Court of Special Sessions, sat with Cooper beginning in

1940. Cooper, he said, berated lawyers for no apparent reason; when Troy suggested he calm down, Cooper would try to control his temper. "Then very suddenly, without any warning, he would explode over some real or imaginary grievance. . . . He would assume someone was talking about him in the court or laughing at him or looking at him. . . . We always felt that he had a persecution complex, that everybody was against him. If you dissented on a ruling by Judge Cooper, as we were compelled in conscience to do, he felt that that was a personal affront to him; that you were questioning his judgement and his integrity." Cooper's conduct eventually became so bad other judges asked they not be required to sit with him.

- When Cooper became chief justice of the Court of Special Sessions he refused to continue handling a normal caseload, even if his absence meant defendants stayed in prison unnecessarily over a weekend because of a shortage of judges. According to Troy, Cooper maintained it would "lower his prestige" to sit as a trial judge.

- Nonetheless Cooper would hold night sessions of a special "probation court" and invite VIP guests to sit on the bench and watch him discharge kids from a rehabilitation program. Jean Cox of the Legal Aid Society called these performances "another indication of exhibitionism" by Cooper. Although the youth offender act was intended to shield juveniles from harmful publicity, she said Cooper's sessions caused the youngsters "to be held up to the gaze of strangers and prominent guests."

- Cooper's courtroom tirades were so titanic that lawyers and aids coined a word to describe them— "cooperized," which meant to be "hauled into chambers and be berated." The experience of Wallace Keyser, a process server, was typical. Keyser tried to hush a talkative police spectator, only to be accused himself of a disruption; Cooper had him physically locked out of the court, and then called him to his office with an assistant district attorney. Cooper made a long speech on the burdens and responsibilities of a judge, then demanded of Keyser, "What have you got to say for yourself?" Keyser said, "I felt like a big criminal, like a big jerk just sitting there in the middle. But I felt if I took the job, and he's the judge, I had better be nice. So I said, 'Your honor, you are right, you do have a big job and we all have to work together to help make it easier for you.' He stared directly at me and screamed 'we, we, we,' about five times, meaning putting myself in his class. 'How dare you say "we"?' Then he started to rave. His eyes started popping. His eyes turned purple. He looked like a reincarnation, the devil or something." The outburst so stunned Keyser he stood and asked if he could be excused. "I felt sick, I was actually sick. He said, 'Go ahead. Get out of here you yellow-livered so-and-so. No backbone, no spine, no spunk, no substance . . . I know what you are. Don't ever let me see you again.' He moved his hands as if he was brushing a roach." Keyser was so shaken that when he reported the incident to his superior "for the first time in my adult life I started to cry. . . . I was shocked and I was humiliated."

- According to other affidavits Cooper loved to parade between his court and chambers, robes billowing as he greeted people. A new bailiff once led him and opened the door to what he thought were Cooper's chambers. "Judge Cooper, without looking, marched into the room and found he was in a porter's closet with mops and brooms. He flew into a tirade, screamed at the attendant and accused him of trying to make a fool of him." Cooper also told the hapless bailiff, "I am sure you were assigned to humiliate me because you are tall and I am short."

- Jean Cox said she had seen Cooper "on the bench screaming, having a tantrum reminding me of a baby in a high chair." He would tell defendants—often Puerto Rican youths who didn't even understand English—that they were "the slime of the earth." Anthony Marra, who ran Legal Aid's criminal division, said, "working for Judge Cooper can best be likened to the dismantling of a time bomb. No one knew when he was going to explode."

- Cooper had little patience with outsiders as well. He once got into a name-calling squabble with bus driver John McNeil on Riverside Drive. By McNeil's account, Cooper yelled "son of a bitch" at him. When he stopped to remonstrate with the judge, a shoving match ensued. Cooper demanded to the bus company that the driver and an official appear in his chambers. Attorney John J. Sweeney went along with McNeil, a neighborhood friend. According to Sweeney, Cooper kept pointing to McNeil and talking about "bums like you" and "punks like you." After an hour-long tirade, McNeil was ready to apologize so he could get out of Cooper's range. But Cooper flung his cigar to the floor and said (according to Sweeney) that he did not "need any apology from any scum like that."

- Which is not to say that Cooper picked his victims by social class. Retired Naval Admiral Dashiel Madeira, a partner in the prestigious investments firm of Brown, Madeira & Company, served on a grand jury that indicted two probation officers in Cooper's court. Madeira and other members met with Cooper to urge that the Probation Department exert more control over its officers. According to Madeira, "Judge Cooper became very incensed and delivered us a browbeating lecture. His face became flushed. His eyes were upturned. He threw out his arms. He walked about and continued to turn and browbeat the committee." Cooper dismissed the jurors without a word of thanks or farewell. Madeira said, "I thought we had done him a favor by bringing the situation to his attention."

To present its case, the opposition to Cooper's confirmation brought in some of the more distinguished brahmins of the Wall Street bar. Herbert Brownell, attorney general under Eisenhower, and then the president of the Association of the Bar of the City of New York, summarized, "If ever a clear case of lack of judicial temperament existed, this is it. If ever a candidacy for judgeship called for refusal of confirmation, I respectfully submit this is the case." Orison S. Marsden, a past president of the ABCNY, and soon to be president of the ABA, opined that Cooper "has been emotionally unstable for a number of years," and said the bar erred in supporting him for judicial appointments on earlier occasions.

The Senate Judiciary Committee was outspokenly hostile to the bar witnesses. Senator John McClellan (D., Ark.), the chairman, didn't like the idea of the ABA trying to blackball a nominee. He did not object to investigations by the ABA, "but I do not presume to let the ABA judgement supersede mine with respect to the [United States] attorneys and the United States district judges in my state. If I know somebody well enough to recommend him, I certainly intend to fight for his confirmation." On such "general interests" benches as circuit courts and the Supreme Court, McClellan said he "would go a long way leaning towards the judgements and the recommendations" of the ABA. "But when it comes to a United States district judge in my state, I do not yield to the ABA in selecting them." McClellan was skeptical of the ABA investigations: "I know how you do it. In my state you send somebody down from North Dakota to talk to four or five lawyers, and come back and make a report. I do not think it amounts to anything. In fact, sometimes it amounts to the reverse of what is right and best and just."

Cloyd LaPorte, a Wall Street lawyer who was the ABA's committee member for the Second Judicial Circuit, didn't impress McClellan in the least. LaPorte maintained he began his investigation favorably disposed toward Cooper because of newspaper accounts he had read over the years. Also, many judges and lawyers had written warm endorsing letters to the attorney general and White House. LaPorte, however, said he found some of the letters had been "solicited with persistence and urging," and that Cooper had asked that copies be sent to him. Resultantly, LaPorte said, such letters tend to be uniformly favorable and "to gloss over the weak points in the candidate's qualifications."

Pressed by McClellan, LaPorte at first refused to say how he learned Cooper generated the letters. He pleaded confidentiality of sources; if lawyers and judges knew their candid remarks to the ABA would be revealed to prospective appointees, no one would talk. This policy distressed McClellan, "The poor fellow that is up for confirmation cannot find out who said it, and what interest he may have had." When a person is refused confirmation, "you can hurt him . . . his character is at stake, his ability is at stake, his suitableness [sic] to serve in a judicial capacity is at stake. I want facts. I do not want somebody's opinion based upon what somebody told them whose name they cannot give. I cannot go along with that."

Relenting, LaPorte gave an example. Florence M. Kelley, judge of the domestic relations court, formerly head of the Legal Aid Society's criminal branch, had written Attorney General Kennedy a letter praising Cooper and asking that he be nominated. But she said the letter should be "read in context" with interviews with the ABA and the Justice Department. Even though she considered Cooper a friend, "I, too, at times was the recipient of his judicial ire in court or in chambers and without, I believe, justification. . . . Valued members of my staff were banished by Judge Cooper from his court or refused to return because of the way in which they had been treated." She felt he lacked judicial temperament for the federal court.

Cooper's defenders conceded the judge was strong-minded. David Peck, a former justice of the New York Supreme Court, called him "somewhat evangelical" on administration of justice, and said, "he is not a placid person, he is not a relaxed person." Another justice, William C. Hecht, Jr., called Cooper "intense" and a "strict disciplinarian." And several court aids testified bar investigators tried to get them to sign misleading statements attacking Cooper.

Cooper, in his testimony, vigorously defended his work on special sessions, a court he found to be a "miserable panorama of horror" when he first went there. Cooper said toughness was required to gain, and maintain, order. "I was not running a popularity contest. It made very little difference to me whether they liked me or didn't like me." He denied any recollection of most of the incidents recited by opponents, although he did sharply criticize several of the legal aid lawyers ("a judge-baiter," he called one woman). He denied personal abuse of either lawyers or defendants. His version of the bus-driver incident was that McNeil was "arrogant and a ruffian" who tried to run him down. Cooper called him to his office for a chat, rather than having him fired, because he had "pity" for a family man.

In the end the bar opposition foundered (even though critics managed to keep the hearings alive from March through August, intermittently). The Senate Judiciary Committee, a great respecter of Congressional courtesy, could muster no enthusiasm for rejecting an appointment pushed by Representative Celler, chairman of its counterpart committee in the House. As the hearings neared their close, with Cooper on the bench almost a year by virtue of the recess appointment, the chief judge in his district, Sylvester Ryan, administered the coup de grace to the opposition. He wrote the Senate that Cooper had been a competent judge who kept his temper and worked hard. That did it. Cooper cleared the judiciary committee without dissent and not a single senator spoke against his nomination when it reached the floor.

Despite the rebuff, one person active on the ABA committee at the time nonetheless argues the opposition did some lasting good. "The Kennedy Administration stopped making those crappy appointments," he said. "That is worth the fight, right there." The ABA man also noted a marked change in the abrasive personality of Irving Ben Cooper. "Cooper was as sweet as an angel on the bench," he said. "That old temper of his just didn't pop out." Not so, retorts a New York trial lawyer. "Cooper's behavior is erratic," the man said. "He's smart enough to behave when the press is present, and he's polite to big-name lawyers. But give him a run-of-the-mill case and he can drive the lawyers crazy."

"If judges don't have the intestinal fortitude to send someone to jail, they should get out of the judge business," Judge Samuel Conti of San Francisco declared to an interviewer in 1971. "This is too good a country to go down the drain with permissiveness." Conti, a hard-eyed little guy with a liking for flashy clothes—a colleague joshes, "He looks like our in-house bookie" —is archetypical of the Nixon judicial appointees: under 50 years of age (which means he will have an impact upon American justice for two decades); certifiably hard-line on "law and order" issues (Conti proved himself with gaspingly severe sentences while a state court judge, before his elevation to the federal bench); not overly intellectual ("This administration wants men who will enforce the law, not rhapsodize about it," notes a Republican lawyer in Washington who helped the Nixonians with judicial recruitment); an active dislike for counter-culture people at any level (at a private luncheon in San Francisco one day I heard Conti issue a firecracker-string of one-line jokes about the sexual lives of such diverse personages as Justice William O. Douglas and Elizabeth Taylor; two other Republican judges at the table laughed uproariously, although some other people there questioned both Conti's taste and sense of humor); and finally, a politically valuable tie with a group with which the administration wishes to be friends (Conti is well known, and seemingly popular, in the Italo-American community in the San Francisco Bay area, collectively Democratic but shaky just before the 1972 elections).

There is nothing clandestine about Nixon's remaking of the federal judiciary. The vast majority of the 142 district court judges he appointed during his first term * were exactly what he promised in a 1968 campaign white paper on crime; jurists who would side with what

---

* During his 12 years, by contrast, President Roosevelt appointed only 194 judges, a record Nixon will have passed by the time this book is printed; President Johnson had 122.

he called "the peace forces" against the "criminal forces." Devotion to "law and order," as defined by the Nixonians, was the litmus test for judicial nominees. The Nixon judges, lawyers generally agree, are for the most part a technically competent bunch. They know the mechanics of running a trial; they are well enough versed in the law that they do not embarrass themselves or anyone else; they have clean, if not particularly distinguished professional backgrounds (as one Midwest lawyer says, "The Nixon judge is more apt to have been president of a Greek letter fraternity than of Order of the Coif or another legal society"). In the opinion of a Washington law professor who is a judge buff, "What Nixon wanted, apparently, was a generation of trial judges who would resist judicial activism, and who would be a weight to swing the entire federal court system in sort of a semi-arc back towards conservatism. I'm disappointed, for I happen to be a lawyer who believes in an innovative judiciary, and I'm fearful that these people will have a long-term stifling effect upon the federal district courts. But, again, Nixon told the American people what he intended to do, and they elected him, and now he's doing it."

Political scientist Sheldon Goldman, in an analysis of Johnson and Nixon appointees to the lower federal courts published in *The Journal of Politics* on August 1972, found many surface similarities. The majority attended private or Ivy League schools, suggesting they came from "at least middle-class backgrounds." Almost half had records of "prominent partisan activism" (48.4 percent for the Johnson appointees; 45.5 percent for Nixon). About two-thirds had either prosecutorial or judicial experience. But there are marked differences as well, Professor Goldman said. About two of five Nixon appointees were affiliated with large law firms (five or more members) at the time of their selection, while only one of five Johnson appointees was so affiliated. Goldman said this figure suggests the Nixon judges "come from a higher socio-economic stratum than the Democratic appointees." The large-firm tilt by Nixon was especially noticeable in the South—two of three appointees. Further, Goldman notes that the "political activists" Johnson put on the bench tended to be drawn from elective officials or candidates, the Nixon appointees from the Republican organization leadership, and particularly in the south. Goldman said this indicates "a manifestation of a Southern party-building strategy, or perhaps a reflection of the fact that Republicans had few other partisan outlets because of the past history of Democratic dominance of that region." Goldman also picked up a religious difference: Johnson appointed 57.4 percent Protestant; 31.9 percent Catholic; 10.7 percent Jewish. For Nixon, the figures are 73.2 percent Protestant; 18.7 percent Catholic, 8.1 Jewish.*

Many Nixon appointees reflected traditional judicial politics. In California, which had no Republican senators to whom he was obliged to defer, Nixon found benches for his former law partner (Lawrence T. Lydick) and also for a bosom political ally of Governor Ronald Reagan (Spencer Williams) who was clobbered when he ran for state attorney general. Williams barely eked past the ABA screeners. Some San Francisco lawyers are astounded at the prospect of practicing before him for 25 years. In the opinion of one activist, "Williams is an ideologue who seems to decide cases upon "*who* you are, rather than *what* you are saying in court." For instance, Williams thinks prison authorities should have carte blanche to run their institutions pretty much as they wish. When inmates at San Quentin protested about alleged beatings by guards after a shooting in the penitentiary Williams didn't even bother holding a hearing before dismissing the suit. By contrast, another San Francisco judge, Alfonso J. Zirpoli, moved his court into a prison for a formal hearing when considering a parallel complaint by inmates elsewhere.

One potential judicial disaster was averted through the combined energies of Senator Gaylord Nelson (D.,

---

* Goldman's report was part of an on-going study of the characteristics of federal judicial appointees—extraordinarily valuable work not performed by any other judicial critic, governmental or private.

Wis.) and the ABA. Representative Glenn R. Davis, a Wisconsin Republican, began pressuring the White House for a judgeship in 1970. A proud and self-identified protégé of the late Senator Joseph McCarthy, Davis is somewhat of a landmark on the farthest-right reaches of the Republican Party. Davis also has some rather unpleasant personal dislikes. During a public wrangle a few years back he publicly denounced an opponent as a "Jewish bill collector" and called another "a professional Jew." Davis has also said similarly unkind things about Italo-American Democrats in the heat of political battle. Nonetheless Davis voted loyally with his party during his 19 years in the House, and the Justice Department, when asked, sent his name over to the ABA for informal screening. Davis flunked. The ABA termed him "unqualified," and the Justice Department so informed him—thinking this would halt his campaign. Davis didn't desist. He went over the Justice Department's head to the White House, and argued loud and long; he asked an exception to the ABA-approval-required rule "just this one time." When the White House stalled, Davis went quasi-public and began telling people back in Wisconsin that "biased members" of the ABA committee were blocking him. Senator William Proxmire (D., Wis.), who generally shows better sense, gave Davis a boost when he wrote a constituent that while "you can say plenty against" the Congressman, putting him on the bench would not necessarily be bad. "As a judge," Proxmire wrote, "he will be subject to appeals [and] he will be surrounded by some of the best judges in the country." * Senator Nelson finally stepped in and said that under no circumstances would he support Davis. Facing a protracted and probably losing confirmation fight, Davis bowed out, and the nomination went to Robert A. Warren, the Republican attorney general in Wisconsin.

---

* *The Progressive Magazine,* which published Proxmire's letter in April 1974, commented, "Under that curious line of reasoning, we suppose, Proxmire is equally ready to award federal judgeships to John Mitchell, E. Howard Hunt, and any lawyer who happens to make the FBI's ten-most-wanted list."

Such is the selection process, the political alchemy through which a lawyer is transformed into a federal district judge. Once the judge reaches the bench, what satisfactions (and work) does he find?

CHAPTER TWO

When the System Works I: Watching Wall Street

On a clear day the morning's first beams of sunshine fall across a conference table in Room 2104 of the United States Courthouse, high above Foley Square in downtown Manhattan, touching first upon a ship model in a glassine case, and then moving to a jumbled variety of judicial flotsam. Open copies of *U. S. Reports,* the hefty, buckram-bound volumes of opinions of the Supreme Court of the United States, marked with scraps of yellow foolscap and stacked one atop the other. Briefs in stiff blue cardboard covers bearing the imprimatur of the ampersand-laden names of big Wall Street law firms. A wayward Christmas card. The Sunday-supplement magazine of the *Tulsa Tribune.* Memoranda from law clerks, some typed, some neatly written in ballpoint pen on pages torn from legal pads. A stack of papers listing assignments of judges to court committees for the Southern District of New York. Indeterminable piles of correspondence and court papers and more law books, spread around three-quarters of the perimeter of the table, which is large enough to accommodate eight chairs.

I sit and sip a cup of tea and peer eastward through the glare of the sun to the Brooklyn Bridge and New York harbor, and then I wander to the south end of the office—past a formidably formal desk that is dusty in places indicating non-use—and look toward the aluminum-chrome-glass-granite outcroppings of Wall Street, a dozen or so blocks distant. It is shortly after

9 A.M., and the money-seekers still on the streets scurry for their offices in the brokerage houses and corporation headquarters from which much of America's commerce is governed. What percentage of the nation's wealth is visible, figuratively, from Room 2104? What levers of power are pulled (albeit invisibly) from within eyeshot of this vantage point on Foley Square?

A bustle at the rear of the room interrupts my idle speculation. Enter David N. Edelstein, a trim, open-faced man in his sixties who carries his head with a slight downward cast, so that when he looks at a person his stare comes up with curious, exaggerated intensity. Room 2104 is Edelstein's private chambers. He is chief judge of the Southern District of New York, which is the largest (27 judges) and busiest (5,520 cases filed in fiscal 1973, a quarter more than runnerup Boston) of the 89 federal benches in the nation. What Edelstein sees when he looks out his south window, as I had done a few moments earlier, is ample explanation of why the Southern District is also considered the most important federal district court in the nation, for it is here that big business comes when it is fighting among itself or with the federal government. ("Wall Street and the corporations," Edelstein mused to me later, "where would our court—and the New York lawyers—be without them?") But the prestigious Edelstein's first concern this morning is a pedestrian annoyance.

"I shall never understand," he announced, "the arrogance of the New York subway system, and why the people who run it don't announce when trains are being delayed, so we can ride a bus or something. Sitting on a stalled train under Forty-second Street is not my idea of an ideal way to commence the day."

Edelstein made mild bahhhing sounds as he shed his topcoat and leather cap and accepted a cup of black coffee from his secretary, Alice Pitman, who clucked sympathy, as if she had heard of subway problems a time or two in the past. As we began exchanging pleasantries the phone rang and Mrs. Pitman called, "This is Judge ―――――. He said it was rather important that he talk to you right away."

The judge's problem became apparent as Edelstein

chatted with him. Edelstein had done the pretrial work on a number of separate civil suits arising from the collapse of a major corporation. With the cases ready for trial, he divided them among other judges, some in New York, others elsewhere. The man on the phone, a relative newcomer to the bench, discovered his old law firm represented one of the parties to the suit he had drawn, hence his call this morning.

Edelstein calmly questioned him about the closeness of his association with the specific attorneys involved and whether he would be uncomfortable handling the case. Did he really know anything about the case other than what was contained in the court papers?

"Huh huh, I see," Judge Edelstein said. "Well, in that case, what is the problem? I think you're clear and that you could take this case in good conscience."

A long pause. Judge Edelstein prides himself on maintaining a non-expressive face, a valuable asset for someone sworn to decide issues on law and facts without tripping over his own emotions. But what he heard now from the other judge brought an audible grunt and an uncontrolled tightening of the mouth.

"No, no," Judge Edelstein said. "I think it would be imprudent for you to call someone in the firm, senior partner or not. Highly imprudent. If you want to know what the firm thinks about your hearing the case, bring all parties into your chambers and lay out the problem for them. But I suggest strongly that you not call a senior partner at ——————— & ———————, regardless of how close you are. That would be most imprudent indeed. I advise against it."

Finished with the call, Edelstein sighed and dropped the phone into the cradle and turned to resume our talk. "That's one of the problems we frequently encounter in the Southern District, although they are seldom serious. Most of our judges come out of big firms, and were active trial lawyers, so consequently they know most attorneys who come into the courts. Myself, now, I've been around New York a long time, and I know the senior partners in the major firms, see them fairly frequently. So where do you draw the line? You can't completely withdraw from society; in fact, I argue that a judge who doesn't circulate, who doesn't talk to people and keep abreast of society, he hurts both himself and justice." Edelstein sighed once again, and then talked about what he intended to be doing during the two days we were to spend together.

For some three years Edelstein has lived alongside an ever-growing, somewhat quaky legal mountain known formally as *69 Civ 200, the United States of America v. International Business Machines, Inc.,* a case that *Business Week* described more directly as "the largest and most complex antitrust battle ever waged." The Justice Department's antitrust division is asking that behemoth IBM be broken into a string of smaller companies, charging that it so dominates the data processing industry that it smothers other companies. IBM, of course, denies doing any such thing: it says, in effect, it is big because it does things better than the other companies. Whatever the truth of the allegations—something that is not likely to be finally decided ere the 1970s end—the case has implications far beyond the computer industry. Its outcome could dictate new antitrust guidelines controlling the growth of future giant corporations. And even in its pretrial stages the IBM case managed to bring Edelstein into testy confrontation with the corporation's lawyers over violation of his orders, resulting in a fine of $150,000 a day until they purged themselves of contempt, an order upheld by the U.S. Supreme Court.

"This case is mind-staggering, no doubt about it," Edelstein said. "Seldom does a judge face a trial with such a volume of documentary evidence, such a wide array of complex issues, such a universality of product, in the sense that it touches so much of American life. Take the evidence factor alone. Today alone the lawyers are taking three sets of depositions, and this has been going on for more than a year, all over the country. The documentary exhibits will number in the millions.

"There are some other peculiar factors. Take the national security thing. At one stage the Justice Department had zero cooperation from government agencies that buy from IBM—the CIA, the National Security

Agency, the Atomic Energy Commission, and others. The Justice lawyers wanted documents, and the agencies said, 'No, you can't have them, they are national security documents.'

"Bosh. My position—and I've told this to the lawyers, so I'm not talking out of school—is that the United States government is not a collection of sovereign principalities. It's all one government, and, damn it, I'm going to accept no nonsense. Is there separation of powers within the government itself? Can one agency of government, such as the AEC, deny documents to another agency, such as the Justice Department, on the grounds of national security? This sort of issue has never been resolved before, and that's one of the things that will keep me busy the rest of the year. In a way this is going to be a Pentagon Papers case in its own right.

"So what I'm in the process of doing now," Edelstein continued, "is clearing the decks so that I don't have anything else before me when the IBM trial begins in October [of 1974]. I am putting aside an entire year for it, and I suppose I'll need it. That October date is something I'm firm about, too. I announced a trial date for October, and if God spares me until then, we're going to trial. Both sides are on notice.*

"For the next few months I'm going to be disposing of a lot of routine cases that have been kicking around awhile, and a couple of rather large ones as well—for instance, there is a case involving commercial paper issued by the Penn Central before it went into bankruptcy. A complex case, and that will take perhaps a month to try. But by the first of summer, I intend to be doing nothing more than the IBM case. So what you'll be seeing the next few days is . . . well, not a typical day, for no day is like another around here. But you should get a feel for the way things work."

The phone had been ringing intermittently, nine calls in an hour. Edelstein disposed of most of them with a

---

* Judge Edelstein didn't meet his October 1974 date. Unforeseen delays developed, and the starting date of the trial was moved by stages, into the late spring of 1975.

few direct sentences, then Mrs. Pitman peeked through the door with a polite reminder, "Judge, they're ready for you downstairs." Edelstein glanced up at the clock, which showed a few minutes past ten o'clock. "Oooops, can't keep the bar waiting, can we?"

Out the rear door of the office, to the judge's private elevator. The tiny car holds only three persons, elbow to elbow, and protocol on its use is strict: a law clerk may ride with a judge but not alone, and some judges are zealous protectors of the privilege. Kevin Duffy, who was only 39 when he went on the bench in 1972 and has the boyish appearance and demeanor of a Fordham sophomore, tells of getting on the private elevator one day with a senior member of the Second Circuit Court of Appeals, which shares the courthouse with the district judges. "This old fellow looked at me sternly and said, 'I don't think law clerks should be riding this elevator. It is reserved for judges.' I looked right back at him without smiling and said, 'I don't think they should either, and if I see a clerk on here I intend to kick his ass off.' He blinked and coughed and that was that; he must have thought I was crazy, or so arrogant he wanted nothing to do with me."

On the ground floor Edelstein pauses in a chill, windowless room behind Courtroom 34. He sits at a chipped wooden desk and flips rapidly through a stack of folders presented by Howard Stravitz, one of his three law clerks. Stravitz has written a capsule summary of the issue raised in each case, but Edelstein impatiently breaks off his presentation. "Nothing too complex here. Let's get on out."

Edelstein's business today is receiving status reports on four civil cases. "Lawyers tend to let these things drag on indefinitely unless you get them into the courthouse occasionally," he said. "Oftentimes the lawyers won't even have a serious talk with one another until they meet in court prior to a hearing. The realization that they actually might be going to trial tends to move them toward settlement."

Which is exactly what happened in the first case called, a patent suit in which the plaintiff had asked more than $100,000. The man subsequently died, and his widow agreed to settle for $26,953. But the lawyers wanted to insure that no claimants existed other than the widow and children, hence they asked Edelstein to make the settlement contingent upon approval by the state surrogate court, which has jurisdiction over estate matters in New York. Fine, said Edelstein. "I don't envy you going through that surrogates court maze, but I think it would be best for all concerned." Total elapsed time: eight minutes flat.

The next case wasn't as smooth. A container of merchandise had disappeared from a freighter, and there was a question of whether the vessel's owner or the shipping agency was responsible. Fortunately for Edelstein, a companion case had already been decided by the circuit court of appeals. The lawyers asked sixty days to see if they could settle on the basis of the other case.

"Why do you need sixty days?" Edelstein queried. Well, the lawyers wanted to submit written interrogatories to the shipper, to insure that all facts were in hand before the bargaining began, and as luck had it he lived abroad. ("Foreign parties show up in about a quarter of admiralty cases," a lawyer told me. "They can be a real pain in the neck—but if you are a stamp collector, you get some good stuff in a hurry.") Edelstein was dubious. "You realize you are investing more time and money in a case that is worth. . . . How much is at issue here?"

"The loss was $23,000 to $24,000, Your Honor," a lawyer replied.

"All right," Edelstein said, "do as you wish. I want all discovery [pretrial gathering of evidence] to be finished within ninety days, and then the case will be deemed ready for trial on forty-eight hours' notice. You understand me? Hold yourself ready on forty-eight-hour notice. I want all witnesses available and all of your documents ready.

"Yes, Your Honor."

Edelstein zipped through two other cases by putting both sides on a 60-day notice and adjourned. In fourteen minutes he had disposed finally of one case and set three on the road to settlement. "We won't try any of those," he said as we rode the elevator back to the twenty-first floor. "They're moving. Once the lawyers start talking, especially when there's so little money involved, they will work to settle rather than tie themselves up in trial."

I remarked on the informality. Although a robe had been available in the anteroom off the court, Edelstein presided in his street clothes, sitting at a conference table with the lawyers. The only formalism was bailiff Rudy Laudante's cry for everyone to rise when he entered and left the room. The lawyers were polite but casual.

"If there's a situation where the issue must be debated at length," Edelstein said, "I'll put on robes and go formal. Otherwise, it's easier to reach the parties on an informal basis. The lawyers are more relaxed when we're at the table, rather than going through all the rigamarole of a hearing. It's faster, too, and I guess you realize by now that a federal judge spends much of his time trying to keep ahead of his calendar.

"And, good heavens, with IBM staring down at me, I *must* get this other stuff out of the way, because come October, I have my work cut out for me for a full year, at the least."

The IBM case. Although Judge Edelstein was months from trial the days I spent with him, IBM was omnipresent. A room in his office suite had been converted into a storage area for documents coming into the court almost daily from the principals, IBM and the Justice Department, and other parties caught up in the litigation, overflowing the filing cabinets into orderly stacks along the wall. Edelstein was holding at least one hearing weekly on pretrial matters. By his order, IBM and government lawyers had moved into the courthouse to take depositions in the cases. Normally, depositions are done in law offices. However, Edelstein learned early on that he should be near at hand to rule in the event either side objected to the questions being asked. So the lawyers bicker among themselves, in one of three courtrooms set aside for the depositions, until they have accumulated a dozen or so points of contention, then troop upstairs to Edelstein for a decision. One of Edelstein's law clerks joked to me, "The atmosphere around here reminds me of a college campus on the eve of a big football game, or the way I felt the night before I took my bar examination. Man, this is living legal history."

The IBM case deserves a detailed examination for several reasons. It is a striking, if somewhat unique, example of the complexity of cases heard by a federal district judge. Edelstein was required to be learned not only in antitrust law but also in the arcane technology and economics of the computer industry. In the IBM instance, the act of *moving* the case to trial was more demanding than the trial itself; the logistical demands upon Edelstein and his courts, not to mention the lawyers, were staggering both in volume and in intricacy. And, again, it is an illustration of judicial power; a $42,500 a year federal judge is in a position to decide whether a corporation with revenues of $9 billion a year should be split into as many as five components. For Edelstein, who was in his sixties when he acquired the case, the IBM litigation was a fitting capstone for his judicial career: a landmark action that could affect the future shape of American industry.

The computer business was the premiere growth industry of the 1950s and 1960s and IBM, with an annual growth rate of 20 percent, simply ran off and left other companies that tried for a share of the market. Even RCA, with the vast resources at its disposal, could not crack IBM's hold on the computer business (although it lost half-a-billion dollars trying to do so). In one antitrust suit settled in 1956 the Justice Department forced IBM to sell data-processing equipment, as well as rent it, but nonetheless IBM continued to crush its opposition, keeping a technological jump ahead of other companies, and making it difficult for them to sell equipment that interconnected with IBM computers. Throughout the 1960s both the Justice Department and the competitors investigated alleged monopolistic practices of IBM. Control Data Corporation, a would-be competitor, was the first to file suit, a private antitrust action brought in December 1968 in the

United States District Court in St. Paul, Minnesota, its headquarters state. Several weeks later on January 17, 1969, the last business day of the Johnson Administration, the Justice Department filed a suit accusing IBM of monopolistic practices in violation of the Sherman Antitrust Act. The government did not specify what relief and penalties it desired; it said, in effect, it needed to get inside IBM and learn more about its marketing and development practices before setting out specific goals of the suit. Other private companies jumped in with their own antitrust suits until a total of nine separate actions was being waged against IBM in various federal courts.

When parallel cases are filed in separate federal districts, the procedure is to consolidate as much of the pretrial proceedings as possible before a single judge. The judiciary learned this lesson the hard way in the 1960s, when separate courts tried to cope with 2,000 suits arising from the electrical equipment price-fixing cases. Officials of defendant corporations found themselves reciting identical depositions as many as a dozen times, and courts were years recovering from massive backlogs created by the cases. With pretrial consolidation, persons give a single deposition for use in all cases, and documents theoretically are for use in all courts—although, as we shall see, such is not always conceded by defendants.

In the instance of IBM, the pretrial assignment fell to Judge Philip Neville * of St. Paul, who had years of antitrust trial experience before his appointment to the bench in 1967, and whose court had received the Control Data Corporation (CDC) suit. Because the Minnesota proceedings later produced such sour, tumultuous aftermaths in Judge Edelstein's court, we must abandon Foley Square momentarily for the United States District Court in St. Paul. Here IBM put forth the legal team and tactics that directed the defense of its very corporate existence.

As America's fifth-largest corporation (and second most profitable manufacturer), IBM has the dollars to

---

* Judge Neville died in the spring of 1974.

afford the services of what many New York lawyers consider *the* best of the best Wall Street legal institutions: Cravath, Swaine, & Moore. Let it be said simply that the Cravath firm, as it is known in lawyers' verbal shorthand, does as well in the legal field as IBM does in the computer field. The firm is large (with more than 160 partners and associates) and experienced (it has toiled for blue-chip organizations since the very beginning of American industrialization). Cravath also practices what could be called, in the lexicon of Nixonian politics, "hard-ball law." Anyone who sues a Cravath client soon learns the firm contests every conceivable point (and, in fact, some that could be considered *in*conceivable). Cravath concedes nothing, and it is unforgiving of opponents' mistakes. "When a Cravath partner knocks you down," a Washington lawyer once mourned to me, in a non-IBM context, "he doesn't help you up—he brings in a couple of young associates to step on you."

For the IBM case Cravath suited up as lead lawyers a Mutt-and-Jeff team. The hardline was Thomas D. Barr, a burly man noted for direct, non-euphemistic speech. The suave partner was F.A.O. Schwarz, Jr., of the New York toy store family, whose Harvard law school politeness almost, but not quite, balanced Barr's bluntness. For backup support Barr and Schwarz drew upon not only their own firm (where more than 20 lawyers got into the IBM cases, to one degree or another) but also IBM's in-house legal talent, led by Nicholas deB. Katzenbach, vice president and general counsel, the former United States attorney general and undersecretary of state.

An accepted and logical stratagem of corporate law is to wear down the other side, financially and physically. When a corporation is sued, the purpose usually is to force it to stop doing things from which it earns immense amounts of money. Hence the longer a corporation can continue business as usual, the better for its coffers. Given the possibly horrible consequences of yielding to the demands of competitors (or the United States government), legal fees and lost executive time are sufferable nuisances—even if dragging out a law suit for years means only postponing the inevitable.

Judging from their actions, such was obviously the thinking of IBM lawyers, and an antitrust case is an ideal place to drag one's feet. Consider, for example, the magnitude of the evidence involved. As part of their pretrial discovery, lawyers for CDC received an order authorizing them to inspect and copy documents in some 60 separate IBM departments, and to go through correspondence and memoranda of 103 ranking IBM executives. A task force of 60 CDC lawyers and computer experts eventually checked out about 40 million documents; of these, an estimated 25 million were selected for microfilming, at a special IBM facility in Nyack, New York, built for that purpose. IBM people, meanwhile, were rummaging through CDC files, examining an estimated 80 million documents. The numbers were overwhelming, but many of the "documents" were low-grade evidentiary ore: sales orders, invoices, and the like. Nonetheless, the opposing parties spent the better part of two years with their noses in one another's filing cabinets.

IBM gave access grudgingly. At one point IBM claimed that 67 cabinets of material were privileged, chiefly because of lawyer–client confidentiality. According to Judge Neville, IBM screeners went through the papers and pulled out anything bearing a lawyer's letterhead. Finally Neville had to appoint a special master who winnowed the contested documents down to about 1,000. (Many of these, Neville remarked later, pertained to such routine, non-computer business as real estate transactions.) Concurrent with the search, CDC attorneys compiled a computerized index to the documents, considered vital to any understanding of the mountains of raw data.

Although the Justice Department's antitrust division was not included in the consolidation order, it received, via CDC, copies of the IBM documents and also participated to one degree or another in the depositions of IBM officials. But the role of Justice lawyers, for all practical purposes, was passive. The reason was pragmatic. The antitrust division has a niggardly annual budget of only $12.8 million, with which it is supposed to ferret out and halt monopolistic practices in all of American commerce. (The Bureau of Commercial Fisheries, by contrast, gets five times as much money.) The IBM case, important though it is, nonetheless is but one of the hundred suits the division has pending at any given time. Hence it was to the government's advantage to "piggyback" with CDC as long as possible, so as to conserve its limited resources for use elsewhere. Too, the antitrust division trial team, headed by veteran lawyer Raymond M. Carlson, felt two separate court orders insured that the government would eventually receive all information CDC found during its discovery activities. The first order, signed by Judge Neville, was on behalf of Telex Corporation, a Tulsa, Oklahoma, computer firm that was pressing an antitrust case against IBM in Oklahoma, and which was covered by the consolidation umbrella. The order read:

> It is further ordered that Control Data, based on its own counsel's statement of willingness to do so, will make available to the counsel for Telex *all IBM documents in its possession and its so-called data base or index* [emphasis added].*

Another order, issued by Judge Edelstein in New York at the government's request, ordered both IBM and the Justice Department to "preserve and secure from destruction all documents, writings, recordings or *other records of any kind* whatsoever" relating to electronic data processings or services. By the antitrust division lawyers' interpretation, the two orders meant that all evidence and documents would be preserved for use in the government case.

Judge Edelstein's order was issued in March 1972,

---

* Telex eventually won a verdict of $259.5 million in United States District Court in Tulsa; IBM appealed. IBM won another of the cases in Phoenix, Arizona, when Judge Walter E. Craig dismissed a suit brought by Greyhound Computer Corporation. Craig found that IBM led the computer industry as a result of "skill, foresight and industry," and that the "mere possession" of monopoly power does not violate the Sherman Antitrust Act.

shortly after he became chief judge and took active charge of the IBM case. For a while he was content to let the government parties continue giving their main attention to the CDC proceedings. By the fall, however, he was restive about progress of the case, and he urged both sides to get along with their work. When the Justice Department pleaded it didn't have the manpower, he suggested that the solution was not to delay but to hire more personnel (something which the Nixon Administration had been unwilling to do). By October 1972 he had goaded the Justice Department into preparing a statement of aims spelling out exactly what it hoped to accomplish in the suit.

With Edelstein now obviously determined to push the suit, the Cravath firm tightened its defenses—and in a way that brought it and IBM into the first of a series of increasingly nasty confrontations with the judge. Thomas Barr argued for a delay of any proceedings until after the 1972 presidential election. Barr feared that political considerations, "the glare of publicity," or other pressures could force Attorney General Richard Kleindienst to produce a "nonnegotiable demand, an ultimatum," rather than a reasoned attempt at settlement. Noting that the suit had been filed by the Johnson Administration, he called it a "political football" and added, "The problem with being a football is, you get kicked."

Edelstein rather snappishly replied that he thought it "appalling" that IBM would argue that politics could affect what happened in his court, or in the attorney general's office. He denied the motion. (A few days later the Justice Department asked that IBM's "enormous market power" be dissipated by splitting its domestic and foreign operations into independent "competitively balanced" divisions, forming perhaps as many as five new companies.) When IBM Board Chairman T. Vincent Learson predicted to a business group that the requested breakup "would never happen," Edelstein haled him into court for a reprimand for violating an order on out-of-court comments on the litigation. Learson's remark, Judge Edelstein said, could give the impression that IBM had some "inside information"

or that a private deal had been agreed on. In so implying, Edelstein said, Learson was close to stepping on
the integrity of his court. "I must state flatly and
firmly," Edelstein said, that "no one, including this
court, is in a position to predict the outcome or hazard
a good guess." And in other remarks Edelstein let it be
known he was impatient with signs of dilatory tactics
on both sides. These exchanges, although individually
insignificant, did amount to a declaration by Edelstein
that he intended to keep firm control of the case, and
that he was not to be cowed by either IBM's money
nor the prestige of its legal force.

Another fear also preyed upon Edelstein's mind: that
the IBM lawyers would rely upon attrition to wear
down both him and the government attorneys, and
that the Justice Department would accept a meaningless
consent decree just to settle the case. Through conferences with Judge Neville, he knew of dilatory IBM
strategies that were delaying the Minnesota case. For
example, IBM wanted a census made of companies in
the electronic data processing business, requiring them
to list their revenues, profits, investments and customers.
(IBM felt the information would rebut CDC charges
that it monopolized the industry.) About 2,000 of
2,700 companies covered by the census responded, providing literally truckloads of documents that swamped
Neville's court. But no sooner had the material arrived
than IBM wanted a rerun of the census: the information gathered, it said, was for 1970; since two years
had passed, a 1972 census should be conducted as well.
"I just finally had to say this has got to cease," Judge
Neville said. "If we are going to do this [a new census]
then it becomes a year old again, and we do it a third
time, and we never get anywhere."

Even more unsettling to Edelstein was the entry
into the New York phase of the suits of a Cravath
partner named Bruce Bromley, one of the more cantankerous members of the New York bar. Bromley, a
bantamy fellow in his seventies, once served a few appointed months on the New York Court of Appeals
(he was beaten when he ran for a full term); he loves
to be called "Judge"; and he has been around the

courts so long that, as one lawyer jokingly remarked, "It's sometimes hard to tell who is in charge—Bromley or the judge." Bromley also cherishes a reputation for legal gamesmanship (for instance, he learned to read handwriting upside down so he could peek at opposing lawyers' papers across a desk), and for an ability to stall cases perhaps longer than any lawyer in Western civilization. Further, Bromley made the somewhat silly mistake of boasting publicly of this ability in a 1958 talk at a conference at Stanford Law School: "I was born, I think, to be a procrastinator. I quickly realized in my early days at the bar that I could take the simplest antitrust case that [the Justice Department] could think of and protract it for the defense almost to infinity." Bromley bragged at length about stretching out for fourteen years a government case against Famous Players–Lasky Corporation, a theatrical and movie booking company. "We won that case, and as you know, my firm's meter was running all the time—every month for fourteen years." Bromley recited with glee how he and fellow lawyers dragged out another action against United States Gypsum for eighteen years.* With Bromley's philosophy about antitrust strategy on the public record, Edelstein was very much on guard as the case progressed.

Then in January 1973 IBM and CDC unexpectedly announced an out-of-court settlement of their case in Minnesota. The nub of the agreement was for CDC to buy IBM's computer-services subsidiary, Service Bureau Corporation, for $16 million, and to receive about $96 million in reimbursements and work contracts over a decade. The computer industry marvelled at the generosity of the terms (one publication called it a "windfall" and a "bargain" for CDC), and wondered why IBM had released Service Bureau Corporation, valued at $50 million, for such a pittance. One conceivable reason—one not stated in the public announcement of the settlement—became apparent several days later: a key part of the deal was for CDC

---

* For further excerpts from Bromley's peroration, see my *The Superlawyers*, Weybright & Talley, New York, 1972, page 190.

to destroy the computerized index to the IBM internal documents, a deed marked by speed and stealth. The IBM and CDC directors agreed to the settlement on January 12, a Friday. The destruction of the index began at 3 P.M. that day and was finished on Saturday. Not until Sunday night did CDC notify the Justice Department of the settlement and the fate of the index. Judge Neville signed the formal out-of-court settlement on Monday.

The Justice Department's lead trial lawyer, Raymond M. Carlson, was so stunned by the destruction that he angrily told an associate, "This isn't lawyering, this is back alley stuff." Carlson dashed off a motion to Edelstein asking him to rule that IBM acted illegally in persuading CDC to destroy the index, and order a reconstruction. His brief bristled with pejorative language seldom used in the arcane world of civil antitrust law. He flatly accused IBM lawyers—that is to say, the Cravath firm—of deliberately violating Judge Edelstein's earlier order on preservation of documentary evidence. Carlson wrote:

The plain fact is that counsel decided to insure the destruction, withholding the knowledge of [the pretrial order] from Control Data and presenting the government and the court with the fait accompli of destruction by doing the deed hastily, thoroughly and clandestinely on the weekend.

Hard-ball lawyering—but Cravath, Swaine & Moore reacted violently to the government's criticism of its professional ethics. Bromley called Carlson's charges an "outrageous . . . attempt to incite public criticism by accusing us in colorful and inflammatory language . . . of wrongdoing." The Cravath firm claimed the destroyed index was a "lawyers' work product" which the government had no right to use.

Judge Edelstein brought in IBM and the government for a hearing, and observers noted "a note of impatience or irritation in some of [his] comments and questions." Given the importance of the index, he asked, should not IBM's lawyers "in the interest of caution" have asked for court guidance before the destruction? F. A. O. Schwarz, replying for IBM, said he and his colleagues "had no doubt of the propriety" of the action, and acted swiftly for fear a disgruntled CDC employee might leak the data.

The IBM arguments did not move Edelstein. On March 6 he ruled that IBM lawyers had in fact violated his order. Edelstein directed strong language against the Cravath firm:

> . . . [S]uch unseemly behavior coming as it does from respected members of the bar of this court is particularly distressing. There appears to be no sound reason why counsel needed to act in this hasty manner.

He order IBM to help the Justice Department rebuild the index.

By reliable account, the IBM lawyers at this point expressed grave private doubts at Edelstein's impartiality. Hurt professional pride was one reason, for classy Wall Street lawyers are not accustomed to having their ethics chastised publicly by a judge.* More importantly, the IBM force felt Edelstein's "entire tone and attitude" showed an impatience with the defense, and a bias favoring the government, conscious or otherwise. Yet even a nastier round of fighting lay ahead.

The issue was IBM's claimed confidentiality of its documents that had passed through CDC to the government. IBM claimed that in the confusion of handling millions of pieces of paper, several thousands of documents covered by the attorney–client privilege were inadvertently released. IBM first attacked the validity of a pretrial order by Edelstein requiring that IBM give the government the same documents it had turned over to CDC. Twice Edelstein ruled against IBM; twice IBM

---

* Although, oddly, the Cravath firm was not identified by name in stories in *The New York Times* and the *Wall Street Journal* announcing Judge Edelstein's decision. The *Times* did not report Edelstein's critical language at all; the *Journal* did, but said only it was directed at "IBM attorneys."

went to the Second Circuit Court of Appeals and lost; finally, on June 13, 1973, the Supreme Court refused to review Edelstein's order.

IBM's sole remaining hope was that when an appellate court reviewed the documents themselves, they would be found to be privileged. In the interim, however, IBM was under binding order by Edelstein to turn the papers over to the Justice Department. And this IBM refused to do. On June 15, Bruce Bromley wrote Judge Edelstein, "I have respectfully concluded that I should not produce the documents unless and until it has been finally determined that they should be produced." Edelstein took up the challenge and ordered IBM to show cause why it should not be held in civil contempt.

Enter now another brahmin of the Wall Street bar, Simon Rifkind, himself a federal district judge from 1941 to 1950, when he resigned with a complaint that he was "unable to maintain a reasonable standard of living" on the $15,000 salary then earned by judges. (As a partner in Paul, Weiss, Rifkind, Wharton & Garrison, he now does perhaps ten times that well.) Rifkind entered the case as counsel for Cravath, Swaine & Moore, with a crafty proposed solution: that Bromley, as counsel for IBM, be held in contempt and fined $100 per day, with payment suspended pending yet another appeal, this one on whether the questioned documents indeed were privileged.

As soon as Edelstein convened court Bromley was on his feet—without invitation from the judge—demanding first say in the proceedings. "Since I asked for this conference, and you have granted it," Bromley told Edelstein, "I think I should first make a statement before the government proceeds with its motion that IBM be cited for contempt."

Edelstein wasn't about to be pushed around in his own courtroom, and he gave Bromley a long, cold stare. Then he curtly said, "I don't think, Mr. Bromley, that I will permit you to make any statement. The first item on this agenda this morning will be the government's motion."

Bromley wouldn't quit. "I thought it would help Your

Honor if I made clear what my position was," he said.

"Your position will become abundantly clear as we proceed," Edelstein said.

When Bromley finally got the floor, much later in the hearing, he was polite but direct. He had custody of the contested documents. "It is my decision and that of my partners that they should not be produced. IBM's instructions to us are they should do with the documents whatever is required by the law. If in our opinion, under the law as finally determined they should be produced, they will be. If in our opinion, under the law as finally determined they should not be produced, they should not be produced." Bromley said he recognized "that this is disobedient of your order and is, as it is intended to be, in form a contempt."

So what should be the penalty? The Justice Department's Raymond Carlson asked for a "coercive sanction sufficient in amount and immediate enough in time of implementation to make it imperative that IBM faces up to the fact that it must comply with lawful pretrial orders." Carlson scoffed at the suggested $100 a day fine. "IBM has perhaps argued this particular matter ten or fifteen times in various courts at far more than a year's cost of the hundred dollars a day that they suggest," he said. The fine should be sufficient, he said, "to require IBM, if, as the government alleges, its purposes are delay, to trade its delay in this case off, and get on with the trial of the case." Carlson felt that IBM was in a "power struggle with the court," and said that the outcome "will determine whether this case, and really whether any antitrust case, can be tried where the defendant's resources are sufficient to carry objections, findings and appeals on for as long as they can find a court to hear them." (Rifkind called Carlson's charge "an unwarranted aspersion on our proceedings.")

How much a fine was required to bring IBM into line? Carlson simply submitted IBM annual reports for 1971 and 1972, showing net earnings of $1,078,846,-907 and $1,279,894,847, respectively. He also noted that IBM had paid $15 million to Control Data Corporation for its legal expenses as part of the settlement in Minnesota. To Carlson this expenditure showed IBM's willingness "to spend money in its defense wherever it might go and the ability of this defendant to pay any coercive sanction."

Edelstein brooded over the case for several days, then slapped IBM with a civil fine that astounded even the government attorneys. He ordered IBM to pay $150,000 daily until it chose to turn over the documents, saying he believed a "substantial fine is required to insure compliance" with the court. And the Second Circuit Court of Appeals, in a two-to-one decision, upheld the fine. (The dissenter, William H. Rivers, argued that "the remedy of a million dollar per week fine clearly demonstrates that its chief purpose was to vindicate the court's authority and to punish IBM if it failed to bow to the court's power." But as the majority noted, "while in absolute terms IBM's fine may seem large, the same percentage of earnings fined against one with a salary of $50,000 would be less than $7 per day.")

The day after the circuit court decision I happened to be lunching with Judge Edelstein in a small Italian restaurant just off Foley Square. Interruptions were frequent as lawyers paused to exchange pleasantries with the judge. Edelstein smiled when one man approached his table. The man said, "I read with considerable interest that opinion yesterday, even though, of course, I did not agree with it." He paused. "I guess you're pretty happy, being upheld."

Edelstein smiled again. "I'm not gloating. Of course, anyone likes to be confirmed, but I don't make my decisions that way. I call them the way I see them and don't worry about the circuit court." The lawyer waved and moved on.

Edelstein chuckled across the table. "That's one of the IBM lawyers. They aren't too happy with me these days, but we're still friendly enough. He just had to give me a little needle."

Judge Edelstein's outward good humor that noon was not a true reflection of what was happening in his mind. He realized that by twice ruling that IBM's

lawyers—which is to say, Cravath, Swaine, & Moore—
had violated pretrial orders, he had stepped on very
prestigious and sensitive legal toes. Establishment law
in New York is clubby and attorneys of the self-im-
portance found in the Cravath firm simply do not
cherish being labelled scofflaws. And Edelstein was
feeling a personal backlash both from his IBM rulings
and other cases as well.

That this is so came up indirectly one evening a few
weeks later as we talked over pre-dinner drinks in
his Park Avenue apartment. Edelstein mentioned the
personal abuse directed at his longtime friend J. Skelly
Wright when he was a federal district judge in New
Orleans.* Supposed friends and churchmen ostracized
Wright because of his rulings in school segregation
cases. "You've got to remember that Wright has deep
New Orleans roots," Edelstein said, "he is a true southerner. But the law was more important to him. Now
that's judicial bravery. For a judge in New York to
make Wright's kind of rulings in civil rights cases—
school segregation and the like—doesn't require any
particular courage, for the mass public here would
agree."

Granted, I said. But what upsets a person is when
his peer group ostracizes him. What sort of adverse
reaction does Edelstein feel when he comes down hard
on prominent Wall Street and corporate lawyers?

"Oh, that's another matter," Edelstein replied.
"White & Case was pretty damned upset when I
wouldn't sever them from the National Student Marketing Case.* You should have heard the talk. 'Goodness,
law firms simply are not brought into things of this

* Now a judge of the Court of Appeals in the District of
Columbia. See Chapter Six, "The D.C. Court of Appeals: The
Mini Supreme Court."
* National Student Marketing, a fast-rising, faster-sinking conglomerate, was sued by the Securities and Exchange Commission in 1972 for painting a falsely glowing picture of its
financial condition during merger negotiations with an insurance company. The SEC's suit accused a White & Case partner
of notifying neither the SEC nor the merger partner that NSM
filed a "misleading" financial statement during the talks. White
& Case emphatically denied the charges.

nature,' gentlemen's agreements and professional courtesy and the like. Lawyers get damned edgy when they are involved in anything that smacks of impropriety."

Edelstein paused a long moment and looked at the whiskey and ice in his glass. "You know, another thing. I lost a friend over the IBM thing, when I held them in contempt last fall. A lawyer involved took it personally, and the word got back that we were no longer friends."

Judge Edelstein's wife spoke up from across the living room. "Oh, Dave," she said, "a person who gets upset like that, I don't think he was much of a friend in the first place."

Edelstein shook his head. "No, I'm simply stating what happened. And some of the IBM briefs have been pretty savage towards me recently. So what do you do? You ignore it, and keep your head, and rule on the facts and the law, and don't worry about it.

"I look at it this way: if I ever start trying to 'please' people when I'm deciding a case, I'm not a judge, I'm something else, and that I do not want to be."

David N. Edelstein's rise to the federal bench began when he took a wartime appointment in the Department of Justice. A native New Yorker, he had practiced law there since his graduation from Fordham. ("My father's idea; he felt the Jesuits gave you the best education in the world.")

Edelstein immediately plunged into heady company. "One of my first jobs in Justice was liaison with Senator Truman's committee investigating war contracts. I'd go over to his apartment in the evening and we'd review what he was finding, and discuss how to handle evidence of criminal violations he would find. Truman was a very human person. He'd be there in his undershirt—we didn't have airconditioning in those days—and I remember the first time I went there he offered me a drink of bourbon. I asked for Scotch. He frowned, in a mock-stern way, and said, 'Mr. Edelstein, in this house we drink bourbon. Now does that suit your pleasure?' Truman was honest about his work, and tough, but also politically realistic. One of the first things he came across was the use of war materials by a senator on some construction on his house. Truman didn't call for prosecution, but he sure made it public. It embarrassed the senator, and kind of put everyone on notice that he meant business."

Other intimates—professional and personal—were FBI Director J. Edgar Hoover and his longtime confidante and associate, Clyde Tolson. Edelstein dined once weekly with Hoover and Tolson in the Mayflower Hotel and in fact was so impressed with Hoover that he urged him to run for president in 1952. "I didn't think much of a general becoming president, and Hoover, I felt, was the only man in the country who could beat Eisenhower. Hoover stopped me cold. 'No law enforcement officer should ever go into politics,' he told me.

"I suppose he was right. One thing that disgusts me about our current Justice Department is its politicalization. Now in our day it was a mark of distinct honor to serve in Justice. We were proud to work for [Attorney General Francis] Biddle—in fact, we called ourselves 'Biddle's Boys.' Biddle was so patrician that even Roosevelt was edgy when he dealt with him. I simply cannot comprehend anyone, even the President, ordering Biddle to use the Justice Department for political purposes. Hell, Biddle would have quit on the spot. The same for Biddle's successors, Tom Clark and Howard McGrath.

"Now, the fact that I worked in Justice *did* result in me being appointed to the federal bench. The way the system worked in my day, a person who had reasonable responsibility in the Justice Department and did his work well could count on a judgeship when he left office, that is, if he wanted it. The assistant attorneys general [Edelstein's last and highest rank], the United States attorneys and their chief assistants—the top people at Justice—got to know you, and I suppose it's natural to turn to people you trust when you are filling judgeships.

"Now of course you are in politics, in the strictest sense. But it's a different sort of politics from the state courts, where the route to the bench is through clubhouse politics and the wards."

Edelstein's colleagues in the Southern District—all

of whom have at least a grain of politics in their backgrounds—illustrate, if nothing else, the rich diversity of the federal bench. There is Dudley B. Bonsal, a Kennedy appointee, whose mother was descended from Thomas Jefferson's sister, and whose father's family, English Quakers, helped found Pennsylvania in 1682. Bonsal, a onetime diplomat, had a classy international practice with Curtis, Mallet-Prevost, Colt & Mosle before his judgeship. On the bench he sits as an equal with Robert F. Carter, youngest of nine children of a black Florida laborer who died when Carter was a year old. His mother worked as a domestic to get him through law school. Twenty-seven times Carter went to the Supreme Court with NAACP cases, 26 times he won.

Or consider Charles E. Stewart, Jr., longtime partner in Governor Thomas Dewey's old firm of Dewey, Ballantine, Bushby, Palmer & Wood, who practiced antitrust law in a 46th-floor glass enclosed office. Stewart spent years defending the duPont Corporation from the government's attempt to force divestiture of its General Motors stock (he lost). Those same years Constance Baker Motley roamed the south as the chief courtroom tactician of the civil rights movement, disarming segregationists with a ready smile, persuasive voice and winning manner. Mrs. Motley was so active in the south that Chief Judge Elbert Tuttle, of the Fifth Circuit Court of Appeals, allowed himself a mild jest one day when a local lawyer unwittingly "introduced" her in his court. "I'll have you know," Judge Tuttle said, "that Mrs. Motley is almost a member of this honorable court." When one of her clients was accused of holding a "frenzied" civil rights meeting in 1962, in violation of a court order, Mrs. Motley offered sweet rebuttal: "Now about those 'frenzied meetings,' Your Honor. Weren't they held in Baptist churches? So there's nothing unusual about that. Everybody knows that Southern Baptists sometimes get pretty emotional in church. We wouldn't want to take that away from them, would we?" The judge smiled behind the back of his hand and ruled for Mrs. Motley.

There is Edward Weinfeld, Edelstein's predecessor

as chief judge, a wiry little guy who, in his seventies, still arrives in his chambers between 5 and 6 A.M.; walks across the Brooklyn Bridge for exercise in lieu of lunch; dons gloves (but not an overcoat) in deference to winter; and is generally regarded as the most astute judge in the courthouse. An example: in 1958, in a non-jury trial he ruled against the merger of Bethlehem Steel and Youngstown Steel & Tube on antitrust grounds. Both sides accepted his judgement without appeal—the ultimate compliment for a judge in a major antitrust case.

There is the Runyonesque Murray I. Gurfein, a self-described "personal and close" friend of Richard Nixon, John Mitchell, and Nelson Rockefeller, who after his appointment in 1971 complained that many environmental, civil rights and discrimination suits were "frivolous and clutter up the court's time"—and who writes Ogden Nash poetry in his spare time.

There are some politicians: Charles M. Metzner was assistant manager of Rockefeller's 1958 gubernatorial campaign; Lloyd Francis MacMahon was national chairman of Citizens for Eisenhower–Nixon in 1956; John M. Connella was a New York City politician/bureaucrat in the 1960s.

And, finally, there is an academician: Judge Marvin E. Frankel, who was professor of criminal law at Columbia until Attorney General Robert F. Kennedy phoned one morning to ask if he would like to be a federal judge. Frankel retains his professorial demeanor in court; he is prone to break into lawyer discussions with the lofty opening statement, "assuming, arguendo . . ." and go into a lecture. Says one courts observer: "Frankel is finicky, and he likes to needle both sides to get out the issues; he'll say such things as, 'I think I may agree with you, but I'm not sure.' "

Edelstein asserts he had little difficulty making the transition from bar to bench. "Anyone who's been around a courtroom, who has common sense and knows the law, can conduct a trial. I have one slight advantage in that my first intention was to go to medical school, rather than law. My undergraduate work was heavy in the sciences—chemistry, math, physics, biology—and I like to fuss around with figures. I find this background of singular value in, say, patent suits. There is nothing mysterious or difficult about the actual substantive law in patents: it's a matter of learning the jargon. The same in computers. Once you learn the language, you just follow the law. In the IBM case, for instance, I had the lawyers prepare a glossary of terms and definitions—a paper, I might add, that turns out to be a basic reference work in the field. I was weary of constantly having to explain terms, some with varying definitions, each time I mentioned them in an opinion. Now I just refer to the glossary, and do not have to go into prolix every time a word is used."

In the years before he became chief judge, Edelstein acquired the reputation of a hard-working jurist who fretted after his cases with mother-hen fussiness. "Dave has a hangup about letting things drag," one of his colleagues says. "Many of us are more philosophical about delay. We'll rationalize, 'It's just another law suit.' Not Dave. He comes from the school that believes man must work—work well, and hard, and long." Edelstein's hurry-along-now approach to trials is reflected in the case of a corporate executive charged with lying to a grand jury and to SEC investigators. After conviction in Edelstein's court, his lawyers complained in an appeal. "The trial was completed in four days, when it was originally expected to take from a week to ten days. . . . [T]he judge took virtually no recesses, opened court promptly each day, and stayed in session until late each afternoon." The court of appeals took these statements as compliments rather than grounds for reversal; it called them "quite descriptive of high judicial conscientiousness, and the argument based upon them is quite frivolous."

During the first years of the 1970s, Edelstein worked hard by necessity as well as by choice, for the Southern District had as many as six vacancies (among 26 judgeships) at a time. The reason was that the White House, the American Bar Association, the New York senators (Jacob Javits, Charles Goodell, and, after 1971, James Buckley) could not agree on appointees. Because Javits is the senior senator and a Republican, much of the public onus for the delays fell on him—although he is quick to slough it off onto the ABA Federal Judiciary Committee. By Javits' account, in 1970 he and Goodell proposed eleven names for ten vacancies in the Southern and Eastern Districts; only two cleared the ABA. A Javits staff man said, "Javits felt this was most unfair. The list included some sitting state court judges he felt were good men. It was embarrassing." The staff man also felt the ABA criteria on age, residency and trial experience are unrealistic for New York. "This might be hard to believe, but it's difficult to get good candidates. A man between forty and sixty is at the height of his legal career. Outstanding lawyers seldom wish to give up their practice at this time; they're not ready to go on the bench. Another problem is that many 'New York lawyers' live in Connecticut and commute. It's hard to find women because of the trial-experience requirement; the way law firms work, few women have extensive litigation experience."

The White House apparently gave Goodell nominees short shrift for political reasons (it marked him for political extinction in 1970 because of his anti-administration stance on Vietnam and other issues, and succeeded). Nonetheless, the Javits staff man professed to see little Nixon interest in the philosophical bent of judges at the district court level. Robert Carter, for instance, had been a trial counsel for the NAACP's Legal Defense Fund, long at odds with the administration on school desegregation. Charles Warren, who handles judicial affairs for Javits, says he was nervous when he told Attorney General Richard Kleindienst in 1972 that Javits wanted to nominate Carter. Warren told Kleindienst of Carter's background. Kleindienst didn't flinch. "Look," he told Warren, "I don't care if he's a left-winger or a radical. If the ABA approves him, he's all right with us." Kleindienst's predecessor, John M. Mitchell, did try to persuade Javits to appoint an old friend to a judgeship. Javits put the man before his own screening committee of lawyers, which rejected him as unqualified. Javits told Mitchell and nothing further was heard of the man. Warren says, "I got the idea this appointment was on the basis of friendship, not politics." *

At any given time the Southern District has pending three to four times as many civil cases as it does criminal cases; and judges' dockets reflect that balance. Edelstein is ambivalent about criminal cases. Intellectually, although criminal evidentiary law is in flux, he finds them a bore. To paraphrase someone or another, once you've heard one narcotics case (or murder case, or postal theft case) you've heard them all, and Edelstein would rather spend his time on more challenging stuff. Emotionally, criminal cases strike to the core of Edelstein's heart—with exceptions. He is coldly objective about repeat offenders. "I have no hesitation about putting the recidivist criminal in jail. Once a man establishes a pattern of criminality, there is little the courts can do with him other than put him away when he breaks the law."

But first offenders are another matter. Several years ago Edelstein heard the case of a New York man, with a long military background, who was guilty of writing a string of bad checks on out-of-state banks. According to the presentencing investigation the man had had an exemplary military career for years, until his wife developed a kinky sexual desire: "Her thing was to make love with other men and demand that he watch. This completely knocked the fellow off his balance, and he got into all sorts of personal and financial jams. The check thing was a direct result of his wife's conduct." Edelstein clearly did not want to put the man

* Nixon appointees to the Southern District appear marked by one or more of three factors: *a prosecutorial background* (Kevin Duffy and Robert J. Ward, both former assistant United States attorneys; Laurence W. Pierce, a Kings County prosecutor; Whitman Knapp, who headed a probe of New York police corruption after years of service as a state prosecutor; and Arnold Bauman, prosecutor and member of the Knapp Commission); *a superfirm background* (Charles E. Stewart, Jr., of Dewey, Ballantine, Bushby, Palmer & Wood; Thomas P. Griesa, of Davis, Polk & Wardwell; and, finally, *relative youth* (Duffy was 39 when appointed; Ward, 46; Griesa, 41; and Charles L. Brieant, Jr., 48. Brieant was Westchester County Republican chairman as well).

in jail; yet he hesitated to release him on probation without any guarantee of professional stability. So what to do? "The man told me he had always wanted to be a newspaperman, and had writing experience in the military. I called two friends of mine—William Randolph Hearst, Jr., and Bob Considine, the [Hearst] columnist—and asked if they could help him. Sure enough, they found him a job on a paper out of New York, and he straightened out and did just fine."

Another case was more complex, and it illustrates both judicial ingenuity and personal clout. New York authorities arrested a 16-year-old Texas girl we'll call Sally, who was wanted for selling hard narcotics in Houston. She was brought before Edelstein for what was to be a perfunctory hearing approving her return to Texas to stand trial. Edelstein took one look at the kid and shook his head. "She was a frail little thing in blue jeans, pretty and quiet, and shook up. Her mother had been a prostitute, and she lived on her own, by her wits, most of her life. She had drifted into the drug thing more by circumstances than anything else. Well, I looked at that kid and decided jail was the last place she belonged. I began looking around New York for an agency to take her in while I decided what could be done for her. No one would take her. I was stymied.

"As it happened, I had a law clerk that year who had been married only a few months, and he got interested in the case. The upshot was that I deputized him as a special United States marshal and released the girl in the custody of him and his wife. She spent evenings and weekends in their apartment, and they cared for her as if she was their little sister.

"The problem was that the United States attorney in Houston was adamant about getting her returned. The way he talked about her, you would have thought she was a major narcotics dealer. He called me and talked rather nasty and said I was not following regular procedures, and that sort of thing. I set him straight in a minute. I told him, 'Look, if you want, I will be happy to call [Attorney General] Ramsey Clark, your boss in Washington, and tell him you are making a fool out of yourself. Ramsey will listen to me because I've known him since he was a teenager * and I don't think he is going to think very much of a prosecutor who makes such a fuss over this case.' Well, the Houston man fumed on, but he didn't press it.

"During the days Sally came downtown with the clerk and worked in my office, doing filing. She was sort of a courthouse secret. Many people knew what was happening, but not a word leaked to the press. Of course, some outsiders thought it rather odd, this frail thing in blue jeans working in my office. But eventually we found a permanent job for her, over in Brooklyn, and a place to live, in a home run by————. She straightened out nicely, and married, and has a child now.

"Funny, though. In the office she avoided me, as if she didn't want to speak to me, or be seen by me. The last day there, though, she wrote out a little note, and left it where I would find it. It said simply: *I want to thank you but I don't know how.*

"Handling kids is a tough part of criminal work. There's the law to enforce—and there are also humanitarian considerations. I once had two young girls in for something or another, a piddling offense that I knew wasn't going to get them any jail time. I told them very sternly that I was going to release them on bond, and that I was trusting them to come back to court on the date specified. 'If you don't come back,' I said, 'I'll lose my job. And you wouldn't want that to happen, would you?' Both girls returned on schedule.

"Another kind of person, the professional criminal, now I have no hesitation about putting them away. I had a case recently involving Johnny Dioguardi [the labor racketeer who gained notoriety in the 1950s for the acid blinding of columnist Victor Riesel]. An absolutely dumb man. Even when he was operating in his own milieu he had problems doing things right. But my case was a stock swindle, of all things, and why Dioguardi ever got involved in such a thing is beyond

---

* Edelstein met Ramsey Clark while serving in the Justice Department under his father, Attorney General Tom C. Clark, later a Supreme Court justice. Edelstein remains a personal friend of the Clark family.

my comprehension. 'Master criminal' indeed. Bosh. The man is a master bungler. Look how long he's been in prison, and how many times.

"Anyway, Dioguardi was accused of participating in a stock jobbing fraud, a deal where people connived to get an essentially worthless stock up to a high price. Although Dioguardi didn't testify, he seemed to dominate the courtroom physically—a handsome, if somewhat arrogant, man. The jury convicted him, and I gave him a fairly stiff sentence [nine years imprisonment and a $30,000 fine]."

About ten days after trial, Dioguardi received a letter from one of the jurors, a nurse's aid at a Fifth Avenue hospital. The letter was on stationery bearing the zodiac sign of Libra and the legend that it was "the heavenly house under which I was born." The woman claimed clairvoyant powers which enabled her to see that Dioguardi was basically a good person—although she believed he was guilty in the stock case, and that his error was associating with bad persons. The letter continued:

When I saw the good within you and how hard your wife was trying; I prayed about it. One word appear before me *repent*. If you repent and run a clean business it is the good within you that will save you, and you will gain what you have lost. Before I continue I must explain something to you. I have eyes and ears that I can see things before it happen. I can tell you about other and what they are thinking and doing. If I am wrong about this it is the first time.

I would like to visit you. I would like to talk to you about what appear before me. I would like to do so when my eyes fully open. They are only partly open. Unfortunate, a curse was put upon them some years ago. I have some people working on them. Everything is being done that can be done. So we will have to wait.

The woman also praised Dioguardi's lawyer and said, "I entain to send him some custom as soon as my eyes open." In the event they could meet, the woman concluded, "I want you to look upon me as a woman and I look upon you as a man and not white man and black woman. Olive agree with me. Let's leave color out, *OK?*" *

Dioguardi's reaction when he received the letter at the federal prison in Danbury, Connecticut, is not recorded. But his lawyers promptly turned it over to seven psychiatrists. All responded in effect that what the woman had written indicated serious mental disturbance, including hallucinatory tendencies and paranoia. But lacking a clinical examination they would not say whether she was incapable of understanding the trial.

"This one really set me to thinking," Edelstein concedes. No similar case had arisen in the second circuit, hence he had had no immediate, local precedent; cases elsewhere also were rare, and in part contradictory. He finally ruled against a requested hearing into the juror's condition at the time of the trial. "The most that can be said of their shallow showing," he said of the Dioguardi lawyers' petition, "is that it invites a 'fishing expedition into a juror's competency.' This cannot be countenanced." When the woman was questioned before being selected for jury service "nothing in her responses and demeanor indicated that her reasoning abilities or mental processes were deficient." And Edelstein commented that courts historically are reluctant to pry into jury deliberations barring *prima facie* evidence of misconduct. The circuit court upheld Edelstein two-to-one, although Judge Henry Friendly remarked to Edelstein later, "My friend, this is one that could have gone either way." The dissenter, Judge Wilfred Feinberg, bitingly commented, "Certainly a defendant is entitled to twelve sane jurors," and he said Edelstein should have called a hearing on the woman's condition.

Edelstein's protestations about careful sentencing

---

* The woman's grammar and spelling are as contained in her letter.

notwithstanding, the Southern District of New York carries the reputation of a "country-club court" in its handling of white-collar criminals—and especially miscreants caught up in funny-money stock schemes in Wall Street. Whitney North Seymour, Jr., while the United States attorney for the Southern District, directed a study that turned up striking disparities in sentencing. Seymour is no crackpot; he is the very model of an Establishment lawyer (he was president of the New York state bar during 1974; and his firm, Simpson, Thacher & Bartlett, represents such people as Lehman Brothers, Manufacturers Hanover Bank, and the Gulf & Western conglomerate) and he phrases his criticisms in polite lawyerese. But his study, issued in early 1973,* was a devastating—and documented—commentary on uneven justice in the New York federal courts.

A brokerage firm clerk who stuffs a wad of stock certificates into his pocket receives a longer prison term than a front-office manipulator who swindles the public of millions of dollars: an average term of two years, eight months for securities *theft* versus an average of one year, seven months for securities *fraud*. During the six months covered by the study, five of ten persons convicted of income tax evasion went to prison, for an average sentence of two months. The average amount involved was $24,000. Concurrently, 14 of 32 persons convicted of inside thefts of mail (chiefly low-level postal clerks) drew jail terms, for an average of five months. Their thefts averaged $200. A person convicted of bribery "faces only a 25 percent chance of imprisonment in the Southern District compared to 55 percent if he were convicted of interstate theft." Overall, Seymour said in the report, "one may conclude that poor persons receive harsher treatment in the federal courts than do well-to-do defendants charged with more sophisticated crimes."

---

* The study, issued in mimeographed form, has been widely reprinted in bar organs; see, for instance, the *New York State Bar Journal* for April 1973. Seymour also incorporated the material into his *Why Justice Fails,* William Morrow & Company, New York, 1973.

One reason is obvious, and cheerfully conceded by Edelstein: federal judges and white collar offenders come from the same social milieu. They belong to the same sort of golf clubs and churches, they dress alike and talk alike, they are from the same universities. Can a federal judge look down from the bench at a man who is the personification of his next-door neighbor— or a mirror image of himself—and see a hardened criminal? Edelstein's position runs roughly as follows on white-collar offenders: The purpose of sentencing is to deter or punish. A white-collar criminal, once he is exposed to the community in which he lives, is tacitly destroyed. What further purpose could be served by locking him up?

Nonetheless the disturbing specific case histories remain, instances which buttress Seymour's contention that "white-collar defendants, predominantly white, received more lenient treatment as a general rule [than] defendants charged with common crimes . . . largely . . . the unemployed and undereducated. . . ." Some cases cited by Seymour's study:

- A white male in his forties, vice president of a Wall Street brokerage house, violated securities laws on sales of more than $3 million, on which he "personally realized unlawful commissions of a good many thousands of dollars." Fined $6,000.
- A father and son, both white and aged 65 and 35, concealed $100,000 in income over three years. Self-employed, they earned $40,000 and $20,000 a year respectively. They pleaded guilty, made restitution, and were fined $2,500 each.
- A 50-year-old IRS agent took a $3,000 bribe. Caught, he testified against two other agents, who were convicted of corruption. The sentence: unsupervised probation for one day.
- A 64-year-old medical doctor, white, who earned $60,000 annually, concealed $80,000 income over three years. Fined $10,000.
- A 40-year-old black who served 14 years in the army, earning a Bronze Star, was charged with transporting $13,000 of stolen United States Treasury checks.

He had no previous criminal convictions. He pleaded guilty and was sent to prison for two years. A 34-year-old black woman accomplice—on welfare and with three children, also with no previous convictions—was sentenced to a six-month term.

- A 31-year-old white male broke into a post office and stole $20,000 worth of stamps. Four years in prison.

So what should be done about sentencing disparities? Why should a selective service defendant stand a 50-50 chance of going to prison if he appears before one federal judge, and only a one-in-25 chance if he draws another? Why should a forger in the Southern District of New York receive twice as long a sentence as a similar criminal in the Northern District of New York? As Seymour notes, the disparities "are not abstract," but concern "real flesh and blood problems involving the sense of justice and fair play of individual human beings." All sorts of goals have been suggested over the years: frequent reports of sentences, so that judges can compare their work with that of colleagues elsewhere; sentencing "institutes" where judges can discuss the rationale behind punishments for particular offenses and particular defendant personality profiles; national conferences aimed at seeking common sentencing policies applicable to all judicial districts.

Judges for the most part ignore such "reform" attempts as unwarranted intrusions on their independence. So long as the law permits a latitude of sentence, judges feel they are as qualified as anyone else to determine what punishment fits what defendant. As one North Carolina judge puts it, "Down here, moonshining is a six-month offense. If some Brooklyn judge wants to put a whiskey-maker away for three years, that's Brooklyn's concern." Nonetheless the Seymour study leaves one with the disquieting feeling that "justice" is not yet a reality in the New York federal courts.

As chief judge of the Southern District David N. Edelstein presides over a congeries of court-related bureaucracies. Bankruptcy judges try to salvage persons and businesses for whom the American free-enterprise balloon went pop. Probation officers try to persuade their wards that the streets of New York, gray though they may be, are more comfortable than the rock walls of Lewisberg penitentiary or even the green lawns of the Danbury "correctional institution." Court clerks shuffle through enough paper to build a stack at least as high as the 27-story courthouse each year. The jury department summons at least 850 New Yorkers every two weeks to sit in judgement on their fellow citizens. More are called for special events: in the winter of 1974, when former Nixon cabinet officers John N. Mitchell and Maurice Stans came to trial in the Vesco bribery scandals, the jury overseers summoned 2,350 prospects, almost three times the normal complement. The courts scheduled four other "major" trials the same week (including a multidefendant narcotics conspiracy case and an offshoot of the Penn Central bankruptcy case) reasoning that even if a potential juror knew enough about the well-publicized Mitchell-Stans scandal to beg exclusion, he could be pressed into service in another trial. The court reporters, who have their own quasi-official partnership association, flick their fingers over Stenotype machines rapidly enough to earn $30,000 to $35,000 a year (meeting even the linguistic challenges of men such as B. Nathaniel Richter, the Philadelphia negligence lawyer whose 400 word-a-minute delivery gives him the title of "fastest tongue in the East"). The federal magistrates conduct preliminary hearings for criminal defendants—a dreary, mind-sickening rote process in which case docket numbers appear in the scared, pathetic form of human beings in trouble.

Although he is charged with overall responsibility for these housekeeping and backup functions, Edelstein shunts as much of the detail work as possible to committees of his fellow judges (there are seventeen panels in all, ranging from courtroom security to hospitality, probation, space and sentencing practices). But Edelstein admits to spending "far too much time" on administrative trivia. And, from the vantage point of Edelstein's elbow, I watched him fuss over matters that could have been resolved several echelons below the chief judge's office. Some examples from our days together:

- Edelstein must approve courthouse parking permits for court employees, a niggling but time-consuming task. (I watched Edelstein bounce back an application twice because the man hadn't filed the right kind of letter.)
- Edelstein must give final approval to any probation officer hired by the court, and during one of our days together the department head brought him two pieces of what the judge later said was "typical" business. He wanted approval to ask FBI background checks on some prospective hirees (granted), and to promote an officer to a supervisory post. Edelstein quizzed him on whether the job should go to a more qualified outsider; the question was never resolved. "Those are the sort of things that eat up your day," Edelstein said when the official finally left.
- So does listening to excuses from persons who think they have valid reason to be excused from jury duty. Hence Edelstein spends part of his Monday mornings listening to citizens recite their medical, transportation, babysitting and business problems.
- As *de facto* landlord of the federal courthouse Edelstein decides how space is allocated in the overcrowded 48-year-old building: whether, for instance, the bankruptcy division should make do with 20,000 square feet at Foley Square, or face an unwilling eviction to the United States customs house, two subway stops south. Edelstein is maneuvering for a sub-courthouse in suburban White Plains, a plan backed by local lawyers who cringe at taking the long commuting trip to Foley Square, but not by the General Services Administration, the federal government's housekeeping and real estate agency. In the interim, Edelstein shoehorns people wherever they will fit. For instance, when his longtime barber, an engaging chap named Mario, lost his Foley Square shop, Edelstein found him space in the bottom

of the courthouse (with a clientele restricted to court employees).

"Those are some of the reasons," Edelstein said, "that a judge can't sit on the bench all the time, or devote his complete working day to conferences with lawyers. My habit is to work either here or at home on Saturday morning, break after lunch to listen to the 'Texaco Opera of the Air' until five o'clock, and then perhaps to work a few hours more in the evenings. I always work on Sunday morning; the afternoon we reserve for the museums and the galleries. Working that schedule enables me to keep current, but not much more."

Edelstein glanced at the wall clock. Almost ten o'clock on our second morning. "Downstairs again," he said, "more conferences on today. Let's see how many of these things will fall off the vine for me."

Once again, the informality of Courtroom 34. I sat in the jury box, immediately behind Edelstein, and watched him tackle the docket. First, a maritime case, out-of-court settlement; one of the lawyers dictates the stipulated terms ($3,500) in less than a minute.* "Thanks," Edelstein says, and he sounds as if he truly means it.

Next, an accident case brought by a peripatetic lawyer plaintiff: a Harvard instructor when injured in 1969, he was later in the Soviet Union with the government, still later a Peace Corps volunteer, and is now a San Francisco lawyer. His lawyer says, "I've been chasing the medical records for two years; if I can't get them in sixty days, I'm going to discontinue the case." "If you please," responds Edelstein.

Another: the plaintiff is in Italy, and the lawyers have tried without success to produce him. "Since 1969?"

---

* Unlike other civil damage suits, a maritime action does not have to involve a claim of more than $10,000 to fall within federal jurisdiction. The plaintiff has the choice of suing in either state or federal court. Most opt for the latter, for they are better run, especially in New York. Resultantly, the federal court is clogged with what lawyers call "nautical fender-bumping cases."

asks Edelstein, incredulously. Yes. "Produce him in sixty days; fish or cut bait." A rash of routine motions, and I sense that Edelstein is becoming restive.

Yet another penny-ante maritime case. A vessel carrying a shipment of oil consigned to Exxon broke up at sea. The owner of the vessel was a "one-ship corporation" that vanished along with the boat. Its erstwhile owners didn't even bother to answer the suit (which is one reason maritime operators put formal title of their vessels into specially-created corporations). Nonetheless the Exxon lawyer wants a formal default judgement entered against the defunct corporation, a proceeding which would require even more court time for an inquest establishing the loss.

"Why go to the expense of an inquest?" asks Edelstein. "Why all this expense for a judgement against a non-existent corporation? Why use your firm's resources on something of this nature?"

Pain and embarrassment. The young lawyer licks his lips. "Your Honor, since we've spent all the time, we feel this would be an appropriate way to close out the case. We represent Exxon on an ongoing basis."

"Yes, but how about the time of the court? Judgement doesn't give you any more than would a discontinuance without prejudice [essentially, dropping the case, but retaining the right to reinstitute it later]."

"Well," the lawyer begins, "my instructions were . . ."

"Aren't you admitted to the bar?" snaps Edelstein. "Go back to your firm, with my suggestion. If you decide not to take any action, we can proceed with default in fourteen days."

The lawyer sighed and gathered his papers and his topcoat and left. Edelstein was muttering something which I couldn't hear, but which brought a suppressed chuckle from the court reporter.

Another maritime case, a longshoreman who fell through an open hatch and was suing for lost wages of $8,500. The accident happened two years ago; nonetheless the lawyer wanted another 60 days before trial. "Why?" demanded Edelstein. "This is an old case. Why not get moving?"

The lawyer, aware that Edelstein was not in the best

of moods, spoke carefully. He wanted the time to take a deposition from the injured longshoreman and his physician. As he spoke Edelstein shuffled through the case folder. He noted that even if the man recovered the $8,500, he would have to repay $6,000 he had already received for workmen's compensation. "There wouldn't be much left after your contingency fee, would there?" he asked the lawyer. (In personal injury cases the attorney fee is one-third to one-half of the amount recovered.) Edelstein unhappily gave the lawyer 90 days—and a suggestion that the insurance carrier settle the case out of court.

And, finally, the epitome of picayune cases: a cargo damage suit claiming $1,200, and the announcement of the lawyer that it had been settled for $500. Edelstein grunted, and as we walked to the elevator I opined the federal courts surely had more important business than listening to small-claims cases. Edelstein agreed. "The problem is that these shipping companies have the lawyers on retainer, and they feel they should do something for their money. So they'll mess around with a case like this. I quake when I think of all the court work, the government expense, the consumer expense that goes into some little case like that, that should be settled in five minutes in the lawyers' offices."

By coincidence, when we arrived back in Edelstein's chambers, the first message was of a phone call from Chief Judge Jacob Mishler, his counterpart in the Eastern District of New York—Brooklyn and Long Island. Judge Mishler, Edelstein was informed, had heard of a new rule the Soutern District was propounding on settlement of maritime claims, and he wanted "coordination" so that the two courts would have a common procedure. New York admiralty lawyers practice in both courts—after all, both abut New York harbor and Mishler's domain is visible, on a clear day, from Edelstein's desk—and the Brooklyn judges thought it would be nice if everyone handled the cases in the same way.

Edelstein frowned mightily as Howard Stravitz, his law clerk, started explaining what Mishler had said. He stopped Stravitz cold. "Look," he said, "it's taken me three years to work this damned thing out, and I'm not about to renegotiate it again with the Brooklyn judges and the other lawyers. Send Judge Mishler an information copy of our rule; tell him it's for his information, it's what we have *already* done. So far as our court is concerned, the issue is closed, the rule is issued. Let Judge Mishler and his people do what they want to do."

After Stravitz left the room Edelstein fumed out loud a few more minutes. "We have about 9,000 civil cases pending in this district, 1,000 of them admiralty cases, and a good many of those are the piddly kind of thing you just saw downstairs. Now if I, as chief judge, can find a way to clear our courts of this sort of thing, I intend to do it. So what we came up with is 'summary determination,' which is a sort of deluxe arbitration—'arbitration' is an unpopular word with lawyers, a real scare word, so for heaven's sake don't use it—for admiralty claims of less than $10,000. I talked with the lawyers for months, and got them to come around, and everyone accepted them. You know, what you have essentially in these cases is a fight between two insurance companies, so there's no reason in the world we can't get down to the facts and settle." The rule permits consenting parties to submit their cases to the judge in either written or testimonial form, and does away with the rigidities of a formal hearing. The judge's ruling may not be appealed. "If this rule works, and I think it will, we should speed up the handling of these cases," Edelstein said.

Lunch time. The Chinese New Year, and Edelstein looked forward to a special treat. "My friend, Andy Lee, who has an insurance agency in Chinatown [just east of Foley Square] likes to get a group of us together from time to time for a special meal." He mentioned a few of the people: Milton W. Mays, president of the Continental Corporation, holding company for the Continental insurance group ("They have assets of around $3 billion," Edelstein said, with a hint of awe in his voice); Dave Gray, Mays' executive vice president and heir-apparent; a vice-president of Manufacturers Hanover Trust Company, 12th largest in the nation, with assets of more than $11 billion, the manager of the bank's Foley Square branch. We walked through Chinatown to the rendezvous. Scores of Chinese youngsters lined Mott Street, tossing exploding packages of firecrackers at one another and at passersby; others cavorted under the cloth frame of a ferocious green dragon, charging at store fronts as people on the sidewalk drew back in mock horror, and hurled even more fireworks. Edelstein strode unblinkingly through the bursts, outwardly oblivious to the fact that Chinatown literally was exploding beneath his feet, and into the restaurant.

Over platters of Chinese delicacies Edelstein probed at the insurance executives on the subject that had troubled him earlier that day. Why is it, he asked, that the insurance companies cannot work out some sort of intramural system for settling damage suits in which both parties are insured? And why shouldn't insurance companies be more realistic about settling cases they don't stand a chance of winning in court?

Edelstein asked these and other questions in mild, polite tones; nonetheless, the insurance men squirmed. One of them rebutted with a horror story about a woman who was critically injured in a Florida freeway accident, and how Continental had been ready to give her the full amount of the policy without question "until some negligence lawyer got into the case and said she was entitled to even more recovery from some of the other parties." So the woman received nothing for several years, until the case was tried.

Edelstein was sympathetic, yet he pressed his thesis: something was wrong with the existing system of adjudicating negligence cases, and as a judge he wanted ideas on how it could be improved.

"That," said Milton Mays of Continental, "is a very complex subject."

"I know it is," said Edelstein, "and that's why it should be talked about."

We took a roundabout route back to the courthouse to give the Chinese food a chance to settle in our stomachs. Edelstein was still thinking about negligence cases. "How many billions of dollars were sitting at that table?" he mused. "Those are the people who could really give a push to the ideas I've been talking about. One dislikes to bring business into a social luncheon—these people are friends, more than anything else—but I see that as part of my job as a judge, to obtain the thinking of as many people in the community as I can." He shrugged. "Who knows, maybe something will come of it."

Although we were veritably in the shadow of the courthouse, on crowded streets, Edelstein passed unnoticed in the crowd—a small man in a black overcoat indistinguishable from any other lawyer or merchant or broker returning from lunch. That afternoon he was to receive a trustee's report on settlement of a one-million-dollar-plus class action claim in a securities case; the next morning he was to spend with that monolith the IBM case. I thought about Edelstein's bemused comment several weeks earlier about the anonymity of federal judges.

We entered the courthouse through the parking garage and had walked perhaps 50 feet when the guard called, "Hey, what are you looking for?"

Edelstein turned and the two men looked at one another full-face. After a few seconds Edelstein said, "I am Chief Judge Edelstein, and I work here. We are going to the elevator."

The guard continued staring a few more moments and gestured that we could proceed.

"As you can see," Edelstein said as we entered the elevator, "judges are rather famous people around here."

CHAPTER THREE

When the System Flops I:
The Shame of Chicago

Their work suddenly done for them elsewhere, the lawyers drifted into the Chicago court in relaxed, casual moods. Earlier that day rail unions had threatened a national strike. Pleading an emergency, the rail companies persuaded United States District Judge James B. Parsons to hear arguments for an injunction at seven o'clock in the evening. In the meantime, however, Congress rushed through legislation ordering the workers to stay on their jobs while negotiations continued. Hence all that remained for the lawyers was the *pro forma* dismissal of the injunction petition, a chore Judge Parsons could handle in seconds.

Only Judge Parsons didn't appear at 7 P.M. The lawyers' conviviality gradually changed to boredom, then irritation, as they thought of missed dinners and wasted time. Finally, at 8 P.M., an hour late, Parsons walked into court—abnormally erect and formal, as if he wasn't entirely sure of his ability to get from his chambers and up the few steps to the bench.

Told that the injunction request was now moot, Parsons sighed and looked at the dozen or so railroad and union lawyers, and the court aides. "So this was a railroad case," he proclaimed in basso-profundo tones. "The railroad industry, ah, yes, a fascinating industry. I have devoted long and deep thought to the railroad industry, and I foresee quite a future for the railroad industry. I envision what can happen to the glorious railroad industry if it is properly managed. I foresee railroad cars carried on tracks ten feet apart for greater comfort, with the carriages suspended far above the tracks for greater comfort. I foresee . . ."

Among the captive audience, total bewilderment. What had possessed the judge? On and on he talked, for a full half-hour, oblivious to the incredulous expressions, half-hidden yawns, and gradually glazing eyes of the listeners. The economics of railroads. The social significance of railroads. The technology of railroads. Parsons seemed prepared to talk all night —"in pure gibberish," in the words of one of the lawyers there.

Then in mid-sentence he paused and stifled a burp. He sipped from a glass of water, and looked down at the lawyers. "Well, gentlemen, since most of our business seems to be at an end, why don't we adjourn and go home?" With a great gathering and flapping of his black robes, Parsons vanished into his chambers.

The Honorable James B. Parsons, the lawyers concluded when he was gone, had presided over court while stone-eyed drunk.

For many years, with only a few saving exceptions, the Chicago federal bench was the most wretched in the nation. Avarice, stupidity, politics, mule-headed pettiness, pathological behavior on the bench, favoritism towards business interests: such were the sorts of evils that could be found in Chicago justice. "When I moved out here from Washington in the fifties," one corporation lawyer told me, "I had a hell of a lot of respect for federal judges. But after two months here," he paused and held his nose, "PHEW! Too many of these guys here were either sick, fixed, or dumb."

Another lawyer, a native Chicagoan: "When I began practicing, the federal courts outraged me. Now I'm as bad as everyone else: I keep a catalogue of the various quirks and prejudices of the judges. If I can trigger one into screwing the opposition, to the benefit of my client, I do it. It's a crappy way to practice law, but what the hell—you've got to make it under the system. An example? Oh, take ——. [He named a veteran Chicago judge.] He is more Catholic than most bishops. Although you could never prove conscious bias, you know where he stands on church issues.

"One time I was cross-examining a witness in a real estate case. I played dumb on the sequence of ownership of a piece of property involved. 'Let me get this straight, Mr. Jones,' I would say, 'this property originally was in the name of your first wife, and after you divorced her, it went to your second wife?' I managed to say the word 'divorce' four or five times, and the other lawyer to this day hasn't caught on to what I was doing. But —— heard. And there was a distinct change in his attitude towards the opposition. He gave me a couple of close ones [rulings that could have gone either way] and we won the case."

Another lawyer, who works with a public interest law group in the environmental field: "Going before some Chicago judges is like playing Russian roulette with all the chambers loaded. You'll get your brains blown out one way or another, so you might as well make a record and hope to hell that the court of appeals bails you out."

These lawyers commented only after I had given them the journalistic equivalent of a blood-pledge not to print their names. On-the-record evaluation of federal judges is rare—a pity, because the worst of the benchwarmers are surrounded by sycophantic court aides and lawyers whose constant praise gives the judges false reassurances of their wisdom and dignity. Chicago is unique in that a study has been made of judges there by lawyers practicing in the federal courts. The study showed widespread opinion among Chicago lawyers that many federal judges wer performing badly.

The study was developed by the Chicago Council of Lawyers, a group of some 1,500 attorneys who tired of the harrumphing, salute-the-flag pomposity of the formal bar and decided to develop some practical ways of improving justice. The CCL devised a 28-item questionnaire relating to integrity, judicial temperament, legal ability, decisiveness and diligence, based upon the American Bar Association's standards for judicial performance. The questions were sent to some 2,400 lawyers who had filed district court appearances in the three preceding years, and to CCL members (some 750) not included in the first group. Of these, 529 responded.

The most important question was, "Viewed overall, do you favor his [the judge's] continued service in his present post?" As a fail/pass line, the CCL chose 60 percent, the vote of the electorate necessary for retention of state court judges under the Illinois constitution. Here is how Chicago lawyers ranked the thirteen judges sitting at the time of the study:

Judge	Percent favorable	Percent unfavorable
Frank J. McGarr *	75.65	2.17
Richard B. Austin	75.94	6.56
Thomas R. McMillen *	67.33	7.43
Hubert L. Will	75.49	9.01
Alexander J. Napoli *	67.28	9.56
Edwin A. Robson	70.82	11.74
Bernard M. Decker	59.48	18.63
Abraham L. Marovitz	56.55	22.62
Joseph Samuel Perry	42.71	34.24
William J. Campbell	40.88	37.59
William J. Lynch	26.12	49.48
Julius J. Hoffman	24.74	57.55
James B. Parsons	15.19	67.13

Another question asked was if the lawyers thought the judges worthy of promotion to a higher court. Only four qualified, in the opinion of lawyers responding: McGarr, Will, McMillen and Napoli. William J. Campbell, long the chief judge of the district, got less than 60 percent scores on six of seven questions pertaining to judicial integrity. William J. Lynch got

---

* Judge Napoli died in 1972, before the poll results were published; Judges McGarr and McMillen, both Nixon appointees, had been sitting only a short while.

less than 60 percent on 21 of 28 questions: all seven relating to judicial integrity; all eight relating to legal ability; and all five relating to diligence. Julius J. Hoffman, of Chicago conspiracy trial fame, was written off as impetuous and rude. Here are the respondents' feelings about Hoffman:

"Does he demonstrate patience and a willingness to listen to all sides?" Favorable, 10.68 percent; unfavorable, 78.13 percent.

"Is he impartially courteous towards lawyers and litigants?" Favorable, 11.98 percent; unfavorable, 79.43 percent.

"We had hoped," said one of the lawyers involved in the study, "that the results would provoke some soul-searching among the judges, and that it might even prompt the worst of them to retire. No such luck. We heard, indirectly, that one of the low-ranked judges was yelling about contempt proceedings against the entire Chicago Council of Lawyers. Nothing came of it."

The quality of Chicago justice was all the more puzzling because of the city's importance as an industrial and commercial city. Chicago feeds, finances, insures and supplies the Midwest; as a corporate headquarters town, it is second only to New York. Given the importance of federal courts to corporations' very existence, why did the Chicago business and legal community tolerate such an incompetent judiciary? I put this question to more than a dozen Chicago lawyers. The reactions were revealing. Several accepted the premise, then stared blankly and said, in effect, "This is the way things have always been; why complain? It does no good." One veteran practitioner, a man in his sixties who divided his life between government and corporate practice, offered a biting (and convincing) summation: "We've had the kind of federal bench we deserved. This district does not have the kind of bar that is interested in the federal bench. The lawyers, even the ones with the big corporations, were satisfied to rock along with a bad judiciary because they were satisfied with the quasi-dictatorial style of government The Machine provides. Chicago has decided to put its fate in the hands of one man, a decision joined in by the Democratic Machine and even the *Tribune*. The bar is spineless. The corporate attorneys were comfortable with the situation as it existed. This amounts to the surrender of an important legal responsibility, for you can't have good administration of justice without good judges."

"The Machine," of course, is the Democratic political organization headed by Mayor Richard J. Daley. During the Kennedy–Johnson years Daley personally approved every Chicago federal judge—for, as one politically active lawyer states, "The Machine long depended upon a subservient bench to dominate Chicago. The state courts, of course, are complete toadies. When that situation occurs elsewhere, you can find relief in the federal courts. Not so in Chicago. You go to court, and even today you may be up against someone who was put on the bench by The Machine for the express purpose of perpetuating The Machine in power. This is a rotten situation. Cases can be decided purely for political reasons, not on the basis of justice. Now let's be specific on one point: this is a bad situation regardless of whether you think Daley is a good boss or a bad boss. Why? The courts are getting away from the law. They exist as tools for suppressing political dissidents, not radicals or revolutionaries, but anyone who disagrees with The Machine."

This lawyer would not speak for attribution. One who did was Robert Bennett, a young professor at the Northwestern Law School. Bennett is no crackpot. He worked as a legal assistant to Nicholas Johnson, the Federal Communications Commissioner, and as an associate in Covington & Burling, the most prestigious of Washington's superlaw firms. He helped form the insurgent Chicago Council of Lawyers and served as an early president. Lean, dark-haired, intense, Bennett sat in a coffee shop adjacent to the Federal Building in downtown Chicago and ticked through the types of "political" cases where a controlled judiciary is important to The Machine.

"There are politically sensitive cases where the Democratic Party has a direct interest in the outcome, such as voting rights and registration. If you get before a political judge, you haven't a chance in hell of winning. The judge will sometimes have the courtesy of going through the motions of a 'fair trial' and pretend he is listening to you. But you were dead from the moment the case was assigned." Cases in which a federal judge has an opportunity to help the Daley Machine are not difficult to find in the record. A prime example: Judge William J. Lynch, about whom much more shall be said in a moment, was a law partner and lifelong personal and political crony of Mayor Daley before ascending the federal bench in 1966. In 1970 Daley wanted to prevent Reverend Jesse Jackson, the black activist, from entering the mayoralty election. Jackson's Operation Breadbasket had won him considerable following in Chicago's black ghettoes, and The Machine feared he would siphon away 200,000 black votes that normally would fall to Daley. So election officers invoked an obscure law that would require Jackson to gather between 48,094 and 92,935 signatures of registered voters—depending upon which way the statute was interpreted—to qualify for the ballot. Under the same law Daley would need only 4,099 signatures (which he could gather without leaving City Hall), the Republican candidate, 2,034. Lynch strictly interpreted the law, thereby preventing the threat of a serious black opponent.

Bennett continued his critique of political judges: "In another type of case, there is no particular political overtone, but 'judicial patronage' is heavily involved, in the form of attorney fees or receiverships or guardianships. A lot of money can be made, and a judge is in a position to enrich his friends. Here I'm not worried so much about politics as about cronyism. Lawyers are picked for important assignments as friends of the judge, rather than because they are the best person. Another danger is that the judge will award too much money for the lawyer's services, to the detriment of the estate or other property."

Judge William Campbell, during more than three

decades on the bench, nonetheless found time to amass a multi-million-dollar real estate fortune. A sometime partner of Campbell was a Chicago lawyer named William J. Friedman. The Campbell family, through his wife and a family foundation (the Argyll Trust, created for his eight children), owned a 37-percent share in the Lytton Building, a prime Loop property valued at $1.6 million. Friedman owned a large share of the Lytton Building, also. Simultaneously, Campbell appointed Friedman as attorney and receiver in a reorganization proceeding for City Savings & Loan Association, an assignment worth scores of thousands of dollars in fees. Chicago lawyers who point to this case do not question Friedman's legal abilities; indeed, one of them said, "Friedman is bound to have good sense. After all, look at the money he's made." But his public friendship with Campbell did cause raised eyebrows.

In 1972 Judge James Parsons handled the bankruptcy of a Chicago company called Cybern Education, Inc. Cybern had assets of $61,000 and debts of $16,000. Without notice to creditors or the Internal Revenue Service (which claimed $63,000 in back taxes), Parsons awarded fees totalling $45,000 to three friendly attorneys he appointed to handle the proceeding. As the Seventh Circuit Court of Appeals commented in overturning the fees, the case was simple and "should have been quickly terminated with little or no expense."

A third flaw of "political" judges—and one which causes the most concern to Professor Bennett—is that they often prove "not smart enough to handle intricate, challenging cases." Bennett told me, "Deficiencies in intellect and judgement, and just plain legal competence, are most apt to emerge when a judge is picked on a political basis." And the shortcomings are not always visible to the casual observer. Bennett points particularly to Judge ———. "It's mind boggling to watch him. He really enjoys the role of judge. You'll watch him for an hour—a big man, with a hell of a lot of dignity and bearing—and realize he hasn't done a damned thing. He loves playing judge, but he won't make decisions on what is happening before him, and when he does, he is very likely to make the *wrong* decision."

Much of the blame for the poor judicial appointments during the Kennedy–Johnson years must rest with Paul Douglas, the state's Democratic senator from 1949 until his defeat in 1966. One of Douglas' Chicago friends, a man who worked on his campaigns, and admires him, told me, "Paul didn't think much of lawyers, he did not appreciate the craftsmanship of the law. Certain skills are essential if you are to be a good judge. Paul never quite got the hang of it." According to this man, Douglas was content to let the Chicago Machine select judges there, because "he felt obligated to them [for votes] and went along with them." In his memoirs * Douglas told of another factor: the willingness of the White House, under both Kennedy and Johnson, to compromise with Senator Everett McKinley Dirksen, then the minority leader, in return for occasional Republican support for key programs. According to Douglas, Attorney General Robert Kennedy twice tried to select Republicans for the district bench in Chicago. Douglas said he told Bob Kennedy the appointments were "intolerable" and "base ingratitude" and suggested the Kennedys ask themselves who had done more for them, Daley, Dirksen or Douglas. Over Douglas' protests a Republican, Bernard Decker, got the appointment. In 1971 Decker wrote a Congressional redistricting decision that cost Illinois three Democratic congressmen. "So the Kennedy–Dirksen alliance gave a final large bonus to the Republicans," Douglas wrote.

One afternoon not too many years ago, a reporter called the city room of the Chicago Tribune with the report that a federal judge had died. The judge had been ill for months, and an obituary was already in type. An editor called across the room to the rewriteman who was composing a lead for the story. "What did ——————— die of?" the editor asked. The

---

* *In the Fullness of Time,* Harcourt Brace Jovanovich, Inc., New York, 1972.

rewriteman, who had spent some time around the federal courts, stood and roared: "GREED!"

What the military would call "operational responsibility" for the politicalization of the Chicago federal bench rests upon the erect, arrogant shoulders of William J. Campbell, chief judge from 1959 until 1970, when he achieved senior judge status at age 65. Campbell is a man not often troubled by self-doubt. Campbell's admirers and critics find common ground in their assessment of him as an activist judge (although one clique calls him "pig-headed" and the other "strong-minded"). Campbell saw himself as a personification of the federal courts (or vice versa) and intimidated fellow judges and lawyers alike through strict imposition of his own definition of how their business should be conducted. Any attack on the courts' authority, or slight on their reputation, was equated with a personal affront to Campbell. Here are examples of some of the personality traits displayed by Campbell during his 30 years on the federal bench:

• Hypocritical. In 1963 Chief Justice Earl Warren dissented from a Supreme Court ruling upholding the contempt conviction of a Chicago narcotics dealer who refused to testify before a grand jury even when given immunity. Warren felt the government had subjected the man to "unjustifiable harassment." Campbell intoned, "It would indeed be refreshing for a change to hear a few expressions of sympathy and appreciation from those strong advocates of the rights of criminals, for the federal agents who daily risk their lives to defend society from the ever-increasing violent activities of such criminals." Quick as he was to criticize the chief justice, Campbell would broach no such behavior from persons who practice in *his* court. In 1965 Edward Hanrahan, then the United States attorney for Chicago, commented sharply on Judge James B. Parsons for a wristslap 90-day jail sentence for a man who stole $55,800 from a savings and loan association. Campbell publicly warned Hanrahan that he would be held in contempt if he criticized any other decisions.

- Thin-skinned. The Chicago Bar Association traditionally sponsors a musical comedy show entitled "Christmas Spirits," each December. The show, which enjoys a large attendance, customarily satirizes public personalities and topical incidents, with emphasis on Illinois and Chicago public officials. The 1969 show, "Heir," included a skit that, in an Alice in Wonderland context, lampooned Judge Julius Hoffman's handling of the conspiracy trial arising from the 1968 Democratic national convention. John C. Tucker, a lawyer who had briefly represented four of the defense attorneys in a contempt proceeding, played the role of Hoffman. Campbell didn't chuckle. He wrote bar officers that he and other federal judges (excluding Hoffman, the butt of the joke) thought the skit "was not only in bad taste, but also constitutes a clear violation of the canons of professional ethics and the long established rules of this court." Campbell felt the skit was "the more flagrant" because of Tucker's role, and he called it "editorial comment on a pending case." Tucker's involvement in the conspiracy case was so peripheral and short-lived that many Chicago lawyers interpreted Campbell's letter as an attempt to gag *any* lawyer from commenting on *any* case. "If Campbell had his way," one lawyer told me, "the only court reporting you'd find in Chicago newspapers would be transcripts approved by the judge."

- Hard-nosed. Campbell, in a 1969 speech, equated the United States Supreme Court's concern for human rights with the postwar "rebellion against authority." When he first practiced law, Campbell recalled with distinct nostalgia, "A defendant who was tried . . . if convicted, stayed convicted. He went promptly to jail and those who appealed invariably had their convictions affirmed with great dispatch and definitiveness." Now, Campbell lamented, the concern for defendants' rights "often reaches a point of great mischief and absurdity." And in testimony to a House committee in 1967 Campbell expressed amazement at public concern about police brutality, and accused the Supreme Court of generally characterizing "all presently used police interrogation methods as being oppressive and violative of the rights against self-incrimination." Campbell felt instances of police brutality are "the unusual and unexpected exception."

Campbell got on the bench after an astute combination of politics and Catholicism. After graduating from Loyola Law School in Chicago in 1926 he set up a ho-hum law practice and got into Democratic machine politics, which in those days was closely aligned with the local Catholic hierarchy. Campbell became very friendly with the liberal-minded Bishop Bernard J. Shiel and helped him found the Catholic Youth Organization. Campbell so impressed Shiel that he soon became a *de facto nuncio* to President Roosevelt on behalf of Chicago Catholics. By one account Campbell "managed to enhance himself in the eyes of the President by emphasizing his friendship with the bishop, while he improved his situation with the bishop by implying a similar friendship with the President." Be that as it may, Roosevelt made Campbell Illinois director of the National Youth Administration and then, in 1938, United States attorney for the Eastern District of Illinois. Campbell received a brush of national attention when the Justice Department chose Chicago as the arena from which to send Moses L. Annenberg, the publishing tycoon, to jail for not paying taxes on income from his racing wire operation. Campbell directed the grand jury in the tax case, and then went after Annenberg's Nationwide News Service, which fed track information to bookies in the United States, Canada and Cuba (grossing $1.5 million a year from Chicago alone). Campbell forced AT&T and Western Union to stop leasing lines to Nationwide, and put it out of business. On October 22, 1940, Campbell was sworn in as a federal judge —at age 37, the youngest then on the bench. "His elevation comes as a climax to one of the most rapid rises in the history of Illinois," marvelled the *Chicago Tribune*.

Based upon his performance in succeeding years, Campbell seemed to many to have found the pinnacle of the federal bench a boring perch. "He's a guy you really never thought about," said one lawyer. "If anything, his reputation was that of a prosecution-minded judge. Oh, it's hard to cite specific instances of unfairness that long ago, but it was generally understood that if a criminal defendant went into Campbell's court, his next stop was likely to be the federal penitentiary."

Perhaps this boredom led Campbell to an unusual secondary career for a federal judge, that of high-level real estate speculator. Campbell came from a family of modest means. His law practice between 1925 and 1938 was minor. As United States attorney he earned $8,000 a year; as federal judge, his salary slowly increased from $8,000 in 1940 to $42,500 in 1973. With eight children, Campbell had heavy financial responsibilities. Nonetheless, from his relatively small earnings and a modest inheritance of his wife's, Campbell managed to construct a massive personal fortune. The exact size of Campbell's family holdings is impossible to determine, for what meager information that is public has come piecemeal and accidentally. Further, when family holdings came to light, Campbell tried to minimize his wealth. In 1969, for example, a company named Mid-Continental Realty Corporation came under investigation because of its supposed holdings of Las Vegas real estate. One investor proved to be Campbell's wife, Marie, who held $350,000 in Mid-Continental stock and debentures. The principal owner of Mid-Continental was John J. Mack, a Chicago real estate man. Campbell explained he had met Mack in 1942 when Mack bid on a property that was being auctioned in his court in a bankruptcy proceeding. Mack became a family friend of the Campbells, who began investing in his ventures using money "from savings," in the judge's words. In 1950, he said, Mrs. Campbell inherited $50,000 from her parents, and used it to buy a five-percent interest in three Mack ventures. Through sales and reinvestments he ran her money up to $350,000 by 1969. Mid-Continental owned downtown office buildings as well as apartment houses at 1150 and 1550 Lake Shore Drive, on Chicago's swank Gold Coast. (Mack all the while was a jury commissioner for United States District Court, responsible for recommending persons for jury duty.) Although Campbell did not say so directly, the implication was that whatever outside wealth his family owned resulted from his wife's investments.

In 1972 Frank M. Whiston, longtime member and president of the Chicago School Board, died. When his will was filed for probate, the Campbell family was revealed as Whiston's partner in real estate holdings valued at $11.2 million. (Campbell and Whiston's son, Jerome, were listed as executors of the estate; Campbell, however, chose not to participate in the probate.) The holdings were in the name of Mrs. Campbell and The Argyll Trust, created by the judge for the benefit of his eight children. The Campbell interests held a 45-percent share in the $4.3 million Carbide and Carbon Building, 230 N. Michigan Street; 36 percent of the $5.3 million Pittsfield Building, 55 East Washington Street; and 37 percent of the $1.6 million Lytton Building, 14 East Jackson Street. The Campbells and Whiston were also partners in The Ohio Trust, which held 50 acres of land in Lordstown, Ohio, near the site of a huge General Motors assembly plant that was completed in the late 1960s. (The will assigned no value to this property.)

No law or ethical canon prohibits a federal judge —or his wife—from making money from real estate ventures (provided, of course, none of the transactions come before his court). Nonetheless, Campbell's accumulation of riches does cause *sotto voce* comment among Chicago lawyers (and distress to at least one of his fellow judges). These persons wonder, "How can a judge devote total attention to his judicial business when he is also caught up in real estate deals involving millions of dollars? And may not such holdings affect his judgement when he hears cases involving similar investors?" One lawyer told me bluntly, "No matter how you fuzz it, Campbell made a fortune while on the bench. If he did it on his own, was he spending his full time being a judge, as he is paid to be? If others did it for him, did he surrender the independence essential to a judge?"

Early in my stay in Chicago a lawyer suggested that I make inquiries on a 1969 suit charging that The Machine required Chicago and Cook County employees to register as Democrats—and vote—in order to retain their jobs. "This is one of the few instances where you have the political bias of a judge documented in court records," the lawyer told me. "But it's a complex situation, so you had best start with the court records. Then you can ask the right questions, once you have the background."

That afternoon I went to the court clerk's office on the twentieth floor of the federal building and obtained the file in case *69-C-2145, Michael L. Shakman and Paul M. Lurie v. the Democratic Organization of Cook County et al.* Shakman and Lurie, both anti-Machine Democrats, had brought the suit, asking that the alleged patronage system be outlawed. I had been told to look for an affidavit in which their attorney, Robert H. Plotkin, asked that Judge Abraham Marovitz disqualify himself ("recuse," in legal language) from further hearings in the case on the grounds of bias. The affidavit, my informant said, contains specific charges of Marovitz's favoritism. The court clerk produced five huge file folders of papers, more than three feet in girth, and for the next two hours I pored through them, looking for Plotkin's affidavit.

It wasn't there.

The next day I went to Plotkin's office and told him what I was doing. Plotkin, a husky, fiercely moustachioed man in his forties, was visibly alarmed that I had sought him out. I told him I knew the bare outlines of his clash with Marovitz, and that I was curious that his affidavit was not in the court file. "I've been in a lot of courts in my life," I said, "and I have an old-fashioned idea that once a paper is filed with the clerk, it becomes a part of the official record."

Plotkin sat and looked at me for a few moments. He knew what I was going to ask of him, and he didn't like it. "Well," he said, finally, "don't think that *I'm* going to give you a copy. All I will tell you is this: Yes, I did file a motion to recuse, and a supporting affidavit. You know that; Judge Marovitz talked about it in open court, in denying it, and he also filed his own memorandum opinion. But the motion itself? Now that's a peculiar story. I took it into the clerk's office one Friday afternoon, and gave it to the clerk, who stamped it and docketed it. But I know it's not in the file. Sometime after I filed it some reporter asked what had ever happened to this idea I had of getting Marovitz out of the case. 'Go and read the motion and affidavit,' I said. I wasn't about to comment out-of-court on this case. 'They're not in the file,' the reporter told me.

"I couldn't believe him. I checked. They weren't —no notation, in fact, that they had even been received. The reporter went to Marovitz, and he says the judge told him, 'Oh, you don't want to bother with all that stuff; wait until I file my opinion, that's the real story.' The reporter didn't press him."

Plotkin was nervous that I was even in his office. "If you came up with a copy of that thing," he said, "Marovitz will know exactly where you got it. Huh-uh, I'm not sticking *my* neck out. If you want to scout around, do so, but I'm afraid I'll have to say, 'Sorry, but no dice.'"

Well, I did scout around, and within an hour I sat in the chambers of another United States District Court judge—a man who has contempt for Marovitz's conduct on the bench—and read Plotkin's suppressed affidavit. In fifteen terse, non-emotional pages he alleged instances of Marovitz's continuing misconduct during negotiations for a consent decree settling the patronage suit. ". . . Judge Marovitz's pressures on us [Plotkin and the other insurgent lawyers] seemed clearly to stem from his concern for the welfare of Mayor Daley (whom he repeatedly characterized as one of his dearest and oldest friends) and/or the Cook County Democratic Organization. It would have been difficult for anyone . . . not to be convinced that the judge was acting as the advocate of the interests of Mayor Daley and/or the Cook County Democratic Organization." Plotkin listed some specific charges:

- Marovitz repeatedly had "unauthorized" private conversations with defendant politicians, including Daley, and their lawyers (one of whom was the mayor's son, Michael). On three occasions, Plotkin said, attorneys made settlement proposals in Marovitz's absence: "Yet at our next appearance before the judge he [Marovitz] would make the same proposal or demand, sometimes in virtually the identical words in which it had been made to us in the private meetings. . . . The only way he could have learned of them would have been in some secret, unauthorized communication with someone on, or connected with, the other side. In addition, Judge Marovitz himself on a number of occasions either expressly acknowledged or made it clear in some other way that he had had private conversations about this case which we had known nothing about." Sometimes these mentions "simply slipped out during our meetings with him." For example, he said, Marovitz admitted two private meetings with Sheriff Richard J. Elrod, a defendant, in which Elrod denied patronage hirings and firings.
- Plotkin's affidavit claimed that Marovitz at one point asked Plotkin's permission to meet privately with Mayor Daley about the settlement negotiations. "He [Marovitz] stated in effect that he believed that his . . . long and close friendship with the mayor coupled with the judge's long background in politics and his knowledge of the legal situation would put him in a good position to move the settlement negotiations closer to a conclusion." Plotkin told the judge to go ahead. "I did so because, first of all, it is difficult for a lawyer to say no to such a request in these circumstances, particularly where a judge has so much discretion over

the case. But the main reason was that it was already clear to us that the judge had already had unauthorized conversations about the case with Mayor Daley. On at least two occasions the judge had acknowledged that such conversations had taken place."

- Plotkin charged that in the private talks Daley used political, rather than legal, arguments against terms of a proposed settlement. Daley talked about "internal trouble and dissension" in The Machine. "The judge stated on a number of occasions that Mayor Daley was having a lot of trouble among the Organization's leaders and officials," who grumbled that the settlement was a "great mistake" and the "Mayor's fault."

- According to Plotkin, Marovitz "strongly pressured" Plotkin not to "cause any commotion" with the suit before the April 1971 Chicago mayoralty election. He specifically was "adamant" that Plotkin not press for a preliminary injunction against patronage abuses—a silly request, in Plotkin's opinion, "since one of the main reasons patronage employment practices should be eliminated was their effect on elections." But Marovitz felt the Mayor deserved more understanding treatment. "He [Marovitz] said more than once that Daley was trying to modernize the local Democratic Party and was trying to do many of the things we wanted, but that he didn't control everyone and everything in the party; that there were other party leaders who opposed these reforms, and that *it wasn't right or fair that the mayor should be subjected to such publicity during his election campaign.*" [emphasis added]

- When Machine lawyers promised to sign an acceptable settlement after the April 1971 elections, Plotkin agreed not to press for the preliminary injunction. Whereupon, Plotkin charged, he was double-crossed—once again with the connivance of Marovitz. Under the consent decree public employees would be notified in writing that they no longer had to pay homage to The Machine to keep their jobs. But Machine lawyers wanted this notice withheld until after the 1972 primaries. Plotkin's affidavit stated, "Judge Marovitz once again supported their position, even though it was contrary to the terms of the settlement. . . . It seemed to be understood by everyone involved that the giving of those notices . . . would have been harmful to the election efforts of the Cook County Democratic Organization, which was involved in a number of bitterly contested primary fights, primarily in the races for state's attorney and governor."

• And, finally, according to Plotkin, Marovitz's opinion deleted a key paragraph which prohibited penalizing government employees for political purposes. All of the persons involved in the negotiations, he said, including Marovitz and The Machine's lawyers, agreed such a provision would be included. Plotkin yielded on many minor points because of Marovitz's promise the provision would be included. Without the provision, Plotkin wrote, the settlement would be "hollow and meaningless."

Denial of the patronage provision, to Plotkin, was the final insult. On September 1, 1972, he filed a motion asking that Marovitz remove himself from the case because of prejudice and political bias. The motion cited Marovitz's long association with the Democratic organization, and his conduct in the patronage case.

Plotkin's action outraged Marovitz. By the account of one (unfriendly) judge, Marovitz grumbled that "Plotkin is through in this courthouse. A lawyer doesn't go around criticizing a judge's *honest* attempts to settle a law suit and get away with it." Remarked the unfriendly judge: "Little Abe might be speaking for Little Abe and one other Daley crony, but many of us were downright delighted at what Plotkin did. *Double* downright delighted, in fact."

Marovitz rejected Plotkin's petition out of hand, in language that was at once defensive and indignant. He called Plotkin's claim "prejudice by association," and said, "it charged me with being a good friend of Mayor Daley, which I certainly do not deny and wouldn't want to deny. I think I am a good friend of the Governor's, too, and of the Senators." But he denied bias in favor of any of these friends. "Like a good umpire, I call them as I see them, regardless of who is out front. . . . I am jealous of my reputation in the community. I come into my chambers and into my courtroom with my self-respect, and I leave with it every day." Marovitz considered it a "compliment" that Plotkin called him "the product of the organization."

He continued: "I don't know how many judges here on this good bench among my brothers haven't come up the same way, and I think that you might have to excuse the entire court maybe save one who hasn't come up through the political ladder. I have said sometimes I climbed Jacob's ladder, that is, Jacob Arvey. So I make no apologies for that."

Marovitz's career deserves some detailed attention because many of his characteristics are typical of how judges get on the federal bench in Chicago. The Jacob Arvey to whom he referred was the pre-Daley Democratic boss of Chicago, and his ladder enabled Marovitz to climb to the bench from one of the city's toughest neighborhoods—the old 20th Ward, long hoodlum-controlled, and a haunt of bootleggers and beer runners during Prohibition days, where, as Marovitz once told a friendly interviewer, "the only significant politics consisted in delivering the vote . . . by bribery, sale, fists or clubs." Many kids from Marovitz's old neighborhood are now in the top echelon of The Outfit, but prideful immigrant parents pushed Little Abe (his pet name for himself) into law school at age 16. Marovitz's first job, a political one, was as an assistant state's attorney, and an older man in the office taught him some of the realities of Chicago life. "Above all he showed me how to keep myself clean, so that I could look anybody in the eye and tell 'em to go to hell if I had to. He showed me that you could do a favor for a man and still not step outside the law or take anything, money or presents or anything from him." Marovitz went into private practice on Labor Day 1932 and immediately picked up five unions as clients—including the Teamsters—and other interesting people as well. There was Gus Winkler, bank robber, gambler, and alleged lead machine-gunner in the St. Valentine's Day Massacre of 1929. There was Ted Newberry, gunman and North Side boss under the Al Capone regime. There was Murray (The Camel) Humphreys, labor racketeer, extortionist and Capone killer. Marovitz, a lifelong bachelor, enjoyed sharing the night life with Mob figures, and he became something of a gangster groupie. "Some of these men involved in big-time crime have a lot of native charm," Marovitz said. "They are generous in their way, especially towards those whose help they think they need." Winkler and Newberry, Marovitz said, "both were really tough but when you did not know their background and merely met them casually you could easily assume they were important business executives."

The associations caused Marovitz an acutely nervous moment in the 1930s. Investigators for the bankers association asked him for help in recovering bonds taken in a Wisconsin bank robbery. They didn't think Winkler was involved, but asked whether he would use his connections without "getting anyone involved." Marovitz said, "I didn't like it, but the investigators [Pat Sherwood and Roy Lapitz] were friends so I talked to Winkler. He didn't like it, but I guess he was fond of me and promised, 'If you want, I'll see what I can do.' A little while later he turned up quite a substantial amount of the bonds and Lapitz took me into Melvin Purvis' office. At that time Purvis was Chicago head of the FBI.

"I was sure Lapitz would thank me for assisting. Instead, when I was introduced, Purvis made some remark like, 'The fellows across the street [indicating the United States attorney's office] may think you are a pretty nice boy, but I know different.'"

Marovitz, surprised, told Purvis he didn't know what he meant. "Well, I'll show you," Purvis replied. He produced a stenographic record of a telephone talk between Winkler and Marovitz. "Well, what bank did you hold up today?" Marovitz opened the conversation. Stunned, he told Purvis the remark was "facetious," and promised, "I'm not proud of this, and it will never happen again." (Marovitz claimed he and Purvis later became friends, and remained so until Purvis killed himself in 1960.)

Meanwhile, Marovitz was scurrying up Jacob's ladder to the state senate, where he had his first close contact with Dick Daley, also a rising young Democratic politician, and Thomas Keane, later head of the city council for Daley. Marovitz adored Arvey, and spoke of him fondly as "more a social worker than a politician" (even as Arvey won 300-1 and 300-2 margins in his precincts). Marovitz had an undistinguished record in the senate. One of his more publicized schemes was for a national lottery to finance pre-Pearl Harbor defense spending. But Marovitz did show flashes of independence. He also got publicity for taking time off from his senate duties to help Willie Bioff, the pimp and labor extortionist, fight extradition from California to serve an old Illinois jail term for pandering. In 1939 he fought a bill (sponsored by the American Medical Association) barring refugee Jewish doctors from working in state hosiptals. Mayor Edward J. Kelly told Marovitz to back away, that The Machine didn't think the issue important enough to warrant a fight with the doctors. "Ed Kelly, you can kiss my ass," Marovitz says he told the Mayor. Kelly, infuriated, told Marovitz he was finished in politics. Marovitz said he would run again "if I only get my own vote and my mother's." Kelly couldn't find a candidate to take on Marovitz, and Little Abe won reelection. In 1943, at age 38, he enlisted in the marine corps (without resigning his senate seat) and went away to war. And, by Marovitz's account, he got an unexpected boost up Jacob's Ladder at an officers club in Manila in early 1945.

Arvey, a colonel, invited Technical Sergeant Marovitz to the club for steaks, and left him unattended a few minutes. Another officer came over and told Abe he had to leave. Marovitz thought Arvey was playing a joke on him. "In my own outfit there was no great fuss about enlisted men in the officers club." Finally, Arvey himself arrived and said, "Abe, this is very embarrassing, but you'll have to go." Another colonel snapped, "We don't care who you are, marine, you'll get out." Arvey didn't follow. Marovitz went back to his unit "crushed."

Marovitz told the story eighteen months later in introducing Arvey at a political rally in Chicago—to Arvey's profound mortification. "Please never tell that story again. I'll do anything you ask, but forget that one," Arvey said.

"Make me a judge," Abe replied.

Arvey did. In 1950 Marovitz won election to the state bench. His union clients helped, as did a campaign promise: "Labor need not fear injunctions with me on the bench." Arvey proudly said of Little Abe at the swearing-in ceremony, "I'll be able to point to Abe as an example that a man can be a good organization man and be honest. In his twelve years in the legislature I never influenced his vote on any bill." Abe's ambitions soared. In March 1952 Arvey almost had him on the federal bench. President Truman, however, caressed Representative Adolph Sabath, the Chicago Democrat who was chairman of the House Ways and Means Committee, by nominating his nephew, Municipal Court Judge Joseph J. Drucker. Arvey had Senator Paul Douglas reject Drucker as "personally obnoxious," but by the time the feud was over poor Abe had been shoved into the wings. The next year gubernatorial visions danced through Marovitz's head. He hired a public relations firm, and tried to persuade Arvey and his old friend, Dick Daley, to support him. Again, no luck.

Marovitz had his troubles on the state bench. His chief adversary was a onetime senate friend, Benjamin Adamowski, the state's attorney, who broke with The Machine rather than whitewash governmental corruption.

• Adamowski claimed Marovitz blocked a probe of a ticket-fixing scandal for fear of embarrassing The Machine. "Instead of being an impartial judge,

Marovitz is fearful the state will uncover more than it already has found. He seems more concerned with thwarting justice than being an unbiased and impartial judge."

- He demanded that Marovitz and another Chicago federal judge resign because of improper docketing of criminal cases. He cited the "remarkable success" of five criminal lawyers—called the "B Boys" because each last name began with that letter—in putting cases before Marovitz and receiving light sentences.

- He petitioned Marovitz to transfer 315 indictments against auto dealers and tax assessment officials from his court. The judge's brothers, Harold and Sydney, "are either partners or associated with firms" representing the defendants, Adamowski said. Marovitz retorted that the "unwarranted implication and innuendoes contained in the state's attorney's motion sets a new low in professional irresponsibility. When I go to bed tonight, I'll pray to the good Lord to forgive you." (But Marovitz transferred the cases.)

Marovitz denied the charges and rode out these criticisms ("Poor Ben is a sick man. I feel sorry for him."), and The Machine buried Adamowski in the 1959 election. Four years later John F. Kennedy made Abraham Lincoln Marovitz a federal judge.

In 1967 Marovitz told Wayne Thomis of the Chicago Tribune *what he thought to be a howler of a story about his appointment. When the FBI began the routine background check, friends called from his old 20th Ward neighborhood: "Judge, I got something to tell you. The Gee's been around asking questions. I didn't tell them nuthin'."*

"It's funny to watch Abe go down the hall of the courthouse," a Chicago lawyer was saying. "Now, some judges deliberately avoid people, because they don't like guys running up and shaking their hand and then telling all the hangers-on what a good buddy they are with the judge. Phil Tone, for instance [a Nixon appointee to the federal bench], ducks his head and won't give more than the time of day to anyone. But Abe—hell, he's like a 25-year-old candidate for the legislature. He handshakes his way through the courthouse, he goes out to eat and he's tablehopping all over the place, glad-handing." Another lawyer is disturbed that Marovitz continues a couple of habits begun when he was a state court judge: sitting in Daley's private quarters on election night, listening to the returns, and then presiding over the quadrennial swearing-in ceremony for the Mayor. "Marovitz is advertising his friendship with Daley as a matter of personal ego," one lawyer commented to me. "Whether you like Daley is not the point. As a mayor and a political leader, Daley is bound to be wrapped up in things that get into court. But this cluck Marovitz goes around with the mayor like a sycophant."

The public image that Marovitz projects is that of a warm-hearted humanitarian, a man whose humble origins give him keen empathy for the poor and the downtrodden, and whose career should be an example for members of minority groups. But Marovitz's pomposity has swollen in proportion to his judicial rank. His name, for instance. As a kid in the 20th Ward, Marovitz was content to be known as "Abe"; as a club fighter, "Little Abe"; as a criminal lawyer, state senator and state judge, "Abraham L." Now, however, he likes to be called Abraham Lincoln Marovitz. His chambers are a veritable Lincoln museum: seven formal portraits of Lincoln, scores of photographs and prints, a bust, a framed copy of the civil war conscription order signed by Lincoln in 1863, volume upon volume of books on Lincoln. On Lincoln's birthday each year Marovitz calls in friends after court and reads aloud from Lincoln's works. A favorite is a quotation on the legal profession: "If, in your judgement you cannot be an honest lawyer, resolve to be honest without being a lawyer." When out-of-town lawyers first appear in Marovitz's court he invites them into chambers for a tour of the Lincolniana. It is impressive. One Washington lawyer told me: "Half-facetiously, I told the judge he should consider hiring a guide for his museum. You know, he took me seriously, and we spent some time talking about the legalities of using one of the bailiffs for the job."

Despite his energetic self-promotion Marovitz cannot cleanse himself entirely of the history of his old underworld clients. Marovitz denies rumors that The Outfit occasionally tugs at his judicial robes when it wants a favor ("Don't believe everything you hear about me and the, uh, Mafia," Marovitz once told the *Chicago Daily News'* Mike Royko), and claims he shouldn't be tied forever to people he represented as a young, hungry criminal lawyer.

Nonetheless, Marovitz has made peculiar rulings in some criminal cases. Consider Robert J. McDonnell, a former assistant state's attorney who became counsel for such underworld people as Sam DeStafano, a loan shark and terrorist who was assassinated in 1973, and then an operating criminal in his own right. Police informants and defecting mob underlings repeatedly claimed McDonnell was a fixer in major cases, both as a prosecutor and a criminal lawyer. In 1966, McDonnell, then 40, was convicted of being part of a ring that sold stolen money orders across a state line. Marovitz gave him five years, but McDonnell moved for a reduction. A government psychiatric report said McDonnell didn't recognize he had done anything wrong and saw no reason to change his mind. "No matter what sentence you give me, it won't matter," McDonnell told Marovitz in open court. Marovitz reduced his sentence to two years. Marovitz has been a good-hearted jurist in other cases as well:

- In 1965 he fined four men $1 each for mail fraud for defrauding 941 citizens of $247,000 in a franchise scheme. Marovitz said the men had "good records" since the theft and were "doing well as law-abiding citizens." Not well enough, though, to think of the persons who lost savings in the fraud; not a cent of restitution had been made.
- In 1966 he gave an eight-month jail term to a police detective caught up in a ring that stole expensive cars and sold them across state lines.

("Incredible!" exclaimed Virgil Peterson, long-time director of the Chicago Crime Commission.)

- He was often lenient with tax cheaters. In a 1966 case a certified public accountant claimed he "forgot" to report a $17,000 fee. "I'd have to be awfully stupid to believe a story like that," Marovitz said. The sentence: a wrist-slapping 30 days in jail.

Enough. Marovitz is an upward-striving and vain man, so close to the Daley political machine that many lawyers think he is incapable of administering justice impartially.

Before beginning my work in Chicago I decided to ignore Julius Hoffman, the judge who presided over that legal maelstrom known as the Great Convention Conspiracy Trial. So many vituperative words have been written about Hoffman's bungling of the case— running the literary spectrum from the underground press to the august Seventh Circuit Court of Appeals, which threw out the convictions—that I felt little new could be said about him. The old judge made a public ass of himself, and his displays of temper and bias outraged the innate decency even of persons hostile to the defendants (Abbie Hoffman, Jerry Rubin, et al). What could be added, I thought, by rehashing the dreary details of Judge Hoffman's foolishness?

But one morning I found myself with an idle hour in the Chicago federal courthouse, and began roaming the corridors, seeing what I could find. Sure enough, there was Hoffman, sitting in a mini-court one-quarter the size of the standard courtrooms elsewhere in the building. He has been in the smaller court since his quasi-retirement into senior judge status in 1971, because of his lessened case load; and I learned later he wasn't happy about losing the trappings of office. But Hoffman wanted visitors to damned well know who they were seeing in action, and that they shouldn't believe all those nasty things they had read about him in the press. Julius Hoffman, so far as I could determine in two years' work, is the only federal judge in the Republic with a praiseful billboard in his court.

It is a poster-sized blowup of an excerpt from the *Congressional Record* of May 7, 1970, a speech by then-Senator Ralph Tyler Smith (R., Ill.), at a dinner honoring Hoffman as the VFW's Man of the Year in Illinois. The speech covers several thousand effusive words; anyone interested in reading the complete text should visit Judge Hoffman's courtroom. One paragraph gives the tenor:

> Judge Julius Hoffman symbolizes to me—to all of us who honor him here tonight—everything that is great and good in our system, and at the same time, that expand and improve it for all mankind. He symbolizes the fact that law and order, in every definition of the phrase, is our first and best line of defense against the destroyers in our midst . . . and I am sure you join with me as we all say sincerely, "God bless you, Julius Hoffman. Well done thou good and faithful servant. You have done much for us, your grateful fellow Americans."

I sat and marvelled at Hoffman's self-advertisement a few moments, then turned my attention to the bench. Hoffman is a wizened gnome of a man, then in his eighty-second year. He seemed pathetically frail sitting there in his black robes, behind the massive bench, scarcely visible to the lawyers standing before him. The lawyers were speaking with on-eggs nervousness, as if they had thrust their hand into this particular buzz saw before, and wanted to keep the hell away from its tearing, biting edges. The years have not diminished Julius Hoffman's meanness, and his rasping whine permeated the room like evil Muzak.

One of the attorneys was offering a routine motion to postpone the taking of depositions in a civil case. "Any objections from you, counsel?" Hoffman asked the young opposing lawyer.

"I object only to the provision that . . . ," the kid began.

Hoffman snapped him to a stop. "You can't qualify an objection like that—either you have objections or you don't have objections. Now what are you *tryyyy-ing* to say, counsellor?"

Confused, off balance, his face flushing, the lawyer had to restate his objection three times before Hoffman admitted to satisfaction.

Next, a habeas corpus hearing in a criminal case, with the defense attorney trying to submit a transcript of his client's arraignment, and written arguments why he thought the man was entitled to release. Hoffman didn't like the way the assistant state's attorney, also a young man, tried to state his opposition to the petition. "You are here representing the *greaaaaaat* state of Illinois," he intoned, "and you must conduct yourself properly." The lawyer replied he thought he was in fact doing so. "Maybe I'm not making myself clear," he said.

Hoffman, flashing anger: "Then get somebody in here who can make it clear. If you want *meeeeee* to teach you the procedural history of habeas corpus, I'll do so." As he spoke he was withdrawing from the bench, leaning so far back in his swivel chair that for all practical purposes he vanished.

The state's attorney started to argue back at one point—"Your Honor, as a matter of fact, last night I *did* read the history of this act . . ."—then thought better of what he was saying, and quit.

"I'll take the matter under advisement," Hoffman said.

"When can we expect a ruling?" the defense lawyer asked, his eyes wandering to two women sitting in the court, kin of the defendant. Hoffman wouldn't say. He would "follow the law and consider the matter promptly." Quite obviously the defense lawyer wanted to have something to tell the women, whether they should wait at the courthouse or go home. "Well, maybe we could look forward to a decision by . . . ?" he left the question hanging. "Sometime," Hoffman said.

I had heard enough. By the time I gathered up my overcoat and briefcase, the state's attorney and the other young lawyer, the one who couldn't phrase an objection, were in the corridor, smoking and talking.

"That son of a bitch," said the young lawyer, jaw clenched. "He's just ruined my whole day. When I come out of his court I can appreciate how people get so mad they commit murders. He's mean. MEAN!" The lawyer stormed off to the elevator.

After this glimpse of the tyrant Hoffman in action I began asking Chicago lawyers about his reputation before the celebrated conspiracy trial. "Oh, hell," one man told me, "Julius has always been a bad ass. No one here was surprised that he blew the case. He's a sadistic old bastard, and if anything he is meaner now that he 'lost' the Chicago Seven trial."

Another lawyer: "Now that Hoffman is a senior judge, with his reduced work load, he sits on cases like an old brooding hen. His court operates like no other in the country. Let me give you an example: A young lawyer filed a civil suit, and a few weeks later Hoffman put it on the status calendar—that is, listed so the attorneys would come to court and tell what progress had been made towards resolving it. Normally several months pass before this is done. But Hoffman, because of his light work load and his obsession with 'efficiency,' telescoped the time span drastically. The attorney, through carelessness, missed the calendar call, and Hoffman dismissed the case.

"So the lawyer goes before Hoffman and asks for permission to reinstate the case. Now almost any other judge would have agreed, because this is one of those meaningless procedural slips that happens to every lawyer once in a while. So the lawyer goofed. Should his client be denied justice? Even the opposing counsel didn't object. Yet Hoffman went into his whine and dance, he would not even let the lawyer talk. Hoffman was going to 'keep his calendar current.' Hoffman quoted Justice Burger to the effect that 'we can't tolerate negligence.' (Well, I'll bet you could find another Burger quote that we also can't tolerate judicial stupidity, but that's another point.)

"This kid finally managed to squeeze in the information that the other side didn't object to reinstatement. So Hoffman rubbed it in. 'That's what *you* say,' he told the guy. 'Come in with opposing counsel next week and orally advise the court you want it reinstated. *Then* we'll see.'

"The horseshit of all this is that it amounts to petty harassment. The lawyer could have refiled the case *de novo* [as a new matter]; there was no statutory bar to doing so. But Hoffman had to kick him around. Some lawyers say this is OK, that it keeps young men on their toes. I disagree. It isn't human. Lawyers go into Hoffman's court, even on a routine calendar call or motion list, as if they are going to wrestle a bear with both hands tied behind their backs."

Another example of Hoffmanism: A criminal defendant came to court with a public defender to enter a guilty plea. Hoffman read a background report on the defendant—family and job status, prior record, and evaluation by the probation officer—as a sentencing guide. His eyes fell on one item, "$12,000 a year this man makes," he stormed, according to a lawyer who was present at the time. "And he comes into this court with a public defender. Outrageous!" The public defender tried to interrupt, "Look on further down the sheet, judge, and you'll see that he has considerable debts, and that he has only $150 per month after meeting his obligations."

But Hoffman wouldn't be deterred. "Why is the government squandering the taxpayers' money by paying the expenses of a criminal who earns $12,000 a year?" He turned to the assistant United States attorney. "I demand that you make an investigation of this matter—right now!" The flustered prosecutor nodded. Several days later he submitted a report—based solely on the background report Hoffman had had before him. An outside lawyer commented: "If Hoffman would have stopped 45 seconds to listen to what people were trying to tell him, he could have avoided this little tantrum. I don't think he *wants* to avoid them; I think they are pathological. A sick man. He shouldn't be on the bench, even as a senior judge."

Hoffman, born in 1895, practiced law in Chicago from 1915 until he became an Illinois Superior Court judge in 1947. His most lucrative private client had been a company, owned by his wife's family, that manufactured billiard tables. President Eisenhower made him a United States District Court judge in 1953. Any judge, if he is so minded, draws swarms of sycophants. Lawyers learned that one ego-caress that Hoffman particularly enjoyed was being called "Julius the Just." (Another Eisenhower appointee to the federal bench, Judge Julius Miner, used to chuckle quietly, "Please call me 'Just Julius.'") Before the conspiracy trial Hoffman was noted for two characteristics: his foul temper, and his antipathy to the United States government in tax cases.

How does such a misanthrope manage to cling to the bench? Surely, I thought, the other judges would contrive a scenario to either embarrass or entice Hoffman into full retirement—or, at least, to clean up his manners. Much of the answer, I concluded, lies in the fact that many Chicago lawyers and judges are frightened by Hoffman. A story about that *Congressional Record* poster is illustrative. The speaker is a lawyer who has been practicing in Chicago for more than forty years: "The courtroom doesn't belong to Julius Hoffman—it belongs to the people of the United States. By what authority does he turn the wall of a court into a billboard for personal aggrandizement? I complained to [Chief Judge Edward] Robson about the blowup, and he was noncommittal. 'Julius is already hurt because he was given the smaller courtroom, and we pretty well leave him alone,' Robson told me 'Anyway, how could I make him take it down?' 'Real simple,' I said. 'Tell the GSA people [the General Services Administration, the federal government's housekeeping agency] to send down a man with a screwdriver, and take it the hell off the wall.' Robson said he'd think about it. He finally told me, 'It's not worth a public row with Julius. Let's just forget it.'"

The poster remains on display.

Enough. Anyone who wishes to know more of Hoffman's conduct—misconduct, more accurately—of the Chicago Seven case is directed to *The Great*

Conspiracy Trial, by Jason Epstein.* Hoffman is a prime example of a judicial cancer that went long unattended until one unique case propelled him into public consciousness.

In the winter of 1972 a lissome 49-year-old divorcee rented a function room at the Ambassador East Hotel in Chicago, bought a $50 wedding cake and a supply of champagne, and invited 50 people to her wedding with Judge James B. Parsons, whose wife had died five years earlier. When congratulations began to reach the judge, he professed to be dumbstruck. He said he "scarcely knew" the woman; that she had called him "out of the blue" and then "repeatedly" thereafter. Whatever she professed their relationship to be, the judge said he had no intention of taking her to the altar.

The divorcee sadly disposed of her cake and champagne, packed away her wedding dress, and lamented to an inquiring reporter: "Jim told me he loved me and wanted to marry me, but something has come between us." A strange situation, indeed.

Increasingly, strange situations tend to happen to Judge Parsons. A handsome, barrel-chested man ("He *looks* like a judge," said one non-admiring lawyer), Parsons nonetheless has a knack for getting caught up in bizarre episodes, both on and off the bench. "The tragedy is," said a man who has known Parsons for three decades, "that Jim isn't going to be remembered for all of his rather remarkable career, but only those last few zany years."

Parsons' career indeed is remarkable. Born in 1911 in Kansas City, son of a minister of the Disciples of Christ Church, Parsons spent his boyhood in Decatur in central Illinois, where he was the only black in his high school class, graduating third of 360. He graduated from college in North Carolina; taught briefly; was the navy's only black bandmaster in World War II; did postwar graduate work at the University of Chicago; and finally became a lawyer at age 38.

* Random House, New York, 1970.

Politically active, he worked as a city lawyer, then moved to the United States attorney's office under Otto Kerner,* a Truman appointee, and did such good work the Republicans kept him on. Parsons was particularly hot on draft cases. During 1953–54, he won 63 convictions in a row, and the Justice Department gave him a special commendation. The Justice Department also picked him as lead prosecutor of Clyde Lightfoot, the Negro leader of the United States Communist Party, not-so-subtly undermining Lightfoot's contention that capitalism deliberately kept blacks from positions of responsibility. In 1960 Mayor Daley, his friend, decided it was time Jim Parsons became a judge, and pushed him through a nominating convention for superior court. The ticket was a slatemaker's delight: Irish, Polish, Jewish, Italian and Negro nominees for the five spots. Attention to ethnic background, said presiding officer Daley, "is the essence upon which our government is built." He called it a guard against the rise of "any aristocracy" in Chicago. The Democratic slate won the election. ("After the Democratic nominees defeat their Republican opponents in the November 8 election, they will be nonpartisan," Daley added.) The "race" was such a non-contest that Parsons spent his campaign time working for Kennedy in black neighborhoods.

In 1961, within a few months after he took office, there was a subtle sign that Jim Parsons had gotten in over his head. He heard the cases of eight Chicago policemen convicted of corruption, and he broke into tears as he sentenced them to jail. Now sentencing is one of the more difficult tasks a judge performs, by their own testimony—but seldom does a jurist lose control of his emotions as Parsons did. However, the episode passed notice, and a few months later the Daley Machine decided it was time Chicago needed a black federal judge, and President Kennedy obliged by tapping Parsons.

The nomination posed a crisis for Parsons. He had

---

* Later governor and a federal appeals judge, driven from the bench in disgrace in 1973; see below.

spent enough time in the Jim Crow South to appreciate the cruelty of discrimination, and he feared the Senate would not confirm him. "I expected the voice of the South to rise up in wrath," Parsons said. He went to Washington anticipating a quiet, private hearing. Instead, as the Kennedy Administration's first black judicial nominee, he got kleig-light, showcase treatment, and lengthy (but friendly) questioning by the Senate Judiciary Committee. Parsons was so nervous that up until the moment of final confirmation by the Senate he feared something would happen to deny him the judgeship.

Judge Parsons' dozen-odd years on the bench have shown instances of erratic behavior and ill-disguised political statements on civil rights issues that benefited his political patron, Mayor Daley. In 1962–63, for instance, the Black Muslim movement was gaining considerable ground among Chicago blacks, thereby theatening to undercut an essential vote block of The Machine. On the eve of a national Muslim convention in Chicago, Parsons said any black who joined was "enslaved" by the movement's leaders. He called the movement inherently evil. "I have contempt for it. It is a dishonest way of making money for its leaders. . . . politically more dangerous to the goals of the Negro people than the Communist Party." Malcolm X, opening the convention the next day, was scornful of Parsons: "They don't call them Uncle Toms any more. Now he [the 'white slavemaster'] calls them 'judge.' All the boss has got to do is say, 'Sic 'em, Judge.' "

To the dismay of civil rights activists, Parsons took a public stand against the civil disobedience tactics of Dr. Martin Luther King, Jr. (although, as a person sympathetic to Parsons' position notes, "As a judge who has sworn to uphold the law, how could Parsons say otherwise? His entire career is based upon adherence to, not defiance of, the law"). When King seized West Side slum properties with the stated intention of holding them until landlords made repairs, Parsons said, "I am not in agreement with civil disobedience or the flouting of good laws. That is a revolutionary tactic." This was in 1966. A year later Parsons spoke out against activist clergymen (in a speech marking a statewide Parsons Day declared by then-Governor Otto Kerner). "Let them desert the streets and concentrate their work in their parishes," Parsons said. (But when a sniper's bullet killed King in 1968, Parsons joined other Chicago politicians in paying him pious homage at a memorial service.)

Parsons took a dim view of other activists as well. Prosecutors in the United States attorney's office breathed a little easier when draft cases went to Parsons' court (for Parsons, after all, had sat at the prosecution table for more than a hundred of these trials). Further, he did not even attempt to hide his bias. Speaking at a law enforcement conference at Great Lakes Navy Training Center in October 1965, Parsons called for "relentless and effective prosecution" of antidraft demonstrators—an indiscreet declaration for a judge who well might be hearing such cases in court. "I have nothing but utter contempt for organizations which are using demonstrations as a smokescreen to weaken our national security and destroy our national goals," he said. And in 1966 Parsons announced that as a "policy" draft offenders would receive no less than four years in jail when convicted in his court, even when they pleaded guilty. But Parsons was inconsistent in applying his policy: in back-to-back cases in 1968 he sent a draft offender who belonged to Students for a Democratic Society to jail for five years, while permitting probation to the son of a Mafia figure who lied to his draft board to avoid induction. Parsons' antipathy to leftwing activists was expressed in other ways as well. In 1965 a youth testified that three Chicago policemen beat him into unconsciousness when they broke up demonstrations against hearings of the House UnAmerican Activities Committee. Parsons interrupted the trial, sent the jury from the court, and told the youth he felt "compelled" to warn him the maximum penalty for perjury was five years in prison and/or a $2,000 fine. In other words, Parsons was telling the man he didn't believe him.

Among Chicago lawyers Parsons developed a reputation for impetuousness. In a 1963 case he wanted to jail all 244 members of a longshoremen's union who refused to obey his order to load two Canadian grain freighters. The union was appealing the order, and Parsons denied it a jury trial. Lawyers managed to get a reversal from the circuit court before Parsons put the entire union behind bars. In another case, Parsons threatened to call out military forces if necessary to hold a court session inside the Illinois State Training School for Boys at Sheridan. Parsons wanted to investigate conditions there, and officials were not enthused about admitting him. If denied admission, Parsons said, "I would come back and get the United States marshal to call in military forces to effect that entrance." Calmer heads intervened, and managed to settle the issue without a third world war.

And the monologues. Parsons has a not-so-articulate penchant for launching into impromptu speeches about the cases before him, such as the railroad-strike case cited at the beginning of this chapter. An example was a case in which a bearded man pleaded guilty to possession of narcotics. His employer, a paint store owner, also bearded, stepped forward to ask leniency in sentencing. The sight of two beards gave Parsons his topic for the day:

> You have a beard, too? What is this? Is it a part of the mores of the new artist colony now? Is it a psychological reaction to certain oppressions which you feel? Does it give an intellectual tone which brings about better artistry? Is it an affectation? Does it demonstrate an attachment to an exceedingly liberal type of life that doesn't conform with the general American way of life?

Parsons was so carried away with his idea that he assembled volumes of research material and secluded himself in his chambers to study the psychology of beards. He would stop people on the streets and in courthouse corridors to ask why they wore beards. A harried legal assistant, instead of helping the judge study important pending cases, spent his working days—and some evenings—in hirsute research. Finished, at last, Parsons waited until another bearded defendant came to his court and called in newspaper reporters to hear him perform. The conclusions of his sophomorish findings—printed and distributed to the news media—can be summarized in two sentences. People wear beards as "a badge of associations, particularly in the fine arts." And beards are "a contemporary fad which invades a social stratum for a period of time."

In another instance, Parsons interrupted a criminal trial to muse: "Some people were tapped by God to have the special ability to distinguish between right and wrong, and to detect whether a person is a criminal or innocent. I happen to be one of those people—tapped by God especially for this role."

Thus the performance of Judge James B. Parsons—a man more pitied than condemned by Chicago lawyers, and his judicial colleagues. But as one man told me, "You can feel sorry for a man in his situation, but he's a judge, damn it, and he should not be tolerated."

When Chief Judge William A. Campbell chose to move into senior judge status in mid-1969 the active judge next to him in seniority was Edward A. Robson. Although only 18 days younger than Campbell, Robson moved up to the chief judgeship anyway. "It is not the easiest of jobs," Robson told a reporter for *Chicago Today,* "but there is no alternative. I have a responsibility to my fellow judges to assume the post." Somehow no one thought to ask why Robson felt this "responsibility," but other judges in the district knew exactly what he was talking about: had he *not* become chief judge, the position would have fallen to the next ranking active judge, James Parsons. As one person involved in court workings said, "It's bad enough having Jim as a judge but chief judge—hell, that's out of the question."

Parsons knew exactly what was happening, but said nothing publicly. There is reliable evidence that at least two fellow judges quietly advised him to retire, which he could do with full pay, and retain his chambers and prestige of office as senior judge. Parsons is said to have refused. According to one source, he angrily told a colleague, "I'm not chief judge because I'm a black man. I'll stay on this bench until I'm carried off of it." This struggle was carried out in total silence, known to a few court insiders but not to the general public. But the situation suddenly came to a crisis peak in January 1972, when a grand jury returned indictments against former Governor Kerner, by now a judge of the Seventh Circuit Court of Appeals. Judge Richard B. Austin, who was acting as chief judge while Robson was ill, referred the case to the court's five-judge executive committee, which in turn asked Chief Justice Warren Burger to appoint someone from outside Chicago to hear the case because Kerner was a hometown judge. Kerner's defense lawyers immediately claimed that Austin, in bucking the case to the executive committee, had preempted the duties of the chief judge. Since court rules specified that the chief judge must be the senior man under 70 years of age, and Austin was 70, the decision should have been made by Parsons. Austin refused, and the executive committee convened to hear the defense appeal. Parsons, angry, complained about being passed over, and sided with Kerner's lawyers. He told them: "You're facing five judges, four of whom are hostile to your position." "You have no basis for that statement," Robson snapped in reply. Parsons argued that all federal judges in the Northern District of Illinois should have been screened to ascertain whether they could have conducted the Kerner trial. He was outvoted, four to one, and he warned ominously that the decision invited overturn of any Kerner conviction. "This district is famous for having very famous and notable cases tried and reversed . . . because of judicial error," Parsons said. And to the consternation of his colleagues, Parsons declared himself to be acting chief judge: "I'm colored, and I don't want to be pushy," he said. "I should have done it a long time ago." He said he intended to carry out a host of physical and procedural innovations in the Chicago courts, including a $3 million closed circuit TV security system for courtrooms and chambers.

The judges quivered with embarrassment for several days, then Robson announced he was well enough to resume his duties as chief judge, and the imbroglio ended. But as one Chicago lawyer told me in early 1973, "We are praying for the health and long life of Judge Robson." In the meanwhile, Judge Parsons sometimes stumbles through his judicial duties, frequently not in his court after lunch, often querulous and unpredictable during the hours he is on the bench, deaf to entreaties from friends and colleagues that the time has come for him to take a nice, long rest.

Richard J. Daley has an astounding ability to predetermine a man's political loyalty; hence, the people he puts into high office, either electively or appointively, normally can be relied upon to do his wishes. For one of these persons to turn on the Mayor, and bite his hand, is such a rare occurrence that Daley doesn't quite know how to behave when it happens.

Richard B. Austin has origins as political as any judge who ever sat on a bench. He was a Democratic assistant state's attorney for fifteen years, until 1948; ran for governor in 1956, and lost; was put on a state criminal bench, then the federal court, in 1961—by Daley. He was dutiful if non-distinguished. During the 1968 presidential campaign, loyal Democrat Austin displayed one goofy mannerism that disconcerted lawyers. When an attorney used that frequent courtroom phrase "I want to make it clear . . . ," Austin would throw up both arms in a V-sign, imitating Richard Nixon's campaign gesture, and whoop, "make it *perfectly* clear." Austin enjoyed intimidating lawyers in court, and was proud of his rough reputation. He kept a pair of mailed gloves on his office bookcase, beneath a poster reading, "Yea, though I walk through the valley of the shadow of death, I shall fear no evil, because I am the meanest son of a bitch in the valley." "Austin dislikes almost everybody," said one Chicago lawyer, "and he has a long memory."

The important point is that, regardless of his little

personal quirks, Richard Austin did nothing to disturb Mayor Daley's tranquility. Then, in 1968, the two men misunderstood one another. Austin felt he had been assured of appointment to the next vacancy on the Seventh Circuit Court of Appeals. Daley remembered no such promise, implied or direct. He wanted the position for Governor Kerner, and President Johnson, as was his custom in Chicago appointments, did as Daley said.

Austin said nothing publicly, but in private he did let some Chicago lawyers in on a secret: at the proper time, on ground of his own choosing, he intended to "teach Dick Daley a thing or two about loyalty."

Austin's opportunity came in the fall of 1971, during Daley's campaign for election to his third term. In the fall of 1971 Daley was determined to win reelection by as large a margin as possible so as to demonstrate public vindication of his handling of the 1968 Democratic convention riots. In such a situation, a politician prefers to put off unpopular decisions until after the voting is over. One project Daley definitely wanted to postpone was a Model Cities program that would have caused low-cost public housing (homes for blacks) to be constructed in white areas. Someone sued to force Daley to go ahead with the project, and Judge Austin said that the mayor had indeed made a mistake, and that the Model Cities program should proceed. Austin said Daley's overseers of the program evaded federal law by delaying the housing. "Daley calls himself a law-and-order mayor," Judge Austin said, "but he ignores federal law."

The next day, by unhappy coincidence, both Austin and Daley attended services marking the investment of a new Episcopal bishop of Chicago. Only two seats separated them. "I spoke to him," Austin said, "I won't comment on if he spoke to me. I would say, though, that he might have his hearing checked." Austin guffawed in telling friends of the Mayor's snub, but a flood of hate mail showed him the political hazards of criticizing the mayor. One of the more sedate letters ended, "God bless Jesus Christ and Mayor Daley!"

Daley has suffered no such indignities from any other

appointees. For one thing, he has taken minimal chances: know the man well, and he'll go along to get along. For sheer audacity, Daley's most political appointment was that of William J. Lynch, in 1966.

Lynch, a hefty red-faced bachelor, is known to the Chicago bar as a man who consults John Barleycorn about as often as he consults Blackstone, and during the Kerner trial he was identified as a chief intermediary in moving racetrack stock between briber and bribee. But these peccadilloes do not affect the relationship between Lynch and his life-long friend Mayor Daley. "Hell, in many ways Bill Lynch is closer to the Mayor than Mrs. Daley is," says one Chicago lawyer. Lynch and Daley grew up within a block of one another in the Archie Bunkerish Bridgeport section of Chicago; they entered politics together, via the old Hamburg Athletic Club (Lynch is a second-generation ward leader. He had his first patronage job before graduating from high school, with the parks district); and they practiced law, as partners, before Daley took over City Hall. There are, in fact, people in Chicago who claim that had not Lynch wasted so much energy reaching for a jug, he would be a better politician than Daley.

The Bridgeport chums were law partners when The Machine put Lynch into the state senate in 1950. He so impressed the capital reporters they voted him the outstanding legislator in his freshman term. He impressed The Machine even more. In 1953, for instance, he pushed through legislation ending the traditional election of state judges on a coalition ticket. The jurists thereafter came directly under political control —and collectively they are an even sorrier lot. In 1955, Lynch masterminded one of the slickest parliamentary tricks ever seen in Springfield. Republicans on the judiciary committee of the senate wanted access to 25 pounds of files that a special crime commission had compiled on links between organized crime, politicians and police in Chicago. The Democrats squirmed mightily; the files contained material that could embarrass several regiments of Chicago politicians. Republican Robert E. Merriam, opposing Daley in his first race for mayor, delightedly cried "coverup," but Lynch deftly extricated The Machine from the hook. When the counsel of the special crime commission appeared before the committee, carrying the files in a sealed box, Lynch moved adoption of a GOP-backed bill authorizing the attorney general to step into lax law enforcement situations. The Republicans, trapped, had to go along. As soon as the bill was approved, there was no business left before the committee, which promptly adjourned. The files remained unopened, and Democrats buried the bill when it got to the floor. The *Chicago Tribune* rated the Lynch maneuver "one of the cleverest parliamentary tactics in recent legislative history."

While a state senator, Lynch continued his law practice (including representation of criminal defendants in extradition proceedings) and as counsel for the Chicago Democratic organization for $10,000 a year. But in 1957, with Daley in City Hall, Lynch quite logically concluded he could make more money by spending all his time in Chicago. He resigned from the senate, and accepted a patronage appointment as counsel for the Chicago Transit Authority. Although the job paid $20,000 a year, it was part-time, and didn't keep Lynch away from his own practice. Daley had to quit the firm when he became Mayor, so Lynch took in another Bridgeport friend, George J. Schaller, and unsurprisingly made a good deal of money—so much so, in fact, that he declined several chances to go on the federal bench after the Democrats regained control of Washington.

During these years Lynch spent considerable time doing work for horseracing clients. At one time or another he either represented or owned stock in the Balmoral Jockey Club, Washington Park Trotting Association, Chicago Harness Racing, Inc., and Chicago Thoroughbred Enterprises. Lynch's connection with the tracks got into print occasionally at annual meetings of the Balmoral Jockey Club, of which he was vice president and director, but no one thought much of it. The connections were not even questioned in 1965, when Lynch finally told Daley he thought a federal judgeship would be an appropriately dignified finale for his career. Daley obliged; the American Bar Association rated Lynch qualified to well-qualified; and both Senators Douglas and Dirksen agreed the Mayor's law partner would be a dandy federal judge. At Lynch's swearing-in ceremony Daley appeared to offer a personal testament: "His family were always wonderful people in our neighborhood. He will never forget the people from whence he came and he will bring great honor and respect to them."

That was April 1966. Six years later, Judge Lynch was suddenly caught up in a judicial scandal of mammoth proportion: the trial of Judge Otto Kerner, of the Seventh Circuit Court of Appeals, for corrupt actions as Illinois governor.

Daily he sat at the corner of the defense table, as erect and unmoving as a gargoyle, steel-gray hair slicked horizontally along his temples, arms tightly crossed over his chest, legs tucked under his chair, careful to be on his feet, courteously smiling, when the jury entered the courtroom, then back to his seat, not doodling nor shuffling—looking, as Bob Greene of the *Chicago Sun-Times* wrote, "like he is posing for the engraved portrait on a $100 bill."

Otto Kerner. One of the most distinguished public figures in Illinois in her generation. Two-term governor. United States attorney. Major general in the Illinois National Guard. Chairman, by appointment of President Johnson, of the National Advisory Commission on Civil Disorders, the so-called "Kerner Commission." And, finally, to cap his distinguished career, appointment in May 1968 to the Seventh Circuit Court of Appeals.

Now Otto Kerner sat in the criminal dock, accused of accepting a bribe while governor from a race track operator, and then lying about it to tax agents and a grand jury. For seven weeks the prosecution laid out a series of transactions so intricate that even United States Attorney James R. Thompson admitted there were "portions of the case I still don't understand."

The jury heard the following story, and found Kerner and a longtime aide, Theodore Isaacs, former Illinois revenue director, guilty:

Marjorie Lindheimer Everett, a tall, outdoorsy blonde, was from a family long prominent in harness racing in the Chicago area. One constant trouble, however, was antipathy between her father, Benjamin Lindheimer, and Illinois Secretary of State Paul Powell, a mysterious downstate Democratic politician reputed to have as much clout as did whatever governor happened to be in office. Powell additionally had a stranglehold on harness racing tracks in Illinois, which he exercised through the Illinois Racing Board.* When her father died in 1960 Marje Everett apparently decided to accept political realities: she would do business with Paul Powell and his friends in Democratic politics. In 1960 she donated $45,000 to Kerner's first campaign for governor. She hired William Lynch and George Schaller, the remaining partners in Mayor Daley's old law firm, as her attorneys. In 1961, when she set about organizing Washington Park Trotting Association to consolidate her father's various race holdings, she was told she needed Powell's approval. The racing board chairman, William S. Miller, arranged an introduction and after several meetings she agreed to give stock to Powell and other politicians. Not openly, however, for this would have put the deals on the public record and this the politicians wished to avoid. As a shield she used William Lynch, who held the stock as "nominee" for a host of political figures: Powell; the Democratic minority leader and the Republican whip in the Illinois House of Representatives; George W. Dunne, president of the Cook County Board (who got the stock while in the legislature); and at least three other legislators.

At Miller's direction, Mrs. Everett also gave stock to Governor Kerner and Isaacs. By Miller's testimony, he met Kerner and Isaacs in the governor's office on

---

* Powell died in 1970. A few days later, more than $800,000 cash was found stuffed in shoeboxes in his Springfield hotel room. Eventually his estate totaled more than $3.5 million. He had no visible source of income other than the public payroll.

November 9, 1962, and told them Mrs. Everett admired Kerner and was "in sympathy with his financial situation." Balderdash, Marje Everett testified: "When he [Miller] told me he wanted to deliver this stock to Theodore Isaacs and Otto Kerner . . . I felt I had been extorted." She spoke of "the tremendous pressure, the point of no return . . . the impossibility I felt of turning down . . . Miller because he was chairman [of the racing board]." Mrs. Everett, aided by George Schaller, drafted a formal memo promising to make shares available to Kerner in Chicago Thoroughbred Enterprises, Inc., her keystone company, for $50,000.

Right away nice things started happening to Mrs. Everett's race operations. The legislature whisked through an omnibus racing bill with several features favorable to her: permitting a racing corporation to own more than one track (Marje held both Washington Park and Arlington Park), to race at a track it didn't own, and to be chartered outside Illinois (Marje's parent company was based in Delaware). Thomas C. Bradley, chairman of the Illinois Harness Racing Commission, said Kerner ordered him to take racing dates away from one track and give them to Sportsman's Park and Washington Park, controlled by Marje Everett. "I refused," Bradley testified. "Governor Kerner told me, 'Well, now, Tom, this is an order.' I remember those words. I was offended."

As Mrs. Everett's profits boomed, Isaacs and Kerner became restless about their promised windfall. According to Miller, Isaacs told him in 1966, "The Old Man and I are irritated about the delay in receiving Marje's stock." So the deal was consummated: Kerner and Isaacs paid $58,958 for 50 shares of stock, its 1962 value. Within weeks they resold it for $300,000. Still later, they purchased 28,000 shares of Chicago Harness Racing, Inc., another of Marje's companies, for $11,200 (far below the market value) and resold it immediately for $56,000. Their profits on these transactions were $285,842. The legislators made similar profits. Representative Clyde Choate, the Democratic house leader, for instance, paid $6,000 for shares that sold for $42,000 four years later. George Dunne, the county

board president, got a $20,000 profit. All these trans-
actions were shielded by the use of Lynch and Schaller
as dummies.

Lynch did other chores as well. In 1966, the same
year he was appointed to the federal bench, Lynch
tried to persuade Modie J. Spiegel, the Chicago mail
order king, to dissolve a voting trust that controlled
part of Marje Everett's operation. Spiegel refused.
Albert R. Bell, a vice-president of his firm present at
the meeting with Lynch, said Lynch "just lost his temper. He said we had better agree to the dissolution of
the voting trust or there would be unhappy consequences. The intimation was that somehow the Spiegel
business might be harmed in some way. The city had a
lot of power over a corporation in this community. He
didn't give the details as to what he had in mind. He
was very vehement." Spiegel still refused.

The stock schemes were revealed in roundabout
fashion. In their tax returns both Kerner and Isaacs
reported their earnings on the stock sales as a long-term
capital gain, rather than ordinary profit, thereby avoiding a higher tax. They claimed to have purchased the
stock in 1962. Mrs. Everett, however, in her returns,
reported the entire transaction as having occurred in
1966, and claimed a deduction for her "loss" (the
difference between the actual value and the price at
which she sold it to Kerner and Isaacs). Internal
Revenue Service agents found Kerner evasive when
they questioned him on the discrepancy. Mrs. Everett,
meanwhile, was in a vicious dispute with Miller, whom
she accused of trying to seize control of her racing
operations. (She finally gave up and moved to California.) Facing tax troubles of her own and disgusted
with Illinois politicians, she decided to tell all to a
federal grand jury. Kerner, Isaacs, Miller, and lesser
state officials were indicted. United States Attorney
James Thompson gave Miller immunity in return for
testifying, and he and Marje Everett (although they
cheerfully conceded they detested one another) succeeded in convincing the jury that Kerner had indeed
accepted a bribe.

Kerner, over three days of testimony, gave a drasti-

cally different version of the stock deal. He denied the
1962 meeting. He said he first learned of the availability
of the stock in 1966, from his state banking director,
and bought it as an investment, on Isaacs' recommendation. He denied any favoritism towards Marje Everett's
race operations. He denied lying either to the grand
jury or to tax agents. And in an emotional peroration
he said the suit "is very important to me. It's my life."
Fifteen character witnesses—including three federal
judges, black leader Roy Wilkins, and General William
C. Westmoreland, for whom Kerner had been a staff
officer in the Second World War—gave superlative-
laden testimony about the judge's reputation for honesty
and integrity.

In the end, however, the jury believed Marje Everett
and Miller, and convicted Kerner of conspiracy and accepting a bribe, and of income tax evasion, mail fraud
and perjury. Isaacs was found guilty of all these counts
except perjury. Kerner took the verdict without flinch-
ing, rode the elevator to his chambers and issued a
statement claiming innocence.

A few weeks later he was fined $20,000 and ordered
to prison for three years. On appeal Kerner asked the
Supreme Court to rule that it was unconstitutional to
indict and convict a sitting judge or other federal
official who is subject to impeachment. The court rejected the argument without comment or recorded
dissent, making Kerner the first federal judge ever convicted of a criminal offense while still holding office.
He went to federal prison in July 1974.

*When Kerner's criminal wrongdoing became apparent
during the grand jury investigation there were suggestions in Chicago that a prosecution would besmirch
the federal judiciary; hence, this argument went, the
former governor should be spared the shame of the
dock. Would not there also be political overtones—for
a Republican Justice Department to proceed against
a prominent Democrat so closely intertwined with the
Daley organization? The hesitation was fleeting, and
United States Attorney Thompson obliquely rebutted
both points in his closing arguments. If the accusations
against Kerner were true, Thompson said (as they*

*proved to be) "he was a corrupt governor and he is
a corrupt judge sitting in judgement of other people."
And he said the prosecution was based on evidence,
not imagination or politics. "They say I am ambitious,"
said Thompson, who by age 36 had already been mentioned as a candidate for mayor of Chicago, for governor, for the United States Senate. "Ambitious prosecutors don't indict federal judges."*

Happily for Chicago, the judiciary is gradually being
upgraded. One by one the old Daley–Dirksen judges
are moving aside, through death and retirement, and
are being replaced by men capable of running decent
courts. The credit belongs to Illinois senior Republican
Senator Charles H. Percy, who has insisted upon quality
appointments, and created the screening machinery to
find good men. The core of Percy's operation is an informal nominating committee composed of practicing
lawyers, bar officers and law professors from throughout Illinois. Some persons who have helped Percy are
Albert Jenner, longtime trial lawyer and ABA power
who in 1974 was named as minority counsel to the
Nixon impeachment probe by the House Judiciary
Committee; Philip Kurland, the conservative legal
academician at the University of Chicago; and Judson
Miner, a young lawyer who served as an early president
of the Chicago Council of Lawyers. Percy's office maintains what is called a "general list" of persons being
considered for appointment (self-nominators are not
included; a lawyer who "volunteers" for a judgeship
is given a polite brushoff letter). According to a Percy
staff assistant, "When a vacancy occurs, we'll pass on
our general list to the committee and ask, 'Please review
these people, and make recommendations. But do not
restrict yourself to these names; if you know someone
better, let us know.' " The contact is informal; sometimes the committee member will simply call Percy or
an assistant and go down the list verbally. The staff
eventually compiles what it calls a "judicial matrix,"
a listing of each candidate with comments of outside
sources, and the staff's "editorial comment" on his
ability.

The last step, and a most important one by Percy's

reckoning, is a personal interview with a candidate. According to one of his staff men, Percy "has a unique skill at an interview. He'll ask such questions as, 'What is the latest book you've read? What do you think the qualities of a judge should be?' He'll ask for comments on Supreme Court rulings. And he'll always ask, 'What effect would a judgeship have upon your family?' Percy considers this to be very important, because a judge has a cloistered life, and not everyone can stand the lack of human contacts." Percy also has the habit of making spontaneous phone calls to persons outside his own committee, for instance, to judges on the Seventh Circuit Court of Appeals who might have seen a lawyer at work. When considering an appointment for the district including East St. Louis, Illinois, a city with a history of racial strife, Percy checked with the NAACP to insure that his selection had the proper sensitivity to black–white problems.

Percy's Chicago appointees to date receive almost unanimously favorable comment from practicing lawyers, even Democrats who could be expected to frown upon "Republican" judges. Said one younger lawyer: "Percy's selections are Republican only in the sense that they register and vote that way; there hasn't been an active politician in the lot." Highest marks go to Judge Philip Tone, an antitrust specialist before his appointment; he is followed closely by Frank J. McGarr and Thomas R. McMillen. "The hallmark of the Percy judges," said another Chicago lawyer, "is that they are fair, and know how to run a courtroom. And, after all, that's what judging is all about."

Chicago is years away from complete recovery from the Daley–Dirksen judges. But given Percy's apparent dedication to good appointees, Chicago is beginning to shake off its reputation as a town where politics, not justice, rule the federal courts.

CHAPTER FOUR

When the System Works II:
The Watergate Judge

*I recommend your full cooperation with the grand jury
and the Senate select committee. You must understand
that I hold out no promises or hopes of any kind to you
in this matter, but I do say that should you decide to
speak freely, I would have to weigh that factor in ap-
praising what sentence will finally be imposed in each
case.*

*Other factors will, of course, be considered, but I
mention this one because it is one over which you have
control.*

*—Chief United States District Judge John J. Sirica,
in imposing provisional sentences of 35 years
in prison on four Watergate defendants on
March 23, 1973.*

An axiom of American politics is that nothing is so
dead as a charge of campaign knavery the morning after
election day. Americans expect their political also-rans
to be good losers. And why should they want otherwise? Listening to the whining and moaning of a loser,
and believing it, is an implicit way of admitting that
a majority of the voters was deceived by a scalawag.
Best that the loser be thrust into that peculiar vacuum
chamber of silence called public inattention, and that
the charge of "cheating" be stored away with him.

Such appeared to be the historical fate of the Watergate affair in late 1972—an episode never explained to
the satisfaction of millions of Americans, but one which

appeared unlikely to fulfill its seeming potential for full-blown scandal. So far as the Nixon Administration was concerned, the case began and ended with the seven persons most directly involved: James McCord, the security director of the Committee to Re-Elect the President (CREEP), who was caught inside the Democratic National Committee offices with four Cuban-Americans, and E. Howard Hunt and G. Gordon Liddy, arrested soon thereafter as straw bosses of the spy expedition. In October, the Justice Department's official spokesman, John J. Hushen, said the grand jury investigation was "over, and there is virtually no prospect of future indictments." Asked whether the Watergate Seven were "acting under the orders of others," Hushen replied, "We have absolutely no evidence to indicate that. Absolutely none." And three weeks later President Nixon referred to the *recently completed* federal investigation of the break-in . . . [which] made the 1948 investigation of Alger Hiss look like a Sunday school exercise [emphasis added]."

Nor would Congress bestir itself. In September and October the staff of the House Banking and Currency Committee, whose investigative jurisdiction (and ability) is limited, raised tantalizing questions about CREEP's shuffling of money between foreign banks and Nixon campaign committees. Yet the chairman, Representative Wright Patman (D., Tex.) could not get enough support from within the committee to hold formal hearings. Senate liberals were similarly stymied: as John Tunney, the California Democrat, said many months later, "It's frustrating to know something is there, waiting to be picked off, but not to be able to get permission to do the obvious things." So Senate Democrats spent the fall and winter muttering among themselves, with no committee showing stomach for a fight with the Nixon Administration.

Outside Washington, press interest in Watergate was minimal.* Of the 1,400 correspondents accredited in

---

* I was travelling in Texas in June 1972 at the time of the break-in. The pro-Nixon *Dallas News* used as its main Watergate story a few days later the fact that two or three of the Cuban-American burglars were registered Democrats in Miami.

Washington, only a baker's dozen pursued the story beyond the actual burglars. And even energetic reporters can go only so far: the press does not have subpena power to compel witnesses to talk, or to put their records on display. The *Washington Post*'s reportorial team of Bob Woodward and Carl Bernstein wrote in general terms of a lavishly financed political intelligence network run by CREEP, but even their sources could not take Watergate beyond the lowest echelons of CREEP, and by no means into the White House itself.

Frustration. Much of Washington smelled a cover-up, *knew* it existed, if for no other reason than common sense. Would such a seasoned intelligence officer as James McCord, who spent 19 years with the CIA, undertake such a mission without authorization from his superiors in CREEP? And would Hunt and Liddy on their own initiative litter Washington with one hundred dollar bills raised through CREEP? But such questions came from the losers. Nixonian Washington cared naught about Watergate; the official capital prepared for the regal inauguration of a president who had just been reelected with the most resounding mandate in electoral history. The Nixon Administration, as 1972 drew to a close, appeared determined, and capable, of keeping the truth of Watergate isolated from the vulgar curiosities of the public.

For Charles Morgan—and, for that matter, the then-unwitting public as well—the low point in Washington came on Friday, December 22, during a luncheon at a Washington restaurant called the Kansas City Beef House, a lawyer hangout just down Pennsylvania Avenue from the Justice Department. The luncheon deserves detail because it shows how deeply Watergate was buried that winter, and how the then-prosecutors were seemingly bent on keeping it just that way. Chuck Morgan is one of the more remarkable lawyers of his generation. A burly, fast-drawling southerner, he did civil rights litigation in the South in an era when segregationists tended to settle issues with dynamite and rifle fire, not fancy words in the courtroom. As a sort of Dixie turncoat, Morgan endured (and survived) more abuse than most men. In 1972, with the civil rights wars dying down, Morgan had come north to run the Washington national office of the American Civil Liberties Union (ACLU). His years of dealing with crafty segregationist lawyers and two-faced judges left Morgan with an astounding ability to sniff out legal deviousness. He watches his opponents' hands without being distracted by their smooth words; he is not a man apt to be euchred in a shell game, whether it is played on a carnival midway or in a federal courtroom.

Morgan's piece of the Watergate case was a civil suit intended to keep confidential the contents of the conversations the Watergate buggers had overheard from the Democratic National Committee (DNC) offices. In the suit Morgan represented both the ACLU and the Association of State Democratic Chairmen, a DNC adjunct. Many of the conversations in question had been over the telephone of the association's executive director, R. Spencer Oliver. Morgan did not want the private conversations unnecessarily spread on the public record, hence his law suit, and the December 22 meeting with the two lead prosecutors in the case, Earl Silbert, the principal assistant United States attorney in Washington, and Seymour Glanzer.

By Morgan's account, the tone of the meeting "was one of cordiality and mutual concern." Silbert wanted to use the contents of the conversations in the trial; in Morgan's words he "seemed unable to understand why the victims of the crime would hesitate to endorse every reasonable step which might lead to a successful prosecution." Morgan and his assistant, Hope Eastman, "sought to convey to him the basic fear of the victims of the crime—that up the ladder of authority from Mr. Silbert, the prosecution and the defense were under a common influence of control"; that is to say, both sides were eager for a continuation of the cover-up.

Then Silbert casually dropped into the conversation his theory of why the break-in occurred, and how he intended to explain away the mysteries so that the jury would be satisfied they knew the whole truth of Watergate. Morgan quotes him: "Hunt was trying to blackmail Spencer and I'm going to prove it."

Morgan is a man street-wise enough not to be easily surprised, but Silbert's statement jolted him to the core. As he said later, Silbert's "blackmail motive had been woven from whole cloth. It became clear that by using bits and pieces acquired from the investigation and by delving into contents [of the monitored phone conversations] he intended to present a non-political and fictitious motive for the crime—personal blackmail and big money," with the blame going no higher than Hunt and Liddy.

To Morgan, Silbert's strategy seemed a crowning, final obscenity, and from an administration so cocksure of its ability to control the trial that the very prosecution would join in harassing the victims of the crime. Morgan feared that jury, judge and press would be so titillated by tidbits about the personal and political lives of persons overheard in the taps "that they would accept Silbert's presentation of the false motive" and place full responsibility for Watergate on Hunt and Liddy. Earl Silbert, rebutting, charged that Morgan saw nonexistent hobgoblins. In a lengthy post-trial defense of his conduct of the trial Silbert called Morgan's charges that he abetted a cover-up "wholly unfounded, inaccurate and baseless." On the specific issue of revealing contents of the overheard telephone calls, Silbert said the testimony was needed to corroborate the otherwise unsupported testimony of Watergate accomplice Alfred Baldwin that the calls in fact were intercepted, "to help authenticate the identity of these conversations, and to help establish motive."

"When you do the kind of law I do," Chuck Morgan said months later, "you get mad a lot, because you are thrown things that disgust you. But this one—well, this was so damnably rotten that I began to wonder, deep down in the recesses of wherever I think such things, whether *anything* would get to the truth of Watergate. You'd run through all the trip wires that normally take care of an injustice: the Congress, the press, the law enforcement agencies, the prosecution. Man, after that day I had about decided that *nothing* was going to work; that this was one damned case that was wired seven ways to Sunday, and back again."

One trip wire the Watergate hadn't cleared, however, was a stubby, crag-faced Italo-American judge named John J. Sirica. And that Watergate did not prove to be "wired seven ways to Sunday," to use Chuck Morgan's phrase, is what a truly independent federal judiciary is all about. Sirica began the case with normal human curiosity—a judge is not required to make himself totally ignorant of the world around him—and he listened to what went on before him, and he refused to permit his court to be used for a sham proceeding. If ever a catalogue of Watergate blunders is compiled, one word belongs at the front of it: *arrogance*.

Arrogance. The mock solemnity. When Sirica asked the obvious questions—why they did it, and who hired them, and what they expected to find up there in the Democrats' office—they put on bland expressions, and stared back at him unblinkingly, and responded, in effect, "Oh, no, Your Honor, we don't know a damned thing, only what it says right there in the indictment."

Behind these answers persons in the courtroom could build their own scenarios: that someone had told the defendants, "You go in there and give a plea. There's not a damned thing Sirica can do; he'll have to accept; that's what the law says he has to do. Now Sirica is a guy who goes off the deep end, and he has a temper, and he might talk tough to you. Don't sweat it, because it's all locked in, regardless of what sentence he gives you." So Sirica, who is not an insensitive man, faced defendants who acted in a way to insult the intelligence of any man—even someone the Watergate higherups might have written off as a little Italian judge they didn't think was too smart.

Playing games with the court. One of the Cubans was asked whether he had worked for the CIA in the past, an allegation that had been bandied about in the press, and even informally confirmed by an agency spokesman. But when Sirica asked the question directly, the Cuban's demeanor became hyperserious, and he replied, "Not that I know of, Your Honor." G. Gordon Liddy, sitting at the defense table, laughed out loud. He didn't even have the courtesy—or sense—to hide the laugh by putting his hand over his face; he just leaned back and laughed, both in and at a United States District Court. Liddy laughed because he thought—and a lot of other people then thought—that they were getting away with something.

Sirica did not show any emotion when Liddy laughed. But in retrospect that was maybe the most expensive laugh in American politics, because once Liddy did it, right there in open court, nothing was going to stop the truth from coming out.

So Judge John J. Sirica went after the truth, using the full panoply of his powers of office. As a trial judge, he insisted that prosecutors go beyond proving the facts of a simple burglary case. When they pulled their punches, he took over the questioning, threw the judicial equivalent of haymakers, and prodded a key witness to say out loud—in open court—the name of two of President Nixon's closest political aides, thereby putting them in the middle of the scandal.

Still not satisfied, as a sentencing judge, Sirica told the defendants in so many words that if they insisted on playing games with his court, he knew a trick or two as well; and so he sent them to jail under 35-year provisional sentences. Anyone who has been there will tell you that the loudest noise in the world is the sound of a jail door slamming shut behind you. Once they heard this noise, all the Watergate defendants save one were eager to give a grand jury the answers they wouldn't give Sirica in open court.

And, finally, as the judge directing the special Watergate grand juries, Sirica swept aside White House claims that executive privilege kept presidential documents sacrosanct even when they contained evidence on criminal violations of the law. Surrender your surreptitious tape recordings, Judge Sirica ordered. The Nixon Administration appealed, and lost, and almost destroyed itself in trying to find a way around Sirica's ruling; in the end, it obeyed.

Sirica is important for another reason as well: he symbolizes the independence of the federal judiciary in an era when other branches of government have run roughshod over constitutional liberties of American citizens. Time and again independent federal judges gavelled down various Nixon Administration schemes—emanating, in most instances, from a politicized Justice Department—that smacked of police state tactics. But in January 1973, when the Watergate cover-up was in its penultimate stages, John J. Sirica hunched forward in his upholstered chair, cast his steel-gray eyes down upon the assembled lawyers and defendants, and snorted to himself, *Unbelievable, unbelievable! You can't do this sort of thing in my court.*

Because of his role in breaking open Watergate, Sirica is at once the best known and most controversial district judge perhaps of all time. That this is so is most ironic, for before the fame of Watergate, Sirica had such a spotty professional reputation that many Washington trial lawyers—and some of his colleagues as well, in deepest privacy—thought him to be somewhat of a bust as a judge. "A calm tyrant," one attorney said of him, "a man who slaughters you without insulting you." Sirica has never claimed, nor has he been credited with judicial intellectualism. From the bench, his sentences sometimes wander around a bit before arriving at what he is trying to say; in relaxed moments, when he is not self-consciously a judge, he is more intelligible because he is more direct, even if his syntax is littered by such repeated conversational stutters as "you know" and "the way I see it." Sirica, in sum, is an instance where the challenge of a particular case brought forth from a federal district judge talents he had not previously displayed.

For Sirica, fame has meant a volley of accolades and brickbats. He is *Time Magazine*'s Man of the Year ("a symbol of the American judiciary's insistence on the priority of law throughout the sordid Watergate saga . . . a testimony to the integrity of the institution he represents"). To Kenneth Clawson, the White House director of communications, gesturing contemptuously towards Sirica at a Washington cocktail party, he "is the pimple on the Republic's backside." To a Tennessee miner who handwrote a letter to Sirica: "For awesome weeks you were the dike that kept the flood water of tyranny from sweeping across our nation." To columnist William Buckley, who worked under Howard Hunt in the CIA, and became such a personal friend that he is godfather to the Hunt children, Sirica is a judge of "singular cruelty"; Buckley called him the judicial equivalent of a medical quack. To Chief Judge Joseph S. Lord III of Philadelphia, "The Watergate case is the epitome of judicial nonpartisanship and a shining reflection of the fact that when you don your robe, you are neither a Republican nor a Democrat but simply a federal judge in search of the truth, no matter where it lies." Columnist Joseph Kraft suggested, in apparent seriousness, that a monument be built in Sirica's honor opposite the Justice Department. To Joseph L. Rauh, Jr., Washington lawyer and a founder and former president of Americans for Democratic Action, "It seems ironic that those most opposed to Mr. Nixon's lifetime espousal of ends justifying means should now make a hero of a judge who practiced this formula to the detriment of a fair trial for the Watergate seven."

The Nixonian dilemma in attempting to discredit Judge John J. Sirica—or even to understand him—is that he so perfectly fits the Administration's prototype of a true-square American: self-educated son of a hardworking immigrant; a political conservative who joined the Republican Party as a young man, even when working in New Deal Washington, because he agreed with it philosophically; a federal prosecutor; partner in a very mercantile Washington law firm, where he specialized in defending insurance companies; and, finally, a law-and-order federal jurist, appointed in 1957 by no less a Republican deity than General Eisenhower himself. That such a man could cause so much unmitigated misery for a Republican president; that he did not see fit to preside over the trial of men caught in a "third-rate burglary," and no more, and then go about his business, while the White House did the same; that he pursued the President to the ends of the Constitution in quest of those surreptitious tapes: does not such zeal surely reveal judicial bias? So the Nixon believers poked around Sirica's background for reasons why he galloped after the president like a one-man posse—discredit Sirica, and all that he has done could be wiped from the public mind.

Throughout the spring and summer of 1973 lawyers with close ties to the White House canvassed the Washington legal fraternity asking for derogatory information about Sirica. Was there anything in his professional or personal background that could be turned against him? Any gripes to the bar grievance committee? Any extra-judicial income or business holdings that could be ballooned into a Fortas-type scandal? How about the fact that Sirica waited until he was almost 48 years old to marry? Were there any, ah, personal reasons for the prolonged bachelorhood? Or any old girlfriends who could recite a gamy story or two about the distinguished judge?

These months of vigorous raking produced only one flimsy story that couldn't even rightfully be called muck. Representative Gene Snyder, a Kentucky Republican, put the "evidence" into the *Congressional Record* on November 29, 1973, in a third-hand manner; an article from a publication of something called The Christian Heritage Center of Louisville that in turn quoted an earlier issue of *The Washington Observer* (unlocatable through the resources of the Chesapeake & Potomac Telephone Company) which supposedly deposed as follows:

In 1957, when John Sirica had mustered enough political support from his native Connecticut for a judicial appointment, he was seeking to fill a vacancy on the United States Court of Appeals. But he was blocked from this appointment by then-Vice President Nixon, so that he had to settle for an appointment to the United States District Court of D.C. He has never forgiven Nixon.

The only flaw with Snyder's thrice-removed demonology is that it is totally wrong. Sirica's "political support from his native Connecticut" is just about as intense as one would expect for a man who left the state at age seven, with a penniless and obscure father, and who never lived there again, or gave it any particular thought. Sirica was an adopted Washingtonian, and the minute District of Columbia Republican Party, from which he drew whatever "political support" he possessed, could fit comfortably into a courtroom (or a jury box, for that matter). Further, Sirica consistently displayed the combative trial lawyer's disdain for the appellate bench; "Better that you are put into a box and buried," he once mused to a friend who was considering taking such an appointment. "Stay downstairs in the court, where the people are; why go batty reading a bunch of books and briefs?" Sirica wanted the district judgeship, and was happy that he received it. His private thoughts about Richard Nixon—past and present—are something he keeps tightly to himself in the Watergate era, but any contacts he had with the president in the 1950s, he has told friends, "were those handshaking sort of things where you go through a reception line and meet some high official or politician and maybe say 'hello, how's the wife?'—the sort of thing that doesn't mean anything at all." And as one of Sirica's friends says, "Anyone who tries to explain or understand John by looking for politics or dirty motives or that kind of mess, hell, they're wasting their time. A guy like this, you've got to understand his origins, the things he's done over the years; that way you know what he stands for."

The Sirica story begins in 1887 when his father, Fred Ferdinand Sirica, arrived in Watertown, Connecticut, at age seven, with his father and stepmother, driven from their native village near Naples by poverty. Watertown wasn't much better, financially. Sirica's father worked as a barber, never earning more than $20 a week, and his mother ran a grocery store; the family (the parents and sons John and Andrew) lived in a cramped room to the rear. In 1911, his strength drained by a tubercular cough, the father took the family on an odyssey southward in quest of warm climes and a better living. Ohio, Georgia, Florida, New Orleans, California briefly, Richmond, finally Washington, on the eve of the First World War.

The elder Sirica never quite made it financially, and the future judge greased cars and worked as a soda jerk to help support the family. Never barbering though, because Fred Sirica often told him, "You learn that trade, and I'll break your arm." He also drummed into the son: "Be honest with people. If they lie to you once, keep your eye on them. The world is full of people who can't talk straight, who'll look sideways and try to con you." Sirica frequently recalls this advice now when he talks about judging the credibility of witnesses in his court; to him, a person who hedges and fuzzes the truth is contemptible. And, in the words of a friend, "John's father had the idea that much of his business misfortune was because of people who lied to him, and cheated him. From the way John has talked about this, the father's experience, real or imagined, is bound to have had a hell of an impact on him."

The Sirica family rooted itself in Washington long enough for John to finish high school there. At age seventeen, despite the lack of college preparatory work, he bravely entered George Washington law school. Sirica couldn't make it. He dropped out after a month, spent a year peddling newspapers from a stand at 9th and D Streets NW in downtown Washington—six blocks from the courthouse he later was to rule as chief judge—and tried again at Georgetown University law school. Once more, failure; once more, a retreat to the newsstand. The next year, haunted by the spectre of his failed father, and "determined to make more of myself than a newsboy, so my parents could be proud of me," he returned to George Washington law. The added maturity apparently gave Sirica the necessary boost: he made respectable grades, and even found the hours to earn $100 a month as a boxing coach at the Knights of Columbus and the YMCA. He graduated in 1926, passed the bar examination his first try, and then joined his still-wandering family in Miami.

During those months Sirica did some boxing that brought him a latter-years reputation he insists he does not deserve. He earned spending money as a sparring partner for a former world welterweight champion named Jack Britton, and he gave lessons to Bernard Gimbel, the department store tycoon and boxing buff. Sirica also won a ten-round professional match, and one of the Miami newspapers adjudged him "a great little mitt artist." But Mrs. Sirica thought—and said, rather loudly—that a head that contained all that law school knowledge should be put to better use than taking punches in smoker matches. Sirica agreed, and returned to Washington to practice law.

Because of his boxing background, and his later friendship with Jack Dempsey (who was best man at his wedding), the Washington press in the early Watergate days spoke of Sirica as if he were an Italo-American Joe Louis, or Muhammed Ali. All of which amused Sirica immensely. As he told the *Washington Post*'s Bob Addie, "It's like a man who sits on the bench in football and then, years later, becomes an All-American." He never put on gloves after leaving Florida.

Sirica had a tough time as a fledgling attorney. The "national lawyer" had not yet blossomed in Washington, and a newcomer needed a tie with a bank, insurance company or an old established firm to get into the money. Lacking business and social contacts, Sirica gravitated to the United States attorney's office in 1930, where he soon acquired a reputation as a competent if somewhat noisy prosecutor. When his biting cross-examination brought a defendant to his feet with a threatening roar, Sirica slipped off his jacket, struck a boxer's stance, and yelled to a restraining court aide, "Let him go, let him go, I'm not afraid to mix with him." Again, Sirica became so angered with the conduct of an opposing lawyer that he impulsively arose and yelled, "Hey, Your Honor, that ain't fair."

Back in private practice, Sirica suffered a few more lean years. For a while he and another former prosecutor shared a $30-a-month room and a $40-a-month secretary; some days, he said later (when the experience was remote enough to be humorous), "we sat around and talked to one another; no clients ever came in to disturb us." Then his career began to move. Sirica had the good sense to recognize that he possessed neither the temperament nor the eye-straining intellect to be an "office lawyer"; better for him the daily bite-and-gouge of the trial court. The word went around Washington: if you can settle, settle; if you must go to trial, hire John Sirica. Trial work is a unique form of drudgery; if a lawyer is good at it, 50 to 75 times a year he goes down to the courthouse and matches wit and witnesses with another lawyer, usually in a courtroom barren of anyone other than the principals. An outstanding trial lawyer is not necessarily famous outside the circle of people who pay attention to such things. But Sirica became known as a lawyer who could win those routine, gray cases that are the daily fodder of the court: whether the bus or the auto had the right-of-way at the intersection; whether the homebuyer should have looked a bit closer at the condition of the retaining wall before he bought the house; whether Partner Doe really looted the business, or was simply a poor manager. Newspaper clippings are a poor gauge of any career—in sports, they tell of the quarterbacks, not the offensive guards; in law, the axe-murders, not the negligence cases. To continue the analogy, Sirica was one of the better offensive guards of the Washington courts in the late 1930s and early 1940s, but only twice did he receive any public attention. In 1941 he successfully defended a Missouri public utilities executive who offended the reigning Democrats by collecting a truly massive political slush fund for the 1940 elections. A year later, Sirica represented columnist Walter Winchell, who had been sued for $200,000 for calling publisher Eleanor "Cissy" Patterson "the craziest woman in Washington," among other things.* No lawyer relishes fighting a powerful local publisher; nonetheless Sirica counselled Winchell to let time and public opinion persuade Cissy to back away. She finally did, on the technical ground that Winchell's sponsor

---

* Winchell also insinuated that Cissy, the editor of the *Washington Times-Herald,* was aiding the Nazis because a senator who had contacts with a German agent had inserted one of her columns into the *Congressional Record.* Cissy replied with an editorial headlined "SQUASH" which read in its entirety: "Nobody likes to step on a cockroach, but occasionally it is necessary in the interest of cleanliness and hygiene."

was obligated to pay any libel losses he incurred. Cissy wanted her blood fresh, not once-removed, so she dropped the case. Thereafter Winchell was Sirica's friend as well as client.

Although Sirica was mildly active in national Republican politics (he campaigned for Wendell Willkie among Italian-American communities in 1940), the Democratic majority on a House Select Committee hired him in 1944 as chief counsel for an investigation of the Federal Communications Commission. Sirica soon turned up evidence that Roosevelt Administration officials tried to use pressure in the transfer of a radio station license, and the Democrats tried to dampen the investigation. Sirica resigned with the blunt outspokenness that was to become so familiar in the Watergate courtroom three decades later:

> There is only one way I can try a case, whether before a Congressional committee or in a courtroom, and that is to present all the facts and let the chips fall where they may. . . . I don't want it on my conscience that anyone can say John Sirica . . . is a party to a whitewash.

In 1949 Sirica joined the prestigious Washington firm of Hogan & Hartson, the largest and perhaps the best "local" office in town. Unlike the superfirms of Covington & Burling and Arnold & Porter, among others, which practice "national" law before the federal government, Hogan & Hartson contented itself with the quiet but profitable representation of Washington banks, insurance companies, utilities and other corporations. Sirica soon was H&H's top trial lawyer, but one with an eye cocked for another try at public life. One chance came in 1951, when a fellow Washington bachelor and racehorse fan named Senator Joseph McCarthy asked him to become chief counsel of his new Senate Investigating Committee. Sirica almost took the job, but backed out at the last minute when his new bride objected. One of Sirica's friends remembers him playing an "if" game several years later: *If* he had taken the job, the McCarthy inquiry might have been a saner venture ("I'd have shut Joe up, or quit him"). *If* he had the McCarthy association, however, President Eisenhower most likely would have looked elsewhere in 1957, when he needed a district judge for Washington. As things worked out, by 1957 Sirica was a 53-year-old trial lawyer who had worked long enough, and hard enough, to look upon the federal bench as a quiet place to close out his career. So he left a $60,000-plus Hogan & Hartson income for what he thought would be a less demanding pace.

Which it was, for more than a decade. The irony of John Sirica is that he made no vivid impression upon lawyers or other courthouse habitués. Lawyers knew that Sirica ran a tight court, and that he didn't hesitate to slap stiff sentences on repeat and serious offenders. Sirica did have his share of problems with the Court of Appeals for the District of Columbia, which is hypersensitive about defendants' rights in criminal cases.*

In a 1967 case, for instance, the appeals court chastised him for giving a five to fifteen year sentence to a man convicted by a jury of trying to rob a bus driver with a toy pistol. When the man came in for sentencing Sirica told him: "Now, the court didn't believe your story on the stand, the court believes you deliberately lied in this case. If you had pleaded guilty in this case, I might have been more lenient with you." Rebutting, the man's lawyer filed an account of a private conversation in which Sirica's law clerk supposedly told him the only way to get a light sentence "was to confess that you did the robbery, apologize four or five times, and to say that you are willing to turn over a new leaf." Put on the stand by Sirica, the clerk denied saying any such thing, although he did concede that from what he had seen in court Sirica *was* easier with persons who pleaded guilty. The circuit court held that forced repentance would have damaged the credibility of the man's appeal; it ordered Sirica to resentence him. (The man died before he got back before Sirica.)

---

* See Chapter Six, "The D.C. Court of Appeals: The Mini Supreme Court."

Sirica's most publicized pre-Watergate case was the trial of a government bureaucrat named Robert L. Ammidown, who hired a Washington hoodlum to kill his wife. The man "kidnapped" the Ammidowns as they left a waterfront cafe, drove them to a secluded spot, then raped and shot the wife as Ammidown watched. During the trial Sirica flatly refused to accept Ammidown's offer to plead guilty to second-degree murder, even though the prosecution did not object. "I would have been the laughing stock of this country in my opinion and I don't think fit to stay on the bench had I accepted a second-degree plea in this case," Sirica said in rejecting the offer. Sirica sentenced the actual killer to death, and said he would have imposed the same penalty on Ammidown had not the jury made a binding recommendation of life imprisonment.

Washington lawyer/journalist Harvey Katz, evaluating Sirica's reputation in a post-Watergate *Washingtonian Magazine* article, called him unfit for the bench, a widespread but by no means unanimous feeling among local trial attorneys. Katz cited "Sirica's careless legal errors, his short temper, his inattentiveness to court proceedings, his misguided view of the purpose of judicial power, his lack of compassion for his fellow human beings," and strange as it now seems, "his lack of interest in the truth." Strong words, but mostly undocumented, and Sirica dismissed them privately as "a bunch of bull shit." Be that as it may, Sirica has displayed occasional and most puzzling symptoms of lacking confidence in his judicial ability. A journalist who once covered federal courts for the *Washington Post* related, "Sirica once motioned me and another reporter into his chambers when a motion was made during trial. He began asking us our impressions of how the case was going. 'What do you think of that witness? Was he lying? What should I do with that motion?' I was flabbergasted. I thought he was putting me on. But we talked about the witnesses, and the motion, and he did exactly as we said. I had the experience several times later. I never could decide whether he honestly felt he needed advice, or whether he was trying to court favor with reporters who wrote about his court."

But Sirica was never hesitant on demanding "the full facts" when he tried a case. In 1966 Washington aerospace lobbyist Fred Black, who was caught up in the Bobby Baker scandals, was tried in Sirica's court for tax cheating. Sirica heard testimony about various payments to Black by firms that wanted to curry favor with Baker, and he lost his temper. He denounced the "dirty work" of some contractors doing government business. "Don't you think these companies ought to have some statements showing where their money went?" he asked lawyers. "It sounds as if these companies are making Mr. Black the scapegoat to cover up their own slimy trail. If these companies hired this man to do their dirty work, they should be here in the courtroom with him."

Thus the background of the judge who on September 15, 1972, assigned himself to try the cases of the seven men indicted on the original Watergate break-in charges (only one of five trials he had accepted since becoming chief judge in 1971). Sirica talked with his fellow judges before taking the case. He could have given it to any one of the fifteen, but the consensus was that he should handle the trial himself. Because of his administrative duties as chief judge, Sirica kept his docket light. Further, and more importantly, Sirica recognized the politics of Watergate: if aggressive questioning proved necessary to bring out the facts, a conservative Republican judge could not be accused of partisanship. Sirica already suspected the whole truth might be hard to find. As he told a group of reporters in an informal chat that fall, he was "asking myself the same questions you are."

But would Sirica try to find any answers? His first two major actions in the case in fact appeared to stifle inquiries into Watergate by either Congress or the press. On October 4, he enjoined all parties connected with the bugging, including the victims, from public comment about the case—an order so broad that Sirica admitted upon reflection it covered even presidential

candidate George S. McGovern. (Sirica tactfully did
not try to apply the order to McGovern, who said he
would ignore it anyway.) But Representative Wright
Patman (D., Tex.) complained loudly the ban could
inhibit a probe he hoped his House Banking and Currency Committee would make of a Minnesota financier
who received a federal bank charter just before the
break-in, and whose $25,000 check wound up in the
bank account of a Watergate burglar. Patman tartly
suggested that Sirica limit the order to the offenses
charged in the indictments and not permit it "to be
used for broader political purposes"—that is, a cover-
up. (As it turned out Patman couldn't muster majority
support for the probe on his own committee, so he let
it drop.) And in December, acting on a motion by
Howard Hunt's lawyers, Sirica ordered the *Los Angeles
Times* to produce a tape-recording of an interview
two of its reporters, Jack Nelson and Ronald J. Os-
trow, held with Alfred Baldwin, who had helped in
the bugging operation. The *Times* refused, and Sirica
cited the newspaper for contempt and ordered its
Washington bureau chief, John F. Lawrence, jailed.
He was released after a few hours when Baldwin personally agreed to give the recording to Sirica, with the
proviso that he would edit out any voice other than his
own.

But in other pretrial hearings Sirica served notice on
the prosecution that he expected it to do more than try
a simple burglary case. His comments on December 4
were a harbinger of what was to come from the judge
during the actual trial.

SIRICA: Now, on the question of motive and intent
in this case, as you know there has been a lot of
talk about who hired whom to go into this place.
Is the government going to offer any evidence on
the question of motive and intent for entering the
Democratic National Committee's headquarters?
SILBERT: There will be some evidence if the court
please.
SIRICA: What do you mean by 'some' evidence?
SILBERT: Well, there will be some evidence intro-

duced. [I]t is up to the jury to accept or reject the evidence that we propose to offer, but there will be evidence we will offer . . . from which a jury may draw, we think, an appropriate inference as to *perhaps a variety of interests*.

Sirica's comments whetted the press's expectations. JUDGE ASKS BROADER 'BUG' TRIAL, the *Washington Post* headlined. WATERGATE JUDGE HINTS AT WIDER TRIAL, said *The New York Times*. Two weeks later, however, prosecutor Silbert attempted to dash these hopes, repeating his plaint that the jury would be asked to choose from a "variety of motives." And Silbert claimed, in effect, that (a) he had no way of deciding for himself what was the true motive; and (b) motive was really irrelevant anyway, for his sole task was to prove the allegations of the indictment. Silbert argued:

I am sure Your Honor is . . . aware the government cannot read any person's mind. There is no device yet known to man by which the government or anyone else can search into the motivation, reasoning or the functioning that makes a person act or commit or engage in any particular line of conduct.

And if, Your Honor, the government is successful . . . in this prosecution in introducing evidence sufficient to prove beyond a reasonable doubt the guilt of the persons charged in the indictment, then I submit . . . that there is no secret then as . . . to the best source of the motivation of the persons and the possible involvement of others.

Silbert's argument was patently specious, for the indictments said nothing whatsoever about motive. And it was during this period, according to Charles Morgan of the ACLU, that Silbert began circulating the theory that Watergate was nothing more than a blackmail scheme put together by Hunt, with the aid of Liddy and CREEP funds.

The trial got under way on January 8 with an accompanying chorus of press reports (unattributed, but totally accurate, as subsequent events proved) that the defendants were under heavy pressure from higherups to plead guilty in exchange for financial support and early clemency. The reports said that the four Cuban-Americans * were being badgered by Howard Hunt, who had got them into the mess in the first place, and that Hunt was striking his own deal with CREEP.

John Sirica hence sat in a somewhat ridiculous position: as a trial judge he was picking a jury to try seven persons for burglary. But as a citizen he read in his *Washington Post* each morning about the under-the-table deals being struck by lawyers and their defendants in his court, not a word of which ever reached the official record. Sirica also was aware, from the pretrial arguments made by Chuck Morgan, that Silbert's enthusiasm for getting to the bottom of the case was considered by some persons to be less than total.*

---

* Bernard Barker, Eugenio Martinez, Frank Sturgis, and Virgilio Gonzalez.

* In retrospect another of Silbert's pretrial actions has an even more suspicious odor than his "Hunt blackmail" theory. In late December Hunt asked for a court order giving him access to papers he had left in his safe in the Executive Office Building for use in his defense. Hunt at the time was threatening "to blow the White House out of the water," unless his monetary demands were met. He claimed he had documentary evidence sufficient to "impeach the president." The material in the safe related to such matters as the burglary of Daniel Ellsberg's psychiatrist. Such papers, quite obviously, would have helped Hunt in his war of nerves with the White House —and they would have been equally valuable to a prosecutor who wanted the full truth about the mysterious Mr. Hunt. Yet Silbert put himself in the peculiar position of urging the court to bar him, Silbert, access to evidence that Hunt himself said was pertinent to Watergate. He vociferously argued that executive privilege covered any material generated by Hunt during his employment by the White House. Silbert has also asserted that there was a "close question" as to whether the search of Hunt's safe was legal, in the absence of a search warrant. Silbert stated further that he did intend to attempt to used the seized documents as trial evidence. CREEP finally met Hunt's monetary demands and the impasse ended without any ruling by Sirica. One can only surmise Sirica's thoughts when he heard a supposedly sincere prosecutor argue against access to material evidence.

In his opening statement, prosecutor Silbert gave the barest bones of the case. He said CREEP officials (he did not name them) had ordered a broad ranging political and espionage operation, and that Liddy had been given $235,000 to carry out various assignments. Only $50,000 could be traced, Silbert said, and he gave no indication that Watergate had been discussed by anyone higher in CREEP than Liddy. In laying the groundwork for his "blackmail" motive, he noted that Spencer Oliver, the Democratic official, once visited the offices of Robert R. Mullen Company, a Washington public relations firm for which Hunt had worked, seeking a job. Oliver met Hunt casually. According to Silbert, Hunt later "voiced his opposition to Mr. Oliver coming to work there because Mr. Oliver was a liberal Democrat and he did not think he would fit well into that company." Oliver did not get the job. In a post-trial memorandum Silbert was even more specific. He said investigators could never determine the "precise motivation" for the break-in and wiretapping, "particularly on the telephone of a comparative unknown, Spencer Oliver. [Watergate accomplice Alfred] Baldwin had told us that McCord wanted *all* telephone calls recorded, including personal calls. They were, many of them being extremely personal, intimate and potentially embarrassing. . . . Therefore, one motive we thought possible was an attempt to compromise Oliver and others, but so far as Hunt and Liddy were concerned, for political reasons, not for the money." Silbert acknowledged there could be a "political motive" for the bugging as well, and that McCord was obviously interested in Senator McGovern "because of his alleged leftwing views." Then Silbert quickly reverted to his blackmail theme: the motives of Hunt and Liddy were not necessarily those of McCord and the Cubans. "Certainly the facts will suggest to you a financial motive here," he said.

Such was the case that Silbert set out to prove. Almost immediately, however, defendants began dropping like so much ripe fruit. First was Hunt, whose attorney, William O. Bittman, said he wished to plead guilty to three of the six counts with which he was charged.

Silbert urged that the plea be accepted, with the proviso that there be entered into the record a "detailed statement of the evidence so that all would know the facts that had been uncovered by the investigation in this case," * and that Hunt tell the grand jury "what knowledge he has, *if any,* as to the involvement of others" in the "so-called Watergate case."

Sirica flatly refused. "Given the nature of this case," he said, "the court is compelled to the conclusion that both the substance and the appearance of justice require that the tendered plea be refused. Anything further?"

Without hesitation Bittman entered guilty pleas to all six counts—various burglary, wiretapping and conspiracy charges. Sirica accepted the pleas, then turned back to Hunt:

SIRICA: Now, in your own words, [Mr. Hunt] I would like you to tell me from the beginning just how you got into this conspiracy, what you did, various things that you did so that I can decide whether or not you are knowingly and intentionally entering this plea voluntarily with full knowledge of possible consequences.

Bittman interrupted before Hunt could answer. He noted Silbert's stated intention of bringing Hunt and the other defendants before the grand jury before they were sentenced, and suggested that would be the proper forum for questioning.

Incredibly, Silbert then moved in to commit Hunt to the prosecution's bobtailed version of the case even prior to his appearance before the grand jury. He asked that Judge Sirica "inquire of the defendant to ascertain . . . whether he accepts the essential accuracy of the facts as outlined in the government's opening satement." Sirica did so.

SIRICA: I will put the question to you as framed by

---

* These stipulated facts, it should be noted, did not begin to approach a full recitation of the case.

counsel: Do you accept those as substantially the facts as you know them to be?

HUNT: Substantially, yes, Your Honor.

SIRICA: You agree with the government's opening statement insofar as your knowledge of the conspiracy?

HUNT: Yes, Your Honor.

SIRICA: And your participation in it?

HUNT: Yes, Your Honor.

SIRICA: Does that answer the question?

SILBERT: Yes, Your Honor, it does.

Thus did Hunt glide out of the case, with a commitment to tell the grand jury nothing more about the Watergate affair than the truncated version which Silbert was willing to pass off to the court—and public—as the entire truth. Hunt knew of many more nefarious activities that led to Watergate: specifically, forgeries of State Department cables to implicate the late President Kennedy in the 1963 assassination of South Vietnamese Premier Ngo Dinh Diem; the burglary of the office of the Ellsberg psychiatrist; and other political black tricks. Hunt's testimony thereafter was to be in the privacy of a grand jury room, and controlled by prosecutors who asserted publicly they had the full Watergate story. (In a brief press conference after his plea Hunt said he would tell the grand jury no higherups were involved "to my personal knowledge.")

Sirica was neither deceived nor satisfied by what was happening. He refused to lower Hunt's $100,000 bail (although Hunt was able to post it, through a surety bond, and went free pending sentencing) and he looked for another chink through which to get deeper into the case.

The four Cuban-Americans followed Hunt's suit a few days later, with Silbert recommending that they be permitted to plead guilty to only three of the seven charges against them. Sirica refused, so they pleaded to the entire seven. Seymour Glanzer, Silbert's trial assistant, noted the press stories about pressures on the men to plead guilty, and said that he had asked them whether "they were coerced in any manner to enter this plea, and they stated they were not."

Sirica spent a fruitless hour trying to wheedle information from the Cuban-Americans. As did any other politically literate American, Sirica knew the Cubans did not wander into the Watergate offices on their own, that someone had recruited them and given them a reason for undertaking the spy expedition. The Cubans, however, chose to play dumb, and gave nothing other than the judicial equivalent of their names, ranks and service numbers. Not until months later did the public learn, through the good offices of the Ervin committee, that the Cubans at this point still received covert expense money via CREEP, and that intermediaries had agreed to support their families—again, with CREEP money—while they were imprisoned. Sirica, of course, suspected to the point of certainty that such was the case, and he was determined to pry as much information as possible from the Cubans. He got nowhere.

> SIRICA: . . . [I]s anyone at this time or *anytime* paying anything to the four of you defendants?
>
> THE DEFENDANTS *(in chorus)*: No one.
>
> SIRICA: Has anyone assured you that if you go to jail, either one of you or the four of you, . . . your families will be taken care of?
>
> THE DEFENDANTS *(in chorus)*: No one.
>
> SIRICA: Was there any statement made to you by Mr. Barker . . . Mr. Hunt or anybody else, that you would be taken care of if you got into trouble or anything like that?
>
> THE DEFENDANTS *(in chorus)*: No, sir.

Sirica had no more success when he questioned the defendants individually. An exchange with Eugenio Martinez shows how tightly the cover-up scheme sealed the lips of the lowest echelons of the conspiracy a full seven months after the arrests.

> SIRICA: I want you to start from the beginning and I want you to tell me how you got into this con-

spiracy, how did it happen that you got involved? Do you understand what I mean?

MARTINEZ: Yes, I understand.

SIRICA: Tell me in your own words what you did, how you got mixed up [in this]?

MARTINEZ: I believe the facts that you have read in the charges are true and are just to the truth.

SIRICA: That is a blanket answer. I want to know specifics.

MARTINEZ: I am sorry.

SIRICA: I want specific answers to my questions. I am not satisfied.

Sirica worked awhile on Bernard Barker, who behaved in court as if he were the top sergeant for the Cuban contingent. Barker admitted that he knew Hunt was a "consultant to the White House," but would say little else. Part of the stipulated evidence was that Barker received a $25,000 cashier's check intended for CREEP and used part of it for expenses on the Watergate foray. Who sent you the money? Sirica asked. "For a definite fact," Barker replied, "I cannot state who sent that money." Sirica was incredulous:

SIRICA: Don't you think it was strange, that amount of money coming through the mail without being registered or anything?

BARKER: No. I don't think it is strange, Your Honor. Like I said, I have previously before this been involved in other operations which took the strangeness out of that as far as I was concerned.

Barker insisted the money arrived one day "in the mail in a blank envelope" and he was never particularly curious about the source. "I don't believe you," Sirica shot back.

Nor did he believe the burglars when they looked askance at his questions about the truth of press reports that they had worked for the CIA in the past. When asked point blank whether he had served the CIA, Martinez replied, "Not that I know of."

Gordon Liddy, who had been sitting at the defense

table with a bemused grin listening to the frustrated Sirica, laughed audibly. Sirica's eyes flickered toward Liddy, and fixed on him momentarily. Sirica did not smile. Nor did he smile at Martinez's flip answer to his question about how he was recruited for the Watergate mission: "Maybe I offered myself." The only substantive answers the burglars gave were that they joined Hunt to help him solve "the Cuban situation." Frank Sturgis said, "When it comes to Cuba and the Communist conspiracy involving the United States, I will do anything to protect this country."

To persons in the courtroom that day it was obvious that Sirica was seething. The guilty pleas reduced drastically the scope of the trial. For instance, it was no longer legally permissible to admit as testimony the details of any conversations they might have had except for the period of the conspiracy alleged in the indictment—May 1, to June 17, the break-in date. Prior to May 1 as it later developed, Hunt had told at least one of the Cuban-Americans that top-level White House aides had advance knowledge not only of the Watergate bugging but other covert missions as well. But Sirica was not to be deterred; if anything, the narrowing of the trial parameters intensified his own determination to get more from the witnesses than the jury was hearing through Silbert's questions.

Sirica's shortening temper—and his damn-the-torpedoes attitude—came through sharply when Gerald Alch, the Boston lawyer representing James McCord, moved for a mistrial after the round of guilty pleas. When the jury returned and saw the men missing from court, Alch said, "no instruction can obviate the inference that these men have pleaded guilty." Sirica said there was ample precedent for continuing the trial. "I'm not awed by the appellate courts," he said. "Let's set that straight. All they can do is reverse me. They can't tell me how to try my case."

Sirica finally found a minor opening during the testimony of Hugh W. Sloan, who had been treasurer for CREEP during Watergate. Sloan was an important witness. He was the conduit through which $199,000 in CREEP money, chiefly $100 bills, was given to Liddy to set up an "intelligence network." Sloan also used Liddy to convert checks drawn on a Mexican bank into cash. And, finally, Sloan told of a hurried conversation with Liddy in a hallway at the CREEP offices the morning after the burglary. Sloan recounted it as follows:

He [Liddy] was obviously in a hurry. He indicated to me at that point he couldn't stop; he said to the best of my recollection: "My boys got caught last night. I made a mistake; I used somebody from here which I said I'd never do. I'm afraid I am going to lose my job."

The prosecution ended its interrogation of Sloan at that point but Sirica was by no means satisfied. He sent the jury from the courtroom and began his own round of questions (ultimately asking 41 of them). Sirica quite obviously felt Sloan knew much more than he was admitting—or had been asked. Didn't Sloan know that Liddy was a former FBI agent and attorney? Sirica asked. Yes, Sloan replied.

Sirica, incredulity dripping from his voice:

Here is a man, a former FBI agent, [who] makes a remark to you, that you claim you didn't know what he meant which indicated to any person I think with common sense that he had done something wrong. Didn't that flash in your mind when he said, "My boys got caught last night. . . ." Didn't that occur to you it was mighty strange about this matter that you didn't see anything wrong with that remark?

"Not at that point in time, no, sir," Sloan replied.

Sirica next asked obvious follow-up questions on Sloan's account of the money-handling. Under questioning by Silbert, Sloan said only that he checked with Jeb Magruder, the CREEP deputy director, when Liddy asked for money, and that Magruder told him the "allocation was in fact authorized." But the prosecutor did not ask what the money was for, and who "authorized" its expenditure. Answering Sirica's questions, Sloan maintained he had "no idea" of the purpose, nor did he question Magruder. Then he added: "I verified with Mr. Stans and Mr. Mitchell that he [Magruder] was authorized to make those [payments to Liddy]."

Having finally received the sort of answer he had been seeking, Sirica used the trial attorney's stratagem of asking a witness to repeat a point which he wanted to impress upon the audience:

SIRICA: You verified it with who?
SLOAN: Secretary Stans, the finance chairman, and I didn't directly but he verified it with John Mitchell, the campaign chairman.

Thus for the first time in public the Watergate break-in was pushed into the highest echelons of the Nixon reelection organization. Maurice Stans, the former commerce secretary, was then chairman of CREEP's financial arm and John Mitchell, the former attorney general, was director of CREEP.*

At another point Sloan was drawn into a discussion of why he had resigned from the CREEP finance committee. With Peter L. Maroulis, Liddy's attorney, objecting strenuously Sloan said he feared he had committed technical violations of the new campaign funds disclosure law and indicated that he was uncomfortable shuffling around checks drawn on Mexican banks and scores of thousands of hundred-dollar

---

* Donald Segretti, who served a jail term for his political sabotage of Democratic presidential candidates, told a peculiar story about Silbert's prosecutorial techniques in an interview April 28, 1974, on CBS's "Sixty Minutes" program. Segretti received the money for his activities from Herbert Kalmbach, President Nixon's personal attorney. When Segretti was brought before the Watergate grand jury, Silbert did the questioning. According to Segretti, Silbert referred to Kalmbach only as "Mr. K," and a grand juror finally had to elicit Kalmbach's full name. "But to be fair to Mr. Silbert, perhaps Mr. Silbert did not know the full story at that . . . point in time. So I don't think it would be fair to go after Mr. Silbert and put a black hat on him completely," Segretti added.

bills. Sirica remarked skeptically, "As a matter of fact, Mr. Sloan, be perfectly frank about the matter. You resigned primarily because you were concerned about the Watergate matter, isn't that the truth of the matter?" Sloan denied that this was true.

All this testimony, it will be remembered, was out of the presence of the jury. The next morning Sirica convened court with the jurors still absent and announced that in reviewing the transcript "I have found a significant portion of Mr. Sloan's testimony" which the jury had not heard. Sirica said he had "concluded that much of it is important evidence and that the jury should hear it. That testimony may have, it seems to me, an important bearing on Mr. Sloan's credibility before the jury." Sirica said he did not "personally intend to challenge the credibility of any witness who has appeared to date or to impugn the integrity of anyone." His "sole interest," he said, "is to see that both sides receive a fair trial. . . ."

Sirica proposed reading the transcript to the jury. He refused to recall Sloan to testify in person, as the prosecution requested. (The defense raised no objection to Sloan in the flesh.) Sirica refused: "Mr. Sloan might have a lapse of memory, I don't know. I would rather read it from the record."

Sirica's remarks about credibility could be taken two ways. His own questions were openly skeptical that Sloan's eyes were as open as they should have been during the time he was passing money to Liddy, and Liddy was mourning "my boys got caught last night." Maroulis, however, had heard enough of Sloan. The fact that Stans and Mitchell had authorized payments to Liddy had nothing to do with the case before the court—that is, the trial of seven men for burglary. Further, as a matter of trial strategy Maroulis wanted to get Sloan off the stand as rapidly as possible, and not give him a chance to repeat, during cross-examination, the hallway conversation. Reading the record, Maroulis argued, would "focus undue attention" on Sloan. He noted the press had called Sloan's testimony "particularly damaging" to Liddy. "I object to any further attention being called to it," Maroulis said, adding that he "exercised his judgement" in not cross-examining Sloan.

Let me tell you one thing [Sirica said]. I exercise my judgement as a federal judge and chief judge of this court, and I have done it on many occasions and in the presence of the jury examined witnesses where I thought all the facts were not brought out by counsel on either side.

As long as I am a federal judge I will continue to do it. As I said, the court of appeals might reverse me in this case. I am not concerned with that. I am concerned with doing what I think is the right thing at the moment and that is the reason I am going to read this testimony to the jury.

I could care less what happens to this case on appeal, if there is an appeal. I am not interested in that. I am interested in doing what I think is right.

Now your client [referring to Liddy] is smiling. He is probably not impressed with what I am saying. I don't care what he thinks either. Is that clear to you?

When the jury returned to the courtroom Sirica explained his reading of the Sloan testimony was "not being done for the purpose to indicate to any one of you jurors how I personally feel about the evidence in this case. That is unimportant." He noted that a federal judge is entitled to say, "I wouldn't believe a word he said. I think he is a thief, I think he is no good, I think he perjured himself." But Sirica said he never made such comments.

I don't think that a defendant or the government can get a fair trial if the judge with a black robe on and with all the power and authority we have can comment upon the evidence in his charge to the jury or during the trial without having some effect upon the jury.

Consequently, even though I have that right and power under the law . . . I never do it, and I don't intend to do it in this case. [If any jurors] have gotten the idea or feeling about how I feel about this case and the truthfulness of any witnesses . . . I want you to disregard it entirely. . . .

Then Sirica proceeded to read the transcript, including Maroulis' objections to questions that indicated Liddy and Sloan violated the campaign finance act in their dealings with the Mexican checks and the $199,000. Maroulis argued such violations were not at issue in the trial, and the prosecution withdrew the questions. Nonetheless Sirica read them to the jury.

In appealing McCord's conviction to the Circuit Court of Appeals for the District of Columbia, Maroulis accused Sirica of exceeding his authority in his use of the Sloan testimony. Although a trial judge has authority to interrogate witnesses, he must do so in a way that doesn't taint the court's impartiality in the eyes of the jury or intrude upon counsel's trial strategy. If the judge thinks a line of inquiry should be pushed, he should call lawyers to the bench, or into chambers, and suggest what he wants done. "That the judge may be able to examine a witness more skillfully than counsel does not ordinarily justify such participation," Maroulis argued. "In this case, the trial judge . . . cast himself in the light of a witness, thus lending the dignity and authority of his office to the words he read to the jury. . . . Sloan's demeanor while giving his testimony was not subject to the jury's observation. The testimony itself was not subject to objection or cross-examination."

Maroulis claimed two other instances of judicial error in his appeal for McCord. Sirica permitted attorney Douglas Caddy to testify that Liddy retained his services for himself, McCord and the Cuban-Americans about five o'clock the morning of the abortive burglary. In his jury instructions Sirica said the jury should draw no inferences from the fact that Liddy exercised his right to hire a lawyer but said it could "consider the time and other surrounding circumstances." Maroulis commented tartly in his appeals brief: "The right of counsel is not tied to the earth's rotation. There is nothing in the Sixth Amendment [which gives a person the right "to have the assistance of counsel for his defense"] to suggest that it is a protection available only between 9 A.M. and 5 P.M." The government retorted that since Liddy hired Caddy not only for himself but the five arrested burglars "he linked himself to these men and their act of burglary and created a rational conclusion that he had conspired with them." Maroulis also objected to Sirica's permitting Robert Bennett, a Washington public relations man, to testify that Liddy told him CREEP had fired him "because of his refusal to cooperate with the FBI" in the Watergate probe.

Sirica's frustration was aggravated when seemingly cooperative government witnesses, try though they might, could not remember all the Watergate details to which they had been privy. One such witness was Alfred Baldwin, a former FBI agent first recruited by CREEP as a security guard for Martha Mitchell, next assigned to help James McCord in the buggers' spy nest in a Howard Johnson Motel across from the Watergate complex. Baldwin, a willing witness, testified at length about helping monitor telephones in the Democratic headquarters. Baldwin said he prepared logs of conversations and usually gave them to McCord. But the one time Baldwin had a chance to tie the bugging directly to someone in CREEP other than McCord, his memory failed. In June, he said, McCord called him from Miami, told him to put what logs he had into an envelope, staple it closed, and deliver it to someone in CREEP.

Sirica had already sent the jury from the courtroom when Baldwin's testimony reached this point, saying, "I don't want them to imply anything or draw any inferences as a result of any questions I might propound." As he said several times during the trial, he repeated that he felt it "perfectly proper, and I think the duty of a judge . . . if he feels that all the facts have not been developed by either side . . . to ask questions in the interest of justice and in the interest of seeing that all of the facts are developed whether it hurts anybody or helps anybody." Then he took after Baldwin, first ascertaining that McCord "gave you the name of the party to whom the material was to be delivered, correct?"

BALDWIN: Yes, Your Honor.

SIRICA: You wrote the name of that party, correct?

BALDWIN: Yes, I did.

SIRICA: On the envelope. You personally took that envelope to the Committee to Re-Elect the President, correct?

BALDWIN: Yes, I did.

SIRICA: And you were under strict instructions from Mr. McCord to give it to the party that was named on the envelope, right?

BALDWIN: Yes.

SIRICA: What is the name of that party?

BALDWIN: I do not know, Your Honor.

SIRICA: You testified before this jury and have gone into great detail regarding the various things that transpired or happened insofar as your recollection is concerned, right?

BALDWIN: That is correct.

SIRICA: But you can't remember the name of the party to whom you delivered this particular log?

BALDWIN: No, sir.

Sirica finally gave up—convinced either that Baldwin didn't know the answer, or that he would not give it. And he indicated he did not think Baldwin was an unwitting participant in the plot as he claimed. He noted, for instance, that McCord insisted that Baldwin use an assumed name when he worked at the monitoring station. "Did that indicate to you some hanky-panky was going on, to use an old expression?" Sirica asked. "No, sir," Baldwin replied solemnly.

As the trial drew to a close virtually everyone still involved in it was in a sour mood. Reporters badgered prosecutor Silbert in courthouse corridors about his gingerly handling of the case. As a *Los Angeles Times* reporter wrote, "A clubby atmosphere has prevailed in federal court" during the three weeks of the trial. "The questioning of Republican officials and others has been more polite than penetrating. Entire areas have been left unprobed." Attorneys Maroulis, for Liddy, and Gerald Alch, for McCord, raged privately about Sirica's intrusion into the trial and on the last day, after the jury had returned guilty verdicts, Alch went public with his complaints. Sirica, Alch said, "did not limit himself to acting as a judge. He has become, in addition, a prosecutor and an investigator. Not only does he indicate that the defendants are guilty, but that a lot of other people are guilty. The whole courtroom is permeated with a prejudicial atmosphere." Alch claimed that Sirica committed at least nine errors that were a basis for reversal of McCord's conviction.*

The dourest party of all was Judge Sirica. Not only had he failed to crack the protective shell of the cover-up, but many of his longtime acquaintances in Washington chided him for "getting out of your place, and acting like an FBI agent, not a judge." One person asked Sirica at a party that winter—jokingly, but the bite was still there—whether "the McGovern people have hired you to try to reverse what happened in November."

So what does a judge do when he is criticized? The good ones react the same way they do to praise. They ignore what is said about them, for, as one judge told me, "You can't try cases looking over your shoulder at *anybody*." Not even if the case the judge is hearing gets close to a popular president of the United States —which Richard Nixon assuredly was in January 1973, when the original Watergate case was before Sirica.

Not that Sirica lacked unsolicited advice on how to handle the trial. People kept shoving the ABA standards for the judiciary into his face, quoting a section they thought applicable to the Watergate trial: "The

---

* Alch never got a chance to test his claim of reversible error with the court of appeals. A few weeks after the trial ended, McCord dropped Alch and retained Bernard Fensterwald, a Washington lawyer. In his appeal for McCord, Fensterwald accused prosecutor Silbert of knowingly permitting Jeb Magruder to give perjured testimony at the trial, and of withholding evidence.

only purpose of a criminal trial is to determine whether the prosecution has established the guilt of the accused as required by law, and the trial judge should not allow the proceedings to be used for any other purpose." John Sirica, of course, had read the ABA standards, as has every other trial judge in the Republic. And had he been asked, he could have pointed to two other sentences in that same section that people tend to skip over: "The trial judge has the responsibility for safeguarding both the rights of the accused and the interests of the public in the administration of criminal justice. The adversary nature of the proceedings does not relieve the trial judge of the obligation of raising on his own initiative, at all appropriate times and in an appropriate manner, matters which may significantly promote a just determination of the trial."

Thus what does a trial judge do when he's up against an obvious cover-up? The first thing is to try to bust into it during the trial, as Sirica did with his questions. If that doesn't work, he waits for the sentencing, the point in the trial when he can give defendants a true incentive for telling the truth—the difference between a long time in jail and being on the street in a hurry.

James McCord broke first. Disgust motivated him. Disgust at the attempts of higherups to shunt blame for the break-in onto the CIA, which he had served for nineteen years. Disgust of the perjured testimony of Jeb Magruder. Disgust of the people who lied to get him into Watergate, and now wanted him to lie to keep the scandal from going further. He typed out a 1,700 word letter and on March 20, three days before his scheduled sentencing, carried it into Judge Sirica's office. As he told the Ervin committee two months later, Sirica "is the lone man I felt like I could depend on in this case. . . . [T]he man is honest and genuine." The surprised judge encountered McCord in an outer office and quickly walked away (Sirica, as is true of most federal judges, as a matter of policy will not talk to a defendant who approaches him before sentencing). When Sirica's secretary reported that he wanted to hand-deliver a letter, the judge told him to take it to his probation officer, who was then busy with a presentencing report.

McCord's visit made Sirica uneasy. As he told friends later, "All sorts of things went through my mind. I wondered if they had put together some more of those famous one hundred dollar bills and stuffed an envelope so they could frame me. Should I receive any kind of letter from him at all outside a regular open hearing? What if it contained some stuff that he said I could not give to the prosecutor?" Sirica fretted around the office, wondering what to do—and also damnably curious, although he intuitively felt McCord's letter was the break he sought—and finally his judicial instincts took over. He called in the probation officer, his two law clerks, and a bailiff, and opened the letter and read it aloud as a court reporter took a formal record. As Sirica listened to McCord's letter he had to struggle to hold down the surge of self-satisfaction: the letter vindicated his courtroom skepticism, but it also signalled grave trouble for the American political system.

Expressing fears of "retaliatory measures against me, my family and my friends," McCord wrote he did not trust the Justice Department or other federal agencies but felt that the court should have "important information" about Watergate. McCord wrote that high officials put political pressure on the defendants "to plead guilty and remain silent." McCord wrote that witnesses perjured themselves during the trial to give a false motive for the Watergate crime. McCord wrote that "others involved in the Watergate operations were not identified during the trial, when they could have been by those testifying."

Sirica read the letter in open court three days later, when the defendants appeared for sentencing, and announced he was turning it over to the grand jury. Since McCord was now willing to testify to his full knowledge of the break-in conspiracy, Sirica deferred his sentencing. Sirica's badgering was finally producing results.

Next Sirica turned to the Cubans and Hunt, still adamantly silent in their grand jury appearances. Sirica didn't waste his time pleading with the five to testify. He said that based on the evidence he had heard "the court has reached the opinion that the crimes committed by these defendants can only be described as sordid, despicable and thoroughly reprehensible." Sirica said he had taken into account the purposes to be considered in imposing sentences:

. . . [I]n view of the foregoing, and taking into account the background of the defendants, it seems obvious to the court that rehabilitation is not the principal purpose to be served nor is it appropriate to impose sentence here with the intent of satisfying someone's desire for reprisal.

In this matter the sentence should be imposed with an eye towards just punishment for the grave offenses committed and toward the deterrent effect the sentences might have on other potential offenders.

Sirica then matter-of-factly read off the sentences, carefully labelling them as "provisional" as he did so: for the four Cuban-Americans, 40 years in prison; for Hunt, 35 years. He suggested again that they make full disclosures to the grand jury and to the Ervin committee, which was preparing for its own hearings. After three months, when the men returned for formal sentencing, he would "weigh as a factor" whether they gave "full cooperation" to the grand jury. Sirica did not say so directly, but he left the strong impression with the Cubans—and with many persons in the courtroom—that unless they did testify fully, he would not hesitate to make the provisional sentences the actual sentences (the terms he imposed were the maximum permitted under law). And Sirica tacitly admitted that the quest for the truth was now out of his hands:

Everybody knows that there is going to be a Congressional investigation. I would frankly hope, not only as a judge but as a citizen of a great country and one of millions of Americans who are looking for certain answers, I would hope that the Senate committee [will] get to the bottom of what happened in this case.

Some good can and should come from a revelation of sinister conduct whenever and wherever such conduct exists.

G. Gordon Liddy was another story. Regardless of what Sirica did, his lawyers let the judge know, he did not intend to talk. Peter Maroulis was confident he could win a reversal of the case because of Sirica's procedural errors. So Sirica made his sentence final: to serve at least six years, eight months and pay a fine of $40,000 before he is eligible for parole. Three days later Liddy refused to testify before the grand jury; Sirica granted him immunity from prosecution for any offenses the proof of which relied upon his testimony; Liddy still refused. So on April 24 Sirica held Liddy in contempt of court and ordered him confined until either he testified or the jury ended its term. (Since Liddy was already in jail the new term had limited punitive utility, although it would have kept him behind bars had the appeals court overturned the Watergate conviction.)

McCord's defection was the signal for the White House/CREEP conspirators to break ranks and run for cover. A steady procession of Nixon Administration underlings marched into the Justice Department and the Ervin committee to offer testimony about various political shysterism and to attempt to strike deals. John W. Dean, III. Jeb Stuart Magruder. John J. Caulfield. Frederick C. LaRue. Robert C. Mardian. Robert C. Odle, Jr. Herbert L. Porter. Names and faces the public learned from the television screens during the traumatic summer of 1973.

How much credit does Judge John Sirica deserve for breaking Watergate? Would the cover-up have collapsed of its own weight? Did not the tangled internal rivalries and fears of White House and CREEP staff members insure that eventually someone would break away from the conspiracy and tell all? Was not "breaking Watergate" a joint venture, with a host of players contributing? (For instance, Senator Robert F. Byrd, the West Virginia Democrat, winnowed admissions from L. Patrick Gray, during his confirmation hearing for the post of FBI director, that he destroyed documents taken from Hunt's safe, and that he warned Nixon of a possible cover-up within days after the burglary.) Were not the prosecutors correct in their strategy to try the actual perpetrators of the burglary first, then force them to testify against higherups later by granting them immunity from further prosecution? Would not the Ervin committee have smoked the truth from witnesses, however reluctant?

Perhaps. But perhaps not. Sirica's strength was that he acted with the authority of law and with the prestige of the institution he represented. His open skepticism gave a tone of legitimacy to criticism of the Watergate investigation; no longer could the questioners be dismissed as "the hostile media" and "Nixon-hating politicians." Sirica's command of the case brought forth "respectable" critics of the Nixon Administration who would support a constitutional confrontation with the President, but not one motivated by partisan politics.

As overseer of the continuing grand jury investigation, Judge Sirica remained immersed in Watergate matters as the case wore on. Careful to keep his own feelings private, time and again he issued rulings that brought the scandal closer to the White House, and made continuing cover-up more difficult. When John Dean broke with the White House he squirreled away incriminating documents (on the enemies' list and the extra-constitutional White House secret police, among other things) in a bank safe deposit box and gave the key to Sirica. When White House lawyers howled for the return of the papers, Sirica not only refused, he gave copies to the Ervin committee and the grand jury. Acceding to a request from Ervin, he granted limited immunity * so Dean and Jeb Ma-

---

* Under the limited immunity Dean and Magruder could not be prosecuted solely on the basis of information they gave

gruder could testify publicly at the Senate. And Sirica denied a prosecution motion to bar live television and radio coverage of the Ervin hearings, thereby literally bringing the Watergate mess into every home in the nation. These cases, however, served as a mere prelude for the court battle that dropped the Nixon Administration into a "fire storm" of public fury, to use the words of presidential assistant Alexander Haig —the tapes controversy.

In July both the Ervin committee and Special Prosecutor Archibald Cox learned that most of Nixon's White House meetings and phone conversations had been secretly recorded since the spring of 1971. Tapes of these talks would be vital evidence in establishing who knew what facts about Watergate and when— whether, in fact, Nixon himself knew a cover-up was under way as early as September 15, 1972, when he supposedly congratulated John Dean for "containing" the case at the level of G. Gordon Liddy. Both the committee and Cox demanded that the tapes be produced for inspection, the White House flatly refused on the grounds of executive privilege, and the battle was joined.† Cox called upon Sirica to enforce his subpena for nine tapes from the immediate post-Watergate period through April 1973, when Nixon finally admitted publicly he indeed did have a problem in his official family.

So Watergate moved from the grubby details of burglary, bugging and campaign finance chicanery to the somewhat loftier level of constitutional debate, with Sirica listening solemnly as White House lawyers and the Cox team tossed around such balancing authorities as Locke, Montesquieu, the Federalist papers, and the thirteenth-century British author Henry de Bracton (who wrote, as Cox emphatically

---

the committee. If prosecutors got identical evidence elsewhere, however, it could be used against them.

† Sirica nudged the Ervin committee out of the race very early, saying, in effect, the courts would not interfere in a fight between the legislative and executive branches. But Cox, who was pursuing a criminal investigation, was another matter indeed.

quoted, "The king ought not to be under any man—but he is under God, and the law"). Charles Alan Wright, the towering Texas law professor representing Nixon, argued that a president was "beyond the process of any court." Wright evoked the spectre of any of 400-odd federal district judges commandeering presidential papers on the slightest of whims: "That, I submit, sir, is a frightening prospect."

Sirica listened, gathered up the voluminous briefs and a small library of law books, and secluded himself, first at his family's vacation retreat on the Delaware coast, then at his home in suburban Maryland. The importance of the decision made Sirica edgy; insomnia drove him from his bed in the middle of the night, and he sat alone at his desk and scratched away at a legal pad with a pencil, revising and rewriting. "The worst part about being a trial judge is having to sit down and play like you're an appellate judge and write some long windy opinion," Sirica had complained to a lawyer friend in pre-Watergate days. "I'd rather take a licking than do the book work. Maybe I should hire a ghostwriter."

Sirica needed no ghostwriter in the tapes case. His opinion, handed down August 29, was an erudite and forceful refutation of the White House claim of executive privilege. Sirica found no constitutional basis for executive privilege:

> In all candor, the court fails to perceive any reason for suspending the power of the courts to get evidence and rule on questions of privilege in criminal matters simply because it is the president of the United States who holds the evidence.

Sirica's chief points:

- The judiciary, not the executive, must finally determine whether privilege is being properly invoked.
- The premise is well-established that the grand jury has a right to every man's evidence, "and that for purposes of gathering evidence, process may issue to anyone. . . . What distinctive quality of the

presidency permits its incumbent to withhold evidence? To argue that the need for presidential privacy justifies it is not persuasive. . . ."
- "That the court has not the physical power to enforce its order to the president is immaterial to a resolution of the issues." Sirica pointedly noted that President Truman obeyed the Supreme Court in 1952 when it declared void his seizure of the steel mills, and said "there is no reason to suppose that the courts in this instance cannot again rely on the same good faith."
- Sirica quoted at length from the description, in Cox's subpena, of a meeting in Nixon's office on September 15, 1972, the day of the Watergate indictments. Dean and White House aide H. R. (Bob) Haldeman gave starkly different versions of the meeting to the Ervin committee. Sirica quoted Cox's assertion that evidence before the grand jury had raised "a substantial possibility" that Nixon claimed executive privilege "as a cloak for serious criminal wrongdoings." The grand jury's showing of need for the tapes he called "well documented and imposing."

In deciding how the tapes should be reviewed Sirica chose a middle course between the White House claim of absolute privilege and "wholesale delivery of the tapes to the grand jury." He ordered Nixon to surrender the tapes for his own private *in camera* inspection, so that he could cull out any material not relevant to the criminal investigation. If privileged and unprivileged material were "so inextricably connected that separation becomes impossible," he would withhold the tapes; otherwise, they would go to the grand jury.

That Sirica agonized over the opinion, and that he wanted his decision cast in a manner designed to gain public support, is evidenced by his use of a question as the concluding sentence. Regardless of what the tapes contained, "would it not be a blot on the page which records the judicial proceedings of this country if, in a case of such serious import as this, the court did not at least call for an inspection of the evidence in chambers?"

The White House's immediate, rather snippish answer was that the president "will not comply with this order," and that it might ignore it altogether, without even appealing. Wiser heads prevailed; a few days later the White House did go to the Circuit Court of Appeals for the District of Columbia, asking that Sirica be reversed. The White House position hardened even further, with lawyer Wright propounding the claim that even if Nixon was engaged in a criminal conspiracy, he could refuse to produce the tapes. "That no president can be indicted before he is impeached is as clear as anything can be. It is not for the courts or the grand jury to say, 'Mr. President, we don't believe you; we think you're a criminal.' "

The circuit judges strained to force a compromise —to avoid what J. Anthony Lukas, writing in *The New York Times Magazine*, called a "constitutional apocalypse." The seven judges asked the lawyers to go over the tapes together to see if they could decide what material should be given the grand jury. Three days of negotiations got nowhere; on October 12 the court sided five-to-two * with Cox and ordered that the tapes be given Sirica for examination. The opinion was a resounding affirmation of Sirica's decision: "Though the president is elected by nationwide ballot and is often said to represent all the people, he does not embody the nation's sovereignty. He is not above the law's commands."

Scrambling desperately to retain control of the tapes without openly defying the courts, Nixon proposed giving summaries of their contents to the aged and friendly Senator John Stennis (D., Miss.), who would decide whether they should be passed on to the grand jury. Cox refused to go along, and the infamous Saturday Night Massacre followed: the discharge of Cox, and the forced resignations of Attorney General Elliot Richardson and his deputy,

---

* The dissenting votes came from two Nixon appointees, Judges George E. MacKinnon and Malcolm R. Wilkey.

William Ruckelshaus. With an outraged nation shouting "Impeachment!" and an avalanche of protest sweeping down upon the White House, Nixon finally realized he had committed one of the more egregious misreadings of public opinion in American political history. And someone in the White House finally got around to reminding the president and his lawyers that the flint-eyed Judge Sirica had a hearing scheduled for Tuesday afternoon on enforcement of his order to surrender the tapes.

An unfailingly fascinating Washington game throughout Watergate has been: What would happen if . . . ? The "if" that October weekend was a White House refusal to obey Sirica's order—for lawyer Fred Buzhardt to come into court and tell the judge, in effect —go shove it, we aren't giving you any tapes. Given his natural civic curiosity John Sirica well might have pondered the White House's possible response himself that weekend. And only minimal imagination is required to project *his* probable reaction had the White House ignored his orders.

There's nothing mysterious about how a judge enforces an order; it's all spelled out in the federal rules of procedure. If the person named in the order doesn't obey, the judge tells him to come to court and show cause why he shouldn't be cited for contempt. If he appears, the judge holds a hearing and listens to his explanation; if it isn't valid, he is cited for contempt. If the person does not appear, he is cited for contempt.

For a judge who is a stickler for procedural regularity, the so-called "compromise" plan under which Stennis was to screen a summary of the tapes had no standing whatsoever, for it lacked one essential element: Cox, the man suing the White House, did not agree to the "compromise." In a legal proceeding, how is an out-of-court settlement possible when one of the parties to the suit does not agree?

Constitutional scholars—and many other persons totally unlearned in the law—had a secondary guessing game the same weekend: OK, suppose Sirica does

cite Nixon for contempt. How does he enforce his
order? Surely he won't attempt to send a United
States marshal over to the White House to attempt to
arrest the president?

Again, the logical answer is found in the procedural
process. John Sirica, who has read the Constitution,
knows that disciplinary actions against a president
originate in the House of Representatives, through
impeachment proceedings. Sirica prides himself on
running an efficient court; if the House made a reasonable and legitimate request of him—for instance, a
record of the tapes dispute, and his contempt finding
—Sirica would have supplied them. And if the House
chose to enforce his contempt finding as a part of
an impeachment proceeding, he had no legal grounds
to object.

At two o'clock the afternoon of October 23, with
the weekend's "fire storm" of citizen outrage still
ablaze, Charles Alan Wright came to Sirica's court
ostensibly to argue for acceptance of the Stennis plan.
Instead, Wright arose and announced that the White
House intended to obey Sirica's original order and
surrender the nine tapes for *in camera* inspection, the
exact course of action which Archibald Cox had been
fired for insisting upon 72 hours earlier. But Wright,
who is a good lawyer, kept a straight face. "The
president," he said, "does not defy the law." James
Reston put it more pithily in *The New York Times* the
next day: Nixon "has saved his skin but not his
honor."

So ended the first phase of the tapes saga—a
controversy that was to sputter on for months, each
new round putting a new strain on Sirica's thinly-
stretched patience. First, the White House told Sirica
that two of the nine tapes—the most avidly sought
pieces of physical evidence in the entire Watergate
case—did not even exist: one conversation occurred
on a weekend, after the tape spools were empty; another, between the president and John Mitchell, was
over a phone not connected to the system. When the
White House brought in the seven tapes that could
be found, Fred Buzhardt, the White House counsel,

embarrassedly told Sirica one of them contained an eighteen-and-one-half-minute buzz—precisely the period that Nixon and aide H. R. Haldeman talked about Watergate during a meeting on June 20, 1972, immediately after Haldeman had received a report from John Mitchell on the June 17 break-in.

Why in heaven's name, asked the exasperated Sirica, had the White House waited weeks to "discover" such an important gap?

Buzhardt argued that Cox's original request called only for the tape of a single meeting: "Meeting of June 20, 1972, in the President's EOB [Executive Office Building] office between the president and Messrs. Ehrlichman and Haldeman from 10:30 A.M. to 1:00 P.M. (approximate)." In a later memo filed with Sirica, Cox further refined the request to include a meeting "from 10:30 A.M. until approximately 12:45 P.M." during which "Ehrlichman and then Haldeman went in to see the president." Buzhardt said he was not aware of this latter description until after the tape gap was discovered; White House thinking, he said, was that Cox wanted only the Ehrlichman portion of the meeting. Buzhardt's explanation left Sirica openly skeptical: "You mean to say it takes a careful reading of that paragraph to conclude that the subpena called for the conversation of Mr. Haldeman and Mr. Ehrlichman?"

"In my opinion," replied Buzhardt, "it takes a very careful reading."

Nor could the White House come up with an explanation for the gap. Rose Mary Woods, Nixon's longtime personal secretary, first said she might have accidentally caused the gap. While transcribing the tape, she said, she paused to answer the telephone. She speculated she might have unwittingly left her foot on the floor pedal and created a gap. But later Miss Woods insisted the phone conversation lasted only "four or five minutes," not the full eighteen and one-half minutes. And in trying to reenact the "accident" she went into a spread-eagled, feet-askew contortion to clutch a phone to her shoulder while simultaneously depressing the foot pedal some seven-

and-a-half-feet distant. Alexander Haig, Nixon's close aide, opined in court that at one time he believed "some sinister force" was responsible for the gap.

Sirica, however, suspected earthly demons, not supernatural ones. Unsatisfied with the White House's lame explanations, he appointed six outside experts (three suggested by the prosecutors, three by Buzhardt) to see if they could determine what happened. Two months later the experts had a cause, if not the responsible parties: five separate erasures, all done manually, and not by Miss Woods' foot pedal. At a January 15 hearing White House lawyer James St. Clair objected repeatedly at prosecution attempts to get the experts to say whether the erasures were "deliberate" or "accidental." "That's just what I would like to know, too," Sirica interjected. But he sustained St. Clair's objections on the grounds that the experts could not answer with certainty. Waving at a mass of 2,800 pages of testimony and almost 200 exhibits, Sirica turned the matter over to the grand jury, saying there was a "distinct possibility on the part of one or more persons . . . of unlawful tampering with or suppression of evidence."

At a social event that weekend Sirica remarked at an ironic juxtaposition of dates: in January 1973 "I was working my butt off trying to get to the bottom of a cover-up. A year later, here I am, still working my butt off on the same case. . . . But the case gets a little more interesting all the time."

March 1, 1974. John J. Sirica, his cragged features locked into his working-day-bland judicial poker face, flipped through the 41 pages of the indictment that had just been handed up to him by the court bailiff. Twenty of the 23 grand jurors who had actively pursued the Watergate truth for seventeen months sat self-consciously in the front of the courtroom, anonymous faces among the kinetic bustle of lawyers, newsmen and citizen spectators. Sirica went through the names. Mitchell. Haldeman. Ehrlichman. Colson. Parkinson. Mardian. Strachan.

Sirica did not grant himself the luxury of a well-earned smile. A United States district court judge had simply done the work that goes with his office. And the nation moved another step closer to the final Götterdammerung *of Watergate.*

American institutions, be they private corporations or governmental agencies, often function as they should because of the lubricant of sheer luck. So be it, in a sense, with the Watergate affair. A nondescript district judge—a man accorded professional esteem by neither his colleagues nor the lawyers who practice before him, with self-acknowledged intellectual and judicial shortcomings, faithful to the political party that put him in office, in the twilight of his career: the qualities, in sum, of a judge who could just as easily have shrugged and tried a burglary case and spent his last active year on the bench in make-work (Sirica marked his 70th birthday a few days before the omnibus Watergate indictments were returned and thus surrended the chief judgeship). But, as we have seen, John Sirica chose quite another course.

Such is not the case for two other district judges who handled cases peripheral to the Watergate matter. According to sworn testimony before the Ervin committee, both men engaged in conduct which tarnishes their judicial integrity; a look at them briefly, for the total federal judiciary did not always match the independence and courage of John Sirica.

In April 1973 the Nixon Administration realized that L. Patrick Gray's admissions that he destroyed evidence in the Watergate case doomed his chances for confirmation as FBI director. The trial of Pentagon Papers figure Daniel Ellsberg was in progress in Los Angeles before District Judge W. Matthew Byrne, Jr., a second-generation jurist (his father is a senior judge in the same district) who was a highly-regarded Democratic United States attorney before Nixon put him on the bench in 1969. Casting around for a replacement for the lamented Gray, Nixon, John Mitchell and John Ehrlichman decided upon Byrne. By Ehrlichman's account, he telephoned Byrne and said:

Judge, I have been asked by the President to call you. I have been asked to discuss with you a federal appointment which is not judicial in character. I do not know whether this is an appropriate time for us to have a conversation like this because I do not know what the present situation in your trial is.

According to Ehrlichman, he told Byrne the matter was not urgent, whereupon the judge replied, "I see no reason why we couldn't talk right now." They made an appointment to meet at four o'clock the same afternoon at the presidential compound at San Clemente. Ehrlichman continued:

When he came into my office I said again, "I am sensitive to the fact that you are trying an important lawsuit. I propose that we take a walk out toward the bluff from my office. If at any point a subject arises that you feel in any way impinges upon your ability to fairly try the case you just turn around and walk away from me and, as I said before, this is not something that needs to be discussed right now. We can talk about it later without prejudice."

He said, "Fine, let's proceed on that basis." So we did.

We walked out to the bluff and back and it was a conversation of perhaps five minutes total. The gist . . . was that I advised him it was the President's conclusion that he was going to have to resubmit a nomination for director of the FBI, that he was interested in knowing whether or not Judge Byrne had an interest in the position. If he did, then obviously any decision on the President's part as to a nomination would finally be the President's, but that it would be helpful to know of his interest.

The judge indicated a very strong interest. He told me a number of his experiences with the FBI . . . he had some ideas about how the bureau was falling short, some ideas about how it might be improved . . . he gave me an expression of very clear interest.

As Ehrlichman and Byrne walked back towards the office area Nixon came out of his own office. Ehrlichman said he "didn't know the judge apparently," and so they were introduced. "They chatted just very briefly, not about the case obviously but about just pleasantries. Their conversation lasted perhaps 30 seconds, and the President went back in his office." As Byrne left, Ehrlichman told him "obviously the President has to reserve his options completely as to whether there is an offer to you or not."

The next afternoon, according to Ehrlichman, Byrne telephoned him, said he had given "a lot of thought" to the conversation, and asked to talk with him again. They made an appointment to meet the following day in Palisades Park in Santa Monica.

> We had a short walk during which he again evidenced very strong interest. He did not press me for an offer. When we . . . finished with the conversation, which again took about five, no more than ten minutes, he got in his car and left. Again no offers had been made, no acceptances, but I took this as an occasion when he wanted to restate his very strong interest . . . in the position.

Senator Daniel Inouye (D., Hawaii), noting the White House's strong interest in the Ellsberg case, asked Ehrlichman whether he felt it was proper to call upon the presiding judge to make this offer. "Didn't you feel it was highly improper, unethical?"

Ehrlichman didn't think so. He said he had "scoured the canons of ethics" for any section he might have violated, and found none.* He claimed he talked to Byrne as the "the President's agent," not as a lawyer, and that "I take some comfort from the fact that I did this with the full knowledge of the Attorney General of the United States." Ehrlichman admitted

---

* Senator Ervin referred him to the catchall canon providing, "The attorney is under duty not to impair the confidence of the public and the integrity of the judiciary."

that he was "sensitive" about the conversation "as anyone would be, because I was not personally as familiar with the progress of that trial as you evidently were from the reading of the press. I had to depend on the judge to tell me the proprieties in this matter." Ehrlichman argued that every federal judge in the country has a case involving the government on his docket. "It may be that the logical implication of what you suggest," he told Inouye, "is that the executive branch should never offer a federal judge a position."

"But this was not an ordinary case," Inouye rejoined. He said that talking to Byrne directly, without going through either government or defense lawyers in the case, was "impropriety squared."

After Ehrlichman's testimony Byrne issued a statement taking heated issue with his account of the contact. Byrne said he repeatedly told Ehrlichman he could not discuss the FBI directorship during the trial. Nonetheless Byrne could not explain away the fact that the approach had been made, and that he said nothing to Ellsberg's lawyers about it. The episode was first revealed by Jeremiah O'Leary of the *Washington Star–News* during the last days of the Ellsberg trial. O'Leary has strong contacts in the FBI (the late director J. Edgar Hoover frequently used him as a conduit to the public) and the general assumption in Washington at the time was that someone in the bureau leaked the information to taint Byrne, thereby keeping him from the directorship. Byrne eventually had to dismiss the prosecution because of the burglary of Ellsberg's psychiatrist's office—a mission, as charged in later indictments, that Ehrlichman approved. (In July 1974 a federal court jury in Washington found Ehrlichman guilty of the charges.).

Byrne's conduct brought biting *sotto voce* comment from West Coast lawyers. One lawyer long active in state and national bar activities told me, "Why Byrne doesn't have the decency to resign is beyond me. I know I'll never have any respect for him again. But, again, a lawyer doesn't go around making stump speeches on the subject, because we have to practice here."

The other jurist whose handling of a Watergate-related case raises serious questions is Judge Charles Richey of Washington, appointed to the bench by Nixon in 1971. Richey came to Washington in 1948 as an aide to an Ohio Republican congressman, practiced corporate law in the Maryland suburbs, befriended and supported Spiro T. Agnew in politics there, and (by reliable report) asked the then-Vice President point blank to get him a judgeship. Agnew obliged.* So what has he done to show his appreciation?

After the Watergate break-in the Democratic National Committee filed a million dollar law suit against CREEP. Richey was assigned the case, and he talked as if he wished to push it to rapid resolution. "I think there is . . . a suggestion implicit in all of this [Watergate] that if something is not done by the courts to rapidly bring this situation to a head one way or another, by settlement or trial, that the integrity of the courts may become subject to question," Richey said at a hearing in late August.

Three weeks later, Richey flatly reversed his momentum, ordering a halt in the taking of depositions until September 20. The depositions were important because Democratic lawyers were using them to get information about covert CREEP financing of various campaign dirty tricks. On September 22 Richey halted proceedings altogether until after the criminal trials.

What happened between August and September that persuaded Richey to put off the case until after the election—thereby denying the public what could have been vital information about Watergate?

According to John Dean, who was White House

---

* A year later, when a *Washington Post* reporter queried Richey about his relationship with Agnew—in the course of an interview stressing Richey's "independence" from the administration that gave him his judicial job—he replied painfully, "I wish you wouldn't ask me that." He went on to say he would "always appreciate [Agnew's] help in enabling me to achieve a lifelong ambition to be a trial judge."

counsel at the time, Richey listened to *sub rosa* administration requests that he put off the suit until after November. A key figure, by Dean's testimony, was a Washington lawyer named Roemer McPhee, one of CREEP's attorneys. Dean told the Ervin committee that he learned in early September that "McPhee was having private discussions with Judge Richey regarding the civil suits filed by the Democrats." Dean said he reported to Nixon on September 15 that "the lawyers down at the reelection committee were very hopeful of slowing down [the Democratic suit] because they had been making *ex parte* contacts with the judge handling the case and the judge was very understanding and trying to accommodate their problems." According to Dean, "The President was pleased to hear this and responded, 'Well, that's helpful.'" * Dean said he learned of these contacts in a meeting in the office of Attorney General Mitchell; he said that "Judge Richey was going to be helpful wherever he could." As late as March 1973, Dean testified, "Mr. McPhee . . . told me he was going to visit the judge in the judge's rose garden over the weekend to discuss an aspect of the case."

H. R. Haldeman, who was at the September 15 meeting, confirmed the thrust of Dean's testimony: "There was some discussion about Judge Richey hearing the civil case and a comment that he would keep Roemer McPhee abreast of what was happening." But Haldeman denied any recollection that Richey was "trying to accommodate Dean's hopes of slowing down the suit."

Both Richey and the CREEP attorneys strongly denied any *ex parte* contacts, and the Democrats in 1974 tentatively agreed to settle the suit for more than $700,000. Thus no evidentiary test has been made of Dean's charge that a United States district judge delayed a civil trial for political reasons.

---

* A transcript of the September 15 meeting released by the White House on April 30, 1974, confirmed Dean's account of the conversation about Richey, with one exception. The transcript does not contain Nixon's supposed remark, "Well, that's helpful."

plate, YA-13, and turned back to Chandler for guidance.

Chandler stood with his hands on the back of his car, beaming delightedly. "Every time I see that license plate," he said, "I say to myself YAAAAAA-AAAY THIRTEEEEEEEEN!!!"

Judge Chandler's yell—yell, hell, a bellow—didn't echo, for that part of Oklahoma City is too flat for sound to find a solid surface from which to bounce. But a flock of pigeons that had been picking through the curbside debris for breakfast left in a hurry; a block and a half away, two guys standing on the corner turned and gawked; and one of the courthouse security guards peeked through the front door glass for the source of the racket.

I stared at Chandler, speechless.

"YA-13," he said. "The thirteenth is my birthday. Everytime I see that license plate, I think of my birthday."

"Oh," I said, and we got into Judge Chandler's white 1973 Cadillac convertible and drove away for breakfast.

That the sight of a license plate would so emotionally stir a United States district judge that he yells in a public street is a happening that, if isolated, could be dismissed as amusing, harmless eccentricity. *Yes, yes, Chandler, a bit exuberant, isn't he?* Chandler, however, finds hidden significance in many happenings around him, and he is besieged by diverse demons. He is convinced, according to what he has sworn in court papers and elsewhere, that he has been the target of "a long existing criminal conspiracy" for the entire three decades he has been on the bench. The changing cast of tormentors, by Chandler's charges, has included judges both of his own court and of the Tenth Circuit Court of Appeals; two United States attorneys; a state prosecutor; some of the most prominent lawyers in Oklahoma City; such public figures as Armand Hammer, the board chairman of Occidental Petroleum Corporation, and a man who negotiates billion-dollar trade deals with the Soviet Union; and even his own court aides. At one time, Chandler alleges, he was so fearful of the conspirators that "I finally got to the point where I wondered if I had better drink out of my water carafe" —lest he be poisoned. He had court aides shuffle three or four cars daily to the court so he could choose which to drive home, thereby foiling any attempted bombing. He felt that Chief Judge Albert P. Murrah of the circuit court and Judge Luther Bohanon of the district court deliberately harassed him in the expectation he would "retire or drop dead, one or the other."

Chandler hurled these charges—none of which he has substantiated—during the course of a series of turbulent controversies that has kept the court in incessant turmoil for more than a decade. "The Chandler Case," as the judge's many woes are summarized in legal circles—"The Chandler Mess" is just as accurate—encompasses both civil and criminal charges. The judge was stripped (temporarily, it proved) of his authority to handle cases. He was indicted in state court (and cleared) of a charge he used public funds and equipment to build streets in one of his real estate developments. On two occasions his detested adversary, the Tenth Circuit Court of Appeals, ordered him out of major cases: once for conflict of interest, once for misconduct. Chandler and a combative Oklahoma City lawyer named W. H. Pat O'Bryan chased one another through state and federal courts for years to achieve off-setting apocalyptic verdicts: Chandler succeeded in disbarring O'Bryan, but O'Bryan succeeded in winning a libel verdict from a state court jury (and $50,000 damages) from Chandler.*

Outside the view of the general public, Chandler wrestled with other grave problems. His real estate

---

* Keeping track of the Chandler-O'Bryan litigation is akin to watching a Ping-Pong game played with four balls simultaneously. In the space of a month in early 1974 O'Bryan won a key decision in the libel case from the circuit appeals court, only to have Chandler gain a rehearing on the point and persuade the judges to reverse themselves. Both parties have made plain, however, that regardless of the outcome at the circuit court level, the Supreme Court will be asked to review the case and make a final decision.

ventures kept him heavily in debt—so much so, in fact, that a nervous bank permitted him to continue pyramiding long overdue loans only because of his judicial office. Investigators used such words as "questionable" and "inconsistent" in describing Chandler's financial statements. In 1965 Chandler became so periodically strapped for cash that in at least one instance a creditor had to go to court to collect $69,000 due on one of the judge's land purchases. Chandler had official dealings with the bank (the First National Bank and Trust Company, of Oklahoma City) as well. For instance, he made the institution the repository for millions of dollars in funds involved in a bankruptcy action pending in his court.

The fact that a public official, even a judge, is a controversial figure is no barrier to his continuing in office. Nonetheless, the Chandler case does raise intriguing problems. What confidence can the citizenry have in a judge who is continuously caught up in feuds with other persons in the community? Can such problems be so distracting to a judge that he cannot function? The American Bar Association's Canons of Judicial Ethics provide in part, "A judge's official conduct should be free of impropriety and the appearance of impropriety; he should avoid infractions of law; and his personal behavior, not only upon the bench and in the performance of judicial duties, but also in his everyday life, should be beyond reproach." Although the ABA Canons have no more legal force than the bylaws of a neighborhood PTA, should not a judge accept them as an expression by the organized bar of the standards that are expected of jurists, and adhere to them? And finally, short of impeachment, what disciplinary action can, or should, be taken against a judge who has repeatedly lost control of himself?

"The Chandler Case" involves a single judge, a man virtually unknown publicly outside his own state; but it is important for several reasons. It is one of the few instances where such voluminous material on a judge's personal and official conduct is in the public domain (chiefly because of Chandler's ongoing litiga-

tion). It is a striking demonstration of just how powerful a federal judge can be when he decides to bring
the full force of his office crashing down upon an
adversary—and how the judiciary establishment, in
turn, can wage its own counteroffensive against what
it considers to be a rogue judge. And it is—or should
be, at any instance—a chilling reminder of the chaos
that can ensue when justice goes awry.

To his admirers—and they are many, both elsewhere in the federal judiciary and in the United States
Senate—Stephen Chandler is the embattled personification of judicial independence. In their view the only
discipline permissible for a federal judge is impeachment. Further, because the House Judiciary Committee looked at Chandler with impeachment in mind,
and found no actionable charges, he should be immune from proceedings elsewhere. These supporters
found particularly appalling the attempt by the Tenth
Circuit Judicial Conference to strip Chandler of his
powers as a trial judge. Because of Chandler's many
eccentricities, some outsiders find it difficult to understand why so many judges formed protective ranks
around him. The answer, of course, is that if the wall
of "judicial independence" is breached at any point,
the entire concept could collapse. And throughout his
many troubles Chandler has fervently—and consistently—argued that the core issue is that of judicial
independence.

In Chandler's view each of his troubles stems directly from the "conspiracy" that, first, sought to deny
him appointment to the bench and, then, to make life
so miserable for him that he would resign (presum-
ably leaving the Oklahoma City federal court dominated by his enemies). The reasons Chandler has
never specified in public, and his admirers tend to
take his charges at face value. They simply rally
around Chandler as a fierce defender of judicial independence. As Chief Judge Martin Pence of the Hawaii
federal court mused not long ago in a letter to
Chandler, "Even among the judiciary, the lambs are
many, the lions are few. I am thankful that we have
still that lion, Stephen S. Chandler, to roar from his

Oklahoma den." Chandler's personal zoological image of himself is yet another feline, the tiger. At one stage of his fight, Clarence Allen, the *Tulsa Tribune* cartoonist, sketched a dripping-wet and most angry tiger labelled "Chandler Case" on the doorstep of the Tenth Circuit Judicial Conference, a weight tied to his neck. In the window a worried judge is whispering to a colleague, "Doesn't look like the tabby cat we kicked out." The cartoon so pleased Chandler that he distributes enlarged prints to visitors. "Just call me," Chandler said during one of our chats, " 'The Tiger Who Drinks Wild Turkey.' " "Wild Turkey?" I asked. "Sure," Chandler said. "You know, Wild Turkey Kentucky Bourbon. My favorite." "Oh," I replied.

Political and personal hatreds of three decades duration are at the core of the Chandler controversy. Chandler and his principal adversary, Alfred P. Murrah, longtime chief judge for the Tenth Circuit Court of Appeals (and now director of the Federal Judicial Center in Washington) are the judicial equivalents of street-brawlers. A confidential report of the House Judiciary Committee once said that each of them "is domineering, strongly individualistic, and self-confident to a point of stubbornness . . . quick to take offense at real or imagined interferences in the business of court management."

One apparent sore point to Chandler is the fact that Murrah, although his chronological junior by five years, went on the bench earlier and attained a more prestigious office. Murrah, born in 1904, was only 32 years old when President Roosevelt appointed him to the United States District Court in January 1937, one of the youngest men ever to receive a federal judicial appointment. Three years later he moved up to the circuit court. Murrah's political sponsor was Joshua Bryan Lee, congressman from Oklahoma from 1935 to 1937, United States senator through 1943, and a member of the Civil Aeronautics Board until 1957. Lee then joined what had been Murrah's law firm years earlier. Another of Murrah's partners was Luther Bohanon, later a federal judge himself, and central in several of the "Chandler Case" incidents.

Chandler had a considerably tougher time getting on the federal bench. In 1940 there were three Oklahoma vacancies to be filled. Senator Josh Lee proposed Royce Savage and Bower Broaddus; Senator Elmer Thomas wanted Chandler. (Some months later Thomas told the *Oklahoma City Times* that Chandler had given $2,500 to his campaign, "more than anyone else," and that he felt an obligation of loyalty to him.) The agreement was that all three names would be submitted as a package. The Justice Department, however, let it be known in advance of the formal nominations that it was cool toward Chandler. The stated reason was that he had not been an active trial lawyer ("more a businessman and operator than an attorney," as one person described him) and that his personal background deserved close scrutiny. Chandler, however, felt the real problem was covert opposition from Senator Lee and persons close around him. The supposed reasons are vague: Chandler suggests, without saying so directly, that attorneys and judges friendly to Lee—Bohanon and Murrah, among others —wanted to control the federal courts, and that he (Chandler) was "too independent." Too, Chandler's law partner had run against Lee in a congressional primary a few years earlier. Whatever the reasons, it became obvious that although Savage and Broaddus could be approved, Chandler would cause problems. And at this point Chandler's suspicions about hidden opposition were reinforced when Judge Murrah, a circuit court judge for only a few months, went to Washington at the request of the chief judge to persuade Senator Thomas that the case backlog in Oklahoma was so large that the vacancies should be filled as rapidly as possible. Thomas agreed to break the package and let Chandler stand or fall on his own merits. Broaddus and Savage were formally nominated and confirmed in swift order, in October 1940. Chandler's name did not go forward until December 1940, too late for action during that congressional session. He was renominated the next year and then for almost two years the nomination hung in limbo, with no action to either reject or approve his appointment.

In the meanwhile serious charges were developed against Chandler. It was alleged to the Senate Judiciary Committee that Chandler had assaulted a stenographer in his law office about ten o'clock one evening in 1937. An Oklahoma City physician, Dr. Dewey H. Walden, wrote the committee that there was no evidence of sexual assault, although the girl was slightly bruised and had a displaced nasal cartilage, which he classified as a "minor injury." Chandler denied any assault, although he did admit to the committee that he paid the girl $3,000 to settle the matter.

During the fall of 1942, when he had almost abandoned hope of the bench, Chandler asserts that he received a visit from Luther Bohanon, Judge Murrah's friend and onetime law partner. Chandler felt Bohanon was working in the campaign to keep him off the bench, providing derogatory information to Washington. By Chandler's account:

> Mr. Bohanon came over and wanted to see me. I didn't know him well, but I knew who he was and he said, "You understand that I could get you appointed tomorrow, don't you?"
>
> And I said, "I am certain of it."
>
> "Well," he said, "I can, and if you will give me twenty-five thousand dollars I will do it."
>
> So I stood up then—I guess I was as crazy as I am now—I could be lulled into doing a lot of things, but I can't stand anything like that. I stood up and said, "Bohanon, you fellows have done everything but kill me. You have tried to ruin my business. You have tried to destroy my character. You have tried to ruin my family. You have done everything but kill me and, by golly, you haven't got the guts to do that. Now, Mr. Bohanon, get out." And he didn't walk away slowly.

In recounting this alleged episode, Chandler stated, "I always considered Judge Murrah as the brains behind it." Both Judge Murrah and Bohanon vigorously deny ever trying to solicit funds from Chandler in connection with his appointment. As Bohanon has noted, at the time of the alleged incident he was in the army in either Salt Lake City or Denver.

When Chandler's nomination finally reached the Senate floor on May 10, 1943, Senator William Langer (R., N.D.) opposed him on the basis of his prior conduct, particularly the alleged assault on the secretary. Langer noted the $3,000 settlement.

Apparently he chose to do this rather than to resist a determination of the issue in court. I do not pass any judgement as to the truth or falsity of the charge made. . . . I do not know why Mr. Chandler chose to pay this sum of money. He might have done so for the obvious reason of avoiding embarrassment or publicity, although innocent. If he did, it would not be an isolated instance. But, as I view it, it indicated a weakness of character that would serve to disqualify him for this appointment. Of course, if he settled the case for other reasons, it would definitely disqualify him. It may be that he was unfortunate. But I believe we have no right to indulge in speculation. The issue is too serious.

Langer failed. With both Senators Thomas and Lee speaking in his behalf and claiming a broad spectrum of citizen support, Chandler won confirmation by the unusually narrow margin of 37 to 28 with 31 not voting.

By Chandler's account, he and Judge Murrah feuded from the very day he went onto the bench. (Murrah would not be interviewed for this book; the record makes clear, however, that the dislike is mutual.) One problem was the close physical proximity of the two judges. Although Murrah's jurisdiction on the circuit court covered six states, he preferred to spend much of his time in his native Oklahoma City, and his offices were adjacent to Chandler's. Murrah's higher rank and more spacious quarters galled Chandler. For his first 15 years as a judge, Chandler once complained, "my office was just a cubby-hole next to his quarters. I didn't even have a toilet." Chandler was convinced that Murrah "has done everything he could to confound me, hurt me, and frustrate me." The judges clashed over appointments of administrative workers in the district and court, over court schedules, even over assignment of parking space in the courthouse parking lot. Lawyers knew of the antipathy, and learned not to speak favorably of one judge in the presence of the other. Nonetheless, these internal squabbles remained out of general public view, and did not affect the working of either court. The energetic Murrah involved himself in national federal judiciary committees, and built a reputation not only as a solid appeals judge but as a man with expertise in court administration and reform. Oklahoma lawyers knew Chandler as a strong-willed trial judge—one whose acerbic tongue made his court "an interesting experience," as one man put it, but who nonetheless handled his caseload competently and with dispatch. Some critics, including Judge Murrah, felt Chandler "forced" settlements because he was afraid to try cases. Chandler, rebutting, says that pretrial conferences are an efficient means of disposing of litigation because they encourage out-of-court settlement. Supporters of Judge Chandler interviewed by investigators for the House Judiciary Committee in 1967 depicted him as a "keen and able man," and a man of "great integrity." These persons said Judge Chandler's troubles arose from his use of "unorthodox procedures and methods," and his continual criticism of "overadherence to fixed rules and procedures." To a Senate subcommittee in 1970, Chandler gave his own view of a trial judge's burden:

He is driving a 20-mule team down a perilous and hazardous road with precipices on each side, with crafty lawyers often trying to inject error into the record, compared to an appellate judge riding in an air-conditioned, ball-bearing Pullman car listening to legal arguments to which he can respond later. The strain is terrific, especially for the first few years, until one has covered the road so many times that it becomes second nature.

Even Chandler's enemies admit he is a hard worker. He normally arrives at the Oklahoma City courthouse before 6 A.M. and he reads briefs far into the night.

In 1956 seniority moved Chandler into the position of chief judge of his district, and put him on a collision course with Judge Murrah and other old and potential adversaries. A chief judge has broad authority over the workings of the entire district court. He can control the assignment of cases and the hiring of court personnel. Although he has no legal control over how a case is handled, he can subtly direct his colleagues; given the proper leadership qualities, a chief judge can transform an entire court into a projection of his personality. The chief judge has prestige as well as power. He sits on judicial committees, and outsiders come to him on matters affecting the court. The job also has the tendency to inflate latent egos; the chief judge is a somewhat more important animal than other judges, and he often acts that way. One of the chief judge's key prerogatives is the control of bankruptcy and reorganization proceedings. As a House Judiciary Committee report once summarized, "Historically, court administration of [these] . . . matters has been an area where the judge, through his power to appoint trustees and to approve attorney fees for the various interests involved in reorganization proceedings, has had an opportunity to dispense largesse and to be responsive to personal interests in the community and bar." And such cases proved to be the wellspring of many of Chandler's future troubles. Although separate proceedings, they had a propensity for producing a maze of controversies that went far beyond the legal questions directly in dispute.

Selected Investment and the O'Bryan Case

In the late 1950s judicial and financial scandals of mammoth proportion staggered Oklahoma citizens. Selected Investment Corporation, financial umbrella for dozens of investment firms in the state with scores of millions of dollars in assets, suddenly developed painful monetary kinks. Concurrently, federal tax agents learned the company's president and founder, Hugh Carroll, had paid a $150,000 bribe to a justice of the Oklahoma Supreme Court for a favorable ruling in a critical state tax case. That proved a mere beginning. The justice, Nelson S. Corn, who was 82 years old and retired when brought to bay, admitted systematic acceptance of bribes for 23 of the 24 years he served on the bench. Corn went to federal prison for tax evasion. Justice Earl Welch was also convicted, and the Oklahoma senate impeached Justice N. B. Johnson. (During one trial Corn claimed three other justices had also taken bribery; none, however, was ever charged.) The tainting of Oklahoma's highest court left the public in shellshock.

As a federal judge, Stephen Chandler initially had only a bystander's interest in the bribery disclosures. But he was soon in charge of attempts to reorganize Selected Investment through bankruptcy proceedings. The legal details of the bankruptcy case proper are too involved for pursuit here. For our purposes, the aftermath of the Selected collapse is more relevant than the actual bankruptcy, for it is here that Chandler got himself into a legal mess of . . . well, let us say, nigh-unprecedented complexity.

Chandler felt the immediate problem in the bankruptcy case was to get as high a price as possible for Selected's salable assets and pass the money along to investors, many of whom were school teachers and retired persons. Because of Selected's admitted bribe to Justice Corn in the state tax case, Chandler looked closely at all phases of this suit. And early on he decided he had found criminal muck.

Here a bit of backtracking: For the first 20 years of its existence Selected was profitable because of federal tax rulings that permitted it to pass earnings on to investors without paying corporate income tax. In the early 1950s, however, the Internal Revenue Service reexamined Selected, ruled the company must change its payout system, and held it liable for millions of dollars in back taxes. Facing ruin, Selected retained several national tax authorities, who opined the company's position was hopeless.

Enter now William Howard Pat O'Bryan, a prosperous, if somewhat nonestablishment, Oklahoma City tax attorney and accountant. When I first met Pat O'Bryan he was fifteen years deep into his fight with Chandler, and he showed it—a man so battered emotionally, so possessed by outspoken hatred of his adversary, that for quite a while I could not take seriously what he told me. At one point in that first chat I jotted in my notes: "Either a certifiable nut or the most persecuted man in Christendom." I had to keep reminding myself that I was speaking with a tax specialist astute enough to have earned $150,000 a year before he became entwined with Chandler—good money for a lawyer whether he practices in Wall Street or in a Washington superfirm or in Oklahoma City. A loner, O'Bryan was not a chum of the ruling mugwumps of the organized Oklahoma City bar, the lawyers who represent the big banks and insurance companies and corporations. For one thing, he was a come-lately lawyer. First an accountant, O'Bryan did not earn his law degree until he was in his thirties and he practiced both professions simultaneously thereafter, causing concerned cluck-clucks among some other lawyers. Further, O'Bryan is brash, the sort of guy who tells fools and other foes to go screw off.*

For Selected's tax problems, however, O'Bryan did see a possible answer. Stymied initially by IRS in Washington, he sued to have Oklahoma tax authorities agree with Selected management on how certain income should be treated for tax purposes. The legal issue involved was abstruse. But the Oklahoma Supreme Court ruled in Selected's favor. IRS then reexamined its own position and said fine, forget about

* Such is the image Pat O'Bryan exudes. There is another Pat O'Bryan as well: after losing his practice he took over operation of a home for children with birth and other defects, mostly kids of six and under who aren't going to live long, and need someone to care for them until they die. Over the years I've seen several of these places, some very good and some very bad. O'Bryan's is the best.

the past tax liability we claimed. But hereafter, Selected must run its business under the new rules—
that is, corporate income tax would be levied before
earnings are passed through to investors.

The tax case was the proceeding in which Hugh
Carroll paid $150,000 to Justice Corn for a favorable
decision. O'Bryan makes several arguments in defense
of Carroll, who ultimately went to jail. First, "It wasn't
a bribe, it was extortion. The people around Corn
told poor Hugh that if he didn't pay, he would lose.
The man panicked. He knew that if he lost, his company went down the drain. So what the hell did he
do? He paid through the nose." Second, O'Bryan insists Selected should have won the case on the merits,
that the $150,000 was a smelly irrelevancy. And,
finally, O'Bryan emphatically says he knew nothing
of the $150,000 bribe. "I'm a lawyer, not a bagman,"
he told me.

O'Bryan also felt the bankruptcy proceeding against
Selected was absolutely unnecessary, and that malice,
or worse, motivated Chandler to break up the company. In an affidavit filed with the Tenth Circuit Court
of Appeals later on in his battle with Chandler,
O'Bryan said Oklahoma banks were responsible for
Selected's troubles. Selected's 30-odd subsidiaries dealt
in chattel mortgages, drawing deposits that otherwise
would have been available to banks. O'Bryan swore
in the court papers: "Thus, Selected was a 'thorn in
the side' of the banking institutions, and from this
standpoint had to be removed." O'Bryan said that
while he was still representing Carroll, officials of a
"large Oklahoma banking institution" came to Selected with the proposition that they handle the reorganization. These bankers, according to O'Bryan,
said they had discussed the deal with Judge Chandler
—even though no formal bankruptcy proceedings had
begun—and that he felt it could be handled within
sixty days. Selected agreed, provided Hugh Carroll
retain control after the reorganization. The bank officers apparently wanted no part of Carroll, and they
refused. Shortly thereafter the bankruptcy action com-

menced in Chandler's court. Declared O'Bryan in his affidavit:

I am confident that the evidence, when developed, will support the proposition that Judge Chandler conspired with this banking institution and perhaps with others to eliminate Selected—and that in so doing he knowingly permitted the investors in Selected to be bilked and defrauded.

Although O'Bryan's affidavit did not name the bank, he was talking about the First National Bank and Trust Company of Oklahoma City (FNBTCO). Chandler dealt with FNBTCO in two capacities. In 1958, he appointed W. M. Harrison, a bank vice president, as court trustee in the Selected case. Harrison took a nonsalaried leave of absence from the bank and worked full time on the Selected case. Chandler designated FNBTCO the depository for Selected funds; during the bankruptcy Selected maintained an average daily balance of $547,377 with FNBTCO. Harrison returned to the bank after the Selected case ended, finally retiring in the summer of 1973. (He and Chandler apparently are warm friends. The judge introduced Harrison to me in an Oklahoma City cafe one day, and they exchanged ribald speculation about a young woman eating there with a lawyer they knew. As Harrison left he called, "I'll give you a call later about that little trip, and when you think we can get away.")

Chandler's other dealings with FNBTCO were as a real estate speculator. Chandler invested in oil and gas properties and real estate both before and after becoming a federal judge, often with FNBTCO financing. Beginning in 1960 his main vehicle was a land development firm named Sims & Company, owned by his daughter, Frances P. Sims, and son-in-law, S. K. Sims. However, Chandler's association with Sims & Company was, in the words of a confidential House Judiciary Committee report, "so intimate as to suggest it has been organized for his personal business." Vera L. Howard, who had been nurse to Chandler's children when they were small, and then became his personal secretary and clerk of the federal court, served as a Sims & Company officer. FNBTCO bank deposit slips were sometimes addressed:

> Sims & Company
> Federal Building
> City
>
> *or:*
>
> Sims & Co.
> c/o Stephen S. Chandler
> Federal Building
> City

Mrs. Howard signed many Sims & Company contracts while working in Chandler's chambers.

The main activity of Sims & Company was developing residential properties on some 103 acres of land Judge Chandler owned outside Oklahoma City. The venture, The Smiling Hills Addition, did not prosper and soon developed such troubles that the judge was a regular caller at FNBTCO's loan department. Between 1961 and 1964 Judge Chandler's indebtedness to the bank rose from $118,800 (of which all but $31,000 was secured by collateral) to $427,590. Valuation of the land pledged as security for Chandler's borrowing varied. FNBTCO consistently valued the land at $160,000. But Chandler, in his financial statements, gradually boosted his valuation from $240,000 to $480,000 (matching the increases in his indebtedness).*

According to internal bank memoranda, Chandler

---

* The House Judiciary Committee found other oddities in Chandler's financial statements: during 1964, for example, Chandler personally paid interest of $16,023 which at five percent interest would indicate a principal obligation of $338,478. In 1965, however, the interest was only $6,570, which at five percent indicates a principal debt of $131,412, and a reduction of debt from 1964 of $207,066. Committee investigators, who had access to Chandler's tax returns, wrote, "Since Judge Chandler's principal income in 1964–65 was his $30,000 salary, such reduction of debt was questionable."

shrugged off criticisms that Smiling Hills lots were overpriced. The situation ultimately attracted the attention of federal bank examiners, who in 1966 classified Chandler's loan as one that "warrants more than usual management attention." A year later, when the loan had not improved, the examiner directed FNBTCO to write it off the books as a statutory loss. The examiner's report said the property's value was "uncertain in view of extremely slow sales . . . attributed primarily to the subdivision's isolated location. . . ." And the report also reflected the preferential treatment FNBTCO had been giving Chandler:

> . . . Latest financial statement of borrower is too outdated for consideration; however, it has become apparent that collection of debt is solely dependent upon liquidation of collateral.
> Borrower has been unwilling to make any attempt toward servicing the debt, even to the extent of not cooperating with potential buyers of the pledged realty, *while management has been reluctant to institute foreclosure proceedings due to his political standing*. Non-liquid nature of collateral, maker's recalcitrant attitude toward servicing, and the absence of forceful collection endeavors render the extended portion a nonbankable asset [emphasis added].

After writing off the loans FNBTCO made occasional oh-so-gentle collection attempts. In a "Dear Steve" letter in February 1968, for instance, a bank officer wrote, "I thought I would bring you up to date on the status of your note accounts with us," and totalled them at $303,007. "I again ask that you give this matter some attention," the officer concluded.

Although much of these dealings with the First National Bank and Trust Company were to come in the future, Pat O'Bryan was acutely aware of Chandler's friendship with bank officers during the Selected case. He and Hugh Carroll, the deposed Selected president, talked openly of their suspicion that Oklahoma banks were behind Selected's troubles, but could offer only tenuous evidence. Chandler, conversely, said that Selected was a hollow shell and that creditors and the SEC were responsible for putting the reorganization into his court.

Once Chandler had the case he paid close attention to any aspect involving O'Bryan because of the lawyer's connection with the state tax suit. O'Bryan charges that Chandler wanted to silence him on the banks: Chandler, the record suggests, decided early on that O'Bryan was involved in the bribery of Justice Corn. And, right away, trouble for O'Bryan.

In March 1958 O'Bryan filed a claim for more than $1,141,700 for attorney fees for his work in the tax case. At first O'Bryan based the claim on an oral agreement with Hugh Carroll for ten percent of any tax savings resulting from his work. Later, he produced a letter contract dated October 1954 setting forth the same terms. Chandler, suspicious at O'Bryan's timing, had the FBI investigate the authenticity of the letter; the bureau found no proof of fabrication. Unsatisfied, Chandler had a private detective check further. He discovered the letterhead contained the name of one of O'Bryan's sons who did not begin practicing law until almost a year later. Testimony from the printer was contradictory as to when the letterheads had been ordered. O'Bryan said the letterheads had been printed in anticipation of the son joining his firm, and then withdrawn when he delayed his graduation.

The discrepancy came out during a hearing on November 3, 1958. Chandler warned O'Bryan of possible criminal charges and set further hearing for November 10. By O'Bryan's account, his lawyer, Gus Rinehart, gave such a gloomy prognosis of the case that he felt a sense of hopelessness. O'Bryan felt Chandler's "hostility" in the earlier hearing was a foreboding preview of what would happen during the disbarment proceeding. According to O'Bryan, Rinehart also passed on some chilling comments from the judge. If O'Bryan didn't abandon his claim Chandler "was . . . going to direct criminal prosecution and disbarment proceedings against O'Bryan and his two sons" (both lawyers, who had helped press the fee claim). By Chandler's account, Rinehart said "O'Bryan had 'come clean' with him; that he could not take the stand and deny the fabrication of the letter contract as denial would constitute perjury." O'Bryan would not challenge denial of the claim; "he asked only that his sons be absolved." Whatever the reason, O'Bryan stood mute November 10 as Chandler denied his claim, ordered him to refund $5,000 in fees already collected, and disbarred him from the federal courts (although, O'Bryan said, he had not been given any formal notice of the statement).

The "truth" of the O'Bryan fabrication is one of the issues in the Chandler affair, and a major one, on which I cannot satisfy my own mind. What is certain is that O'Bryan did the legal work in question, and that a ten percent contingency fee in such cases was the accepted practice. If indeed O'Bryan was innocent, he lost vital tactical ground by not fighting the charge head-on, for thereafter he was a professional leper—a disbarred lawyer. And this taint handicapped him severely in subsequent cases in which the record makes clear that Stephen Chandler stepped beyond the bounds of an objective jurist to become a veritable prosecutor of Pat O'Bryan.

For Chandler was not satisfied with simply disbarring O'Bryan and denying his $1.1 million claim; he wanted O'Bryan jailed. And he was disturbed and surprised when Paul Cress, the United States attorney in Oklahoma City, told him that in the opinion of the Justice Department, the evidence would not support an indictment. (Conceivably, Cress did not care to charge "fabrication" of the claims letter when another branch of the Justice Department, the FBI, said fabrication could not be proved.) Concurrently, O'Bryan regrouped, psychologically and legally. After a year he hired a new lawyer and asked Chandler for a rehearing, claiming that the fabrication had not been substantiated, and that Chandler had not followed court rules in the disbarment. Chandler turned him down, and the Tenth Circuit Court of Appeals dismissed O'Bryan's appeal as untimely. When Chandler gave materials on the disbarment to the Oklahoma Bar Association for action, O'Bryan sued him for libel. However, Chandler established that he did not write the supposed "letter" quoted in O'Bryan's suit as the basis for the libel, and the case was dismissed. O'Bryan was ultimately disbarred in the state courts as well.

Nonetheless, O'Bryan continued to fight, and he denounced Chandler to anyone who would listen. Chandler also escalated. Upon appointment of B. Andrew Potter as the new United States attorney in 1961, Chandler dragged out his old O'Bryan file and once again tried to get him indicted. By Chandler's account, Potter first agreed, then backed away, saying his superiors in Washington felt the case did not have "prosecution popularity."

At this point Chandler passed over the pale from judge to prosecutor. As he said later, he thought Potter's opinion was due to his "youth and lack of experience as a lawyer." So Chandler tried to set him straight. He had his law clerk compile a new dossier on O'Bryan for Potter. Potter, unmoved, let Chandler know he did not intend to present the case to the grand jury.

Chandler would not desist. When an old friend, T. B. Hendrick, was appointed foreman of the grand jury that met in November 1961, he briefed him privately on the O'Bryan case. As chief judge, Chandler convened the grand jury for its regular business. When it had finished, Chandler came to its chambers —at Hendrick's request—in street clothes (rather than judicial robes), declared the room to be "a United States courtroom now instead of a grand jury room," and launched a lengthy and one-sided account of O'Bryan's role in the Selected case. He repeatedly said he was not urging that O'Bryan be indicted: "Whether or not you indict anybody couldn't make the least bit of difference to me." The words rang hollow, because in the next breath he spoke of his obligation to direct the jury's attention to criminal

violations. Further, Chandler spoke with the full prestige of a chief judge, and the blue-ribbon citizens who
make up federal grand juries were not apt to misread
his obvious, if unspoken, opinion that O'Bryan should
be indicted.

Which is exactly what happened. The specific
charges were filing a false and fraudulent claim for
professional services, and for concealing $20,200 from
the Selected trustee by hiding it in a private bank
account. (O'Bryan and Carroll claimed these funds
to be Carroll's personal monies; they returned the
money upon challenge of the trustee.) The case went
to Judge Fred Daughterty. When O'Bryan moved for
a dismissal, United States Attorney Potter wrote a
brief, at the court's request, stating that Chandler's
conduct sufficiently blurred the line between the judiciary and the prosecution to invalidate the indictment.
Potter found "pressure was put on the grand jury to
indict." Judge Daughterty held that Chandler's conduct was technically irregular, and dismissed the
charges without prejudice (meaning a new indictment
could be sought if the prosecutor so chose).

The action infuriated Chandler. Potter thereafter
was not a naive young lawyer, but part of the supposed Murrah-Bohanon conspiracy—by now (1962)
very much out in the open. Or so felt Judge Chandler, at any rate, for he saw a grand design of malice
behind some things happening in and around his
court. The O'Bryan episode was far from over, but
for the purposes of chronological coherence, let us
leave O'Bryan in limbo for a moment and turn to
the second major component of the Chandler Case.

The Occidental Petroleum Case

During the late 1950s Parker Petroleum Corporation,
an Oklahoma-based firm, was in reorganization in
federal court. Despite its cash crisis, Parker owned
valuable oil properties both in the United States and
South America, and several major oil companies offered to shore it up financially in hopes of putting

these assets to profitable use. One such plan came from Occidental Petroleum Corporation, headed by Dr. Armand Hammer, the venerable financier who has been a major world trade figure since the 1920s. Hammer hired Luther Bohanon and Bert Barefoot, Jr., partners in Judge Murrah's old law firm, to present the plan to Judge W. R. Wallace, who then had the case. Wallace approved it, whereupon Occidental invoked its rights under escape-hatch language and withdrew from the deal. At about this time Judge Wallace died and Judge Chandler took over the case, and didn't like what he found. He felt Occidental had used the prospect of acquiring Parker to help float a big securities issue. As he said later in court papers, approval of the plan had been "obtained by fraud practiced on Judge Wallace and the shareholders and creditors of Parker by means of misrepresentation made by Luther Bohanon and Bert Barefoot, attorneys hired for that specific purpose by Dr. Hammer"— an assertion vigorously denied by the two lawyers. (In fact Bohanon did temporarily withdraw his firm from the case because, according to Chandler, his clients "double-crossed" him.) Chandler held that Occidental could not withdraw; the Tenth Circuit Court of Appeals reversed him and said it could—to Chandler's displeasure—and ordered him to proceed with fresh reorganization negotiations with Occidental.

Luther Bohanon, meanwhile, had some good fortune. In large part at the urging of his old friend Judge Murrah, Senators Robert Kerr and Mike Monroney nominated him for the federal district court in August 1961. The background investigations raised questions about his fitness. The Justice Department concluded that although Bohanon had "demonstrated an astute business sense, his legal ability was not considered exceptional by other lawyers." Bohanon knew how to attract legal business, but the success of his firm depended on a strong backup lawyer. Justice Department files also showed "considerable doubt as to Judge Bohanon's professional integrity and ability." * And the American Bar Association's standing committee on the federal judiciary concluded unanimously that Bohanon was "not qualified" for appointment. Nonetheless the Senate approved him without debate twelve days after the nomination. And, despite past differences that were soon to erupt again with public fury, Chandler wrote a glowing letter of endorsement for Bohanon: "I know of no Oklahoma lawyer of wider experience, of greater ability, or higher integrity . . . a well-considered and fortunate choice."

The rapport was shortlived. By fall Bohanon was arguing with Chandler that bankruptcy and other reorganization cases should be split equitably among the four judges of the Western District. Bohanon also felt Judge Chandler's relationship with Vera Howard, the district court clerk, was too close to permit impartiality of treatment among the court's judges. (Mrs. Howard, it will be remembered, had been nursemaid to Chandler's children, his personal secretary, and an officer in Sims & Company.) Bohanon suggested that she be replaced by a friend of his. Judge Daugherty took a middle position, saying the clerk should have no previous social or business relations with any judge. Eventually the judges agreed on a neutral choice and Mrs. Howard returned to Chandler's chambers as his secretary. The judges also quarreled over appointment of a United States commissioner, a court officer whose main function is to conduct preliminary hearings in criminal cases. Bohanon succeeded in getting the job for a friend who also happened to be a private detective, prompting a charge by Chandler that Bohanon wanted to plant a spy in the court. (The man resigned almost immediately.)

According to Bohanon, Chandler gave him an ultimatum in 1962 to choose between friendship with him

---

* None of these misgivings were made public, and the hearing on Bohanon was perfunctory. The quoted language is from the House Judiciary Committee confidential report on the Oklahoma feud.

or friendship with Judge Murrah. By Bohanon's account, Chandler required him to either "hate Murrah and cuss him" like Chandler did or else Chandler and Bohanon could not be friends.

With such acrimony in the background, Occidental was pressing forward with a new reorganization plan involving infusion of $2.5 million of new capital into Parker Petroleum, this time in conjunction with Western Oil Fields, Inc. Bohanon's former partner, Bert Barefoot, represented Occidental, Western, Hammer, and a promoter named Marvin Hayutin, whom Chandler referred to as "Hammer's money-finder." Chandler initially liked the plan, but after many delays, mainly at the request of Barefoot, he decided the Hammer combine had deliberately laden it with defects so as to squeeze more favorable conditions from Parker Petroleum. Chandler accused the parties of "attempting to perpetrate another fraud" (the language of a Supreme Court brief he filed later) and he called a meeting in his chambers in January 1962 to discuss the situation. Chandler excluded Occidental officers and lawyers from the meeting, most of which he devoted to denouncing Hammer and warning Western officers they risked being cheated. Chandler said he would listen to no defenses of the Hammer plan.

> You're not going to be able to talk me out of anything. I'm not going to change my mind on any of this. I couldn't be hoodwinked into changing my mind about the conclusions that I have come to about Hammer at all. I don't want my intelligence impugned. If you have got something you can do and want to say "I can do this," I'll listen to you, but there is no use in your making an argument to me. You can't sell me a nickel's worth of anything. I've got my mind made up and I know what the facts are about this whole deal. I am just as sure as if they were written up there in blood on the wall where we could see them.

Chandler said he felt Hammer was trying to "choke this company to death . . . so that they can milk it.

. . . I intend to say that from the bench because I verily believe it to be true." He accused Hammer of trying to "take" assets such as drilling equipment, buildings, and half a million dollars of South American properties.

Warming as he continued, Chandler denounced Hammer in pungent billingsgate. Speaking sympathetically to a Western officer whom he felt was being victimized, Chandler said, "It's the damnedest thing. There is something about it when a judge sees a son of a bitch undertake to ＿＿＿＿＿＿ ＿＿＿＿＿＿ just because the other man is good. They would just as soon rob your company and take it over as ＿＿＿＿＿. . . . He's a wolf, and I wouldn't want even to take his money . . . these vultures . . . these shady characters . . . they are absolute pirates. When you get in a position to have to deal with them, you need a bodyguard and a lawyer and everything else." (Despite the thunderous language Chandler did not cite any specific instances of Hammer's supposed infamies, nor did he pursue the matters elsewhere. Nor did the charges affect Hammer's reputation as a respected and trustworthy businessman.)

At the conclusion Chandler seemed uneasy that word of the meeting would leak to Occidental. If the participants were asked about it, they should be careful of what they said. "Mr. Hammer [would] likely sue me for slander" if he got a transcript, Judge Chandler said.

As Chandler feared, Occidental did hear of the meeting, and its lawyers filed a battery of petitions. First, they asked that Chandler disqualify himself from any further hearings in the case involving Occidental, and that another judge be assigned. Before Chandler had a chance to rule, the lawyers went to the circuit court and asked that Chandler be barred from participating in the case, charging that his conduct was "more than mere 'mental bias' but overt acts of such gross misconduct and judicial impropriety as to scandalize the administration of justice." Jockeying thereafter was rapid. Chandler refused to disqualify himself, saying the charge of bias was unfounded, but that he would not hear Occidental matters anyway. The circuit court, concurrently, set a hearing in Denver, invited Chandler to offer oral rebuttal, and subpenaed Chandler's stenographer to bring notes of the January hearing.

Chandler tried desperately to keep the transcript from Occidental lawyers. According to the stenographer, Russell H. Ingram, Chandler ordered him to bring in "everything that I was going to bring to Denver" in response to the subpena. Chandler "picked out the notes that they [Occidental] do not have a transcript of," and told Ingram, "All right. Now, I've had possession of these all this time."

Ingram said, "I went home and I was scared and I was confused and I was mad." That evening Ingram decided he must be a "man or a mouse," in his words. He returned to Chandler's home and told him: "I'm going to go out there [to the circuit court] and I'm going to tell the truth on what happened. I've got this subpena . . . asking for everything that I had in my possession, and all that stuff was in my possession. I'm going to say that they were taken."

According to Ingram, Chandler became irate. Ho told the stenographer that if he had the notes he had them "illegally," that the January chambers session "wasn't a hearing or a proceeding," that somebody "must have got to me, and I had sold out." Ingram quoted the judge as asking, "How much have they paid you?" and then telling him, "All right, boy, you're on your own. The only person you have to fear is me."

"Either I'm going to take those notes with me or you're going to order me not to take them," Ingram said.

"All right," Chandler replied, "I order you not to take them."

Ingram went on to Denver without the notes and told the circuit court what Chandler had said to him. The same day Chandler told the court by telegram that he indeed had ordered Ingram not to produce the notes, because they were of "conversations" in his chambers, not a formal hearing. He claimed they "legally" belonged to him, even when Ingram took them for transcription. But he agreed to surrender the transcript anyway, sending them to Denver by courier. (Contrary to Chandler's claim, the transcript made plain that the meeting was much more than "conversations." For example, he said at one point, "I'm going to make another statement, and I make it as . . . in my official capacity as a judge.")

The transcript dispute, however, was a sideshow to the main issue of Chandler's bias. Citing a matter of "commanding importance," the judge declined to appear personally during several days of hearings, basing his defense upon written denials of the Occidental charges and support from attorneys from numerous other parties in the reorganization, including the Securities and Exchange Commission. Only Occidental accused him of bias and supported his removal. Obviously aware of the explosiveness of the case, the circuit court decided the decision should be made by the full judicial council—the circuit court plus the chief judges of the other districts within the circuit—and bucked it there for hearing on April 20. Chandler was advised "that it is the wish of the council that you be present at such council meeting if you can conveniently do so."

Chandler put his defense in the form of a counterattack. In a letter to the council, he demanded that Judge Murrah disqualify himself from passing on Occidental's application. He said Murrah "is so actuated by malice toward me and has been so vindictive toward me for more than 20 years . . . that he is disqualified to sit on the bench or in conference to exhort his colleagues in a decision of the matter now before the court." Chandler also had words for Luther Bohanon, by now a federal district judge. Chandler maintained that Murrah's past association with Bohanon was a further reason for Murrah to bow out of the case. Chandler claimed that when he moved against Occidental, Bohanon's attitude "changed from warm friendship to bitter and active, vindictive hatred in an attempt to discredit me." Chandler professed not to understand the reason for Bohanon's turnabout,

although he did advance one rather eye-popping
theory:

> This whole matter is very sinister. Great forces
> of evil are apparently involved. A lawyer in whom
> I had complete confidence, Bohanon, as is conclu-
> sively shown by the record, and whom I tried to
> warn and protect has gone utterly berserk, which is
> something beyond my comprehension unless he has
> been hypnotized by his clients, Dr. Hammer and
> Mr. Hayutin, and I want to say to you that my
> knowledge of this subject makes me know that such
> a thing is possible by use of post-hypnotic sugges-
> tion. Unless such be true, his actions certainly are
> reprehensible. His wild, frenzied urgency I cannot
> understand.

Chandler's letter was dated April 19, and his attorney was supposed to deliver it to judicial council
members the next day. Through an inexplicable error
the letter was not delivered. The next day, April 20,
the circuit court, acting on the recommendation of the
judicial council (there is some overlap of members),
removed Chandler from the case, citing three grounds:
his closed hearings without the presence of Occidental
attorneys; his attempt to prevent Ingram "from the
performance of his official duties"; and his "personal
enmity, hostility, bias and prejudice against Occidental." Judge Murrah signed the order.

Three days later the circuit judges received Chandler's April 19 letter. Murrah, by reliable account, was
livid at the attacks on his integrity. He told a colleague that the time had come to make Chandler put
up or shut up, since he had gotten the idea he could
make all sorts of irrational, vicious statements and
get away with them. The council ordered Chandler to
appear on April 25 to make his charges in person.

The Chandler testimony, in the privacy of a circuit
court conference room, surely must rank as one of
the more bizarre episodes of American judicial history.
Never has so much judicial dirty laundry been so
defiantly displayed. His delivery emotional, his syntax

and stream of thought often confused, his attitude fiercely unrepentant, Chandler harangued the council for almost an hour. He recounted at length the Parker reorganization, and his negotiations with Hayutin, Bohanon and Barefoot. He told of Bohanon's supposed $25,000 solicitation. He traced Murrah's longtime "bias." One excerpt gives the pathos of Chandler's tortured, emotional presentation:

The building [the federal courthouse in Oklahoma City] is full of rumors and you would be surprised at the little mysterious notes I got and things of that kind as to what was going to happen and this and that, that I was going to have a nervous breakdown, go to the hospital, and Judge Bohanon would be the chief judge and so forth. Of course about a year and one-half ago the chief judge of this court [Murrah] learned that I had high blood pressure and coronary deficiency, and I will assure you that since that time, you might not believe it, but it has just seemed to me that he thought maybe by keeping the tension on that I would drop dead, because it has been on every minute. . . .

Chandler also attacked Judge Bohanon. Despite their period of friendship "he began spitting in my face and he took charge of the court and entered orders and it was pretty bad. And in that atmosphere —you couldn't imagine how dire it was, and I am not going into details but I know that every telephone I had was tapped and I knew there were bugs and I knew that everything I did was watched. . . ."

At one point during the Parker reorganization, Chandler asserted, "I finally got to the point where 'I wonder if I had better drink out of my carafe' because to me it was that dire. It meant prison for more than one person."

Judge John C. Pickett incredulously interrupted Chandler. "You were afraid someone might poison you?"

"It was that dire around there," Chandler replied, "with this in my possession if they knew it." Chandler didn't amplify, and no one pursued the question of what incriminating evidence he held.

At another point Chandler accused Murrah of interfering in his cases. One involved the condemnation of land needed for the construction of a new federal courthouse in Oklahoma City, a cherished project of Judge Murrah. Chandler raised the price of one parcel by $10,000 over the value set by a special condemnation commission. Chandler said privately he thought Murrah pressured the commissioners to set a low figure because of his zeal to get the new courthouse built. Murrah, rebutting, said Chandler raised the price because a friend owned the land. (Chandler denied knowing the owner or ever talking to him.) In any event, as Chandler told the story to the judicial council, after he announced his decision Judge Murrah called him into his chambers and said, "Now, you have just got to change that. You can't do that. You are going to delay our building here."

"I said, 'Well, judge, that is a judicial decision and it has got to be. I don't talk to anybody, I just do it.'

"He jumped up and he said, 'You goddam yellow son of a bitch, you. I have worked for seven years on this building and here you do that and we don't get it.' And I sat there and smiled and I said, 'Judge, it is a judicial decision and there is not anything I can do about it.' " (Murrah vehemently denies trying to persuade Chandler to change the decision.)

In another case, Chandler said, a disgruntled lawyer went to Murrah's chambers after an adverse ruling. A few minutes later Murrah emerged and told Chandler, "I want you to set that order aside." Chandler said he refused. "He said, 'Well, every other judge of the circuit does what I tell them to. I don't know what the hell is wrong with you that you won't.' I said, 'If I would, life would be a lot easier for me, but I just have to be like I am.' " (Again, Murrah denied this allegation.)

The judges heard Chandler out and the next day declined to withdraw their order dismissing him from the case. Chandler spent several years trying to reverse the order in the United States Supreme Court, re-

peating his old claims about the Hammer–Hayutin–
Bohanon–Murrah conspiracy, and throwing round-
house swings at anyone who got in his way. Under
normal circumstances, Chandler argued at one point,
a judge should withdraw from a case "when there is
the slightest ground" to support a charge of bias. But
he maintained a judge had an obligation *not* to withdraw when disqualification "is an attempt to run him
off the bench for the purpose of obtaining another
judge" when the party realizes it is about to lose the
suit. And this is what he charged Occidental and its
lawyers with doing: "To discredit me by obtaining
wide publicity in the out-of-context, seemingly scur-
rilous and careless language used in the informal conferences . . . and thus bluff or scare me off the
bench."

Ah, yes, that langauge at the chambers conference.
Because of the transcript Chandler could not deny
the harsh things he had said. But he pooh-poohed its
significance: "common, ordinary, everyday descriptive
terms," he said of his billingsgate, and claimed most
was justified. "As to all of the terms, they are in the
language of the street, and are quite accurately descriptive of the kind of person the evidence in the
Parker case shows Dr. Armand Hammer to be. They
may be even more accurately descriptive of him than
my finding from the bench using judicial language
that he did not possess the requisite integrity and
moral character to be trusted not to make away with
the assets of Parker and Western worth millions of
dollars."

The Supreme Court refused to hear Chandler's appeal. Another judge concluded the Occidental case,
which is just as well, for Stephen Chandler was
under siege elsewhere.

Stephen Chandler's multi-track troubles began to
converge in 1965. Before the year ended he was
under siege in civil and criminal cases, and from his
fellow judges.

The collapse of the old Selected indictment—the
one Chandler had pressured the grand jury to return

—gave Pat O'Bryan a toehold in his fight with the judge. When the time limit for reindictment passed with no further action, O'Bryan sued Chandler in the state courts for $10 million damages for malicious prosecution, libel and slander. He alleged that Chandler's appearance before the grand jury, and his distribution of derogatory material, were done "not as a judge but as a private citizen." Chandler had the case removed to federal court,* where Judge Roy W. Harper held that a federal judge is immune from civil liability for judicial actions, even if taken maliciously and in excess of his jurisdiction, unless there is a clear absence of all jurisdiction. Harper did not rule on the issue of whether Chandler's action was actually malicious.

Despite Chandler's seeming invulnerability, O'Bryan still would not quit. In a motion asking Judge Harper to reconsider the immunity decision, he attacked Judge Chandler as "corrupt" and "immoral." The fifteen-page affidavit—shrill and emotional, veritably reeking with outrage—attacked both Chandler's personal and professional conduct. It revived the 1938 episode where Chandler supposedly paid $3,000 to his secretary in the assault case. The bulk of the affidavit, however, dealt with Chandler's handling of the Selected case. Essentially, O'Bryan claimed that Chandler wanted to discredit him so that a wide range of conspirators could put their hands on Selected's assets. He cited a 77.2 acre tract in northwest Oklahoma City (known locally as Capitol Gate) sold during reorganization for developing as a shopping center and hotel/office complex. The purchaser, United Founders Corporation, was formed by members of the law firm of Mosteller, Fellers, Andrews and Loving, which had been one of the attorneys for

* Chandler removed the case to federal court under a provision of the United States Code that provides that the federal district courts have jurisdiction over actions against "any officer of the courts of the United States, for any act under color of office or in the performance of his duties."

the Selected trustees. A partner, James D. Fellers,†
in fact had been largely responsible for uncovering
the supposedly fabricated O'Bryan letter contract;
the firm received fees of $118,000 for its 4,000 hours
of work on the reorganization. The chain on the
transaction went as follows: in September 1959, with
the Selected reorganization virtually complete, Judge
Chandler ordered Capitol Gate and other properties
turned over to Mid-America Corporation, successor
to Selected. Thereafter Capitol Gate was free of court
jurisdiction or trustee supervision. In June 1961, almost two years later, Mid-America sold Capitol Gate
to United Founders for $750,000, for a capital gain
of approximately $300,000. Later United Founders
resold the land for $3,400,000, and its chairman,
Gerald G. Barton, told Oklahoma City newspapers
the company made a profit "in excess of $2 million"
on the transaction. In rebuttal to O'Bryan, United
Founders principals noted that Capitol Gate had not
been involved in the reorganization for almost two
years before they purchased it. For this reason they
denied any conflict of interest.

What O'Bryan was attempting to do with his blun-
derbuss charges, he told me several years later, was to
show an ongoing pattern of conduct by Chandler.
O'Bryan recognized that Chandler carried the *ex officio* respect of his judgeship, and that appellate
courts would be inclined to accept his word over that
of a litigant—especially when the litigant was a disbarred lawyer. Hence O'Bryan decided to play mean
—to try to disclose what he considered the totality of
Judge Chandler's personal and professional career,
in the hope that the appeals judges would give the
case more than cursory attention.

But O'Bryan didn't get a chance to argue his motion. Chandler's attorneys asked that Judge Harper
deny an oral hearing to prevent O'Bryan from pleading "voluminous wholly false, irrelevant, obscene and

---

† A pillar of the establishment bar, Fellers became president
of the American Bar Association in the summer of 1974. Previously he headed the Oklahoma bar.

scandalous matter for the purpose of calling same to the attention of the news media and obtaining publicity and libelling [Chandler] in an area where media and defendant are immune from libel laws." Judge Harper, after one horrified look at the O'Bryan affidavit, ordered it suppressed. O'Bryan blandly sent basically the same document to the circiut court, again calling Chandler "corrupt" and "guilty of violation of federal criminal laws."

Retaliating, Judge Chandler laid out his version of the Selected case, with Pat O'Bryan cast as a criminal conspirator. And Chandler did so in a manner to insure maximum publicity, without the risk of having his statement suppressed by the courts (the fate of both O'Bryan petitions). Rather than following Circuit Court of Appeals rules and submitting a formal brief in response to O'Bryan, Chandler wrote what he termed an "informal Official Statement" covering some 32 printed pages. Chandler had a first draft of the "official statement" printed and circulated it among friendly lawyers and editors for comment. On Sunday, August 15, Chandler called John Claves, managing editor of the *Oklahoma Journal*, to his chambers and gave him a copy of the statement. According to Claves, Chandler said he intended to file the document with the circuit court on August 18. With a good story in hand, editor Claves went right to work, and the *Journal* ran his article August 19 under an eight-column front-page banner: O'BRYAN CALLED "BRIBE MASTERMIND."

The lead paragraph said Chandler disclosed that he furnished evidence to prosecutors in 1961 showing "beyond any reasonable doubt" that O'Brayn was "an accomplice if not the mastermind" of the $150,000 bribe in the Selected tax case. The story ran almost a full page of type. Apart from the "mastermind" allegation, it consisted essentially of what Chandler had already said about O'Bryan in court and elsewhere.

Unfortunately for the *Journal*—and for Chandler —the version of the "official statement" given to Claves was not filed in court. Chandler rewrote the draft once again, and in doing so he deleted some of the saltier language.

These charges and countercharges, it will be recalled, were made during O'Bryan's appeal of dismissal of the $10 million indictment libel suit. On November 30 the circuit court upheld dismissal, saying Chandler had judicial immunity. A week later, however, O'Bryan tried again. He sued Chandler in state court in yet another libel suit, this time on the basis of the "official statement" and the *Journal* story. (He brought a separate action against the *Journal*.) And, once again, Chandler pleaded judicial immunity and sought refuge in federal court. Judge Richard B. Austin (a Chicago judge sitting by special assignment, since no Oklahoma jurist would pass on a case involving a colleague) rebuffed Chandler. He held that Chandler's acts were not "done under color of judicial office," and that since no federal issues were involved, the case should be tried in state court.

Chandler could not prove the "mastermind" charge. During pretrial examination he spoke vaguely about "documentary" evidence, but never produced it. At the trial he wrangled constantly with Judge Laverne Fishel (later, in a motion for a new trial, Chandler lamented that Fishel told him to "shut up" when he tried to speak in court) and presented a defense of sweeping generalities. The jury, asked to choose between a disbarred lawyer and a federal judge, opted for O'Bryan. It returned a verdict of $40,000 in compensatory damages and $10,000 in punitive damages.

Pat O'Bryan at last had had his day in court, and he had won. But events elsewhere were proving once again the astounding resiliency of Stephen Chandler.

Chandler's charge about O'Bryan being the "bribe mastermind" was headlined in Oklahoma City newspapers on August 19, 1965. Exactly one week later Chandler had some banner headlines of his own: CHANDLER CHARGED WITH FRAUD.

The criminal case, filed by the Oklahoma County prosecutor, Curtis P. Harris, accused Chandler of conspiring with an Oklahoma County commissioner to build private roads benefiting his Smiling Hills development with public funds and equipment. Although Chandler and the commissioner, Edwin Lee Kessler, ultimately were exonerated (they established that the county had owned the roads since 1957), their chase through the courts kept the story on the front pages for three months. And throughout the case Chandler displayed his propensity for doing things differently than other people:

- When Chandler failed to appear for his scheduled arraignment, a justice of the peace ordered deputy sheriffs to find the judge, arrest him, and bring him to court. The deputies looked for Chandler all day. At 8:30 that evening, as the justice was dining at the swank Twin Hills Golf and Country Club, Chandler walked in with his lawyer and asked that he be arraigned on the spot. The justice postponed his steak dinner and obliged Chandler.

- Chandler next went after prosecutor Harris. In court papers he demanded that Harris be disbarred, and that the grand jury remove him from office. He accused the county attorney of "intolerable and un-American abuse of his powers of public office." Although Chandler never got around to explaining any motive, he alleged Harris was "out to get me" at the behest of unnamed Oklahoma City attorneys.

- In an action apparently unprecedented in Oklahoma history, Chandler succeeded in having grand jurors brought into a hearing for questioning on the evidence on which they based their indictment of the judge.

- For another preliminary hearing, Chandler arranged to slip into the county courthouse at 7:15 A.M.—about two hours before normal business hours—to enter an innocent plea to an indictment, thus avoiding press and television coverage. Judge JoAnn McInnis, who permitted the unusual procedure, had been Chandler's law clerk before she went on the bench. The *Oklahoma Journal* editorialized that the "special treatment accorded . . . Chandler cannot help but rankle in the breast of all who have been nurtured in the American way of life which teaches us all men are equal under the law."

After the months-long legal chase, a state judge exonerated Chandler and Kessler. He ruled that the roads in question were public and that hence Chandler and Kessler had violated no law.

The acquittal brought little solace to Chandler. As his troubles accumulated during 1965, the Tenth Circuit Judicial Council made known its concern over the impact on the court. For one thing Chandler's hatred of Judges Murrah and Bohanon was unabated, and he frequently denounced his old adversaries; for instance, he even claimed that his attempted prosecution on the state charges was part and parcel of Murrah's "criminal conspiracy" to drive him from the bench. He continued to flood the United States Supreme Court with appeals and reappeals on his disqualification in the Occidental case, each time repeating his accusations against Murrah. He was caught up in yet another disqualification suit, this time in a $25 million civil action against Texaco, Inc., for an alleged breach of contract. The plaintiff's lawyer also represented Chandler in one of the O'Bryan libel suits. Texaco became upset after a series of unfavorable rulings and claimed that Chandler was so closely related to the opposing lawyer that it was improper for him to sit on the case. Chandler for months refused to disqualify himself, and Texaco had to take the case to the appeals court. Another judge was assigned to hear the case.

Upon appointment of Luther Eubanks to the court in August 1965, the judges fell into brisk debate over division of the workload. Bohanon and Fred Daugherty felt the newer, younger judges should carry the bulk of the caseload, and that Chandler should handle only one-eighth the civil cases, rather than one-fourth. Chandler refused, prompting a letter from Bohanon which reflected the acrimonious atmosphere on the court:

It is my sincere conviction that the litigants and the lawyers of this court should have better treatment than they have been getting in the cases assigned to you, in that you do not give them an opportunity to try their cases. . . . You should take a year's rest; you need it, and there is no question about that.

Bohanon concluded that the "honor of our court" was at stake. (Bohanon thought better of the letter the next day, and sent Chandler a note of apology for "things I wish I had not said.")

As the fall wore on, the appeals court began an apparent concerted effort to persuade Chandler to accept senior status and retire. Murrah, understandably, could have nothing to do with any matters concerning Chandler, so the negotiations fell to Judge John C. Pickett, next senior man on the appeals court. The pressures on Chandler came from two sources. A spate of articles in Oklahoma City newspapers in September and October said flatly, although without attribution other than to "courthouse sources," that the council would move to strip Chandler of his powers. The articles were legitimate speculation because Oklahoma lawyers were concerned about the turmoil in the federal court, and what the appeals judges would do about it. Nonetheless they bore the distinctive scent of deliberate leaks from persons who wanted to give Stephen Chandler a nudge. Chandler charged flatly that Murrah and Bohanon inspired the stories "for the purpose of hampering [Chandler] in the performance of his official duties and precipitating his retirement so that co-conspirator Bohanon can succeed him in control of [the district] court as chief judge and thus facilitate their corrupt designs in controlling decisions of the court." Concurrent with the press attacks, Pickett had a succession of lawyers friendly with Chandler—including former Governor J. Howard Edmondson—meet with the judge to urge him to retire. Several times Chandler appeared on the brink of doing so; each time, however, he drew back.

The council lost its last shred of patience with

Chandler on December 13, 1965. As one of the judges said later, the collective judgement was that "something had to be done with Judge Chandler." Several took offense at his charge in the Occidental case that Murrah's supposed "conspiracy" even included members of the appeals court who had stayed aloof from the feud. Meeting in secret, and without notice to Judge Chandler (although he had asked to be heard), the council passed an order noting that it had been concerned with conditions in the district for four years, and that Chandler had been a defendant in both civil and criminal litigation. The order made three findings: Chandler was "presently unable, or unwilling, to discharge efficiently the duties of his office"; a change must be made in the division of business and assignment of cases; and Chandler should take no action in matters pending in his court, which were to be divided among his colleagues, nor was he to be assigned any new cases.

Five of the six judges attending the council meeting signed the order; the sixth, David T. Lewis, protested the council did not have authority to promulgate such an order, and refused.

Armed with the still-secret order, Pickett made one more attempt to get Chandler off the bench peacefully. He told the judge's lawyer that if he retired voluntarily, the order would not be entered into the public record. Chandler refused. "Surely you can realize that under these circumstances I could not have [retired] honorably . . . ," he wrote Pickett. On December 27, therefore, the council had a United States marshal serve the order on Chandler, and released it to the press.

As its authority, the council cited a provision of the 1939 law which created judicial councils: "Each judicial council shall make all necessary orders for the effective and expeditious administration of the business of the courts within its circuit. The district judges shall promptly carry into effect all orders of the judicial council."

Events tumbled swiftly. Chandler asked the U.S. Supreme Court to stay the order. When it refused, he took actions in several pending cases so as to assert his legitimacy in office, and notified lawyers he would act on any "urgent" matters that arose, the circuit court's order notwithstanding. In his appeal to the Supreme Court Chandler asserted that the council had no authority to issue such an order. As he said in one of the many briefs that flowed from his chambers, "The twists and turns of this case should not obscure the principal issue: Do judicial councils have authority to discipline judges?" Chandler did accept the portion of the order barring him from accepting new cases. But he adamantly opposed surrendering pending cases, saying that to do so was tantamount to accepting "impeachment" by the council.

The record suggests that the judicial council felt Chandler would yield his office once the order was publicized, and that his resistance embarrassed it into a backdown. In any event, both the Tenth Circuit Judicial Council and the Supreme Court squirmed mightily to avoid answering Chandler's "principal issue" question. Responding to Chandler's appeal to the Supreme Court, the council said (through Solicitor General Thurgood Marshall) that the first order was preliminary, and said it intended further proceedings under a section of the law providing for removal of a judge because of physical or mental disability. Marshall's brief spoke ominously of "material" in court files which "warrants the most careful examination." Once raised, the issue of physical and/or mental disability was never pursued; when investigators from the House Judiciary Committee made an in-depth examination of the material later, they found nothing which "could form a conclusion that Judge Chandler was not fit to sit as a judge." In the committee's language, "Although certain statements made by Judge Chandler, and documents signed by him . . . are extremely intemperate and reflect mental distress or even exceptional feelings of persecution, there is no evidence or responsible opinion (confirmed by personal interviews with the judges) that would establish that Judge Chandler . . . has a permanent mental or physical disability. . . ."

The Supreme Court quite happily kept out of the dispute, denying Chandler's request for a stay, and not passing any judgement on the legality of the council order. Justices Hugo Black and William O. Douglas dissented. They argued that the council was "completely without legal authority to issue any such order. . . . This is clearly and simply a proceeding by circuit judges to inquire into the fitness of a district judge to hold his office and to remove him if they so desire." The council gradually retreated, agreeing to let Chandler keep his pending cases, and finally surrendered altogether.

By the time the Supreme Court got around to ruling on Chandler's appeal the judge had regained his powers; hence the court declined to get into the case on grounds of lack of jurisdiction. The majority opinion, by Chief Justice Warren Burger, suggested the council order was not judicial in nature, and that Chandler should have sought relief elsewhere; by acquiescing in parts of the order, he forfeited the right of challenge.* Dissenting vigorously, Justice Douglas called the order a *de facto* impeachment and said he saw no constitutional power "for one group of federal judges to censor or discipline any federal judge and no power to declare him inefficient and strip him of his power to act as a judge." Douglas continued:

> The mood of some federal judges is opposed to this view and they are active to make all federal judges walk in some uniform step. What has happened to [Chandler] is not a rare instance; it has happened to other federal judges who have had perhaps a more libertarian approach to the Bill of Rights than their brethren. . . . All power is a heady thing as evident by the increasing efforts of groups of federal judges to act as referees over other federal judges.

---

* Burger's ruling was consistent with his longtime advocacy of tight regimentation of district judges by the judicial councils, the Judicial Conference of the United States, and the Administrative Office of the United States Courts.

As Chandler stated in his many defense briefs, if he had sinned, punishment must be through impeachment. Such a process must be initiated by the House Judiciary Committee, which in modern times has been most reluctant to move against federal judges. The last impeachment was brought in 1936 against District Judge Halsted L. Ritter, of Florida. The House charged Ritter with accepting $4,500 from a former law partner who had received a $75,000 fee in a receivership appointment made by Ritter; with practicing law while on the bench; and with using his authority for his private benefit in a case involving a light and power company. The Senate convicted Ritter and he was removed from office.

In succeeding years the Judiciary Committee discreetly averted its eyes from several outrageous jurists —drunks and incompetents and borderline-cheaters— and its first inclination was to ignore the Chandler Case as well, even when Chandler indirectly accused his esteemed brethren of contemplated murder. But Representative H. R. Gross (R., Ia.), who makes a career of asking embarrassing questions, called for an investigation of the Chandler matter in floor speeches in January and February 1966. Failure to get at the truth of Chandler's charges of "malicious persecution" was a travesty which destroyed public trust in the judiciary, he said. When Representative Emanuel Celler (D., N.Y.), the committee chairman, would not respond, Gross introduced a resolution demanding an investigation. This action forced Celler's hand. The next day he announced the Judiciary Committee would get into the case, via a special three-man subcommittee headed by Representative Jack Brooks (D., Tex.). As special counsel the subcommittee retained Washington lawyer Walter D. Hansen.

Hansen spent some two years interviewing principals and studying documentary evidence. Hansen's final report, given to the committee April 30, 1968, was labelled confidential, and has never been distributed publicly (although bootleg copies are tolerably easy to obtain, as I discovered during research for this book). Hansen concluded that actions of the principal figures—Judges Murrah, Bohanon and Chandler—"brought discredit to them personally and has demeaned administration of justice in their courts." However, he continued:

- "Although . . . some of the actions of the judges were sharp, if not discreditable, . . . no evidence available at this time . . . would support a charge of impeachment against any of the judges investigated. . . ."
- The judicial council's action in stripping Judge Chandler of his power to hear cases "was equivalent to his removal as a judge . . . [and] completely beyond the legal authority of the council. . . . Confronted with seemingly complete opposition and exasperated by intemperate, if not unreasoning, attacks on their judgement and integrity, the circuit judges let themselves be goaded into action that was not within their power to undertake."
- "The bitterness and animosity" between Judges Murrah, Bohanon and Chandler "has impaired their future usefulness and brought discredit upon their courts."
- The Chandler Case underscored "the need for a new mechanism, other than the impeachment process, to resolve questions of judicial behavior and fitness to continue to hold judicial office."

Despite the exoneration, the House report directed sharp language toward the judges. Many of the actions against Judge Chandler were "vindictive" and "motivated more by malice than by merit. . . . The plotting and intrigue among the participants in this feud ultimately resulted in a political cabal which does no credit to any of the parties involved." The report called Chandler's real estate speculation "inappropriate for a member of the federal judiciary. There is a wide difference between this type of business activity and the mere investment in securities of a public corporation whose stock is widely held. A federal judge is not given the security of a lifetime appointment at a salary that cannot be reduced to enable him to build a fortune on outside speculations. A person with such ambitions should not accept judicial appointment." However, the report found no wrongdoing in Chandler's relations with the First National Bank and Trust Company, nor in his appointment of a bank officer as a trustee in the Selected Investment Corporation bankruptcy.

With Hansen's report the House Judiciary Committee happily washed its hands of the dispute in the tenth circuit. The report's harsh language had scant effect on the three judges criticized: the inexorable process of seniority elevated Bohanon to the position of chief judge of Oklahoma's Western District. Chandler moved to senior status. Murrah, to the surprise of many persons in the judicial establishment, in 1970 was named director of the Federal Judicial Center in Washington, charged with developing and adopting improved administrative techniques in the federal courts. The job is prestigious (the first man to hold it was retired Justice Tom C. Clark) and powerful (the center is an integral part of Justice Warren Burger's goal of rearranging the federal judiciary so that it is run from the top). Stephen Chandler, however cheering the finding that he had committed no impeachable offense, continued life much as he had in the past—mired in litigation.

We left Pat O'Bryan savoring a $50,000 verdict in his libel suit over Chandler's charge that he was the bribery "mastermind." O'Bryan felt at this point, in early 1967, that at last he was on the brink of clearing his name, and even overturning the old disbarment ruling. "This was the first time I'd had an impartial hearing, where someone other than Steve Chandler ran things," he told me years later.* "Well, I got overconfident. Chandler is a mean fighter, and

---

* Not exactly accurate, for after Chandler's action, the Oklahoma Bar Association initiated its own disbarment proceeding to strip O'Bryan of his state law license. These hearings were conducted over several days and were reviewed by Oklahoma courts.

he can pull stunts as a federal judge that are beyond the powers of a mere citizen." In this instance, what Chandler did was to remove his case—the one he had just lost in state court, in a jury trial—back into federal district court notwithstanding Judge Austin's earlier order that it did not belong there. When O'Bryan filed a motion to bring it back to state court, the action was assigned to yet another visiting judge, Frank J. Battisti, of Ohio. And right away all sorts of strange things happened.

Battisti is a judicial heavyweight, a scholarly lawyer and Harvard law graduate who knows how to run a courtroom. Ohio lawyers apparently love him; several whom I interviewed at random say he is one of the smartest federal judges in their state. Unfortunately for O'Bryan, however, Battisti's pet subject is judicial independence. He subscribes enthusiastically to the Almighty-God concept of a federal judge, and a key theme runs through his writings: a federal judge should be answerable only to Congress for his personal and official conduct. Meddlers such as judicial councils and court administrators, even when ordained by law, should not interfere with how a judge runs his court. Battisti once wrote that as a chief judge in Ohio, he would not dare to demand that his colleagues handle their cases promptly, or act civilly towards litigants; each judge, he said, is entitled to set his own standards of conduct. Further, Battisti is on record as an unabashed supporter of Chandler in the judge's struggle with the Tenth Circuit Judicial Council.

Battisti's interests are cited because of the extraordinary legal ballet he performed to rescue his fellow judge:

- Going directly into the face of Judge Austin's earlier, contrary ruling, he held that Chandler was judicially immune from the libel suit. He ordered the state court to expunge the verdict favoring O'Bryan, and enjoined it from proceeding further.
- Under a specific federal statute, a ruling of the sort entered by Judge Austin is nonappealable. Battisti

managed to circumvent this obstacle by granting
Chandler a "bill of peace" against O'Bryan. The
bill of peace is a legal rarity seldom encountered
in modern law. It is intended to protect a person
from repeated, baseless litigation on an issue already resolved by the courts, by barring further
proceedings. In this particular phase of the O'Bryan-
Chandler feud, however, O'Bryan had won both
rounds, before Judge Austin and in the state trial.
No problem for Judge Battisti. He held that the
entire string of cases, dating back to the initial
disbarment and continuing through the libel actions,
should be treated as a unit. Chandler had won judicial immunity from the first libel suit. The so-
called "official statement" (the basis of the second
libel suit) had been filed during appeal of the first
libel suit. Ergo, the immunity was transferrable to
the second case, regardless of Judge Austin's findings to the contrary.

If Battisti's logic appears acutely circular, consider
the plight of O'Bryan, who felt at this point as if an
omnipotent Federal Judges Mutual Protective Association was crushing down upon him. Undaunted, he
plodded up to the court of appeals again, which for
the first time saw things his way. The court scoffed
at Battisti's bill of peace. That Chandler would even
ask for one, it considered to be a "rather unique
contention." Though Chandler claimed the prolonged
litigation hurt his effectiveness as a federal judge, the
court remarked tartly that the worst thing that could
happen to him would be to have a decision reversed,
"and this is but one of the hazards of the judicial
occupation." The court held that Battisti should have
left the case in state courts, rather than interfering
with Austin's ruling.

When I spoke with O'Bryan and Chandler in the
summer of 1973, more appeals (from Chandler)
were churning towards the United States Supreme
Court. Chandler fended off specific questions about
the O'Bryan litigation; because he declines direct

quotation on anything he says off the bench, suffice
it to report that his public posture towards the case
is that a disbarred lawyer is stirring up a needless,
silly fuss, and that justice or God or something
eventually will do right in the matter (that is to say,
make Pat O'Bryan go away). Serious citizens should
pay no attention to O'Bryan—Chandler never called
him by name, only by the epithet "disbarred lawyer."
The main issue, to Chandler, remains the attempt of
judicial councils to dominate and intimidate district
judges.*

O'Bryan, meanwhile, cheerily computed six percent
interest on his $50,000 libel judgement (returned in
February 1967) and fantasized what he would do
should the Supreme Court go against Chandler in the
final appeal. "The $50,000 is nothing, pure nothing,"
he said. "Once I establish that Chandler was persecut-
ing me—as this case would do—I'm going after his
ass for malicious disbarment, and for that $1.1
million fee that was rightly mine." He showed me a
computer printout of his work on the Selected Investment tax case—enough paper to cover the walls of
my home, and most of the lawn as well. "What I'm
going to show is that a ＿＿＿＿＿＿ can't tromp
on Americans just because he happens to be a
＿＿＿＿＿ federal judge. And put that in your
＿＿＿＿＿ book."

By this time I had heard Chandler and O'Bryan
harangue their many enemies at such length that my
inclination was to forego writing about them. Could

---

* In the spring of 1974 Chandler found himself yet another
set of adversaries. On March 10 he disbarred William R. Burkett, the United States Attorney for the Western District of
Oklahoma, four of his assistants, and an Internal Revenue
Service regional counsel, on charges of conspiring to conceal
the whereabouts of a witness in a tax evasion case. The order
would have barred the six attorneys from practicing in the
federal courts in the 44-county district. Within hours, however, the Tenth Circuit Court of Appeals suspended the order.
Burkett and the other attorneys vigorously denied any wrongdoing, and the Oklahoma City *Daily Oklahoman* commented
that Chandler's action "raised anew the long debated question
of whether judges should be appointed for life."

I truly find credible O'Bryan's charge of an oppressive judiciary, of judges so loyal to their brothers of the bench that they move against a colleague only when he violates lodge rules, and that the trampling of a mere citizen is not sufficient cause for sanction? Or could I give credence to Chandler's equally vehement claim of victimization by a conspiracy including parties so diverse as Judge Murrah and Pat O'Bryan?

Then one morning, as I sat chatting with Judge Chandler in his chambers—*listening*, to be more accurate; conversations with Chandler tend to be one-sided—he did something that brought me up with a start, that made me realize there are times when it is wiser for a reporter to sit and listen and permit his subjects to perform naturally, rather than try to get at the truth through conventional questioning. Chandler had been inundating me with copies of printed briefs and photostats of various pleadings (*"Just one more time, Miss,"* he called to his secretary at least half a dozen times in directing her to feed something through the Xerox machine). We had finally gotten to the area of judicial independence, and I casually asked Chandler to recommend some good background reading. "Bring me that Battisti file," he called to the secretary.

"Battisti?" I asked.

Yes, Battisti, the guy who tried to straighten out that disbarred lawyer for me.

"Oh, you know him?"

Sure. We write back and forth, and he's done some good work in judicial independence. He knows what they are trying to do to me down here. We've even set up our own informal group of district judges to fight these goddamned judicial councils. Battisti is very big in this field.

The secretary put a fat file on Chandler's desk. As he rummaged in it I could see letter after letter signed by Battisti. Chandler finally gave me reprints of two Battisti speeches containing highly favorable resumes of his troubles, and supporting his position. *A great judge, this Battisti,* Chandler mused, *he isn't afraid to fight.*

And, I thought to myself, how can Chandler and Battisti justify such a close relationship when they are thrown together, not as judge-and-judge, but as judge-and-litigant? Technically the O'Bryan libel case was still before Battisti, remanded there by a Circuit Court of Appeals order in May 1971; if the Supreme Court refused to review the case, Battisti would be compelled to rework his own ruling in O'Bryan's favor. Indeed, Battisti commented favorably on the embattled judge's side of "The Chandler Case" (words he used in his texts) in public speeches at the Boston College Law School Forum in November 1971 and eighteen months later at the dedication of the Roscoe Pound Library at the Harvard Law School. During this time Battisti was actively involved in the Chandler litigation, and one of the several orders he issued gives the flavor of his feelings. At one stage the circuit court had ordered Battisti to remand the libel case back to state court. He complied "with deep regret," according to his order (dated December 20, 1972) and added, "It should never be forgotten that Judge Chandler has been persecuted by a disbarred lawyer for more than a decade, and only the learned courts of the great State of Oklahoma can remedy this injustice." Yet at the same time Battisti was conducting a friendly exchange of correspondence with Chandler (according to several brief passages Chandler read to me) and cited "The Chandler Case" (of which the O'Bryan suits most definitely are a component) as an example of judicial courage. Judicial independence, of course, is a perfectly legitimate area of concern for jurists, and at the time Battisti was making his statements several proposals for curbing judicial activities were before Congress. Lawyers friendly to Battisti say that the judge indeed has a keen interest in protecting jurists' constitutional status. Nonetheless, here were these speeches, referring to a man caught up in a case which Battisti might well be deciding in the future. Stuff and nonsense, I said to myself as I sat there in Chandler's chambers. O'Bryan might be just what Chandler claims him to be. That is a question I cannot resolve even in the privacy of my own thoughts.

Nonetheless O'Bryan is deadly accurate on one of his core claims: an individual citizen who offends a federal judge had best find shelter and stay there.

Enough. I began my quest for whatever truth exists in the Chandler Case by talking with the judge. Now I had filled a briefcase and a file box with stuff from both Chandler and O'Bryan, and listened to both men at length, and gone through more court and other records than I care to remember, and interviewed whatever people I could find who cared to talk about the imbroglio. My inclination was to get out of Oklahoma and sort through what I had learned, and attempt to make sense of it. As a parting gesture, however, Stephen Chandler wanted to show me something.

I followed him from his chambers and across the corridor through an inconspicuous door (Chandler had to unlock it first) that opened into his courtroom. *Sit up there,* Chandler said, gesturing towards the bench, *that's the best seat in the United States of America. . . .*

I did, and I enjoyed the sensation, even though Chandler and I were the only persons in the room. No one, by God, looks down on a federal judge, because they have the highest seat in the house, and all the other chairs, even those of the jury box, seem to have this subtle slant that makes them face toward the bench. (When I checked later I found I was wrong; the chairs are not slanted. Alas, a delusion of power.) I swivelled around in Judge Chandler's chair and (approvingly, I thought) noted the United States flag was in order, and I inspected the top of Judge Chandler's desk (40-odd pencils, two containers of paper clips, a doodle pad). Chandler let me play for a moment, then walked to the lawyers' lectern some 20 feet in front of the bench, gripped both sides, and nodded formally.

"If it may please The Court," he said (pronouncing the words with capital letters).

"You may proceed, counsel," I replied.

"It is my intention, Your Honor, to argue to you

this morning the importance of judicial independence in our republic, and to summarize for you. . . ."

Yes, I thought to myself as I listened to Chandler, the Oklahoma federal judiciary is something that definitely belonged in my book.

CHAPTER SIX

The D.C. Court of Appeals: The Mini Supreme Court

When a bomb exploded in a restroom in the United States Capitol in 1970, Senate Minority Leader Hugh Scott (R., Pa.) angrily commented that even if the bombers were arrested and convicted, the United States Court of Appeals for the District of Columbia "would find some way to get them out." Aside from enhancing Scott's reputation as one of Washington's more odious masters of the political cheap-shot, the remark capsulized the court's reputation among Congressional conservatives. The D. C. appeals court is what politicians have in mind when they rant about mollycoddling judges who dream up ingenious excuses to free criminals from jail. The court's proximity to Congress—three blocks distant, via Pennsylvania Avenue—makes it a visible irritant to law-and-order enthusiasts, a daily reminder that the Bill of Rights is interpreted by a judge, not by the cop on the beat.

And to the conservatives, the D. C. appeals court is personalized by a rather interesting character named David Lionel Bazelon, its chief judge since 1962. A reclusive intellectual who is so private he is almost invisible in the capital (one acquaintance says, "Dave Bazelon isn't 'chummy' with more than half-a-dozen people in this town, including his wife and kids"), he has had an extraordinarily civilizing impact on criminal law in the United States, and especially as it pertains to psychiatry. The seminal episode for this interest came in the late 1940s when Bazelon was a young bureaucratic lawyer in the Truman Administration. A Washington psychiatrist named Harry Stack Sullivan, proponent of the interpersonal school of analysis, was much in vogue among New Dealers and their successors in Truman's Fair Deal. Briefly, Sullivan rejected inner Freudian drives as the imperatives for a person's development, and stressed outside influences. Together with his friends William O. Douglas, the Supreme Court justice, and Abe Fortas, then a Washington lawyer (and later a justice himself), Bazelon underwent prolonged psychoanalysis with Sullivan at the Washington School of Psychiatry. Sullivan's message, essentially, was that an individual's behavior could be altered by changing the environment in which he worked and lived. His thesis, of course, dovetailed neatly with the political philosophy of the Roosevelt–Truman Administrations, and it had unmeasured but apparently profound impact upon many intellectually-bent government officials. And Sullivan's influence is directly reflected in what is perhaps Bazelon's outstanding single contribution to criminal law.

For a century the test of insanity in a criminal case was whether the accused knew right from wrong (the old M'Naughton Rule). In 1951 a confused young Washington burglar named Monte Wayne Durham, who had a long history of mental disturbances, broke into a Georgetown home. Despite his obvious mental defects Durham could not convince a district court jury he did not know right from wrong. On appeal (with Abe Fortas serving as Durham's court-appointed attorney) Bazelon completely dashed the M'Naughton Rule. "The science of psychiatry now recognizes," Bazelon wrote, "that a man is an integrated personality, and that reason, which is only one element in that personality, is not the sole determinant of his conduct. The right-wrong test, which considers knowledge of reason alone, is therefore an inadequate guide to mental responsibility for criminal behavior." His decision laid down a new rule: "that an accused is not criminally responsible if his unlawful act was the product of a mental disease or defect."

The United States Supreme Court used a Bazelon

opinion as the basis for its key ruling, in the Mallory case, that the police must take a criminal suspect before a magistrate for warning of his rights before he's hustled off to the back room of the station house for interrogation.* Other Bazelon decisions, although not national landmarks, show the thrust of his thinking. Under his tutelage the D.C. appeals court required mental hospitals to treat criminal inmates, not just store them away indefinitely. It classified skid-row winos as sick persons, not criminal misdemeanants, and ordered that they be treated, not jailed. It put tight curbs on police searches of private dwellings. It forbade the federal government to fire civil servants solely on the ground that they are homosexuals. It struck down the prosecutions of some 12,000 persons arrested in Washington during the massive May Day antiwar demonstrations of 1971, saying nothing warranted the Nixon Administration's tacit declaration of martial law in the District of Columbia.

The list is seemingly endless; in fact, the D.C. appeals court's activism in criminal law tends to overshadow another function that makes it, in the opinion of many lawyers, the second most important court in the United States—a "mini supreme court," in the words of a Boston attorney. The accolade stems from the court's jurisdiction over appeals of decisions of a host of key federal regulatory agencies, and over appeals of the many federal cases arising in the United States District Court in Washington. (The district court draws these cases for the logical reason that the government is based in Washington.) As national power gravitated to Washington during the 1930s, the regulatory agencies acquired awesome authority over the lives and fortunes of Americans. Since only a minute percentage of cases go to the Supreme Court, for all practical purposes the D.C. appeals court is the final reviewing authority over regulatory agency

---

* Bazelon couldn't sell his thesis to fellow judges on the appeals court, who upheld Mallory's conviction on a rape charge. Mallory's lawyers went to the Supreme Court and won reversal in a decision that tracked Bazelon's dissent.

decisions. A listing of the agencies involved indicates the staggering diversity of the issues that come before the court: the Securities and Exchange Commission, the National Labor Relations Board, the Civil Aeronautics Board, the Federal Trade Commission, and the Federal Power Commission. The D.C. appeals court shares with the ten other circuit courts appeals from the Federal Communications Commission, the Atomic Energy Commission, and the Post Office.

Yet for all its prestige, the D.C. appeals court is a cockpit, one whose judges insult one another in private and in printed opinions, and which is attacked frequently—and bitterly—by lawyers and district court jurists in Washington. The target is Judge Bazelon. An outnumbered conservative clique on the court thinks him to be absolutely daft and so soft-hearted he should be a social worker, not a jurist. Warren Burger, who served with Bazelon on the court before his appointment as chief justice of the United States, regularly called in court reporters for the Washington newspapers to listen to not-for-attribution lambastings of his colleague. As one of these journalists told me, "Burger would say things like, 'Poor Dave is so misguided he's pathetic. He's a menace to society himself, let alone the people he keeps turning out of jail.' There was a visible gut hatred. Burger would even call reporters directly to make sure they gave space to his dissents when he disagreed with Bazelon."

The Bazelon-conservative animosity is revealed in ways other than the behind-the-back-biting. Consider the seating arrangements in the judges' dining room in the Washington federal courthouse. "The Bazelon people will take one table, the conservatives another, at the opposite end of the room," states a Washington lawyer who formerly clerked for the court. "Poor Judge [Carl] McGowan felt this kind of implicit side-choosing put him on the spot, because he was frequently a swing man between the blocs. For a long time he just disappeared at lunch, and no one knew where he went. Finally, someone saw him one day at the cafeteria in the Federal Power Commission Building, a few blocks from the courthouse. Judge Mc-

Gowan seemed embarrassed, and he said, 'Somehow it's more comfortable over here, away from the feuding.' "

The animosity spills down into the D. C. district court, whose judges are frequently outraged at being reversed. During fiscal 1973, for instance, the appeals court reversed 16.3 percent of district court findings: 12.1 of the criminal cases, 21.7 of the private civil cases, 16.7 percent of the federal civil cases. District judges, as humans, don't like being told they are wrong, especially by men who are, after all, other mortals. Loudest in his anger is Judge George L. Hart, Jr., Republican chairman for the District of Columbia before President Eisenhower put him on the bench in 1958. Hart has been upset with the court of appeals more or less constantly for the last decade; he is unique, however, in that he likes to rake off the Bazelon faction publicly, rather than toss brickbats out of the darkness of anonymity. Hart's outcries deserve attention not because of his stature as a jurist (many Washington lawyers write him off privately as a sort of screwball) but because in his own loud way he summarizes what many other persons think of the Bazelon court, and their frustration in trying to override the majority.

During 1971 the Department of Interior and the American Civil Liberties Union squabbled constantly over government attempts to curtail protest demonstrations outside the White House. Interior, which controls grounds near the White House, wanted to limit demonstrators to 100 on the sidewalk, and 500 in adjacent LaFayette Park. Hart upheld the 100/500 limit three times; the court of appeals reversed him three times in successive cases. Finally along came a group wanting to mount a "daily death toll vigil" outside the White House. This time Hart threw up his hands and refused to issue the government any further injunctions. "The court of appeals has said the Secret Service is not going to be the arbiter of how you protect the President of the United States," Hart thundered from the bench. "It doesn't appear to me that anyone who goes to the White House with anything less than heavy guns is to be banned." Hart said he would not grant the injunction "unless somebody is trying to wheel 16-inch guns up there [to the White House] . . . unless it is so patently dangerous that even the most extreme liberal thinks something should be done."

The same year the court of appeals ordered an unwilling Hart to examine secret government documents concerning a nuclear test blast under an Aleutian island. Hart was willing to take the AEC at its word that the test wouldn't harm anything. Environmentalists, however, felt the documents would reveal dangers of the blast. Hart was holding a hearing on a peripheral issue when someone slipped the appeals court's decision before him. As someone in the courtroom at the time later said, what followed could hardly have been more dramatic than if Bazelon himself "tiptoed up behind Hart and tapped him on the shoulder" and told him he was wrong. Hart read the opinion and exclaimed, "This is the most outrageous thing I think I've ever seen. I gather from this that there's no damned thing that the court can't ask for from the President. Heavens above!"

In yet another instance a Bazelon decision blocked construction of a controversial bridge between Washington and suburban Virginia, one that would decimate waterfront parkland on both sides of the Potomac. Hart, who had given builders the go-ahead for the span, protested that Bazelon's "economic, political and sociological ideas" prompted the reversal, and then offered the supreme judicial insult: Bazelon, Hart said, "believes the bridge should not be built. I think he is distorting the various applicable laws to reach this private conclusion of his." (One of Bazelon's colleagues on the appeals court agreed with Hart. Judge George MacKinnon, in a dissent, accused Bazelon of taking a "partial and slanted view of the facts" in the case.)

Bazelon's most outspoken adversary on his own court is Judge Edward Tamm, a former FBI agent who served on the district bench from 1948 until his elevation to the appellate level in 1965. A dissent in a 1971 racial covenant case attacked what Tamm felt was a continuing unsatisfactory trend by the Bazelon majority:

> These strained contortions of the meaning and the nature of the record in this case illustrate again the unfortunate practice of some members of this court of attempting to wrench far-reaching social changes without regard to the facts, the law or precedents . . . and in absolute disregard of separations of powers [between the judiciary and Congress].
>
> The practice of choosing the philosophically eclectic rather than the established legal precedents is unfortunately a pursuit of abstract liberalism for its own sake rather than an adjudication of the law governing an individual case.
>
> The dangerous illusion that the courts, upon the pretext of ruling upon a particular case, may articulate with great sympathy and understanding upon all of the social evils of the nation, is implausibly fashionable in some areas of judicial rulings, with a resulting horrible economy of law.

Such commentary is typical of the billingsgate heard around the Bazelon court on any given day. Public commotion in the judiciary is such an extraordinary phenomenon that it cannot be ignored, especially when a feisty character like Hart unloads on a higher court with such vehemence. But as one long-time academic observer of the D.C. appeals court mused during our discussion of the court, "What upsets me, I guess, is that so much of the criticism is personal. The fact of the matter is that many people in Washington do not like David Bazelon. Were he another sort of person, you might have the same kinds of philosophical disagreements over the direction of his court." The man paused a long moment. "But at least, we'd be shed of the hatred. And that's what it is on the part of many people—sheer hatred of David Bazelon."

The evolution of the United States Court of Appeals for the District of Columbia as a liberal bench was "by accident rather than by design," according to a legal scholar who watched the bench closely for almost two decades. Because the court was considered a "national bench" and Washington had no senators with whom appointments must be cleared, a president technically was free to go anywhere in the country for nominees. But as a matter of practice local conservatives dominated the court through the 1930s and 1940s—men drawn from the D.C., Maryland and Virginia bars, and reflecting their southern, business-oriented backgrounds. The more energetic Washington lawyers, the men used to the top-dollar pay of the superfirms, were hard to lure onto the bench, even when presidents tried. President Roosevelt once sought out Dean Acheson, who worked briefly in the Treasury Department early in the New Deal before returning to his old firm of Covington & Burling. Acheson declined, and FDR asked why. "I told the story of the old boatrigger at the Yale boathouse," Acheson said. "We said to Old Charlie, 'How do you prepare yourself to row a four-mile race?' He said, 'The first thing you have to do is to learn to sit on your behind that long.' " Acheson, as was true with most Washington lawyers, was a doer, not a sitter. The court did produce two Supreme Court justices—Fred Vinson and Wiley B. Rutledge—but the legal fraternity ranked it as a so-so, do-nothing bench.

Things began changing in 1949 with the appointments of men with strikingly different personal and professional backgrounds—David Bazelon and Charles Fahey. From the perspective of history, my legal-scholar source submitted, these disparities contributed heavily, even if obliquely, to the acrimony that has swirled around the court the past two decades.

Fahey, born in Rome, Georgia, of an Irish father and a Jewish mother, became the archetypical professional Washingtonian. He came to the capital immediately after high school and took a menial government job to work his way through Georgetown law school at night. The bureaucracy and the Congress, as well as the D. C. bar, is well-larded with men of such humble legal origins. During the New Deal Fahey did distinguished service as general counsel for the National Labor Relations Board and then served as solicitor general, the ranking legal position in the government. (Among other chores, Fahey did the constitutional legerdemain to justify President Roosevelt's 1940 trade of destroyers to the British in return for United States use of naval facilities in Bermuda.) He served on the Truman commission that integrated the postwar armed forces and then, in his late fifties, was tapped for the appeals court. The importance of this Washington background is that the D.C. bar considered Fahey one of its very own.

Not so with Bazelon, who went on the court as a rank outsider. Reared in poverty in Chicago, Bazelon worked his way through Northwestern law school as a store clerk and movie usher. He served briefly as an assistant United States attorney in Chicago, trying tax cases, then went into private practice. During the Second World War he "really coined it," in the words of one longtime acquaintance, earning an estimated $50,000 a year and contributing handsomely to Democratic campaign funds. In 1946 President Truman brought him to Washington as an assistant attorney general, at $10,000 a year, then moved him over to head the Office of Alien Property. Here Bazelon got his first whiff of political grapeshot. Critics charged the office with rewarding Democratic contributors with directorships and other sinecure positions in firms which the federal government had seized from enemy owners during wartime and continued to operate. In 1949, with his division a half-step ahead of a Senate investigation of favoritism in the disposition of enemy assets, Bazelon was boosted on to the appeals bench by his old Chicago political friend Senator Paul Douglas (D., Ill.). His appointment was effective one day ahead of that of Fahey. Bazelon was 40 years old, then the youngest circuit judge in the federal courts. The then chief judge, Wilbur K. Miller, was 57, thirteen years shy of the mandatory retirement age of 70. The actuarial tables gave great significance to the day's difference in the date of appointments. According to my legal-scholar source, "This meant Fahey could never be chief judge, and that Bazelon would become chief judge early enough in life to have some influence. The general feeling of the Washington bar, and of the district trial bench, was that Fahey got screwed in the appointment. Fahey was considered the 'grand old man' of the Washington bar, and here you had an outsider, a Chicago lawyer nobody really knew anything about except that he had had a piss-ant job at the Justice Department."

Another factor was that Bazelon was Jewish, and at a time when the D.C. bar contained an inordinate number of plain, old-fashioned bigots. "All of this," the legal scholar said, "is a roundabout way of saying that Bazelon went onto the bench with the ill-feelings of a substantial number of influential Washington lawyers. Because they treated him as an unwanted outsider, he tended to keep his own counsel, to draw within himself, to act as an intellectual superior. God knows but he *was* the superior of most lawyers in town, but he never established that essential rapport with the bar. Had he done so, I think a lot of his controversial decisions would have been swallowed much easier."

As proof the scholar points to the fact that once on the court Fahey and Bazelon had virtually indistinguishable records. Fahey, however, maintained his popularity, while Bazelon rubbed lawyers and other judges the wrong way veritably from the very moment he put on his robe. Although there are nine judges on the appeals court, most of its work is done by three-man panels, drawn by lot by the court clerk. One of Bazelon's longtime colleagues says, "Dave somehow never developed the power of persuasion. He'd come into a conference and announce where he stood; his mind was made up, and he wouldn't argue. And as is true of many bright people, his thoughts outrun his tongue, and he's not very good in this sort of give-and-take. Most of his big decisions, by my reckoning, came when he had a built-in philosophical majority on a panel."

Be that as it may, Bazelon consistently displayed a compassion for criminal defendants—although it was an intellectual one not based upon practical courtroom experience. Again by contrast, Fahey knew accused criminals as people, not names in appellate briefs. As a young lawyer he worked five years to overturn the death sentence of a man who had been held incommunicado for twelve days until he "confessed" a murder. Fahey often told friends, "I never looked at criminal 'law' in the same light again." Bazelon's philosophy, as expressed in his opinions, is based heavily on his deep-rooted belief in the efficacy of psychiatry as a tool of criminal justice. Recurrent themes are found in his opinions: that society should treat those who are not mentally responsible for criminal acts, not punish them; and that the public should relate crime to the conditions in which it breeds—and if it is unwilling to do so, at least it should not sit in such righteous judgement on those who are less fortunate. Further, justice is not served when a court treats equally the rich and the poor, the strong and the weak, the brilliant and the feeble-minded. "We should all be prepared," he once said, "to recognize the irony in the remark of Anatole France: 'The law in its majestic equality forbids the rich as well as the poor to sleep under bridges, to beg in the streets and to steal bread.'"

For a judge so bent, the D.C. appeals court was an ideal place to work. The federal district court in Washington had jurisdiction over cases such as robbery, murder and narcotics violations that elsewhere are tried in state court.* Hence appeals went directly to the federal circuit court rather than to a state appeals court, giving Bazelon and his colleagues a greater opportunity to "make" new criminal law. Another factor was a surge of interest in activist criminal law during the late 1950s and 1960s at the George-

---

* The district court's jurisdiction was cut sharply by a D.C. courts reform act in 1970, legislation attributable directly to hostility towards the Bazelon court by the Nixon Administration and congressional conservatives.

town University and George Washington University law schools. At Georgetown, for instance, Professor A. Kenneth Pye ran a legal internship program in 1960–61 in which students helped defend criminal cases in the district courts. Pye gave each student a hefty black spiral notebook listing procedural questions that should be raised during hearings and the trial. "The basic notion was that criminal law had been standing still; it was inevitable that it would be moving again because of concerns for racial and social justice. Our thesis was that cases should not be tried solely on the facts—now, of course, you have an ethical consideration here, in that you don't evade or tamper with the facts—but in a context where we would raise questions when we thought the existing procedures were wrong.

"A student would bring up ten points on procedure in a case. He put the district judges in a situation where if he granted all ten, he would go against existing law and accepted procedure. He also might free a guilty man. But if we were overruled, we would choose two points of the ten, and we'd go up [to the circuit court] with a reasonable assurance of getting a reversal."

In the first year of the program, according to Pye, students won some 90 percent of the cases they appealed. "We were going after cases with the same methodology as you would in trying an antitrust case: pick out the weak points of law, concentrate there, and win." Pye acknowledged that some guilty men went free as a result. But the long-range effect was to bring police procedures into tolerable conformity with the constitution and the statutory law.

Police and trial judges, however, felt as if they played in a game in which the Bazelon court constantly changed the rules, unpredictably and in midcourse. After decisions stressing post-arrest warnings of defendants, for example, the Washington police printed a form entitled "Warning of Your Rights" which was given to each suspect before questioning. The form told the person he had the right to remain silent, and to request a lawyer. It warned, "Anything you say can be used against you in court." In October 1966 a man named Frazier was arrested for the robbery of a food carryout shop. Detectives gave Frazier the warning form, and he read it. He also read (and signed) another "Consent to Speak" form which repeated the warnings, and concluded:

I know what my rights are. I am willing to make a statement and to answer questions. I do not want a lawyer. I understand and know what I am doing. No promises or threats have been made to me or used against me.

When detectives began their questioning, Frazier interrupted to tell about another robbery with which he and a friend had been charged, but which he, Frazier, said he actually committed alone. When the detective reached for a pencil and paper Frazier said, "Don't write anything down. I will tell you about this, but I don't want you to write anything down."

The detective complied, and Frazier proceeded to confess yet a third robbery, one for which he was eventually convicted and given a five-to-fifteen-year sentence. The trial judge ruled Frazier was aware of the effect of his oral statements and had "validly waived his privilege against self-incrimination."

Judge Bazelon disagreed. Frazier's refusal to permit note-taking created the "strong implication . . . that [he] thought this confession could not be used against him so long as nothing was committed to writing." Bazelon noted that Frazier was "of at least low-average mentality," and added, "When . . . police . . . are dealing with ill-educated and uncounseled suspects, they have a special obligation to be alert to signs of misunderstanding and confusion." Court of Claims Judge Phillip Nichols, Jr., sitting with the circuit court panel on special assignment,* dissented.

"I am not aware that it is a common misconception

* By law, any federal judge may be assigned to sit with a United States Circuit Court of Appeals, both to give them appellate experience and to relieve work loads.

that the words 'anything you say may be used against you' really mean not what you say but what is written. Anyone who so believed would certainly have a wonderful capacity to disregard plain logic."

Bazelon doesn't deign to answer these and other criticisms. His opinions, he tells anyone who asks, speak for themselves. But he does occasionally point out to visitors a china turtle on his office desk. Written on the underside is the legend: *Consider the turtle. He makes progress only when his neck is out.*

After the Durham decision Bazelon completely submerged himself in psychiatry, so much so, in fact, that he became recognized as one of the nation's leading lay experts. He taught on the medical faculties of George Washington and Johns Hopkins Universities and at the Menninger Clinic and served on the boards of many research groups and foundations involved in mental health. The American Psychiatric Association came to regard Bazelon as somewhat of a legal godhead, and once gave him a commendation for removing "massive barriers between the psychiatric and legal professions." As Dr. Harry C. Solomon, the association's then-president, said, "Bazelon's Durham decision made it possible for a psychiatrist to testify and give a realistic appraisal of the total nature of the defendant's illness, without adhering to the narrow limits of criminal sanity."

Unfortunately for both Bazelon and the psychiatrists, the Durham case turned out to be a mouthful of ashes. And no one was more disappointed than the judge. Given the chance to bring their professional expertise into the courtroom, the psychiatrists bolted and ran. As Bazelon lamented in an interview with Washington journalist Julius Duscha:

I had hoped that the decision-makers in psychiatry would willingly open up the reservoirs of their knowledge in the courtroom, and that this knowledge would have a significant impact on the fact-finding and value-judging tasks of the law.

What I saw instead was that psychiatrists in court quickly adopted a protective and defensive stance.

They refused to submit their opinions to the scrutiny that the adversary process demands. Psychiartists' current response to the public's concern parallels the defensive reaction which I observed in court. The profession's refusal, or perhaps its inability, to submit its expertise to public scrutiny has generated much of the current crisis which is rapidly undermining confidence and trust in the profession.

The Durham Rule proved unworkable because psychiatrists could never agree on a definition of a mental illness or disease. So in 1972 Bazelon somewhat glumly put his name on an opinion throwing out Durham in favor of another standard for criminal insanity, one developed by the American Law Institute. The ALI criteria hold that a person is not responsible for a criminal act if, as a result of mental disease or defect, he lacks substantial capacity either to appreciate the wrongfulness of his conduct or to conform his conduct to the law.

His disappointment notwithstanding, Bazelon continues to be protective of the psychiatric profession. He shows curt contempt for yahooish badgering of psychiatric witnesses by district court judges in Washington. By requiring a psychiatric witness to describe in isolation the most minute "symptoms" on which a diagnosis rests, an interrogator "may succeed in making these symptoms seem trivial or commonplace," Judge Bazelon once wrote. When this occurs Bazelon unhesitatingly slaps down the trial judge; his bias, if any, is on the side of psychiatry. Many of the trial judges, conversely, consider psychiatry so much hocuspocus. In a 1970 case, for instance, a psychiatrist was establishing that a sex offender had recovered sufficiently to be released from Saint Elizabeth's, a District of Columbia mental hospital. Judge Edward Curran broke into the examination of two psychiatric witnesses; his doubt literally drips from the transcript. The psychiatrist, among other things, maintained that the fact the man saw female genitalia and breasts in a Rorschach test was normal. Judge Curran was undisguisedly dubious:

> JUDGE CURRAN: Is there anything in the Rorschach test that will lead a normal person to determine that there was a female organ involved?
>
> THE WITNESS: Yes, Your Honor.
>
> JUDGE CURRAN: There is?
>
> THE WITNESS: Yes. Female breast is a good, plus response.
>
> JUDGE CURRAN: There is nothing about a female breast in the Rorschach test. You are a clinical psychologist and you are telling me that as a result of looking at these ink spots there is a female breast in there?
>
> THE WITNESS: I didn't say there was a female breast there. I said it is not abnormal to see a female breast.
>
> JUDGE CURRAN: There isn't?
>
> THE WITNESS: Female breast by standard, statistical analysis has been shown to be a frequent response of normal people and it is a good, plus response.
>
> JUDGE CURRAN: A normal person looks at a Rorschach test and sees a female breast, right?
>
> THE WITNESS: Not every normal person, but it is not abnormal to do it. Many normal people do it.
>
> JUDGE CURRAN: That's all. Step down.

Judge Curran was also rough with the next witness, a staff psychiatrist from Saint Elizabeth's.

> JUDGE CURRAN: Do you agree with the clinical psychologist that as a result of the Rorschach test that a normal person gets the idea that there is some female organ there?
>
> THE WITNESS: I would agree that . . .
>
> JUDGE CURRAN: No. I didn't ask you that. Are you familiar with the Rorschach test?
>
> THE WITNESS: Yes, sir.
>
> JUDGE CURRAN: As I am. Are you going to tell me that a normal person looking at the Rorschach test is going to find anything resembling a female organ?

THE WITNESS: Your Honor, the only way I can answer is to say that some normal people will and some won't.

JUDGE CURRAN: You don't know then. You are the psychiatrist and you don't know. Right?

THE WITNESS: I can't answer your question.

JUDGE CURRAN: That is pretty good. You can't anwer the question.

In an earlier case the Circuit Court of Appeals for the District of Columbia had held testimony of a clinical psychologist was relevant in determining the sanity of a person. Judge Curran, however, disagreed. "I don't think a clinical psychologist has any competency to tell me what a man's mental condition is. The court of appeals says he does. I am not going to release him."

"Judge Curran," asked the man's lawyer, "when are you going to release him, may I ask?"

"I may never release him," Judge Curran replied. "Take it up to the court of appeals. I am not going to release him."

When the man's attorney pointed out he had already been at Saint Elizabeth's longer than any term he would have served upon conviction, Judge Curran shot back, "He is not serving time. He is at Saint Elizabeth's."

"Your Honor," the lawyer responded, "I am not sure he would make that distinction so clearly."

"That could be," said Judge Curran. "If I am wrong, the court of appeals can turn him loose. If they turn him loose, there is nothing I can do about it. But I am not going to turn these people loose that are convicted of this type of a crime."

Reversing Judge Curran, Bazelon said he had disregarded both higher courts and a statutory mandate of Congress on the release of persons acquitted of criminal charges by reason of insanity. Because of his close scrutiny of cases involving Saint Elizabeth's inmates, he has prevented the mental hospital from becoming a permanent dumping ground for persons involved in criminal offenses. In one case he required

Saint Elizabeth's to provide treatment, not just confinement, for the criminally insane.

Bazelon has said, in several forums, that he thinks one prime function of an appellate court is to "lay things open on the table." As he once wrote, "The true measure of the quality of a judicial system is how many hidden problems it brings into public view and how well it stimulates the responsible officials and agencies into doing something about these problems." And in reviewing decisions of government regulatory agencies, Bazelon has written that courts no longer will "bow to the mysteries of administrative expertise." Another analogy of which Bazelon is fond is "lifting up the rug and getting at the problems that society has hidden there." To which Bazelon's critics retort: he is not just lifting up the rug, he is attempting to renovate the entire room, and by judicial fiat, not by legislation.

Further, many responsible critics of the court feel decisions are preordained once a three-judge panel is selected to hear an appeal. As noted earlier, the court normally sits in three-judge panels drawn by lot by the clerk of the court, but by a majority vote the court may elect to hear a case *en banc* with all active judges and senior circuit judges sitting. Numbers of cases are put into a tin drum. A clerk draws the names of three judges, and then three cases. The skeptics' view is that if the Bazelon faction has two judges on the panel, a criminal conviction is apt to be reversed for trivial error; if the conservatives have a majority, they are likely to affirm the lower court decision in the absence of glaring error. The President's Commission on Crime in the District of Columbia noted in 1966 that it was "concerned by the widespread community feeling that the outcome of a particular case too often depends on the choice of judges. We believe that the court should be sensitive to the effect of judicial dissension on the public." It recommended increased use of the *en banc* court. A hardline faction of critics goes a step further: they charge that Bazelon somehow is able to rig the composition of the three-judge panels so as to insure a majority in cases that interest him (particularly ones involving psychiatric issues). Several statistical snippets appear to support the claim. During one six-month period in 1969, for example, the court issued written opinions in seven cases in which mental health or critical insanity was the central issue. Bazelon was on the panel in each case. Judge Edward A. Tamm, the most outspoken conservative on the court, was on only one of them. Significant? Perhaps, but perhaps not. The conservative faction has a tendency to dispose of many of its cases without written order by simply affirming the lower court; Bazelon tends to write opinions in cases that interest him. Court functionaries heatedly deny any rigging. When Washington lawyer Norman Littell asked at a judicial conference several years back why "sociological" cases always seemed to go to "liberal" judges, court clerk Nathan Paulson replied, "I would have been fired" had he stacked panels.

Campaigning in 1968, Richard Nixon said crime in the District of Columbia was a "national disgrace" and promised steps to "restore freedom from fear in the capital of the world's greatest democracy." He favored "eliminating technicalities that favor the criminal," and appointment of judges "thoroughly experienced and versed in the criminal law and its problems." Although Nixon did not criticize the Court of Appeals for the District of Columbia by name, his appointments have obviously been intended to recast it in the same conservative mold he wanted for the Supreme Court. And as was true with his predecessors, Nixon has gone beyond Washington to find appointees he considers suitable for the court.

His first selection, to replace Warren Burger in 1969 when Burger moved to the chief justiceship, was George E. MacKinnon. A Minnesotan (and a friend of Burger), MacKinnon first met Nixon in the 1940s when they served together in the House of Representatives. He worked as research director for Nixon's 1952 campaign, and as a special assistant attorney general late in the Eisenhower Administration. In the interim he made a good deal of money as general counsel for Investors Mutual Funds of Minneapolis, an affiliate of Investors Diversified Services. Mac-Kinnon farmed out some work to Nixon's Wall Street law firm of Nixon, Mudge, Rose, Guthrie, Alexander and Mitchell, when the President was a partner. In fact, MacKinnon kept doing legal (and political) work for IDS even after his nomination for the circuit court in the spring of 1969, but before his confirmation by the Senate. According to evidence gathered by the Senate Banking Committee, Mac-Kinnon suggested to IDS directors that Hamer H. Budge, then the chairman of the Securities and Exchange Commission, be recruited as IDS president for $80,000 a year. Some senators found this offer peculiar, for at the time the SEC was drafting tight new rules to regulate mutual fund companies such as IDS. Also, what were the proprieties of a person just nominated for a judgeship making such approaches to the chairman of a regulatory agency on behalf of a client with regulatory problems? But MacKinnon explained he had known Budge since they were in Congress together, and admired him as a lawyer and administrator. As it turned out, Budge declined the IDS job, and the flurry didn't deter MacKinnon from gaining the bench.

MacKinnon promptly picked up Warren Burger's old cudgel and set about flailing Judge Bazelon. In 1971, for instance, Bazelon ordered a new trial for a narcotics defendant who had not been permitted to show that the 36 capsules of heroin he carried were a one-day supply for an addict, and not (as a layman might have thought) a peddler's stock. Mac-Kinnon, outraged, stormed in a dissent that "a convicted felon, who appears from evidence to have been caught red-handed on the public streets blatantly pushing a choice of narcotics . . . goes free for another trial wherein the interests of society will be hazarded more than usual by government evidence that has grown stale with the passage of time."

Nixon's next appointee, Roger Robb, is described by one activist liberal lawyer as "very, very conservative and very, very bright." Lawyers see Robb as an intellectual counterweight to Bazelon. "It's not enough," one man said, "to have a staunch conservative on the bench. What Nixon needed was a smart lawyer who could out-argue Bazelon on the facts, and a guy who is aggressive enough to exert leadership. Robb is definitely that man." Robb acquired a local reputation as a blood-and-thunder prosecutor during the 1930s, winning 23 first-degree murder cases. His father, Charles, meanwhile, was on the appeals court, serving from 1906 to 1939. He attracted national note as special counsel to the Atomic Energy Commission during the proceedings that branded famed physicist J. Robert Oppenheimer a security risk. Although his clients as a Washington lawyer have included such prominent conservatives as Senator Barry Goldwater, Fulton Lewis, Jr., and Otto Otepka, Robb points with professional pride to his successful defense of Earl Browder, the Communist leader charged with contempt of Congress in 1951. Robb served by court appointment, but Browder wrote later that he "displayed such a pride of his profession and what may be called a 'spirit of sportsmanship' that, despite his pronounced political opinions, which I would call reactionary, he proved of substantial, not merely formal, assistance." As an "uptown lawyer" with a lucrative private practice, Robb did not court criminal cases. It was ironic, therefore, that such a case delayed his judgeship by more than a decade. In 1958, when his name was being bandied about as a prospective district judge, Robb defended Bernard Goldfine, the New England textiles tycoon who got into trouble for giving presents to Sherman Adams, Eisenhower's White House chief of staff. Not only did Goldfine draw a jail term, but as the *Washington Post* commented after the trial, "The feeling is that Robb cannot now be nominated [for the United States District Court] without creating the impression that the nomination is a payoff for that defense." Once he did make it to the appeals bench, in 1969, Robb confounded court conservatives by refusing to be a knee-jerk hardliner. "Knowing Robb's predilections before he went on the bench," said one lawyer, "I felt he would bend over backwards to uphold all criminal convictions. He has been a strict constructionist, but he also demands that the prosecution play by the rules." A couple of examples:

- In the trial of an accused robber, Judge Oliver Gasch, a district bench hardnose, used the so-called "Allen charge" in an attempt to blast a jury out of deadlock. Under this charge a trial judge says a dissenting juror, when the majority is voting the other way, "should consider whether his doubt is a reasonable one which makes no impression upon the minds of so many jurors, equally honest, equally intelligent with himself." In this instance, the holdout juror wanted acquittal. When the jury still couldn't agree, Gasch went even further. He refused to declare a mistrial; he said he was "sure you ladies and gentlemen know we have a substantial backlog of work, and to spend another day before another jury retrying this case just doesn't make sense to me." After another day the jury voted guilty. But the circuit court, sitting *en banc*, reversed the case 5-4, Judge Spottswood Robinson writing, "Any undue intrusion by the trial judge into [the] exclusive province of the jury is error of the first magnitude. . . . While there is need to expedite the work of the courts, this cannot be at the expense of the call of conscience." The Allen charge is used sparingly because it pressures holdout jurors to accept a majority vote; the Third and Seventh Circuit Courts of Appeal do not permit its use. But as Robb noted in a crisp dissent from Robinson's opinion, the D.C. circuit on three occasions had upheld its use, as had the Supreme Court twenty times in five years. "Since the Supreme Court has not disavowed the charge," Robb wrote, "it is not for us to do so."
- But in a burglary trial, the defendant was warned that character witnesses would be examined about his reputation for drunkenness if they took the stand. They did not testify, and he was convicted. The circuit court reversed, Robb writing, "We do

not believe that convictions for drunkenness are relevant to a reputation for honesty and integrity."

For his third appointee Nixon picked a corporate lawyer, Malcolm R. Wilkey, general counsel of the Kennecott Copper Corporation. "In this instance," in the view of a Washington attorney whose firm represents blue-chip corporate clients, "the administration was looking for a conservative who would be the focus for pro-business sentiment. Business takes a licking when regulatory agency rulings are appealed to the circuit court. Let's face it—the climate in Washington is such that all you have to do is yell 'smoke' and the consumer nuts (and I include the circuit court) pour a bucket of water on whatever company is blamed." Based upon his business background Wilkey could be expected to give industry a sympathetic hearing. And, as a former United States attorney for the Southern District of Texas, he votes with the court's anti-Bazelon block on criminal justice issues.

So, too, does Edward A. Tamm, a Johnson appointee who went on the bench in 1965 as part of a compromise deal with conservatives on the Senate Judiciary Committee. Johnson had two vacancies to fill. For one of them, he wanted Harold Leventhal, the general counsel for the Democratic National Committee, and a partner in a superlaw Washington firm with David Ginsberg, who had headed a presidential crime study commission; and Meyer Feldman, a White House counsel for President Kennedy. Leventhal was a brilliant lawyer: a Phi Beta Kappa graduate of Columbia, where he led his class and edited the law review; clerk for Chief Justice Harlan Stone and Justice Stanley F. Reed; a stint with the solicitor general's office. But Senator James O. Eastland (D., Miss.), chairman of the Senate Judiciary Committee, wasn't excited about putting Leventhal on the bench. "Hell, he's nuthin' but a pint-sized David Bazelon," Eastland told one Justice Department man with scorn. Eastland threatened to "sit on Leventhal until Christmas" if Johnson sent his name to the Senate for confirmation. The administration's solution was to reach down to the district bench in Washington and promote Ed Tamm as a sop to Eastland.

Tamm certainly possessed the proper law-and-order credentials. He served with the FBI from 1930 to 1948, lastly as the top assistant to J. Edgar Hoover. When President Truman nominated him for the district court in 1948 the D.C. bar association raised a mighty clamor. The stated reason for the opposition was that Tamm had no experience in the active practice of law, and because of his background he would be partial to the federal government. The real reason, of course, was that the D.C. bar wanted the job for one of its own members. During the 1948 confirmation hearings Tamm had his feathers ruffled by a charge—which was not substantiated—that he had forged documents to gain admission to the bar almost two decades before. Once on the bench he proved a diligent judge—in one estimate, the best trial jurist in the district. "By God he learned the stuff, and he had guts," said a man friendly with the Bazelon faction. Tamm was instinctively sympathetic to prosecutors and police but "ran a fair courtroom," according to a defense lawyer. "Tamm was particularly good at making police officers keep their testimony flowing in a straight line," this man said. "But I'll admit it was disconcerting to me, as a defense lawyer, to have him listen to me at sidebar [out of the jury's hearing], and then dismiss me by saying, 'Oh, that's nonsense and you know it, and we aren't going to waste time on it.' " Tamm was hardline enough to satisfy Eastland and the Senate mossbacks, but not such a zealot that he outraged civil libertarians in the District of Columbia. So he and Leventhal went to the circuit court in a package: "Mr. Hard and Mr. Soft," by one description.

Leventhal's strength on the court is his expertise in administrative law. He has a pro-bureaucratic reputation, and regulatory agencies are generally pleased when appeals from their rulings go to his court. But he has kept his mouth shut, and keeps out of the newspapers, and votes with the Bazelon majority more often than not.

Another Bazelon ally is Spottswood W. Robinson III, "Spots" to his fellow judges and to lawyers casual enough to ignore judicial formality. Renowned as one of the top civil rights lawyers in the country during the 1950s, Robinson helped win Supreme Court decisions on school desegregation, and racial discrimination in interstate transportation and real estate ownership. He fought segregation with the fire of a Southern black (Robinson was reared in Richmond, Virginia) who has met Jim Crow face to face. "A Negro lawyer practicing in some of the outlying county courts had a hard time finding any place to eat," Robinson once said. "To be safe I'd always carry my lunch." For eleven years Robinson was on the law faculty at Howard University, the black school in Washington, the last three as dean. In October 1963, President Kennedy flouted Southern segregationists who had long kept the D.C. bench lily white and nominated Robinson as the court's first black judge. But Virginia's two Democratic Senators, Harry F. Byrd, Sr., and Willis Robertson, refused to submit approval slips; since Robinson was a Virginian, this blocked the confirmation, and the Senate adjourned without acting. About half an hour before the next session convened on January 7, 1964, Johnson submitted a new nomination—this time as a recess appointment, meaning Robinson could serve until the Senate either acted or adjourned. He was sworn into office and began his duties. The opposition dragged through the spring. The D.C. bar association, through president Oliver Gasch (now a United States district judge) objected to Robinson, saying the bar preferred an attorney who had practiced before the D.C. courts. The bar finally gave Robinson a formal, if grudging, endorsement and President Johnson persuaded Byrd and Robertson to turn around. Robinson was approved in June 1964.

As capable a trial lawyer as he had been, many Washington attorneys consider Spots Robinson a bust as a trial judge—to the disappointment of his friends.

"He was a terrible district judge," said one man who is friendly to Robinson. "He would take three to four days on routine decisions, and a jury trial could drag for days. This appalled the personal injury lawyers (the really liberal element in the civil trial field). There are cases where they simply cannot afford to spend that much time in court—they can't charge their clients fees big enough to cover the cost, and it's a waste of time." So Robinson, in effect, was promoted to get him out of the way. In 1964 President Johnson wanted a black on the D.C. appeals court because of the large number of Negroes whose cases are heard there. "The blacks would be happy with Spots on the higher court, the white trial bar wanted to get him the hell out of the way so the district courts could get some work done," my informant said. "That's the way federal judges are made." Spots Robinson has done well in the quieter atmosphere of the appeals court, where he is under no pressure to make quick decisions.

Another Bazelonite, J. Skelly Wright, is a Louisianian who figuratively fled the South one step ahead of a racist lynch mob. Wright served as a federal district judge in New Orleans during the mean, nasty civil rights fights of the 1950s, when Dixie mobilized its legal and strongarm forces to keep its schools segregated. Wright faithfully and courageously enforced integration mandates of the Supreme Court in his district, and resisted attempts at evasion by local officials. The South fought hard. In 1956, for instance, Wright barred officials in Orleans Parish (New Orleans) from operating segregated schools. Racists invoked every legal wile known to Southern man to circumvent Wright's order. The legislature passed no fewer than 23 separate acts; the school board declared "holidays" each time blacks approached; the governor seized the schools. Wright patiently slapped down each delay. Even so, not until 1962 did black children enter the first grade. Hatred swirled around him: Southern politicians called him "Judas Scalawag Wrong," and anonymous mail and phone calls constantly carried death threats to his home. Federal marshals kept Wright and his family under guard for months.

In 1962 the Kennedy Administration wanted to reward Wright for his courage by promoting him to the Fifth Circuit Court of Appeals, which covers most of the Deep South. But Senator Russell Long (D., La.) told the president that he (Long) could not be reelected if he permitted Wright to go to the appeals court. So Kennedy instead sent Wright to the D.C. circuit court, thereby solving Long's political problem, but at the same time depriving the south of Wright's accumulated wisdom in the protracted conflict of civil rights. As a replacement the South got a safe man: Frank Ellis, a genial if oafish Louisiana politician who had been Kennedy's state campaign manager in 1960, and then director of the Office of Civil Defense Mobilization.* "Now if we approve you," Senator James Eastland (D., Miss.) asked Ellis at the confirmation hearing, "you are not going to be another Skelly Wright, are you?" Ellis promised to behave. One of his first orders halted the first-grade integration Judge Wright had spent six arduous years achieving.

One person who has watched the courts at work from an insider's position, as a legal clerk, suggests that Wright "is a stronger man with the other judges than Bazelon, in the sense that he operates with considerable tact, and he is very persuasive in conferences." The clerk continued: "The conservative bloc respects Wright, because they feel he listens to their arguments even when they are in a minority. Bazelon tends to brush them aside."

Easily the most controversial decision to come from Wright's pen since he joined the court was an order banning the so-called "track system" in Washington

---

* Kennedy promoted Ellis in exasperation over his puppyish enthusiasm. Theodore Sorenson wrote in his presidential memoir that Kennedy had to dissuade Ellis from flying to Rome to get Papal endorsement of his fallout shelter plan. Kennedy also wondered aloud how he would survive being closeted in a shelter with Ellis, an *ex officio* member of the National Security Council, during a national emergency. The judgeship solved the problem.

public schools. Early in their schooling pupils were classified as to their academic potential and put on "tracks" leading either to a liberal arts curriculum or one heavy with vocational subjects. A high percentage of black children landed on the vocational track, and civil rights activists (and a number of educators) protested that the system was self-perpetuating, that it shunted successive generations into "a training program for mediocrity," making it harder for youngsters to break out of the lower economic class. They sued to scrap the track system. The federal district judges, who at that time appointed school board members in Washington, were included among the defendants. Hence it fell Bazelon's lot to designate a local judge to hear the case. He chose Wright, and all sorts of noise erupted.

First of all, conservative Washingtonians who were content with the system felt they faced a stacked deck, that given Wright's past background in civil rights cases he would surely rule for the plaintiffs. Washington lawyer Norman Littell, a New Deal era assistant attorney general who is a hairshirt of the local judiciary, complained of "clever legal maneuvering whereby . . . Bazelon could appoint a judge with a preconceived point of view to hear this case." *The Washington Star,* after poking around in Wright's past opinions and public speeches, decided it was "perfectly evident that he had anything but an open mind on the very issues which lie at the heart of the law suit." The city corporation counsel's office, defending the school officials, asked Wright to withdraw from the case because he was not able "to fairly hear and impartially weigh the evidence, and render a completely unbiased ruling and give the defendants a fair trial." Wright refused, listened to the evidence, and threw out the track system, ending the last vestiges of *de jure* segregation in the District of Columbia.

Wright's continuing interest on the court has been the use of the law to protect the poor. As he wrote a few years back, "a law may be consistently and evenly applied, yet systematically work a hardship on . . . those least able to withstand it. Rather than helping the poor surmount their poverty, the law has all too frequently served to perpetuate and even exacerbate their despair and helplessness." Wright formed these opinions after smelling some of the commercial messes that come through Washington courts. A couple of prime examples, and what he and the court did about them:

- In a 1965 case a woman complained to city officials about conditions in her apartment, and inspectors found 40 violations of the housing code. The landlord, instead of fixing up the place, threw her out. The district court deplored his action—but in the next breath held that evidence of his retaliatory motive was irrelevant; that a contract was a contract, and relief lay in the Congress, not the court. Nonsense, said the circuit court. And no longer could D.C. landlords evict tenants who complained to housing authorities.

- In another instance, a cut-rate store loaded an indigent mother with $1,800 of furniture and appliances even though she was on relief with seven children. Somehow she managed to pay all but $170 of the $1,800 (from her monthly relief check of $218). Whereupon the store persuaded her to buy a $515 stereo set, and added it to her original purchase agreement. Fine-print language in the contract said that unless she paid for each item, *all* could be repossessed. Which is exactly what happened. The district court again mourned the misfortunes of the ignorant poor but did nothing. Again, the appeals court came to the rescue. It held that courts have the power to refuse to enforce an unconscionable contract. As Wright has said, "Though our most pressing social, mortal and political imperative is to liberate the urban poor from their degradation, the courts continue to apply ancient legal doctrines which merely compound the plight of the poverty-stricken. These doctrines may once have served a purpose, but their time has passed. They must be modified or abandoned." And Wright is willing for the courts to throw the "out-

worn" doctrines into the trash can: "The failure
of the legislature to live up to its responsibility was
not reason for the courts not to live up to theirs."

The circuit court in Washington, as is true of the
other ten circuit courts in the country, portends to become an even more important part of the judiciary in
the future. Chief Justice Burger has made plain he
wants a decrease in the volume of cases for the Supreme Court, which jumped from 1,429 in 1952 to
3,171 in 1973. Without changes, Burger feels, within
a decade "we may well see the nine justices facing a
caseload exceeding 7,000 cases a year—nearly one
new case every hour of the day and night, weekdays
and weekends included." If Burger indeed succeeds in
limiting appeals, the circuit courts increasingly would
be the "court of last resort" for the areas they serve.

For the D.C. court, this fact poses an additional
challenge, that of overseeing a district court for such
uneven quality that most Washington lawyers take a
deep breath before approaching it.

*"This is a hard damned thing to talk about without
sounding like a bigot, which I think I'm not, but one
reason our bench is so putrid is that for years it was
dominated by a clique of Irish-Catholic lawyers who
ran local bar politics." The speaker was a Jewish trial
lawyer, a man in his late thirties who spends perhaps
as much time in the courtroom as does any attorney in
Washington. We were sitting in a downtown bar miles
distant from the courthouse—his choice, because he
said he wanted to talk frankly about judges, and didn't
care to be overheard by other lawyers when he did so.*

*"There were no Jewish lawyers here to speak of
until after World War Two, when you had the influx
of people from the government and the military service. At its lower levels, the government discrimi-
nated against Jews as much as it did against blacks.
The Protestants were too interested in making money
to bother with the judiciary. The Irish-Catholic clique
was composed of guys out of Justice and the United
States attorney's office. Catholics have a tendency to
go into government; look at the fire and police depart-*

ments, for example. So you had this flow: they'd work as a prosecutor, then gravitate onto the bench after dabbling in private practice awhile.

"Hell, run through the list of the oldtimers; it sounds like roll-call at the Holy Name Society. McGuire, Curran, McLaughlin, McGarraghy, Walsh, Keech. You know how black this town is. Do you realize Washington didn't even have a black judge until Spots Robinson in 1964?

"Let's get this straight. I object to these guys because, first, they were mediocre lawyers, and, second, because they go on the bench with pretty fixed notions about society. Take [John Lewis] Smith. He can overlook gambling or stealing, but don't bring a rape or abortion case before him. Lem Walsh is a good old man who never did anything particular in life but get elected president of the Touchdown Club [a claque of sports boosters] and the bar association. As a federal judge he's making more money than ever in his life.

"Or [George] Hart. His old man was in Hart and Harkins, the stenographic firm that used to be official reporter for the Republican National Convention. George got to know politicians, and so eventually they gave him a judgeship. No particular reason, other than that he was a guy who was around, and in the clique."

The lawyer swished his glass around a minute. "I don't particularly give a damn who goes on the bench, just as long as they are professionals who'll give you a fair trial. But the tragedy of this damned town is that when you run through the whole fucking list, you got three, maybe four who sit up there with an open mind and listen to you and the other lawyer, and decide the case based on the law and the facts, and not some damned political or cultural notion they've picked up in the past. End of speech. Good luck, my friend, because what you're going to see on the bench here is not very damned pretty."

My lawyer informant spoke from anger and disgust, but his characterization of the Washington federal district court proved painfully accurate. The court is fortunate in having three top-flight judges: William B. Bryant, Gerhard Gesell and William B. Jones. From there the quality trails off quickly to mediocre and awful. It deserves attention, therefore, not for judicial quality, but because of the importance of the cases it handles. For it is in Washington federal court that the government is frequently obliged to justify executive and legislative actions, and hence the decisions frequently have national impact: the legality of the Alaskan pipeline, overbooking by airlines, the impounding of funds by the president, the constitutionality of government-required safety equipment on automobiles. Such is the stuff on which the Washington court feeds daily.

Only many of the judges aren't able to digest such a demanding diet.

After watching Chicago courts a few weeks, and talking with lawyers and other persons, I concluded the sorry quality of the bench there was attributable to a combination of bar apathy and politics. Such is also the case in Washington. Seldom will a prominent "national" lawyer step down from the six-figure income that partners earn in superfirms for the $40,000 salary of a judge. One prominent exception is Gesell, who was earning upwards of $200,000 annually when he left Covington & Burling in 1967 for the bench. But as one of his friends told me, "Gerry was bored silly. After you've won all the big ones, and you're not even 50 years old, and you have all the money you can ever spend, what's the excitement about law? I don't think Gerry 'left' Covington; I think he just decided he wanted a new career."

More often the appointees are politicians who didn't quite make it on the national scene, or attorneys whose practices were marked with more hustle than riches. Unadulterated politics are frequently a factor. During Lyndon Johnson's vice-presidential years, for example, one of the few old friends who stayed close to him was the fabled Washington lawyer–lobbyist Thomas G. (Tommy the Cork) Corcoran. So when Johnson succeeded to the White House he did Tommy the Cork a favor by putting his brother, Howard, onto the district bench, even though his courtroom experience was minimal. A more complex deal put Luther

W. Youngdahl of Minnesota on the D.C. bench in 1951. Youngdahl, a popular Republican, was just finishing his third term as governor when President Truman made the appointment. As a *Washington Times-Herald* editorial bitterly observed, with Youngdahl's name on the ticket for reelection in 1952, "the chances of the Democrats seemed about nil. The New Dealers reasoned that if they bought off Youngdahl with a judgeship, they would improve their chances." *

Or, again, a president might simply want a person of a certain background, race or sex. Such was the case with Judge June L. Green, who was a pleasant but undistinguished lawyer specializing in divorce and auto accident cases (both in Washington and nearby Annapolis) when the Johnson Administration decided in 1968 that it wanted to give women a chance at high-level government jobs. The women's liberation movement was coming into full voice, and national politicians hadn't decided just how to handle it. The reflexive instinct of an administration is to toss out a few jobs, if they are available, and see if the mob will quiet. June Green had been active in bar affairs (as president of the women's bar in Washington, and as one of two women bar examiners in the United States) and in Maryland politics (among her close friends was Daniel Brewster, then the Democratic senator from Maryland). Her husband, John, also a lawyer, worked in the Office of Emergency Planning, a White House agency. So when the administration began looking, she was visible enough to be noticed.

Which turned out to be a pity, both for June Green and for justice in the District of Columbia. There is no way to say this nicely. There are lawyers who consider the woman a disaster. She has so fouled case after case that even defense laywers weep and sneak

---

* Truman made the appointment even though Youngdahl confided he was considering retiring as governor because of high blood pressure. Youngdahl minimized the health problem at his confirmation hearing. "I can do 50 situps without bending my knees," he said. "I can take on any member of the committee." He proved to be a first-rate (and healthy) judge and continued active even after reaching senior status in 1966.

out for a midday drink when they learn they must go
to trial before her. After listening to attorneys rant
about her shortcomings for several days ("stupid" and
"not enough sense to understand what was going on"
were two recurring gripes) I decided to explore for
myself Judge Green's track record. So one afternoon
I went to the law section of the Library of Congress
and browsed through a dozen volumes of the *Federal
Reporter,* which publishes appellate decisions from
each federal circuit court. Judge Green's deficiences as
a jurist were laid bare in page after printed page. Some
notable cases, gleaned from some two years of appellate oversight of her competence:

- A man charged with robbery had not seen his
  lawyer for the six months preceding trial, and
  tried to fire him several times. He wanted a new
  attorney. Judge Green refused, and forced him to
  trial; he was convicted. Reversed.
- A man confined at Saint Elizabeth's was accused of
  killing a woman employee on the wooded hospital
  grounds. Ten days later, while under heavy police
  suspicion, he confessed to a doctor, who relayed
  the statement to officers. The circuit court held
  he had not been properly warned, and that the
  confession was therefore inadmissible. Reversed.
- A man was charged with carnal knowledge of his
  ten-year-old daughter. Judge Green raised an insanity defense over the objections of his lawyers;
  the jury agreed, and ordered him confined. The
  circuit court held there was a "substantial possibility" the jury would have acquitted him had not
  the insanity issue been presented, because there
  were no corroborating witnesses other than a "confused" nine-year-old brother. Reversed.
- A robbery victim told the defense attorney in private conversation that another man forced the defendant to aid in the crime. He recanted on the
  witness stand. Judge Green refused to permit the
  lawyer to withdraw from the case and testify about
  the conversation. Reversed.
- Once testimony is completed, and lawyers finish

their closing arguments, the judge must instruct the jury on the applicable law, and outline what must be shown to support a particular verdict. Judge Green has had considerable trouble convincing the circuit court that she always knows what she is doing when she instructs juries. In the case of a defendant named Wharton, Judge Green muddled through instructions on both manslaughter and murder as possible verdicts. The jury convicted Wharton of murder. The circuit court wasn't even diplomatic. "We find that the instructions were doubly erroneous. . . . Both passages were erroneous and we have so held in a number of recent cases. . . . What we face is bad advice twice given to the jury." The court changed the conviction from murder to manslaughter and reduced Wharton's sentence.

- In another case, a man named Washington was charged with car theft and transporting a stolen vehicle. The sole evidence was that he had been found with the car in Pennsylvania about half a year after its theft. Appellate courts have held repeatedly that such evidence is not sufficient to sustain conviction on the specific charges faced by Washington. Again, botched instructions, and a conviction, and a reversal in tart language: the circuit court ordered acquittal, and told Judge Green she should have known better.

- But Judge Green's most notorious case involved a man named James Skeens, accused of robbing the popular Duke Zeibert's Restaurant in Washington of $14,000. Washington lawyer/journalist Harvey Katz, after a review of the case, commented that "Judge Green made so many contradictory rulings and committed so many errors that the court record reads like a chapter from Dickens." Much of the evidence against Skeens came from an informant who identified Skeens as the gunman, told police where to find a shotgun used in the robbery, and warned of a plot to kill a government witness. The defense wanted the informant identified so that he could be cross-examined. Fearful for his life, the informant refused even to meet Judge Green in her chambers *in camera*. Judge Green wanted to dismiss the case, but the court of appeals ordered her to complete the trial. The jury found Skeens guilty. She set aside the verdict and acquitted him —without giving the United States attorney the opportunity to argue against her ruling. Judge Green reconsidered, and ordered a new trial (although this is improper unless requested by the defendant; Skeens' lawyers had made no such motion). Eventually the circuit court said the original jury verdict should have stood. Skeens went off to jail.

"Were June Green a younger person," a trial lawyer told me, "I wouldn't worry so much about her, because she might learn the ropes. But she's been on the bench for six years now."

Through geographic accident, Judge Green's next-door neighbor in the United States courthouse is a man generally listed as one of the best three men on the fifteen-judge bench, Gerhard Alden Gesell, whose erect carriage, white hair and round ruddy face (now beginning to sag with the weight of his 61 years) would satisfy a television casting director were he in need of a judge to hear Perry Mason's cases. Gesell is one of those rare judges who can be tough with lawyers without offending them. "When I try a case in Gesell's court," one criminal lawyer told me, "it's he, me, and the other side. Because I know him, I'll occasionally get off a flippant remark. He takes off his glasses and glances down, and he doesn't have to say a word—I know he's mad, and I apologize and move on." Because of his lofty corporate background and his zeal for rough-and-tumble tactics on behalf of business clients * Gesell was not uniformly trusted by many

---

* During the early 1960s Gesell saved General Electric uncountable millions of dollars in potential antitrust damages by arranging criminal pleas in such a fashion that company directors and top management were absolved of any "knowledge" of illegal price-fixing. The complex story is detailed in my *The Superlawyers*, Weybright and Talley, New York, 1972.

Washington lawyers. In the opinion of a civil practitioner, "To me the question had two parts: whether Gerry would be bored silly by the daily tedium of the bench, and whether he could forget that he used to work for the kinds of corporations that were going through his court. After six years I have no doubt about him—he's first-rate. He's independent."

Gesell's independence is one born both from wealth and the self-assurance of a professional. Gesell has never had to give money a second thought; he's always had it. His father, the late Arnold Gesell, was an earlier-generation Doctor Spock, and his Gesell Institute at Yale University did pioneer work in child psychology. Gesell *pere*'s *The Child From Five to Ten* and other book royalties kept the family comfortable. Gesell learned his law at Yale and as a trial attorney for the Securities and Exchange Commission, where he toiled five years before joining Covington & Burling. According to friends in the firm Gesell was the workhorse sort of lawyer who could spend a day in court, concentrate on strategy all night, and then shave and change his shirt, and be "as bright and chipper as a boy scout when court opened at nine." A Democrat, Gesell took two presidential assignments in the 1960s: to study the impact of racial factors on servicemen and their families, by President Kennedy; and to help reorganize D.C. courts, by President Johnson. In late 1967, when he tired of law, he simply let the fact be known at the Justice Department and in bar circles; sure enough, soon the Johnson Administration offered him the appointment. In the words of one lawyer, "Justice was so damned happy to have a first-rate man in Washington that they jumped at his 'availability.'"

In his two most-publicized cases Gesell showed a willingness to look beyond precedent in situations involving changing national mores; and to resist government and other pressures. In 1969 he wrote a bold, reasoned opinion legalizing abortions in the District of Columbia, one of the forerunners of the historic Supreme Court ruling. And when the Nixon Administration sought to enjoin the *Washington Post* from publishing the Pentagon Papers, Gesell came down strong on the side of freedom of the press. (Because of Gesell's liberal reputation, and his past representation of the *Post* while at Covington & Burling, government lawyers would have preferred that the case go elsewhere. When Justice Department lawyer Joseph Hannon learned in the court clerk's office that Gesell had drawn the case, he clasped his hand to his forehead and exclaimed, "Oh, my lord.") Gesell had two chances to rule in the case; both times he refused to restrain the *Post* from publishing articles based on the Papers. "What is presented is a raw question of preserving the freedom of the press as it confronts the efforts of the government to impose a prior restraint on publication of essentially historical data," he said. At one point government lawyers asked for a 24-hour delay in an order to give them time to file an appeal. Had Gesell granted it, of course, the ban on publication would have been extended for another day. Gesell glanced at the courtroom clock. It showed 4:40 P.M. He said curtly, "Gentlemen, the clerk's office upstairs [in the circuit court of appeals] closes in twenty minutes," and walked off the bench. (The Supreme Court ultimately sided with the *Post* and *The New York Times*—and Gesell—on the prior restraint issue.)

After the Pentagon Papers case had ended, Gesell confided to friends, "I wasn't going to give the government an inch, because I recognized the implications in this case. I was determined to make them prove a case, if they had one." He paused a minute. "I wasn't going down in history as the judge in another John Peter Zenger case" [referring to the pre-Revolutionary era editor whose jailing helped establish the American tradition of freedom of the press].

Gesell was also tough on the government in the Watergate-related cases he handled. An example: the government asked for a postponement of sentencing of Donald Segretti, the young California lawyer who had pleaded guilty to illicit campaign tactics on behalf of the Committee to Re-Elect the President. The argument was that Segretti would be needed to testify against other defendants, and that putting him in jail would cause logistical inconveniences. "Oh, come now," exclaimed Gesell. "What if he *is* in prison? You can fly him anyplace in the country in twenty-four hours. The man had pleaded guilty, and it's time to sentence him." Which he did, to six months in federal prison. And during pretrial manuevering in the Ellsberg psychiatrist burglary case Gesell accused President Nixon of courting dismissal of the charges by reneging on a promise to permit former White House aide John Ehrlichman free access to his old files so he could prepare his defense. At one point Gesell thought he had struck a compromise with White House lawyer James St. Clair. But when Ehrlichman went to the files he was told he could not take notes or copies; instead, he had to read and remember what he could, then "come out and regurgitate . . . into a dictating machine." Gesell demanded of St. Clair: "You are saying that [the President] will not comply with the court's order?" "I think that's a fair reading," St. Clair said. Gesell snapped that Nixon was "pointing for" dismissal of the case and started a fact-finding hearing preliminary to taking "appropriate action under the contempt statute." He sternly scolded St. Clair: "You agreed to it [the compromise] and you were vetoed, and it's wrong. We all know it's wrong. It is an obvious affront to the process of justice . . . It is offensive, sir—it borders on obstruction." The White House backed down sufficiently to permit the trial to proceed, thereby averting any contempt citation against the President.

Lawyers use the word "intellectual" in speaking of Gesell. For Judge William B. Bryant, they have another term: street-wise. Gesell's background is prep school/Yale/superlaw/Washington society. Bryant's personal and professional origins could not be more disparate. He was born in rural Wetumpka, Alabama, in 1911, to impoverished but rebellious parents who fled the South a year later to escape the hopeless future of most southern blacks. Bryant worked at menial jobs to get through the Howard University law school and taught there until the Second World War. One significant side project was aiding Ralph Bunche, then a Howard professor (and later United States ambassador to the United Nations) on a study of the Negro in American political life. The findings later became a part of Gunnar Myrdal's classic treatise, *An American Dilemma*. Bryant spent much of the succeeding decade on race relations. As an army legal officer (he achieved the rank of lieutenant colonel) Bryant studied the racial impact of military installations on North Carolina, Indiana and Mississippi. After his discharge in 1947 he worked with sociologist Joseph D. Lohman on the study, "Segregation in the Nation's Capital," that was a major impetus toward the end of official discrimination in Washington.

Yet despite this background Bryant decided against making civil rights his career. As he once told an interviewer, "I guess I just got frustrated by the slow process of chipping away at discrimination. Besides, a lot of other lawyers were already on their own in that field. Maybe I came along ten years too late or ten years too early." So Bryant turned to criminal law, representing the lower-income blacks who constitute the bulk of defendants in Washington courts. Such a practice, in the words of a man who has done it, requires two things of a lawyer: the instinct to get at the core facts of a story that is almost always absurdly complex, and told by barely-literate persons who are suspicious of anyone involved in the criminal justice system, including their own lawyer; and "to keep your own hands clean," in street vernacular. Bryant succeeded on both counts. "Bill Bryant could talk to poor blacks because he had been a poor black himself," says a lawyer friend. "When he had a 14th Street case [referring to the core artery in the Northwest Washington ghetto] he could put himself in the shoes of the dudes who were in jail; he knew what they were talking about, and he could sort out the lies from what really happened."

But there is little money in such cases, hence the constant temptation for a criminal lawyer to step across the line and become a *de facto* partner of felons. (An example: a criminal lawyer acquaintance of mine in Dallas, now deceased, once confided he took a weekly retainer from a group of safecrackers who specialized in large chain stores and pharmacies. Each time they left for a series of out-of-town burglaries they gave the lawyer an itinerary of cities where they intended to work. If they did not return to Dallas by a set date the lawyer was to call the police in each of the towns to see if they were jailed there. He would then make bond for them. "Sure, I knew what they were doing," the lawyer told me. "But the police were in the wrong, too, because when you get out in those country towns in Texas and the South, a guy in jail doesn't get that famous 'one telephone call' you hear about in the Constitution and the movies.") Anyway, Bryant avoided such entanglements; in fact, one lawyer friend tells a story that indicates Bryant was oblivious to, if not outright ignorant about, the fees a lawyer can legitimately charge.

Judge George L. Hart, Jr., a law-and-order jurist who cared not a hang for the types that Bryant customarily represented, nonetheless respected Bryant's legal abilities. He appointed him as executor of the estate of Daddy Grace, the flamboyant leader of a black religious cult in Washington. The estate was tangled with farflung potential claimants (including some in Africa) and obscure and hidden assets (one way Daddy Grace raised money was to lie in a coffin and exhort followers to cover him with dollar bills). Bryant worked on the case for two years, found that Daddy Grace had assets of $30 million, and satisfied all claimants: For his final report to the court he drew up a draft bill and showed it to a friend for comment: "Do you think this is too much?" he asked. To the friend's surprise, Bryant asked only $30,000, although, under law, it could have been up to $300,000, one percent of the assets. The friend notes, "You can bet your ass that some other lawyers in this town would have run up the meter on this one: trips to Africa, trips to the West Coast, that sort of thing. Bryant played it tight and honest. He's that kind of guy."

Although much of Bryant's practice was what lawyers call "nickel and dime law"—that is, a succession of similar, petty criminal cases—his scrappy tenacity for clients put him at the center of several landmark criminal law cases. And foremost among them was that of Andrew Mallory, mentioned briefly earlier in this chapter.

In 1954 police arrested Mallory, a 19-year-old itinerant black from Alabama, as a suspect in the brutal rape of a Georgetown woman. Washington at the time was a transitional city, with much racial tension as the number of blacks steadily rose (from 30 percent in the 1950 census to now well above 70 percent). Community feeling was intense. The police held Mallory for seven and one-half hours before taking him before a committing magistrate; during this time he supposedly confessed to the crime.

As Bryant has told friends, Mallory was "crazy as a loon" and should have been found not guilty by reasons of insanity. But the trial judge, Alexander Holtzoff (now deceased), feared such a finding would result in Mallory's eventual release, and he considered him too dangerous to be on the streets. Holtzoff belittled a psychiatrist who testified Mallory was insane and when the jurors asked a question about the consequences of an insanity verdict, the judge told them, in effect, that he well might go free soon. Whereupon the jury voted a death sentence. So on appeal Bryant attacked the prolonged police questioning and he won both in the circuit court (in a decision by Judge Bazelon) and in the Supreme Court, which held: "The police may not arrest upon mere suspicion but only on 'probable cause.' The next step in the proceeding is to arraign the arrested person before a judicial officer as quickly as possible so that he may be advised of his rights and so that the issue of probable cause may be promptly determined." *

For his work on behalf of Mallory, Bryant got only the minimal fees of a court-appointed lawyer. At one point Mallory's family in Alabama collected $50 or $75 from church friends and offered it to Bryant. The

---

* 1958, while Congress debated legislative negation of the Mallory rule, Washington police searched for "three young Negroes" wanted for a cafe holdup. They arrested 90 persons of that general description and held 63 of them overnight. None proved to have any connection with the incident.

lawyer gently refused. "You keep the money," he told them, "you need it more than I do."

In another case, that of an accused killer named Killough, Bryant went through three trials and two appeals before winning freedom for his client on the grounds police had illegally obtained a confession. His total fee was $1,800. As a lawyer friend says of Bryant, "he was an old time lawyer. He starts a case with you, he doesn't walk out on you just because your money runs out."

By 1965 Bryant had been practicing law in Washington for seventeen years, and according to what he told friends, in no year did he earn more than $25,000 —that is to say, his income was less than what a superfirm partner could expect after three or four years. Hence when the Johnson Administration began casting around for another black district judge for Washington, Bryant was available. A longtime friend and Johnson confidante, Abe Fortas, was among his sponsors; so, too, were Ralph Bunche and A. Phillip Randolph, president of the Brotherhood of Sleeping Car Porters. Because of his background in criminal defense work, especially that of the Mallory case (a decision which the police establishment considers the Pearl Harbor of law enforcement, or worse), Bryant's nomination drew much underground opposition, especially from the Washington field office of the FBI. According to reliable accounts from within the Justice Department, the FBI report contained so much unconfirmable adverse rumor that Bryant's appointment was fleetingly in doubt. But when department officials finished sorting through the information, and evaluating it, "there wasn't a piece of dirt the size of a toothpick." So in 1965 Bryant became a district court judge.

As is the case with many trial-lawyers-turned-judges, Bryant must constantly struggle to restrain himself from plunging into the proceedings. He has the professional's impatience with incompetent cross-examination and he expects lawyers to be tolerably familiar with rules of procedure. A judge who interjects questions during examination of witnesses risks "taking over" a trial to the extent that he irritates everyone, including the jury. But Bryant, by the testimony of lawyers who practice before him, knows when to shut up—and also when to throw light on a murky factual situation.

One such instance is related by Sol Z. Rosen, an aggressive criminal trial lawyer who knows his way around the courtroom, but who is smart enough to admit that he occasionally overlooks something. Rosen once defended one of seven black youths accused of a particularly nasty rape. The victim was a white woman with a master's degree, who lived in a commune near Dupont Circle. She was subjected to at least 21 separate acts of rape and sodomy over a period of hours in three locations. Rosen's client denied involvement, and during examination the lawyer found one conflict in her identification. The girl said the man she thought to be Rosen's client had a pockmarked face, with conspicuous lesions, and that he was hyperactive "as if he was on dope or something." "My client had a face as smooth as a baby's ass," Rosen related, "and he was so silent that I could barely communicate with him." Bryant, too, noticed the discrepancy. "During two hours of hearings," he said, "this man has barely moved. This doesn't sound like the same person to me." He began asking questions. The police, it developed, had located the house where the sequence of rapes began, obtained a picture of Rosen's client, who lived there, and shown it to the girl. She said he was one of her attackers.

But had the police shown her any other pictures? Such as the man's brother, who also lived there, and who in fact *was* hyperactive and pockmarked? Well, no. Whereupon the police staged a lineup including the brother. The victim said he was her assailant, not Rosen's client. "No one had even thought to ask the right questions—not even me, the defense lawyer," Rosen related. "That's what I mean about Bryant being street-wise—he can smell a bad spot in a story, because he knows reality. He chips away in a law suit until he gets down to the truth."

Another example: during 1970–72 Bryant heard

the challenge by insurgents in the United Mine Workers of America to the reelection of President W. A. Tony Boyle. The insurgents claimed that Boyle supporters had misused funds and miscounted ballots to defeat challenger Joseph A Yablonski. Stated a lawyer observer: "Bill Bryant knew as much about labor law as you or I know about being an astronaut. Well, I loaded him up with a lot of law review articles and background stuff, and he worked, and he learned, and he held his own in a courtroom where pretty sharp labor guys were around, lawyers like Joe Rauh." Some early Bryant decisions in the case were reversed; eventually he ordered a new election, which the anti-Boyle forces won. One Boyle witness had been a man named Albert Pass, a UMWA functionary from Kentucky. Bryant watched him closely on the stand and was struck by the coldness of his demeanor. Later he remarked to an aide in his office, "When I saw the steel in his eyes, I decided he was either a deacon in the church or a man who could commit murder." A year or so later Pass was indicted and convicted of complicity in Yablonski's murder.

The third judge on the D.C. district bench whom lawyers rank as outstanding is a dour-faced man named William B. Jones, a Notre Dame law graduate who was a trial lawyer and health association general counsel before going on the bench in 1962. Although lawyers praised Jones, no one seemed to know any anecdotes about him. "He's just a guy who does his work and keeps his mouth shut," said one man; further, he hasn't been involved in any cases that excited public interest. So one winter Friday morning I dropped by Jones' court to see how he did his work. Friday is a regular sentencing day for the federal courts in Washington, a gloomy chore that judges told me they dread more than any other duty, and particularly so on this day, with freezing rain falling through the gloom outside, and the courthouse lights dimmed to conserve electricity.

Jones' business this morning was a 29-year-old man named Whitaker, a slightly built fellow in a reddish knit suit sporting an Afro the size of a bee hive. A jury earlier had convicted him and his wife, Jackie, on a narcotics charge. Now, with the probation reports before him, Jones was trying to decide what to do with the couple.

Whitaker was blunt and nonapologetic about his background. "I grew up in the courts," he said. "I had all the usual childhood troubles because of my inner-city background. But since my nineteenth birthday I've tried to turn myself around. I got a job, and married, and started a family—something I never had when I was a child myself. My first job out of jail, at nineteen, I earned $50 a week, and I worked myself up to supervisor at this printing company and I now carry home $319.

"I guess I ran out of strength in dealing with the kinds of things that got me down before. I have to accept the [jury] verdict, but at no time have I sold anybody anything. I feel guilty because I let my wife down, I let my family down. There is a flaw in me, and the problems got to me."

After Whitaker mentioned "problems" several more times Jones bore down on him. "What is this thing you've got this mad on about? What kind of 'problems'? Get specific with me."

"As I got up in this printing company, I had more contact with racial hatred and bigotry, and took petty humiliations from people with this kind of sickness, who like to nibble you down." Whitaker shook his head. "I couldn't take it."

"You should have enough pride that those nickel and dime things don't bother you," Jones said. "You have come a long way, you have nothing to be sorry about."

"Well, it's this way," Whitaker said. "I have pride in my accomplishments. But I also have pride in my being. The belittling gets to me. I'd come home at night so mad and disturbed that I couldn't eat, that I couldn't be nice to my wife and kid. This other stuff got to be a sedative for me, you know, a kind of tranquilizer?"

"You mean the heroin?" asked Judge Jones.

"Yes, the heroin," Whitaker replied.

So what does a judge do with a man convicted on a narcotics offense in a city where the addiction rate has been estimated as 20 percent of black males under 30, and where drugs are considered responsible for some 75 percent of the crime? Men sentenced from Jones' court go to a reformatory in suburban Virginia named Lorton, a hellhole of a jail that is so tough, so overcrowded, that the keepers have tacitly surrendered control to the inmates. Criminal lawyer Sol Z. Rosen once told me, "It's easier making a buy [of drugs] in Lorton than on the street; once a guy hits there, there's no return. His life is over."

Judge Jones sighed, his sad face seemed to sag even more as he shuffled through the papers before him. What should he do?

I got up and slipped out of the courtroom and tried to make my own decision. I didn't talk to anyone about the case, not even my wife or friends, but I thought about what Whitaker had said. And I also thought about hard narcotics, and what they do to people. On Monday morning, I called Judge Jones' chamber and inquired as to the sentence.

"Oh," the secretary said, "the Whitakers. Yes, that was a sad case, one the judge gave special thought to. For Whitaker it was five years probation, for the wife two years, both with pretty tough restrictions to keep them away from future involvement with narcotics."

A good decision, I said to myself. Or, more accurately, what I would have done with the couple.

I think so, anyway.

CHAPTER SEVEN

Judging the Judges

*His white panama suit hanging limply from his frail
body, the old man tottered several feet from the curb
into busy Gaston Avenue in a residential section of
Dallas and peered at the morning-rush traffic roaring
close by him. Many persons honked, braked and
swerved to avoid hitting the tottering fellow. Finally,
a driver stopped and called, "Get in, Judge Atwell,
I'll drive you down to the courthouse." That evening,
United States District Judge William Atwell performed
his perilous hitchhiking once more at a garage near the
federal building, standing in a traffic lane until someone recognized him, and offered him a ride home. Although Judge Atwell, in his eighties, had long since
taken senior judge status, he still heard cases and filed
opinions. I picked him up one day (this was in the
late 1950s) and mentioned I wrote for* The Dallas
News. *He asked that I give his regards "to my dear
friend George Dealey." I didn't think it polite to remind Atwell that the publisher—one of Dallas' most
prominent men for half a century—had been dead for
thirteen years.*

The aged judge. What is to be done about a federal jurist who, through the fault of nothing more than
the calendar, teeters over the brink into senility, and
cannot recognize his condition? "Get rid of the aged
judges," remarks Chief Judge John Brown of the Fifth
Circuit Court of Appeals, "and you get rid of most
of the problems of the federal judiciary: drunkenness,

incompetence, senility, cantankerous behavior on the bench."

Well, not totally, for younger judges are capable of mischief and unseemly conduct as well, activities that in one way or another cast a shadow on the federal judiciary. Because this chapter is concerned with such activities, let us begin with several qualifying caveats:

Outright corruption on the federal bench is rare. More than 2,000 persons have served as federal judges; only eight have been impeached by the House of Representatives, and of these, only four were convicted by the Senate and thrown from office. By contrast, that many members of Congress have been convicted as felons in a single session. The low number of ousted judges is all the more striking because grounds for impeaching a judge are much broader than for other constitutional officers. Judges are governed by the general impeachment section, which means they can be removed from office for "treason, bribery, or other high crimes and misdemeanors" (Article II, section 4) and also by the tenure provision of Article III, Section I, which provides that they hold office *"during good behaviour."* However, what constitutes "good behaviour" has never been rigidly defined. Fifty-five judges have been subjected to formal investigation leading toward possible impeachment: eight were censured but not impeached; four were impeached but acquitted by the Senate; 17 others resigned at one stage or another of the investigation; the remainder were absolved. Washington lawyer/writer Joseph Borkin, the foremost student of judicial corruption, maintains the conviction rate is not truly reflective of the extent of misconduct. The four convicted judges, Borkin says, were "far less culpable than others whose judicial crimes were greater and whose guilt was clearer." In many instances, Borkin says, the offending judge resigned and impeachment proceedings were dropped. "Whenever testimony and evidence were not conclusive; whenever malice and the probity of witnesses are difficult to distingush; whenever evil intent and poor judgement cannot be separated—here a hapless judge may elect to fight the issue through and stand trial before the Senate. As a result, the evidence points to the inescapable conclusion that an impeachment trial as a practical and historical matter has been reserved for the less flagrant cases of judicial abuse." Be that as it may, not since 1936 has the House undertaken a fomal impeachment proceeding against a judge.

Strictures on outside business activities of judges imposed in the past decade removed much of the opportunity (and temptation) for financial misadventures. Several scandals precipitated the new rules. First was the disclosure by the *Wall Street Journal* in 1963 that numerous federal judges served on the boards of banks and other profit-making institutions. The most questionable was Judge John C. Knox, Sr. (now deceased), of the Southern District of New York, who earned $111,425 between 1948 and 1961 as a director of the Equitable Life Assurance Society. Several years Knox's fees from Equitable almost equalled his judicial salary, only $15,000 a year at the time, and he attended as many as 119 meetings a year, almost every other business day. Other judges served banks, insurance companies, coal companies, a steel mill, and various lending institutions.

That many of their brethren held such directorships was surely no secret to the judiciary. Nonetheless, not until the *Journal* exposé, by reporter Jerry Landauer, did the United States Judicial Conference pass a rule forbidding federal judges (including Supreme Court justices) from holding such positions in profit-making corporations. Next were two scandals involving Supreme Court Justice Abe Fortas: his acceptance of $15,000 in legal fees, chiefly from corporate clients of his old law firm of Arnold & Porter, for lectures at American University in Washington; and the covert arrangement under which he was to receive $20,000 annually in "consultant" fees from the family foundation of financier Louis Wolfson, agreed to at a time when Wolfson was in grave trouble with the law. Finally, there was the turmoil around Judge Clement Haynsworth, of the Third Circuit Court of Appeals, whom President Nixon wanted to put on the Supreme

Court. The evidence against Haynsworth was thin. He had served as a director of a vending company which did $50,000 business annually with a textile mill which benefited from a favorable labor relations decision in his court; and he bought $16,000 of stock in the Brunswick Corporation—as did 40 other persons serviced by the same broker—soon after ruling in Brunswick's favor in a minor business case, but before the decision was published. (Brunswick did $400 million worth of business annually; the decision had minimal impact on its earnings. Haynsworth paid $16 per share for the stock, the same closing price the day the court ruling was made public.) Nonetheless, given the post-Fortas temper of the nation, and the ferocity of Haynsworth's opponents, the episodes were sufficient to cost him the appointment. In the words of one court observer, he was a victim of the "appearance of impropriety rather than the reality."

A minute but increasing number of trial lawyers is willing to criticize judges publicly, and to point to possible reasons for judicial bias. A striking, if somewhat disastrous, example: Famed trial lawyer Melvin Belli won a $900,000 jury verdict for a 14-year-old District of Columbia girl who became blind after treatment at Children's Hospital. Both Belli and the trial judge, John Lewis Smith, Jr., felt each other's trial conduct was outrageous. Belli accused Judge Smith of pressuring him in pretrial conferences to settle the case for "peanuts." Smith, in turn, denounced Belli for supposedly letting the jury know the hospital was heavily insured against such medical accidents (an unlikely ignorance, but one upon which defense lawyers insist). So Smith set aside the verdict and ordered a new trial. A few weeks later Belli went on the Merv Griffin television talk show and, before a national audience, accused Judge Smith of bias. He said Smith should not have heard the suit because his son was the attorney for the D.C. Medical Society, and that the judge had excused himself from similar cases involving Children's Hospital. Smith, angry, retorted that his son didn't represent the hospital, and that his earlier disqualification was by choice, not request. The D.C.

judges told Belli henceforth to keep out of their court, and asked the bar in his home state of California to start disciplinary proceedings. But Belli was philosophical about the putdown: "One reason I started taking these negligence cases in the District," he told me, "was to get some decent verdicts for people. The only way to do that is to shake up the existing system, to let some of these judges know that they can't stomp on plaintiffs and lawyers simply because they don't like them."

Judges presiding over a plethora of so-called "movement cases"—those involving war resisters and civil rights activists—came to realize that defendants weren't hobbled by the traditional notion that a jurist is beyond reproach. Much of the movement-inspired criticisms were ghost-under-the-bed paranoia. But judges went on guard against the most oblique of criticisms. A district judge in California told me: "I was once trying a case of some people charged with violence directed against a corporation that had contracts for equipment used in the Vietnam War. Now their defense was purely political: they didn't deny the acts, but they were appealing to this thing they called 'the higher moral authority.' When court resumed one afternoon one of these kids asked me how I had enjoyed my lunch at the ———— Club, and what 'war criminals' I had sat with.

"Now I just ignored him, I didn't even answer him, court hadn't started, and there was no reason to. Then I got to thinking. As a matter of fact, I had sat at a table with six or seven men, and one of them was an executive of one of our aerospace companies that certainly does war work. We didn't talk about the war or anything remotely connected with it, and certainly not the trial; best I recall, it was the sad quality of Stanford football. But maybe this young fellow was right —maybe I should keep away from 'war criminals,' as he would call them, when I was trying a case in which opposition to 'war criminals' was a factor (or so the defendants claimed, anyway).

"For the rest of that particular trial I stayed away from the club and either had a sandwich with my clerk or walked over to one of these little courthouse cafés and ate by myself. Sure, it's hypersensitivity to criticism, but I didn't want to give those guys one iota of grounds for thinking I was biased."

There is a considerable amount of personal self-policing among judges to avoid ticklish situations. For instance, before coming on the Sixth Circuit Court of Appeals, Judge George Edwards served two years as police commissioner of Detroit. Hence he decided to screen all criminal appeals from Michigan to ascertain whether they came from cases developed by the Detroit police while he was commissioner; if so, he disqualified himself, even if he had no recollection of the case. Regardless of the remoteness, Edwards says, "the defendant would never be able to regard the head of the police force which arrested him as impartial in the appeal of his conviction." Edwards reacted strongly to any hint of conflict by other officials as well. He once reversed a postal theft case in which the district court judge who conducted the trial had been the United States attorney at the time the person was arrested and subjected to a preliminary hearing. Although the actual trial came months later, Edwards ruled the judge was tainted because of his office's participation.

So much for the caveats. Regardless of formal rules, court traditions, and individual ethical standards, far too many judges are regularly caught up in situations that reflect adversely upon their offices. Simon Rifkind, who was a district judge in New York for ten years before he left the bench in hot pursuit of money, once told a Senate committee that "to be a model judge it is not necessary that the judge go to bed in his robes, or that he substitute a halo for a nightcap." But 'Rifkind did caution: "Consciously or unconsciously the public recognizes that a judge ought to represent one of the forces of stability and moderation. In short, it is not the judge's wife who ought to be the first to try on a topless bathing suit."

What judicial flaws are most often encountered among the 603 federal circuit and district judges around the country? Unwillingness to admit senility. Wanderlust. Foul tempers. Drunkenness. Mental erraticism. Delusions of personal grandeur. And, finally, downright meanness.

The oldest living member of the federal judiciary at this writing is Senior Judge Joseph W. Woodrough, of the Eighth Circuit Court of Appeals, who marked his one hundredth birthday on August 29, 1973. A whimsical man, Judge Woodrough is totally lacking in self-pomposity. When President Wilson appointed him to the district bench in Nebraska on April 1, 1916, he quipped, "It was the best April Fool's Day joke ever played on me, but I'm not sure about the public."

Judge Woodrough's good friend Senator Roman Hruska (R., Neb.) tells of the time the Judge wandered into a pool hall in Little Rock, Arkansas. "While he was playing a game with the natives," Hruska says, "a migrant magician walked in and began a series of magic tricks that delighted the Judge. It was only later that the Judge realized he had been the victim of the magician and had had his watch taken from his pocket. When asked why he did not report it to the police, Judge Woodrough replied: 'How would I have looked reporting that an Eighth Circuit Court judge had his pocket picked in a pool hall while watching a magician?' "

When Judge John Biggs, Jr., was appointed to the Third Circuit Court of Appeals in 1937 the average age of the incumbents (excluding Biggs) was 77 years. Most of the judges were "old and ill," Biggs recollected. The senior judge, Joseph Buffington, was 86 years old, and senile. "He was blind and could not read and had great difficulty reading," Biggs said. "And he would not employ a law clerk. This made for very considerable difficulties." Indeed it did. Despite Buffington's helpless condition, decisions bearing his opinion poured from the court between 1935 and 1939. In five instances the "Buffington opinions" reversed a trustee-in-bankruptcy and rendered decisions favorable to William Fox, the movie mogul, whose empire was falling apart. As has been noted by Joseph Borkin, the scholar of judicial corruption, "One would have to be blind himself not to see that a malign influence was at work in the third circuit." The malign influence, it was later established, was Judge John Warren Davis, who wrote and sold the decisions ostensibly produced by Judge Buffington in return for bribes from Fox totalling about $27,000. Davis was subsequently sent to jail. The pitiable Buffington was allowed to retire.

The case of Buffington is unique only in that his senility resulted in criminal corruption. But the aged judge poses problems other than criminality. Lawyers dislike to name names when they talk of sitting judges who have let age get the best of them; to do so is, in effect, to criticize a person for a condition over which he has no control. Nonetheless lawyers' tongues occasionally do point to judges who have yet to realize time has overtaken them. A New York attorney: "For years one of the best trial judges in the Eastern District [Brooklyn] was Leo Rayfiel. His mind apparently is still as sharp as ever. But the poor fellow is in his eighties and the fact of the matter is that he can't hear. Hell, the courthouse could fall on his head, and unless he happened to be looking he would never notice." Why, then, hasn't someone suggested that Rayfiel stop hearing cases? "Tell you what," the attorney countered. "I'll give *you* his phone number, and *you* give him a ring and *you* tell him to retire."

Lawyers who practice before Rayfiel feel sorry for him. No such sympathy is detected for another aged judge, Willis Ritter, of Salt Lake City, Utah. "You know," a California lawyer told me, "I'd call old Ritter the 'meanest son of a bitch east of the Pacific Ocean,' but sure as I did, he'd take a liking to the name and try to live up to it even more than he does now."

So far as can be determined by the existing record Ritter is ecumenically mean, which is to say he seems to dislike most persons who come into his court, be they defendant, government lawyer, private trial attorney, or ordinary citizen. Ritter is also selective about his fellow judges. He was once so estranged from another Utah federal judge that they wouldn't ride on the elevator together, much less speak; for a while the court clerk divided cases so that they didn't have to appear in the courthouse on the same day. Ritter, who is 75 at this writing, has been on the bench since 1949 (previously, he was a lawyer in Salt Lake City and a law professor at the University of Utah). Ritter is one of the few federal judges in the nation who becomes so emotionally involved in his hearings that appeals courts often order him not to retry cases when they are reversed.

Some of the cases are petty, others are not. Ritter was the original trial judge in a case in which the federal government sued to force El Paso Natural Gas Company to divest itself of a competing pipeline company in the Pacific Northwest. The competitor's entry into the market had forced El Paso to cut its own prices by 25 percent; hence it was eager to restore its previous monopoly of the market. At the close of a three-week trial Judge Ritter announced from the bench that the government had lost. He instructed the El Paso lawyers to prepare the findings of fact and conclusions of law, which he signed unchanged. "I shan't write an opinion in this case," Ritter loftily announced and adjourned court. When an appeal reached the Supreme Court, Justice William O. Douglas wrote "we would have to wear blinders" not to see the patent illegality of the merger. The court took the rare step of ordering immediate divestiture of the pipeline company by El Paso without even a further hearing.

But even with clear instructions Judge Ritter could not—or would not—follow the high court's mandate. He permitted El Paso to file a divestiture plan so botched that it would have been allowed to keep many of the benefits gained through the illegal merger, while the spun-off company would have incurred heavy tax and other liabilities. According to what one observer told a Ralph Nader study group that examined the El Paso case, Judge Ritter "practically spat on the government and outside witnesses." The Supreme Court, unsurprisingly, rejected the Ritter divestiture plan as grossly inadequate, and also directed him to take no further part in the case. In the words of the Nader study group, Judge Ritter's activities "earned him the dubious distinction of being one of the few district judges ever to be removed from a case by a Supreme Court opinion."

"The fact of the matter is," says a West Coast attorney, "Willis Ritter simply doesn't like the United States government. I do a lot of tax work, both criminal and civil, and going up before Ritter as a defense attorney is like shooting craps with loaded dice—*your* dice." But the lawyer adds, "Nonetheless, it's an unsettling experience. You are always on edge, because you never know when he's going to turn 180 degrees and come after someone else. A typical bully. He has power, and he misuses it." Two cases on the point:

- In a 1971 drug trial the defendant originally said she was indigent, and Ritter appointed an attorney for her. Later friends loaned her money and she wanted to hire another lawyer. Ritter not only refused, he spent some time bullying the second lawyer, saying that in fact *he* needed an attorney. This exchange followed:

THE LAWYER: I don't think I need one, Your Honor.
RITTER: You ought to hire yourself a lawyer.
THE LAWYER: I resent that, Your Honor.
RITTER: You can resent it as you please.
THE LAWYER. I am a member of the bar and quali fied to practice before this court in this state.
RITTER: There is some question about that in my mind.
THE LAWYER: There is none in mine, Your Honor, and I resent those comments.

- The circuit court held that Ritter's conduct "demeaned" the lawyer in front of the jury, thereby denying a fair trial. It reversed the conviction.
- In another case Ritter gave a young man five years probation after he pleaded guilty to selling stimulant and depressant drugs. Later the youth saw the arresting officer, Federal Agent Charles H. Bullock,

in the hallway and said "hello" with what Bullock took to be a smirk. Bullock admittedly lost his temper and vowed he would "get him again." The youth's lawyer complained to Ritter, who summoned Bullock into court, told him the remarks constituted "criticism of the court for its sentence," held him in contempt, fined him $250, and levied a 90-day jail term. Ritter ignored the statutory procedure for a contempt hearing: he neither notified Bullock of any charge nor did he give him a formal hearing. He simply administered drumhead justice. Judge James E. Barrett, reversing the contempt conviction for a unanimous Tenth Circuit Court of Appeals, called Ritter's proceeding "a clear-cut example of judicial abuse of the most basic assumptions of procedural due process, i.e., reasonable notice and opportunity to prepare and be heard."

For sheer judicial whiffleness, collectors of what lawyers call "Ritterisms" point to the "Indian pony case" —one in which Ritter gave full and vigorous head to his emotions. The aggrieved parties definitely were a mournful lot: an impoverished group of Navajo Indians who maintained herds of burros and horses in southeastern Utah, off their reservation. (The plaintiffs included Widow Sleepy, Shorty Smiles, Little Wagon, Slim Todachennie, Mary's Boy, and Suzy Sleeps, among others.) Because the Indians did not have a grazing permit for the federal land, agents of the Bureau of Land Management drove off the animals, killing many of them. The Indians sued for $100,000. Ritter held that the roundup and destruction was "willful, wanton and malicious," and part of a plan to drive the Navajos from the range.

The Tenth Circuit Court disagreed. It ruled that the federal agents had committed no errors in enforcing an "abandoned horse" statute, and remanded the case back to Ritter with orders to rule for the defendant. The court commented, "The record discloses that the case was tried in an atmosphere of maximum emotion and a minimum of judicial impartiality." The Supreme Court, in turn, reversed the circuit court, and held that

the federal people indeed had violated the law, and remanded the case to Ritter to fix damages.

Ritter, on retrial, gleefully gave the Navajos almost
double what they originally asked—$186,017 rather
than $100,000. The circuit court found this out-
rageous enough ("We think it quite clear that the sum
given each plaintiff was wholly conjectural and picked
out of the air. . . ."). It also commented at length on
Ritter's loss of emotional control:

> A casual reading of the two [trial] records leaves
> no doubt that the district judge was incensed and
> embittered, perhaps understandably so, by the gen-
> eral treatment of the plaintiffs and other Indians in
> southeast Utah by the government agents and white
> ranchers in their attempt to force the Indians onto
> established reservations. This was climaxed by the
> range clearance programs, which the court referred
> to, during trial, as "horrible, monstrous, atrocious,
> cruel, coldblooded depredation and without a sense
> of decency."

Several times during trial Ritter suggested a presidential or congressional investigation of the Bureau of
Land Management, and even threatened to conduct
one himself. "A public appeal on behalf of the plaintiffs was made for funds and supplies to be cleared
through the Judge's chambers." The court said Ritter
could give "calm, impartial consideration" to the defendants during a new trial and suggested that he
"should step down." In applying the law, the court
said, "everyone should be treated the same. Racial
differences merit no concern. Feelings or charity or
ideological sympathy for the Indians must be put to
one side."

Ritter noted the court's "suggestion" that he withdraw by saying he did not "intend to follow that suggestion so you can lay that to one side." So the government formally moved for disqualification, and after
much more wrangling both the circuit and the Supreme
Court told Ritter to get out of the case.

Lawyer Bernard Segal of Philadelphia recollects a

hearing before a judge of the Third Circuit Court of Appeals who was both aged and dipsomaniacal. After both lawyers finished their arguments "suddenly the judge put out his light on the bench and left," Segal said. "We thought he had left for some temporary purpose. So there we sat in the courtroom with our clients. After we had done so for almost an hour, it dawned on us, with the speed that things sometimes dawn on lawyers, that perhaps the judge was not coming back. And it developed that if we had sat there for the next week, he would not have been back. He just disappeared for the ensuing week, indulging his tragic addiction."

So why is the judiciary—and eventually all of us— cursed by the continuation in power of such persons? In the opinion of many constitutional authorities, much judicial unfitness falls outside the impeachable offenses of "treason, bribery, or other high crimes and misdemeanors." As has been stated by former Senator Joseph D. Tydings (D., Md.), who devoted much of his career to judicial reform, "It is uncertain whether senility, insanity, physical disability, alcoholism, or laziness—all of which are forms of unfitness that require remedial action—are covered by the impeachment process."

The judicial code provides two avenues for retirement because of disability. A judge "who becomes permanently disabled from performing his duties" may retire by presenting the President a certificate of disability signed by the chief judge of his circuit. If the judge has served ten years, he receives full salary for life; if not, half-salary. When a judge is disabled and refuses to request retirement, a majority of the members of the judicial council of his circuit may petition the President to retire him, and appoint a successor. In this case, the judge receives full pay for life, regardless of his length of service. Judge John Biggs, Jr., who is perhaps the judiciary's ranking in-house expert on disability, says the "involuntary" retirement procedure has been invoked only once—and then, oddly, at the request of the target judge. According to Biggs, the judge had not served ten years; hence if he retired voluntarily, he would receive only half-pay. So the judicial council performed a bit of subterfuge by going through the motion of an involuntary retirement request, which the President accepted. Thus the judge was able to retire at full pay. Perhaps because of the questionable legality of the episode, not to mention the apparent breach of any number of ethical canons, Biggs refused to name the judge or the circuit. The net result of the charitable scheme was to give the judge twice the pension to which he was legally entitled. Biggs felt the procedure worthwhile. Nonetheless it illustrates the mutual backscratching endemic in the judiciary, for one wonders whether a court would similarly bend the law to double the pension of a rank-and-file government worker.

Another idea with which reformists have toyed over the years is to require judges to go into senior status at age 70, and to permit appointment of full-time replacements. Both the judges and the Congress are hostile toward such a requirement. As one judge remarked, "When you retire, you see death standing over in the corner." Congressional objections are practical as well as philosophical: With a majority of committee chairmen in both houses well beyond 70 years, the legislators are in no mood to establish an age at which a person becomes legally decrepit.

Given these narrow guides, what does the judicial establishment do about judges felt to be unfit for reasons not warranting impeachment: the senile gaffers who drool from the bench, oblivious of both the law and common sense; the drunks who might or might not make it back to court after the luncheon recess; the mentally sick jurists who rant at lawyers and litigants? Uncomfortable though it may be, the favored route is an attempt at gentle persuasion. One judge in the West who asked anonymity described the psychological pressures involved, both on him and the person who was the target of the nudge: "We had this situation develop in the 1960s where a judge in our district went into what I suppose you could call a second childhood. His first wife had died a few years back, and this man suddenly burst forth like an aging teenager. He got a mod haircut and started wearing the wildest damned clothes imaginable.

"Now in a sense this was good because I believe a man is only as old as he feels. But our good brother overdid it. First thing you know, he was pestering young secretaries in the federal building for dates, and bringing them flowers and candy. For a while they sort of tolerated it, and I think two or three of them might even have had lunch with him. Then it took a nasty turn, and he made it plain to several of these young ladies that he wanted more than a meal with them—downright blatant in what he said to them, according to what went around the courthouse. They started treating him like a dirty old man, and apparently he deserved it.

"What was worse was his courtroom behavior. He had been a good lawyer and judge. I know, because I knew him for more than thirty years. But here he was, no interest whatsoever in his court. He made the silliest procedural errors imaginable, and daydreamed, and he took a strong dislike to the United States attorney's office and everyone who worked there. He also began making remarks to women jurors and witnesses that were just a shade on the questionable side.

"Well, the upshot of it was that the rest of us decided he needed some rest, and it fell my lot to break the news to him. Here I was, talking with an old friend, trying to tell him as indirectly as possible that his colleagues thought he was incapable of sitting any longer. He fumed and stewed, and he said some rather nasty things to me, but in a couple of months he came around and took senior status.

"How is he now? Hopeless. The man is so out of touch with reality that he couldn't tell you where he lives. He's out of the mod dress phase—now when you see him downtown you'd think he was some bum who had wandered in from the freight yards. Sad, but I'd rather have him walking around the streets talking to himself, than sitting on the bench."

Judge Peirson Hall of Los Angeles faced a similar situation several years back, when he was chief judge of that district. "We had a judge who became so senile he could not do his work. The rumbles were so bad in the bar association that it was going to break out in a public scandal unless something was done." Hall, through discreet inquiries, learned the main barrier to retirement was the judge's wife. "I went to see her and the judge, and told her it would be a shame for such a brilliant man to wind up with a scandal at the end of his career. She said she would think about it and talk to him. I told her, 'Do it now, while I'm here.'

"It turned out the old man wanted to keep his chambers, bailiff and secretary. Now circuit rules at that time required that a judge do a 'substantial amount of work' to keep his staff. I promised he could keep them. 'OK,' she asked, 'what about your successor as chief judge? Will he keep the bargain?' I picked up the phone and called him and he said fine by him. Now this was a matter of using a little ingenuity, tact and diplomacy, and of saving the man's pride." *

Many Los Angeles lawyers take sharp issue with Hall's conduct towards the late Judge Thurmond Clarke. Late in his career, Judge Clarke (who died in 1969) behaved far more leniently to criminal defendants than the United States attorney's office felt was warranted. There was namecalling in the newspapers about "wrist-slap sentences," and "silly prosecutions for cases where no one was really hurt." Clarke was an immensely wealthy man—he married into the family that once controlled the vast Irvine Ranch south of Los Angeles—and he was both a hard drinker and an egotist of no small renown; in short, the kind of fellow who is confident enough about himself that he goes through life at a gait of his own choosing. Clarke's conduct was often boisterous.

---

* A Texas judge, speaking from anonymity, tells a similar story—but one with an unfortunate ending. An elderly associate became so senile he could not remember what he had done from day to day. Veiled suggestions that he retire were to no avail, so he sought out the judge's wife and asked her help. "What! And have him here under *my* feet all day! Not on your life!" The judge remained in office until he died.

"After a party at Thurmond's place one night," a Los Angeles lawyer told me, "he got out in the driveway hogass drunk and began directing traffic. Wow. He had cars backing into one another and into the ditch and all over the place, and he stood in the middle of things hooting and yelling and waving his arms. Quite a spectacle, even for your friends." Two episodes finally got Clarke * into the deadly crosshairs of Pierson Hall's judicial sixshooter.

- In a celebrated mail-fraud case involving chinchilla ranching, Clarke put all defendants on probation. Soon thereafter his bailiff went to the press room in the federal building, called the defense attorney, and told him, "The judge says you owe the press room a case of whiskey because he gave these defendants six months probation, and by the way, add another six bottles for me." Judge Hall said, "As soon as I heard that, I called down the newsman—the fellow at the desk where he used the phone—and I said tell me what happened. He said, 'You know you cannot question the press.' I said, 'Well, did something like this happen, and tell me whether or not I am a good guesser.' So I repeated it and he said (my nickname is Pete), 'Pete, you are an awful good guesser.' So I called the lawyer on the phone and said, 'How many times has Judge So-and-So called you and had you send cases of whiskey down to the press room?' He said, 'Only once. What do you want to ask me that for?' I said, 'You have given me the information, that is all.'" Hall called together an ad hoc committee with two other judges and they agreed the bailiff should be fired that night. "We told him, 'Get out of this building tonight and never come in it again.'" Clarke protested loudly, "You have no right to do this." Hall said he re-

---

* Hall did not use Clarke's name in telling these stories, either in my interview with him in Los Angeles or when he alluded to them during 1970 testimony before a Senate Judiciary Subcommittee. I learned that Clarke was the figure through interviews with other persons in California, and Hall confirmed that he was the judge in point.

plied, "I don't care whether I have a right to do so or not. There's nothing to talk about."

- Clarke had unusual ways of accelerating his docket. "He would call a defendant or a lawyer on the phone and say if he would plead guilty to tax fraud, say, he would give him six months probation." Clarke did much the same in open court. According to Hall, "When he had the criminal calendar lining up in the way of thirty or forty people every arraignment day, he just pronounced generally, 'Anybody who wants to plead guilty, I will give him probation.' And he would."

Hall wanted to ease Clarke away from important criminal and civil matters without "making a so-called federal case out of it." So the judges in the district passed an order providing that nothing be assigned to Clarke, as Hall told a Senate subcommittee, "except immigration and naturalization cases, where he cannot take anything away from anybody, and bankruptcy cases." Clarke yielded to the order—unhappy, to be sure, but nonetheless willing to accept the judgement of his colleagues.

Such is not always the case. According to Chief Judge Paul C. Weick of the Fifth Circuit Court of Appeals, "We had trouble . . . for about fifteen years" with Judge Mell G. Underwood of Columbus. "The particular judge just was not doing much work, and a number of mandamus cases * were filed against him in our court." The circuit judges eventually asked Underwood to retire. He retorted: "They have no authority to remove me, and they've found that out. I told them to go to hell. . . ." Weick and the other judges decided to play rough. "We kept after him and the largest newspaper in Ohio, with statewide circulation, published some accounts concerning the way he was handling his work, and he finally called me up and said his name had been 'dragged down in the mud far enough,' and that he would retire." (A better way to handle the matter, Weick said, would have

---

* Petitions asking Underwood to act in a case.

been for the circuit council to be empowered to subpena both Underwood and his physician "to substan-
tiate that he was under disability," and force his retirement. The case could have been handled with no
publicity. Since no such subpena authority existed,
and Underwood wouldn't yield voluntarily, the other
judges had to go public with the charges.)

Chief Judge Walter E. Craig of Phoenix tells of a
similar episode involving "a judge who was inclined
to abuse the use of alcohol to some extent." Chief
Judge Richard Chambers of the Ninth Circuit Court
of Appeals visited the man and tried to persuade him
to take senior status. Although the man was aware
of his alcohol problem, he nonetheless insisted to
Chambers that he was "just as good as he was the
day he went on the bench and there was no intention
to take senior judge status." Chambers thought a moment and replied, "Well, I am awfully glad to hear
that, because Nevada is in a little difficulty and, you
know, we can sit in Elko [a remote mountain town
with 6,298 population] and I think it would be nice
if you went down to Elko for six months and helped
those judges down there." The judge quickly replied,
"You know, Dick, I think I *will* take senior judge
status."

In another instance, according to Bernard Segal of
Philadelphia, the Justice Department insisted on appointing to the bench a man who had "suffered a
drastic heart attack and apparently would not fully
recover." The ABA Federal Judiciary Committee,
which Segal headed at the time, objected, but to no
avail. "Within weeks after he got on the bench the
judge suffered a drastic stroke ·and began to deteri-
orate," Segal said. Segal tried to persuade lawyers in
the district to give him a statement so that he could
urge the chief judge to move against the jurist. "We
could not get a lawyer, even anonymously and on a
blank piece of paper, to give us what we needed. Then
one day I received a call from a lawyer at a considerable distance from that state, who said, 'Bernie, look
at our dilemma. The attention span of his judge is one
hour per day. Here we are, a large number of counsel

from various parts of the country, coming to try an antitrust case before him. Before a judge who would sit five days and perhaps a sixth morning and perhaps a few evenings a week this case will take four to six months. None of us will live to see the end of the case before that judge.' " Even with this specific complaint, months of persuasion were required before the judge stepped aside.

Joseph D. Tydings, an active trial lawyer before his election to the Senate, knew well the pitfalls of judicial self-policing. As United States attorney for Maryland he learned about the judicial incompetents and misfits, and occasionally wondered out loud what could be done about them. One source of information was Chief Judge Biggs, of the third circuit, a longtime Tydings family friend. (Biggs got his appointment through the good offices of Joseph Tydings' father, Millard, a Maryland senator from 1932–50.) Tydings held some cautious hearings on judicial fitness beginning in 1966 ("It is not our intention to conduct an exposé of the federal judiciary," he carefully explained at the outset), and eventually came up with a proposal for a "commission on judicial disabilities and tenure." The commission would have been composed of five judges appointed by the chief justice of the United States. It would have been charged with enforcing the constitutional provision that judges hold office during "good behaviour," and with determining whether a judge was mentally and/or physically capable of service. ("Habitual intemperance" would have been considered a disability.) The commission could have retired or removed a judge after a formal, confidential hearing, subject to review by the Judicial Conference and the Supreme Court.

Another part of Tydings' reform act would have permitted retirement of judges at age 65 with ten years service. Existing law gives judges several options. They may resign at age 70 with ten years service and continue to draw, as a pension, their full salary. (If active judges receive a pay raise, however, the resigned judge's pension is not increased.) More frequently, however, judges "retire" into senior status (possible at age 70 with ten years service, or at 65 with fifteen years service) and receive the "salary of the office" for life; that is, they share in raises. The senior judge does only as much work as he chooses, upon assignment of the chief justice of the United States or the chief judge of his circuit.

Tydings' bills got nowhere. A majority of the federal judges opposed the bill, calling it an infringement upon the Constitution. Many considered it a personal affront; after all, as one of them stated during Tydings' hearings, "You don't have a similar mechanism for removing a Congressman who is drunk or goes crazy." "Only the ballot box," Tydings replied dryly. Eventually the three senior members of the Senate Judiciary Committee—James O. Eastland, Sam J. Ervin, and John L. McClellan—invoked an unspoken but very real rule that governs the Senate establishment: resist firmly any tinkering with the United States Constitution. Ervin held his own round of hearings (entitled "The Independence of Federal Judges," a not so subtle rebuttal of Tydings' position that Congress could pass laws judging the judges) at which witness after witness lambasted the commission idea. If Congress wanted to impose guidelines on judicial behavior, Ervin said, it should do so through constitutional amendment, "not the glowing language of making improvements in the administration of the courts." Tydings' reform bills were quietly buried.*

In 1851, when Supreme Court Justice Peter Daniel took a three-month, 5,000-mile trip around his judicial circuit, from western Pennsylvania down to Arkansas and Mississippi, he came into revoltingly close contact with his public. In a letter he described one stage of his journey on a riverboat:

> The discomfort of being about in immediate contact with all sorts of people, some of the most vulgar and filthy in the world, women more disgusting

---

* So, too, were his parallel efforts to require judges to report their extracurricular activities and income. See below.

if possible by their want of cleanliness than the men; with squalling children and being required to use in common two tin basins encrusted with filth, and one long towel for the whole male establishment, is a misery beyond which my imagination can scarcely picture any earthy evil. My washing, therefore, was limited to wiping my eyes and mouth with my linen handkerchief, but I neither took off my clothes nor slept during this purgatory.

More than a century later, another federal judge made a trip. Rather than holding court in his own chilly jurisdiction of Philadelphia, Judge Albert B. Maris spent the months of November and December in the pleasant climes of the Virgin Islands—for the stated purpose of helping clear a backlog of cases. But Chief Judge John Biggs, Jr., of the Third Circuit Court of Appeals, who assigned Maris to this genteel duty, conceded that no particular hardship was involved. "He [Judge Maris] rented a house and went down there and spent a honeymoon. I would not call that a great personal sacrifice." Judge Maris, Biggs said, "spends a great deal of his time in the Virgin Islands."

Maris was not unique. Many federal judges display much the same travel patterns as migratory birds. One whiff of cool air in the winter, and they pant for special assignments to Florida, Southern California, Puerto Rico and Hawaii. In the summer, the judges afflicted with wanderlust have an especial talent for finding assignments to cities that other Americans visit as vacationers: Washington, San Francisco and Denver. There is one difference, however: the lay vacationer pays his own expenses. The "visiting judge" travels as a guest of the taxpayer, regardless of how much actual time he spends on the bench during his "special assignment."

Defenders of such judicial travel point to the fact that much of it is done by senior judges (as was true of Maris) who are not required to do any work whatsoever. By volunteering for out-of-town assignments, the senior judges help overburdened districts. Further, for health reasons, many of the elderly judges are able to function better in places such as Florida and the Virgin Islands. Critics of travel—and especially the Senate judiciary subcommittee headed by Senator Quentin Burdick (D., N.D.)—suggest the senior judges could be put to better use in their home towns.

The way the judges tell it, the resort assignments are arduous. One jurist who is particularly defensive of them is Chief Judge Richard Chambers, of the Ninth Circuit Court of Appeals on the West Coast. Chambers has authority to send judges as far as Guam, and the district and circuit judges beholden to him are the most peripatetic in the nation. During 1968, to cite a not untypical year, Chambers permitted two San Francisco judges to spend 45 days in Hawaii; the next year, Chambers asked the Senate to create two new judgeships for San Francisco because the existing number could not handle the work load. Senator Joseph Tydings (D., Md.) thought this request a bit odd. One of the visitors, he noted, had gone to Hawaii to replace a judge who was disqualified in a case, but stayed around for several weeks. Chambers did not consider this to be unusual.

CHAMBERS: If you send a man over for the disqualification you don't say, "OK, get yourself out of there" after he finishes two days' work.

TYDINGS: What do you do, let him stay for a little vacation?

CHAMBERS: Vacation nothing. There again those two men may have worked on cases that were . . .

TYDINGS: You say they worked a couple of days. What did they do there the rest of the time?

Chambers said he could not give an immediate answer because Judge Martin Pence, one of the judges involved, "for the last three weeks . . . has been down in Australia and travelling around." "Oh," replied Tydings.

Other reports given the Tydings subcommittee noted that three other judges from Chambers' circuit sat in Hawaii during 1968, even though Hawaii had the lowest caseload of any district court in the circuit. One of the "special assignments" was to a judge who stopped in Hawaii a week en route home from Guam. "The indication from the statistics," Tydings told Judge Chambers, "is that they were not needed in Hawaii, and they were sent out there as some sort of a reward because they were in your good graces."

"Mr. Tydings, you could not be any more wrong," Chambers replied.

"I am anxiously awaiting your detailed explanation," Tydings said. He accused Chambers of poor judicial management. "All anybody does when they get a backlog, is they run in and ask the Congress for more judges at $250,000-a-judge * while the circuits themselves are not taking the steps they ought to be taking."

The aggrieved Chambers still could see nothing wrong in the resort assignments. In a memo he sent later to Tydings he asserted he was "sure that no judge loafed on the beach at Waikiki. . . . I might note that service in Hawaii for a federal judge does not come up to the blandishments of the travel posters. Most of the year air conditioning is needed in the courtrooms and offices. In the present courthouse, the air conditioning is abominable." Chambers continued, "I know, I have been there many times. . . ."

In fairness to Chambers, other circuits have their wandering jurists as well, men happiest when sitting behind someone else's bench. Some examples:

● Judge Ted Dalton, of Roanoke, Virginia, needs regular infusions of ocean air and beach sunshine, and especially that found around the comfortable beach resort of Wilmington, North Carolina. According to a lawyer who has been an eyewitness, "Old Ted would go down to Wilmington on the Fourth of July and ceremonially open court—clad sometimes in shorts and a sun hat—and immediately adjourn so he could go fishing or lounge on the beach." Dalton also enjoys Puerto Rico; he spent 22 days

---

* The $250,000 was the current estimate of the expense involved in staffing a new judge's office.

there in 1970 and 34 days in 1972. Judge Richard Kellam is another Virginian who appears frequently in Wilmington in the summer, although his home chambers are but a clam shell's throw from an equally attractive ocean front at Virginia Beach.

• Yet another Virginian, Judge Walter E. Hoffman, cheerfully admits he decides where he wants vacation, and then hustles an assignment. In 1972, for example, Hoffman chose San Francisco. "I decided to be a postman and go on my vacation by holding court there. I did the same thing in San Diego this past summer and spent a month . . . assisting in that very busy . . . district," says Hoffman.

• Mutual backscratching is another factor. In 1972 Judge Frank H. McFadden of Alabama served on a judicial committee with Judge Alexander A. Lawrence of Georgia. McFadden mentioned he intended to vacation with his family in Hilton Head, South Carolina, a resort community just across the state line from Lawrence's court in Savannah, Georgia. At Lawrence's suggestion, McFadden turned the trip into a work/play affair, spending part of his days in court, the remainder in Hilton Head with his family. Thus he was able to bill the government for both travel and per diem expenses.

• A district that can't offer surf and a warm sun is not inundated with visiting firemen, and in fact has trouble persuading judges to sit on special assignment even when they are sorely needed. That this is true is commentary on the judges' pious claims that they travel for the good of the judiciary, rather than for pleasure. Chief Judge Wesley E. Brown of Wichita, Kansas, laments, "It is a lot easier in the summertime to get visiting judges in Colorado than it is in Kansas; to get a judge out into Wyoming, particularly if he is going to Jackson Hole, than it is to attract one to Kansas. Now, we love Kansas weather, and we love Kansas, but the facts of life are just that way." Resultantly, Kansas relies almost exclusively on judges from bordering states.

• Another judge who follows the "work-vacation" pattern is Chief Judge Robert C. Bellioni of Portland, Oregon, and he says "it is very difficult for me to be apologetic." In four of six years Bellioni received a month's special assignment away from Portland and took his family along with him. "For example, I worked in the District of Columbia for a month one summer. I took my family, we had a nice vacation, my teenage children received an education being in the nation's capital." Bellioni notes he takes no other time off during the year. Between 1968 and 1972 Bellioni spent 149 work days out of his home district, an average of almost 30 per year.

Travel records maintained by the Administrative Office of the United States Courts confirm a claim long made by the Florida Chamber of Commerce: Florida is a pleasant place to spend the winter months. A handful of veteran federal jurists have veritably found a second home in the central and southern districts of Florida. "The winter judges," local lawyers call this well-tanned band of aged visitors—men who begin arriving in December, and linger until February or March, when the northern and western snows have ended. Consider Judge Richard M. Duncan of Kansas City, the dean of the winter judges. In 1968 he spent 76 days in Florida's central district (which belts the state, from Tampa to Cape Kennedy); in 1969, 65 days; in 1971, 69 days; in 1972, 78 days. Or Judge C. William Kraft, Jr., of Philadelphia: 122 days in Miami in 1971; 121 days in 1972.

Florida lawyers are of two minds on the visitors. One school sees the use of "winter judges" as a means of keeping senior men active long after most men go into full retirement. As one lawyer said, "What's wrong with Kraft having a winter home here and doing some work, rather than sitting around in retirement and drawing full pay anyway? Hell, the man wouldn't go outside in Philadelphia during the wintertime—here he can get around." The winter judges supposedly keep the Florida courts from sinking under the weight of docket backlogs. The time they spent in Miami in 1970, for instance, was the equivalent of having an extra one and one-half judges in the district.

But the winter judges are also a considerable nuisance both to lawyers and local jurists. A Tampa lawyer: "These people have no rapport with the local bar. They want to do things the way they are done in Missouri and Pennsylvania and what have you, and heaven help the lawyer who crosses one of them." Another lawyer, from Orlando: "The problem with the visitors is that they can't keep their minds off the golf course and beach. They daydream; they aren't here to work, they are here to play. One of these characters—and I'm not going to give you his name, although I will say that he's from Pennsylvania—anyway, we were in a rather tedious pretrial conference, and he suddenly broke off saying, 'Gentlemen, my wife and I are down to play in a bridge tournament at three o'clock, so let's resume this meeting next Tuesday.' Now that is patently absurd."

Chief Judge Charles B. Fulton of Miami cites another drawback to the influx of winter judges: "We feel, as active permanent judges, that we have some obligation to entertain these people. And they bring their wives with them, usually, and we certainly would not have these people in our court unless there was a necessity for it." So the local jurists smile, often a bit tightly, and host the winter judges at festive luncheons and cocktail parties and dinners while their wives act as tour guides in the afternoons. Peirson Hall, the former chief judge in Los Angeles, asserts that visitors can be obnoxiously demanding. He cites the out-of-town judge who filed a formal complaint with the Senate and House Judiciary Committees and the Ninth Circuit Judicial Council about "the treatment accorded this judge by the Honorable Peirson M. Hall." His problem? "He complained about sitting in this ragged old chair, that he had low-ceiling chambers, and he had to sit in this terribly dumpy old chair." Hall simply responded that the visiting judges' chambers were outfitted with furniture supplied by the General Services Administration, and the matter was dropped.

In Arizona, the flow of judges is two-way. During

the winter months as many as fifteen visiting judges settle into Phoenix and Tucson for periods ranging up to eight weeks. Judge John Bowen of Seattle, for example, managed to wheedle 223 days in Arizona during the five-year period 1968–72; in a typical year (1970) judges came into the state from Delaware, Montana, Idaho, Northern California and Washington. Chief Judge Walter E. Craig of Phoenix, a dapper man who is one of the most popular federal judges in the country, cheerfully acknowledges that "these Northern judges like to come down [to] get out of the snow from Alaska and Washington." In the summer, however, the traffic is reversed, with Arizona judges scurrying for San Francisco, San Diego, Hawaii and Guam. According to Craig, Arizona judges take regular assignments out of the state for three to four weeks each because "the exceptionally hot weather in Arizona . . . is not conducive to the trial of cases." Lawyers don't like to try cases from July through mid-September because of the heat and unavailability of witnesses, according to Craig.

Senator Quentin Burdick (D., N.D.), who heard this story as Craig pleaded for creation of a new judgeship in Arizona in 1973, was skeptical. "For the record, Judge, we find that these assignments for the most part have been to Hawaii, Guam and San Diego. The climate in those areas is also oppressive in the summer months. How do these courts manage to try cases in hot summer months?"

Craig contended that the San Diego and Hawaii weather wasn't all that bad, but alas for Arizona. "When you run one-hundred-five degrees to one-hundred-ten degrees for maybe a month at a stretch, you don't find people wanting to go out in the street very much."

The Burdick subcommittee counsel, William P. Westphal, wasn't satisfied. "Judge, I practiced law for twenty years in Minnesota, and I can remember times when the temperature never got above zero for 30 days, and frequently went down to 25 to 30 degrees below zero. If your car doesn't start, you have to take a bus or a taxi in order to get to your office and get over to the courthouse. Your witnesses have to do the same thing.

"I don't recall that the courts in the State of Minnesota ever suspended because the temperature was so extremely cold."

Craig demurred. Even with air conditioning, he said, the "whole town shuts down." If cases are scheduled in the summer, lawyers contrive excuses for postponement. "The court," Burdick reminded the judge, "runs the court." "But if you are going to run the court, you need the cooperation of the bar," Craig retorted.

Judicial goof-offs and junkets are not universal. According to court records, a number of judges are veritable workoholics. Some examples of industrious jurists:

- Chief Judge Frank M. Johnson of Montgomery, Alabama, said in 1973 he had not had a vacation in twelve years, and didn't anticipate one in the foreseeable future. His normal work day was ten hours.

- Judge William T. Beeks of Seattle lamented that he had only four weeks vacation between 1966 and 1973. "I am in my office regularly at 7:30 A.M. I schedule pretrial conferences for 8 A.M. and 8:30 A.M. I start the trial of cases at 9 A.M. and recess no earlier than 4:30 P.M." In 1972 Beeks finally "collapsed on the bench from physical exhaustion." Despite Beeks' arduous schedule, other judges in his district accepted assignments elsewhere—generally in warm winter resorts—rather than help him cope with the court's high caseload. Judge George Boldt spent 48 days in Puerto Rico in 1968; 50 days in Southern California in 1970; 43 days in Hawaii, Alaska and San Francisco in 1971. Judge William J. Lindberg spent 50 days in Florida and Arizona in 1968; another 26 days in Arizona in 1969; another 35 in 1970.

- The three district judges in Denver have taken a *total* annual vacation of as little as 25 days. The chief judge, Albert A. Arraj, has never taken more

than 15 days annual vacation during his fifteen
years on the bench.

• Judge Henry Graven, of Iowa, now deceased, ran
pretrial conferences until nine o'clock in the evening. Frederic M. Miller, former president of the
Iowa Bar Association, says an out of town lawyer
once called Graven a few days after one of his
marathon conferences and said, "Judge, I understand you set the Jones case for a pretrial at one-
thirty." "That is right," Graven replied. The lawyer
continued, "Is that one-thirty P.M. or A.M.? Your
order doesn't say."

The hard worker, unfortunately, is not universal.
For all too many judges, the security of the lifetime
appointment is a license to work as little as he pleases
—and in as comfortable a city as he pleases, provided
a friendly chief judge hands him the proper travel
orders.

*The very memory of the demonstrators set Judge
A. Andrew Hauk of Los Angeles aquiver with inner
fury. He had been telling a group of judges, meeting
in Washington in conjunction with the American Bar
Association Convention in August, 1973, how he dealt
with "bum lawyers" and "long-haired, hippie-type
lawyers" and "great civil liberties lawyers" (the latter
pronounced with inflections that were not compli-
mentary) and "screwballs" who came into his court.
But one day these "hippies and screwballs"—Andy
Hauk had to pause a moment to compose himself
before he could even spit out the words—anyway, a
group of these people saw the sign he had posted
on the courthouse door in downtown Los Angeles
reading, "No Placards or Demonstrations on United
States Courthouse Property." And they ignored it!
They read Andy Hauk's sign, and they picked up
their own placards, and they turned and marched up
and down the courthouse plaza.*

*So Andy Hauk gathered his judicial robes about
him and puffed downstairs at a gallop with a United
States marshal, and he told them where to head in.*

Yes, Andy Hauk did. And the memory of the triumph began to warm Andy Hauk, and he smiled, and he shouted to dramatize for the audience how he handled the situation: "Now you guys here parading, you are violating a court order. NOW GET THE HELL OFF THE PROPERTY! GET THE HELL OFF OR GO TO JAIL! WHICH DO YOU WANT?"

Andy Hauk stopped and grinned, and then he mimicked one of the demonstrators. " 'Eeeeeuuuuu! We have freedom of speech, we have the freedom to demonstrate.'

" 'Yes,' I said, 'out on the sidewalk. But not on the plaza.' " *Andy Hauk's eyes gleamed at his shrewdness, and he continued:* "The beauty of this is, by arrangement with the chief of police, once they are on the sidewalk, they are not our responsibility, they're not the marshal's responsibility. The city police have tact squads [tactical squads] which know how to handle demonstrators—if they don't march in a certain line, why, you go into the paddy wagon."

Hauk smiled again, as if envisioning dozens of bum-lawyers and hippies and screwballs looking forlornly through bars at the back of the van, their long locks hanging limply, as the Los Angeles cops drove them away to jail.

At this writing the federal courts appear to be ending The Years of the Big Scare—the era in which politically-oriented defendants used their trials to debate flaws of the American system, rather than the facts (and law) at dispute in their immediate case. For the first time in their existence the American courts dealt with persons who paid no heed whatsoever to the hoary traditions of the judiciary. People who didn't snap to their feet and chorus, "Good morning, Your Honor," when the judge arrived. People who used street langauge on the witness stand, and called the judge by his first name. People who wore whatever garments happened to be lying around in the morning: jeans and denims and mumus and old army fatigues and lumberjack boots and sandals and often no shoes at all—a happy, chaotic affirmation of an up-yours attitude that, put most simply, drove many of the learned judges batty. Chief Justice Warren Burger, in a speech in May 1971 at the height of the fright, castigated "adrenalin-fueled" lawyers who appeared to think that "the zeal and effectiveness of a lawyer depends on how thoroughly he can disrupt the proceedings or how loud he can shout or how close he can come to insulting all those he encounters, including the judges." Soon thereafter the American Bar Association put out new suggested guidelines for controlling "unruly" lawyers, including censure, contempt, removal from court, and temporary suspension from practice.

Rattling the calm of the existing order is what a political defense is all about, really—to put the judicial system and the people who run it off balance, to accept its punishments with a laugh, as a means of pointing up the supposed absurdity of laws on the draft, on marijuana, on governmental secrecy, on military discipline. And, in perspective, the guerrilla defenses worked. The militants and their attorneys demonstrated that unconventional courtroom tactics can embolden supposedly conventional jurors to vote in unexpected ways. As the 1960s ended the government was striking at the very heart of the political left in America with such prosecutions as that of Dr. Benjamin Spock and friends for advocating draft resistance; of the Chicago Eight for the 1968 Democratic convention disorders; of the Berrigans for the Kissinger "kidnap" caper; of any number of individual war protesters. But as the 1970s move toward their middle years, jurors working within the established framework have cried "Enough! No More!" to political prosecutions, refusing, for example, to convict a group of Philadelphia antiwar activists for invading the draft-board office in suburban Camden, New Jersey, and eight members of the Vietnam Veterans Against the War for alleged plans to disrupt the 1972 Republican national convention. (Enthusiastic FBI informers pushed along planning of both "plots" and the jurors apparently considered them provocateurs rather than intelligence sources.)

But the Years of the Big Scare had a somber edge as well—the fear, by many judges, that militant defense-conduct inevitably would degenerate into physical violence directed against the court. Bomb scares. Courtroom scuffles between marshals, defendants and spectators. Seizure of weapons in and near courtrooms. In a single month, according to William R. Sweeney, deputy director of the Administrative Office of the United States Courts, guards found in a single courthouse a ten-inch fish knife, a .38-caliber pistol, and a .22-caliber rifle, "and this in a 'quiet section' of the country." The violence threats were from non-political defendants as well. In the words of Hauk, "Two of our [Los Angeles federal] judges have received serious death threats. Contracts have been put out for them by bums they sent up for twenty-five years, and who are boasting around prison they put out $25,000 contracts on their lives. One judge in particular was really concerned about it and got protection from the United States marshal's service until things seemed to blow over." * Finally, the kidnap-murder of a state judge who was presiding over the prison murder trial of black defendants in Marin County, California, sent a shiver of I-could-be-next anxiety through jurists around the country.

That the judicial system survived both the new defense techniques and the violence is a tribute to its resiliency. But the cost was high: many judges equated militancy with violence, and in the name of "courtroom security" imposed Draconian rules that damaged the Constitutional right of fair and open trial. At off-the-record seminars † federal judges were

---

* Hauk is so excitable a fellow that not everyone takes him seriously. He declined to identify the two threatened judges on "security grounds." Speaking on the same program, William Sweeney of the courts administrative office said, "I don't know any judge who is really afraid despite the fact we have threat after threat after threat against judges, and that we have some really violent people."

† A federal official permitted me to read a syllabus for one of these seminars, conducted under the auspices of the Federal Judicial Center in Washington. But he refused to permit notes

schooled in techniques for keeping the so-called "political" trials from getting out of hand.

- Defendants were not to be permitted to serve as their own defense counsel, for those who did so "shouted political speeches to the jury" and asked "immaterial political questions of witnesses." Defense attorneys were to be "admonished strongly at the outset of the trial, in chamber," that they would be held liable for the courtroom conduct of their clients and sympathetic witnesses. If the client was disruptive, the lawyer should be threatened with contempt.
- Marshals and bailiffs were to exercise strict crowd control. No spectators were to be permitted in the first two rows of the courtroom, so as to deny them physical proximity to defendants and lawyers. "Unconventional and outlandish dress" would not be tolerated in the audience. Identification would be required for admittance to the courtroom, and marshals, at their discretion, would frisk spectators at the door. Plainclothesmen would sit in the audience so as to provide quick identification of persons who became disruptive.
- Regardless of public interest in a trial, the judge should hold it in as small a courtroom as possible to keep down attendance. Under no circumstances should the judge use the outsized "ceremonial courtroom" found in most metropolitan courthouses. Persons standing in line for admittance should be required to wait outside the courthouse; bad weather, the judges learned, discouraged crowds.
- Counsel and defendants should be put under strict gag rules about out-of-court comments at the outset of the trial. The media should be encouraged, through personal contacts by the judge if necessary, to avoid advance stories on "political" trials until

---

to be taken, on grounds that plans for courtroom deployment of marshals and certain other security techniques should remain unpublished "in the public interest."

the jury was empanelled, and to ignore out-of-court statements by both parties. Television and still cameramen should be kept as far from court as possible. An example: prior to 1969, a Chicago rule forebade photography on floors of the federal building which contained courtrooms. A week before the start of the Democratic convention conspiracy trial, the judges passed a new rule extending the ban to the "environs" of the "courtroom," including the ground floor and "the plaza and sidewalks surrounding the courthouse." The Seventh Circuit Court of Appeals, acting on a suit brought by editor Ron Dorfman of the *Chicago Journalism Review*, held the rule violated the first amendment and ordered that restraint on the press "must be confined to those activities which offer immediate threat to the judicial proceedings and not to those which are merely potentially threatening." The appeals court noted the rule would have prevented Senator Charles Percy, who has offices on the eighteenth floor of the courthouse, from holding a press conference and discussing any judicial topic.

Marshals and other federal agents, meanwhile, received their own special schooling. The marshals service invested heavily in metal sensory devices for screening spectators, closed-circuit video systems, miniaturized walkie-talkie radios for inconspicuous courtroom use, bomb detectors, and other sophisticated gear. Much of this equipment could be justified for practical security reasons; other items, however, are questionable.

Covert surveillance of militant defendants and their lawyers was an underlying (but unadmitted) factor in one politically-oriented trial, in which the judge used his contempt powers to wreak vengeance upon an attorney who offended him. The case is a stark illustration of how unconventional defense tactics so unnerved some federal judges that they lost control of their emotions and struck out at their supposed tormentors blindly—and often illegally, as proved true here.

The defendants were nine antiwar activists, including former Catholic priests and nuns, who ransacked the Washington office of Dow Chemical Company in 1969 to protest the company's manufacture of napalm for use in Vietnam. The lead lawyer for their defense was Philip J. Hirschkop, a feisty, outspoken guy who well could be the best criminal attorney in the nation. (Some other well-known criminal lawyers get publicity; Phil Hirschkop, although not uninterested in seeing his name in print, gets acquittals for his clients as well.) Hirschkop's combative trial techniques and plain speech brought him into frequent confrontations with judges, and he spent much time fending off disciplinary actions by bar associations. Hirschkop never lost any of these proceedings; he joked about them privately as "the annual disbarment rites of spring."

The judge in the case was John H. Pratt, who some local lawyers feel has rather basic flaws. They maintain that he is mean, and he is hardheaded, and he behaves as if God or another deity gave him special duties for weeding out and punishing people who don't behave as he (Pratt, not God) feels desirable. "Say what you will of Judge Pratt," a lawyer remarked to me, "he has the courage of his convictions. Why, once Pratt makes up his mind, he never changes it—not even after the trial gets under way, and he begins hearing the evidence." Another lawyer attributes Pratt's martinet behavior to his marine corps background. Pratt lost part of an arm in the Pacific during World War Two, and he combined a military and administrative practice in the postwar years, serving as judge advocate general for the Marine Corps Reserve Officer Association. A devout Catholic (one of his daughters is a nun), Pratt sometimes remarks in court about taking communion daily regardless of his trial schedule. President Johnson put him on the bench after a term as head of the D.C. Bar Association.

The Dow defendants cheerfully admitted the break-in; in fact, they had called the press while it was in progress and asked for coverage. Their intention, they said, was to use the trial as an antiwar forum. They wanted to argue a defense of "nullification," that is, to persuade the jury to vote against judge and law, and "express the community conscience" on the war and companies such as Dow who helped wage it. They wished to conduct their own defense, and make antiwar speeches to the jury in lieu of closing arguments.

In pretrial conferences Pratt was unsympathetic to the defendants' plans. He told lawyers he had called the city desks of Washington newspapers to ask they not print stories about the trial until the jury was selected. He issued an order against out-of-court comments and demonstrations in proximity to the courthouse. Pratt said he "was meeting with police authorities and hearing rumors about plans concerning demonstrations and activities of the defendants." And he flatly refused to permit Hirschkop to withdraw from the case, as the defendants had requested, so they could conduct their own defense.

In the minds of the defense, Pratt had already prejudged the case. Hard evidence soon confirmed their suspicions. Allen W. Scheflin, an associate law professor at Georgetown University, represented some of the defendants in a related civil matter. Marshals guarding the trial courtroom refused to let him enter save as a spectator, and said he would be arrested if he persisted. Outraged, Scheflin went to Pratt's chambers to protest. Pratt made a long speech about his "concern for political trials" and his strategy for conducting the Dow case, based upon procedures he had learned at a seminar at the Federal Judicial Center. According to Scheflin, Pratt said, "In a multi-defendant trial, you *never* let the defendants represent themselves." In "this kind of case," Pratt said, "You keep the courtroom loosely attended. In other words, you don't fill all the benches. You keep the first two rows of benches clear. You pack the room with marshals. You don't hold the attorneys in contempt until the trial is over."

As Scheflin recounted later, Pratt "sounded to me like . . . well, the attorney *is* going to be held in contempt, it is just a matter of time." Pratt showed Scheflin a file card containing a notation about an earlier contempt proceeding against Hirschkop in Virginia, saying he "had this card in case he needed it."

During the first trial day Pratt formally refused to permit the defendants to represent themselves. He was not interested in why they wished to do so, but did take the time to inquire of their status in the church, and grunted unsympathetically when Art Melville said that he had resigned as a priest in the Maryknoll Order and that, yes, his wife was a former nun. (The two met while serving in Guatemala as missionaries; they quit in protest of orders from their superiors to stop associating with *campesino* and student groups hostile to the government.) And he denied motions by Hirschkop to move to a larger courtroom (persons stood outside for admittance, even though several rows of seats were vacant) and to conduct an open hearing on the gag rule. Finally Hirschkop gave voice to his frustrations in a toughly-worded, fifteen-minute statement in which he complained that Pratt "made your mind up before you . . . heard anything this morning" and refused to let the defense state its objections to his rulings. By going through the *pro forma* motions of a hearing, Hirschkop said, "we . . . demean our system." The only thing to be resolved, he said, was the "length of the sentence." He continued:

I am afraid of making this system rotten by not being able to do my job, and that is representing people, and that is what I am here for. I am not here to grease the wheels of the court. I am terribly afraid that you have made up your mind that you are going to dispatch this case as expeditiously as possible. I am not here to expedite it. I will do it with all the dignity of a lawyer and all the sanctions of the bar in mind, but I will not take part in greasing the wheels, not of justice, but the wheels of expeditiously packing these nine people off to jail as quickly as we can.

During the three-and-one-half-day trial Hirschkop and Pratt sparred frequently but politely. Pratt was hostile throughout but only one time did he even hint that he was considering holding Hirschkop in contempt (telling him, during an argument over the defendants' jury speeches, that "you are treading close to the line.")

Internally, however, Judge Pratt seethed with rage against the defendants—and, in a sense, justifiably so. Pratt indeed was receiving reports from "police authorities" about "activities of the defendants," the words he used in a chambers conference with attorneys. An investigative agency installed electronic eavesdropping devices in a house used by the defendants and their coterie of supporters, and the conversations they picked up in the evening were dutifully transcribed and submitted to Pratt. And what Pratt read can charitably be described as offensive.

With black-humor viciousness several of the defendants jested about the prosthetic device Pratt wore because of the loss of his forearm during the war. They called him "Captain Hook" and joked about "the iron hand of justice." To Pratt's frustration he could make no direct use of the transcripts. And the defense, even when it learned of the covert eavesdropping, dared not raise objection lest the derogatory commentary become a part of the formal record.

But as the presiding judge, Pratt was in a position to reap his revenge, and he attempted to do so from the detested hide of lawyer Hirschkop. Immediately after the jury returned guilty verdicts against seven of the defendants (two others had dropped out of the trial and pleaded guilty), he summoned Hirschkop to the bench and cited him for criminal contempt. The next day he handed Hirschkop a generalized bill of particulars (chiefly the use of "insulting, derogatory and disrespectful" language) and ordered him jailed for 30 days. Pratt gave Hirschkop no opportunity to speak in his own defense. The same morning Pratt appeared before the D.C. Bar Association grievance committee and demanded that Hirschkop be disbarred.

Hirschkop promptly appealed to the circuit court,

which held Pratt had no summary contempt powers once the trial had ended, and that he should have given the contempt citation to another judge for formal hearing since he, Pratt, was the complaining witness. Upon rehearing, Judge Frank A. Kaufman of Baltimore (sitting by special assignment because no Washington judge would touch the case) acquitted Hirschkop. After reading his opinion Kaufman walked over to Hirschkop, who was sitting at the counsel table, and said, "If I had been trying this case, and you acted like that, I would have called you up to the bench, and chewed you out, and that would have been the end of it."

Meantime, the bar grievance committee (whose three members were aged 82, 78, and 68 years) accepted Pratt's recommendation that Hirschkop be disbarred. But a three-judge panel of district judges held that, because of Hirschkop's "exemplary" record, disbarment was too severe a punishment. It did censure him for "discourteous" conduct.

But the irrepressible Hirschkop was not yet free. Asked by a *Washington Post* reporter for a comment, he said the district judges censured him as a "face-saving gesture for Pratt." He continued: "It was a slap on the wrist when Pratt was trying to cut my head off." Whereupon the three district judges went back to the bar and asked that yet another contempt proceeding be started. Hirschkop's supporters in the Washington bar inundated the committee with affidavits defending the propriety of his defense, and the matter eventually died of ennui.*

Because of what Edward Lumbard, the former chief judge of the Second Circuit Court of Appeals, has called "a tradition of isolated splendor and almost unlimited power," the federal bench has spawned what he gently describes as "many unforgettable characters." In reminiscing about these judges, Lumbard

---

* So, too, did the felony convictions of the original defendants. The circuit court threw out their convictions because of Pratt's refusal to permit them to conduct their own defenses—tacitly endorsing what Hirshkop had argued all along. They then pleaded guilty to misdemeanor charges.

sounds pleasantly nostalgic, as if practicing before them was a privilege (even if an unrecognized one) for a young lawyer. Listen to Lumbard:

> They were cantankerous, strong minded, and ornery; they lent color to the American scene. Men like Charles M. Hough did not merely preside; they literally scared you to death. Bold spirits like Felix Frankfurter and Emory Buckner † walked around the old federal building three times before they dared to visit Hough. Fortunately, behind the bellow and the rough manner was a kindly and friendly spirit and a great judge.
>
> Judge Hough, of Vermont, was such a character, in New York as well as in the Green Mountains. It was a sight to see and hear him administer criminal justice. At the end of the government's case he usually summoned the marshal and in stentorian tones he commanded: "Mr. Marshal, open the window! Out goes another government case!"

The judges were so independent, Judge Lumbard continued, that often they did not bother to be civil with one another. Lumbard tells of the chief judge in a two-judge district who, by accident, met his colleague in the elevator after not seeing him for many months. "The junior judge summoned a smile and said, 'How are you today, judge?' After a long pause, the senior replied, 'It's none of your damn business, and I wouldn't tell you that much if I hadn't known you for thirty years.'"

Early in research for this book I began assembling what I labelled my "Expletive Deleted file," material on judges who are so nasty, so savage, in their courtroom conduct that in a less civilized society they would have been taken out behind the barn and knocked in the head. One tribute to lawyer restraint in our republic is that no offended barrister has ever taken after a federal judge with a pistol, dirk or

---

† Hough was a judge in the Southern District of New York; Buckner, a leading New York trial lawyer for three decades.

horsewhip; many certainly have deserved a quick, brisk thrashing, or worse, for deportment that offends the standards by which decent men live. Lawyers are an oddly masochistic lot. As youngsters they are subjected to judicial hazing not unlike that inflicted on college fraternity pledges, or marine recruits. They cry about it among themselves, and to their wives and friends, and they toss and turn at night and wonder if that slow abdominal burn is really the start of an ulcer, and the next day they slink into court for yet another flogging. Then, in their golden years, they compose charming memories of "unforgettable characters," to use Judge Lumbard's euphemistic phrase, while yet another generation of judges torments and berates the new class of young lawyers.

After a year my Expletive Deleted file bulged with names and case histories. Let's begin in my home area, northern Virginia. Judge Oren R. Lewis of Alexandria, in the words of a man who practices regularly before him, "has done more to increase the incidence of lawyer high blood pressure and ulcers than any other force in nature. Blue Cross should give him a finder's fee." Lewis, 70 at this writing, and in senior status, is rude and abrupt. One perverse specialty is embarrassing lawyers in front of juries (and clients) with such questions as "How long you been practicing law anyway, young man?" or "Exactly what are you *trying* to prove, counsellor?" The modern age does not disturb Judge Lewis; he simply ignores it.

Harvey Katz, a onetime Justice Department trial lawyer, tells of the time he defended the government against several civil suits brought by a lawyer in North Carolina. A Virginia judge was to hear the cases by special assignment. Because of high settlement demands Katz could make no progress on out-of-court disposition. Then one day the North Carolina lawyer called. Katz recounts the conversation:

N.C. LAWYER: I accept your offer on these four cases.

KATZ: I haven't really made any.

N.C. LAWYER: Make it a fair one and I'll take it.

KATZ: What's the story?

N.C. LAWYER: Haven't you heard? Judge Lewis is coming down, and you've got me over a barrel. My clients are black.

Because the Pentagon is located in his district, Lewis heard cases of scores of antiwar demonstrators arrested during the late 1960s. Lewis could not understand why all citizens did not support such an important national undertaking as the Vietnam War. During one 1967 trial, that of a young man named Howell, Lewis took over the interrogation and asked questions for a full 13 pages of transcript, brushing aside attempts by defense counsel to intervene. As the Third Circuit Court of Appeals commented in reversing the conviction, Lewis "lectured and chided Howell, asked time and again why 'an honor student at Harvard University' would participate in events which occurred during the demonstration but which were not the subject of charges brought against Howell." The circuit court said Lewis "gave every indication that he had already decided the case adversely to Howell. . . ." In another case arising from the same demonstration, the court reversed Lewis for interrupting defense counsel's closing argument with "chiding, critical language."

Another egregious Southerner is Judge Robert E. Varner, a Nixon appointee in the middle district of Alabama, and a protégé of former Postmaster General Winton M. Blount. (Varner's appointment suffered an embarrassing delay when information turned up that he owed $45,000 to $60,000 in estate taxes on an inheritance from his father. No wrongdoing was involved, but public announcement of the appointment was withheld while Varner scurried around Montgomery and borrowed the money.) As a former president of the Montgomery Bar Association, Varner saves most of his barbed comments for out-of-state lawyers and the dwindling band of civil rights lawyers working the South. "People like this," he once said of a black bank robber, "jail's the only thing left for *them*.

And don't give me any sociological rubbish either, counsellor." Varner's outlook towards justice is best revealed in affidavits through which the Montgomery Community Action Committee, Inc. (MCAC), a predominantly black poverty unit, tried to persuade the judge to disqualify himself in a suit brought by local officials.

As the basis of their petition, MCAC attorneys cited a conversation Varner had with United States Attorney Ira DeMent and three of his assistants prior to starting a round of criminal trials in rural Opelika, Alabama, in the spring of 1973. According to affidavits, Varner asked DeMent and the other prosecutors to "strike Negro jurors because the white people in that area had not accepted the idea of eating with Negroes; and that if a jury had to go to lunch together, the white jurors would not like to eat with the Negro jurors. This . . . would upset the white jurors." DeMent rejected the "suggestion" out of hand, and black jurors were not purged. Nonetheless MCAC lawyers cited the episode as evidence of Varner's bias, and hence unfitness to hear their case. When Varner read the papers he called MCAC lawyer Morris S. Dees, Jr. According to an affidavit Dees filed later in court, Varner did not deny the substance of the conversation with DeMent. Dees' motion continued:

> He [Judge Varner] told Mr. Dees that . . . the things alleged in the motion were true except for the conclusion that he was biased. Mr. Dees asked Judge Varner whether his clients would be allowed to have a hearing on their Motion to Disqualify in order to have proof, other than Judge Varner's admission, in the record to support the motion.
>
> Judge Varner stated that he doubted if a hearing would be allowed because there would be no contest about the facts alleged in the Motion to Disqualify.

Enough of Dixie. Let's prowl the Eastern seaboard for a moment. Former Chief Judge Thomas J. Clary of Philadelphia is renowned for possession of a quick temper and tongue. But he does make an effort to control himself. Once, when a lawyer offended him during a closing argument, Clary got up from his chair and walked out of the courtroom, slamming the door with a resounding bang that left no doubt proceedings had been recessed. Another time Clary heard that a postal inspector had talked to a juror after a not-guilty verdict. He called the inspector into court and held him in contempt. The *Philadelphia Inquirer* reporter wrote, "Judge Clary conducted the hearing in unconcealed fury, speaking at the top of his voice and shouting down interruptions. 'What do you think you did? Are you trying to get convictions in other cases?' " (To his credit Clary didn't put the hapless fellow in jail; he turned him free after chewing on him half-an-hour or so.) Some of Clary's friends in the Philadelphia bar say he's not that bad a guy at all; that what the public sees are the natural foibles of an aging man. Nonsense, retorts a Philadelphia trial lawyer: "Tom Clary's been mad more or less constantly for the last twenty years."

One man who felt the sting of Clary's anger—and survived, and prospered—is J. Shane Creamer, former first assistant United States attorney in Philadelphia. In the 1960s Creamer won convictions of racketeers who ran a high stakes dice game featuring chauffeured limousines that brought in big spenders from a 200-mile area around happy-go-lucky Reading, Pennsylvania. Later, the gamblers filed a motion for reduction of sentence with Judge Joseph Lord. The judge set a hearing, and a parade of character witnesses, chiefly politicians, testified the gamblers were really rather nice people and well-respected in their home towns. Oddly, no one ever sent a notice of the hearing to Creamer or anyone else in the United States attorney's office, hence prosecutors didn't have the opportunity to bring out the long and unsavory records of the defendants. Lord reduced the sentences.

Philadelphia newspapers got word of what had happened, and their stories featured the lack of notice to the prosecution. Lord became livid. So, too, did Chief Judge Clary. They called in Creamer and his boss,

Drew J. T. O'Keefe. Clary blamed Creamer for leaking the story to the press and "crying to the newspapers." (Creamer denied doing any such thing.) "You have held this court up for contempt," Clary told Creamer. "You have worn out your welcome in this court, young man!" Clary told O'Keefe he did not want Creamer to prosecute any more cases in Philadelphia.

Since a prosecutor's job is just that—to prosecute people—Clary's edict effectively put Creamer out of the United States attorney's office. O'Keefe, whose professional well-being relied upon good relations with the judges, would not support him, and he resigned. Clary was not yet satisfied. When he heard Creamer was negotiating a position with a big Philadelphia law firm he sent word of his dislike for the young prosecutor. "Sorry," the firm told Creamer, "we can't buck the judge." (In due course Creamer went on to become attorney general of Pennsylvania and is now a partner in a major Philadelphia law firm.)

New York's prime wild man, Judge Irving Ben Cooper, we encountered earlier, in the chapter on judicial selection. Aside from Cooper the New York bench has tolerably good manners. One sometime backslider is Judge Thomas Murphy, who was New York police commissioner and United States attorney (he prosecuted Alger Hiss) before going on the bench. When Murphy hears a criminal case, defense lawyers have been heard to complain they feel outnumbered two-to-one, that is to say, the Honorable Judge can't forget his former occupation of cop and prosecutor. But as one criminal lawyer puts it, "Murphy's problem isn't meanness as much as it is callousness." Another attorney, Martin Garbus, cites a good example: Garbus once sued the New York Welfare Department for cutting off aid to two kids without investigating whether the mother was receiving money from a man whom social workers reportedly had seen at her apartment. Garbus asked for a preliminary injunction but Murphy wouldn't even read his papers. Garbus quoted Murphy as saying, "She's managed all right for the past two weeks. She can wait until the case is reached in its normal order. . . . She can borrow money from her boy friend."

But do any of these judges—Oren Lewis of Virginia, Robert Varner of Alabama, Thomas Clary of Pennsylvania, Thomas Murphy of New York—qualify for the title of ultimate Expletive Deleted judge of the federal courts? At one point I had decided that Judge Willis Ritter, the perpetual-fury machine of Salt Lake City, deserved the honor. Ritter's bad temper, however, seems to be fired by age and whiskey more than by innate meanness and, as is true of any ricocheting object, he occasionally lands on the right side of an issue. Let me say that again: Ritter sometimes makes a humanitarian decision, but maybe only because he is madder at the bad guys in the case than he is at the good guys.

No, the ultimate Expletive Deleted must be a man of such misanthropic vigor that he spends a good portion of his court day haranguing lawyers, defendants, and anyone else who comes into sight; who has brains enough, and is lawyer enough, to know better, but who nonetheless behaves like . . . well, a real so-and-so, and is proud of it.

I found my man in Los Angeles.

His name is Charles Carr, and I began hearing stories about him from California lawyers even before I got to the Los Angeles courthouse. Sadistic. A tyrant. A smart lawyer who is so convinced of his own intellectual superiority that he wants to conduct both sides of the trial and act as judge as well. Vindictive. Cross him early in the trial, and he'll bide his time and retaliate when he can *really* hurt you. But he is fair: he mistreats both sides. Such are the things California lawyers said of Charlie Carr.

I went to watch Carr perform. A suburban Los Angeles "tax consultant," a frightened, gulping little man in a nondescript brown suit, was on trial for allegedly falsifying deductions on returns he prepared for clients. Carr, florid-faced with deep jowls, his hue as deep as the crimson fabric backdrop of his court, stared down at the guy as he testified in response to questions from his own lawyer.

Or tried to testify, anyway. The problem was that Carr could not let him proceed for more than a minute without butting in with his own questions. Much of the ragging was semantical quibbling. At one point, for instance, the consultant maintained he didn't remember preparing a specific return but that he "knew" he used information supplied by the taxpayer.

"How do you 'know' when you say 'you don't remember'?" interjected Carr. The man tried to explain that he "knew" because he "always" relied upon the taxpayer's documentation. "You can't have it both ways," Carr said, and shrugged and waved his hand at the lawyer, a sign he could proceed.

A bit later, interrupting the prosecutor's cross-examination, Carr computed that the charitable deductions claimed on each of the questioned returns amounted to five percent of the total income. He asked the consultant to comment on the "coincidence." He questioned whether taxpayers had been warned that the high deductions—$2,300 on a gross income of $6,266, in one case—would not be a "red flag for the tax bureau."

"Most taxpayers don't get one-half the deductions to which they are allowed," the consultant protested. He nervously ran his tongue over his lips and adjusted his tie. "You see, Your Honor . . ."

"That's all," Carr said, "you may proceed with your questions."

Jesus, I thought to myself, sitting in the back of the courtroom, not knowing anything about the case other than what I heard in that half-hour, *Jesus, this guy is guilty as hell.* And, I decided later, I reached the conclusion solely because of the impact of Carr's intervention—his choice of language, his tone of voice, his raised-eyebrow response to the answers; even when silent, Charlie Carr is a demonstrative person. And if Carr had convinced me, a wandering stranger who entered the courtroom *skeptical* of his fairness, what effect had his comments had upon the jurors?

That morning session was atypical only in that Carr selected only one person—the defendant—for hazing. Reporter David Shaw, of the *Los Angeles Times,* once saw Carr explode in four successive cases in no more than 40 minutes:

- As the attorney for a convicted bank robber asked for a reduction of his 25-year sentence, Carr snorted, "It's just too bad they did away with the death penalty." When the attorney challenged Carr on a procedural point, the judge said, "Let's don't get me off in some position where some great liberal on the appellate court is going to find some way to get this man free . . . so-called liberals; I call 'em pseudo-liberals."

- When the prosecutor of a man arrested for selling LSD mentioned he also was charged with possession of marijuana, Carr sneered, "Well, that was one cigarette, and I suppose some of the professors down at the college are smoking one cigarette today. In fact, the way some of them act, you'd think they were smoking two or three."

- The third defendant was also a bank robber asking for a reduced sentence. "Well, we got another bleeding-heart situation," Carr said. "Here's a man committed how many bank robberies?" "Four, Your Honor," replied the attorney. "Is that all?" Carr snapped. "And now he's writing me these gushing letters about how religious he's become. It's amazing how reformation sets in the minute they get behind the bars. I had one bank robber who insisted he was reformed even before we sentenced him. Said he got religion, saw Jesus. I told him he'd be seeing Jesus through bars for a while."

- Next, a young attorney who had not followed court procedural rules in filing motions. Carr demanded, "You think I'm going to jump up and tear down here on Monday morning just to give special attention to your case, do you?" When the attorney stammered an apology Carr cut in: "Counsel, apologies don't mean a thing to me. Rules are the thing that count. I practiced law for thirty-six years and I don't ever remember having to go in and apologize to a court."

The root of Judge Carr's problem, in the opinion of several West Coast lawyers who know him well (including one man associated with him as long ago as the mid-1930s), is that he considers society's increasing liberality as a personal affront. Carr acquired some rather arch-conservative political and social views during his rural southern boyhood and, by god, no outside demons are going to tamper with his faith. "Charlie's conservatism has increased in geometric proportion to the progress of the rest of the world," opines another California jurist. "If he was at the same place politically as he was, say, in 1945, that would be fine. But he is rolling the clock back every year. Right now he's coming up hard on 1875—in reverse, that is." Carr's dislikes include, in no special order or degree of intensity, most appellate court judges (he won't even call Justice William O. Douglas by name. He refers to him as "that idiot up at Goose Prairie," meaning Douglas' vacation retreat in Washington State *), newspapers, pornography, bureaucrats, abortion, new trends in religion ("You can say 'bikini' in court these days, but not 'Bible,' " he once remarked from the bench), most lawyers, and the quality of contemporary legal education ("I am down here to try law suits, not educate you young jerk lawyers," he said during a tirade).

The pity of it is that Charles Carr was a first-rate lawyer, even if a cantankerous one, for some 30 years before President Kennedy put him on the bench in 1962. Born in Coahoma, Mississippi, son of a prosperous merchant, he attended Yale law school, practiced briefly but none too profitably in Memphis, and finally drifted to Los Angeles in 1929 with a couple of bucks in his pocket. Carr's private practice didn't do too well, so he took a political appointment as an assistant United States attorney in 1933. He won his first major trial, the conviction of a state judge who had demanded $50,000 to fix a case, and his career

---

* The quotation comes from a Los Angeles lawyer who later held a high position in the Ford Administration. Carr denies saying any such thing.

soared. The Justice Department made him a special roaming trial attorney, from 1936–40. He broke briefly for private practice, then returned to government as United States attorney in Los Angeles in 1943. His most famous case was the trial of comedian Charles Chaplin on charges of violating the Mann Act for transporting a young woman to New York for "immoral purposes." Carr says now that Chaplin wasn't guilty, and he knew it when the charges were brought, but prosecuted him anyway. "There were rumors going around that I'd been offered $50,000 to dismiss the charges, so I had no choice; I had to go ahead."

Carr returned to private practice in 1946 and, by his own estimate, built a practice that brought him $300,000 a year. For a moralistic southerner, Carr had some interesting clients during those years. He was president and counsel of the Delmar Turf Club, a race track, in the 1940s and he also represented (and won acquittals for) a number of gambling, social and political figures in tax evasion trials. One client was Wilbur Clark, the Las Vegas gambling figure. Stanley Mosk, then the California attorney general, used this representation as a basis for calling Carr "a mouthpiece for gamblers" when he was nominated for the judgeship. Carr retorted, "The trouble with Stanley Mosk is that he has a big mouth and a small brain."

But Carr's most profitable undertaking—and the one that ultimately got him to the bench—was his successful plea before the Los Angeles planning commission for permission for Twentieth-Century Fox to drill oil wells on its property in West Los Angeles. Carr's client was Universal Consolidated Oil Company, the firm that wanted the drilling permit. Quite understandably, many citizens didn't care to have an oil field in an urban neighborhood and the fight was prolonged and bitter. Ultimately, however, Carr won. By the account of a leading California political figure —now a prominent jurist himself—Carr's victory also gained him the lasting gratitude of Joseph Schenk, a Twentieth-Century executive and a powerful money-politician for the Democratic National Committee. In due course, Senator Clair Engle sponsored Carr for a federal judgeship. Schenk was dead by this time, but my judicial-politico source insists that he gave Carr the first, most important push towards the bench.

That Kennedy, Engle and the Justice Department had made a mistake became obvious almost as soon as Carr put on his robes. The Ninth Circuit Court of Appeals said as much, in polite language, in one of the first appeals it heard from a Carr trial. The case involved the conviction of a securities dealer who fraudulently pumped up the price of stock in a new charcoal company. The dealer's lawyers appealed on grounds Carr kicked them around so capriciously that their client was denied a fair trial. An example: the federal rules of procedure say a judge "shall" inform counsel of the instructions he intends to give the jury. Carr told the lawyers that when he was practicing he "never insisted on the court doing it" and suggested strongly that they waive the requirement also. When one of the defense lawyers demurred, Carr moved to retaliate:

CARR: Then I will cut some of the instructions I am going to give for you. They are very favorable. Those go out. So I'll tell you now what I'm going to give.

LAWYER: Just a moment.

CARR: I'm going to give them to you.

LAWYER: We will withdraw our objection.

CARR: No. I'm going to give them to you now. The issue has been made. . . .

The circuit court cited this exchange, and others, as a "sort of petty tyranny on the part of the judge," but said the threat was not reversible error because it took place in the absence of the jury, and Carr did not carry it out. And Carr's conduct toward the defense, the court held, was more than overbalanced by his mistreatment of the prosecution. The court recognized the impatience a new judge with a long trial background might have with an inexperienced prosecutor or defense attorney. And it offered some advice for

Charlie Carr, in the wishful expectation he might listen:

> We feel confident that with increasing experience upon the bench the trial judge will decide, as others have before him, that it is the better part of wisdom to refrain from unnecessary interference with counsel in the presentation of their case. Such interference may destroy a perfectly valid strategy, it may ruin a cross-examination which would otherwise be quite effective, and above all, it may give the jury a false impression of partiality which in a particular case may be so serious as to require a retrial of the case.

But listen to Carr ten years later, berating an assistant United States attorney during the trial of a marijuana smuggling case:

> DEFENSE ATTORNEY: I object. The prosecutor is leading the witness.
> CARR: Yes, he is. He can't help it, counsel. I don't know how you can cure him, counsel. I just don't know how it is possible. . . . Ladies and gentlemen [of the jury], leading means that the suggestive question suggests the answer, and that is not permissible in a court of law. This has been in effect for the last three hundred fifty, four hundred years, and I do not think counsel has found it out yet.
> [A bit later the prosecutor attempted to put some photographs into evidence.]
> PROSECUTOR: What is depicted in the picture, Government's Exhibit Number 12?
> CARR: Counsel, the picture speaks for itself. Anybody who can read plain English can read what's in that picture. I could read it by the time I was three-and-a-half years old, and I hope you could. . . . What I cannot get over to the United States Attorney's Office is that the proper way to try a case is to offer exhibits at the time they become admissible, and if they are admissible they may be shown to the jury so that the jury, the poor

jury, may keep up with what is going on in the case.

Carr finally summarized his discontent with the prosecution: "You know, ladies and gentlemen, I am sorry you can't see a case tried as it should be tried. It can be a real art. I mean from the standpoint of prosecution, short questions, the most marvelous things in the world, the easiest things in the world to understand—who, when, how, where and what."

Carr also took sideward swipes at the defense attorney, Michael D. Nasatir, of Beverly Hills: When Nasatir said a question was intended to impeach a hostile witness, Carr chimed, "Well, I don't really believe you, but I will let you do it." When Nasatir asked that a package of marijuana that had been opened in court be replaced by an unopened package before being offered into evidence, Carr remarked, "Let it be said that you never close a day without complicating something. I am glad we are not in a hospital. I can just imagine that the doctor would be put to sleep instead of the patient." The circuit court called these and other comments "improper belittling."

Carr cheerily declares he pays no attention to such criticisms. He berates "those damned childish opinions from appellate court judges who never tried a case in their life" and "high-sounding opinions that turn criminals free to pillage and plunder innocent people." He calls them "lying bastards," and worse. At a private dinner party a few years back, according to a lawyer who was present, Carr proposed "rather seriously" that after five years' service, appellate judges (including those on the Supreme Court) should be subjected to a secret referendum ballot of district court jurists. The lawyer quotes Carr as saying, "We would vote out that old freak [William O.] Douglas on either of three grounds—lechery, senility, or stupidity." The referendum, Carr maintained, "would put some backbone into the spineless nothings on our circuit court, make them pull the rose petals out of their noses and smell life."

My last day in Los Angeles, my Expletive Deleted file swollen with Carr anecdotes, I slipped into his courtroom for one final look at the man. Carr's calendar that day was pretrial motions in civil cases, and some unfortunate lawyer had already put him into a huffing rage.

"What do you *mean,* you want more time on this little two-bit case?" Carr was demanding. "Counselor, have you told your client he is in all probability wasting his money on this matter?"

"Judge, if you would let me explain, I think . . ."

"Don't beg with me," Carr said. "You are a lawyer. You can talk to a judge without putting on that whiney voice."

"Your Honor, that is what I am trying to do. If you would just hear me out for . . ."

"When I was practicing law, a man came into the courtroom prepared, and he was *man* enough to stand on his own two feet," Carr said. "He also did his paperwork properly, and didn't insult a judge—*yes, insult a judge*—by expecting him to understand some kind of stuff like this." Carr made a face and flipped a brief some six inches into the air. The lawyer's shoulders rose as he took a deep breath, and he clenched his hands so tightly behind his back that they whitened.

"OK, young man. If you feel you are capable of trying this law suit—and I am not convinced that you are—I am setting this down for thirty days." Carr bent forward to scrawl something in his docket book, and the lawyer murmured, "Thank you, Your Honor," and left—rapidly and unhappily.

Judge Charles Carr looked at his clerk and called, "What further nonsense must we dispose of this morning?"

The Abe Fortas scandal in the spring of 1969, followed closely by a firecracker-string of other episodes that threw the federal judiciary into disrepute, finally drove the judges into serious self-examination. With the public and the congress in sour moods over the Fortas mess, Chief Justice Earl Warren convened the

Judicial Conference in June with a firm suggestion: unless the judges did some immediate policing, Draconian laws were a nigh certainty. The country, Justice Warren said, simply would not tolerate "anything that has the appearance of impropriety on the bench." Warren spoke from a high (and earned) moral position. Not since entering public life in 1925, as district attorney in San Francisco, had he accepted any income other than his official salary. Perhaps no other high official in Washington lived as frugally as did the chief justice—which is one reason that Fortas' grasping acquisitiveness, even while on the bench, disgusted him. Further, the Fortas scandal meant that the chief justice's reign over his prided "Warren Court" was to end in an atmosphere of sordidness.

Warren's resolution, which passed after considerable (but closed-door) debate, imposed the strictest financial rules ever for federal officials, elective or appointive. A judge was not to accept "compensation of any kind" for services other than his judicial duties. The only exception would be activities that the circuit judicial council found "are in the public interest or are justified by exceptional circumstances," and did not interfere with his work as a judge. The language was intended to enable judges to continue part-time teaching at law school, and to serve such quasi-official bodies as the American Law Institute. Each judge would be required to file an annual statement "of his investments and other assets held by him at any time during the year," plus a breakdown of income including the source, and a listing of liabilities. The reports could be published if determined by the Judicial Council "to be in the public interest."

The resolution recognized that although it could issue rules it did not have authority to force unwilling judges to, obey them. It directed a committee to write legislation for submission to Congress "that would ensure the conference being able to enforce the motions we have today passed."

Reaction from the nation's judges was swift, and mostly angry. Many thought the resolution to be self-flagellation. Why should the judges be bound by a rule

—and a self-imposed one, at that—that went far beyond any covering the legislative and executive branches? If the judges must put their assets and income on public record, why not the president and congressmen also? One West Coast judge wrote Warren: "Why are you demanding that we judges dance naked in the streets to appease a mob? You have gone too far—*too far!!!* Your resolution is personally insulting and professionally unacceptable, and I fervently advise you to go read your Constitution, Mr. Chief Justice. I, for one, do not intend to count my pennies, few though they may be, in public." The judges objected that the "reform" resolution did not apply to justices of the Supreme Court—the source, after all, of the furor over ethical standards. A majority of judges in the second circuit, in the northeast United States, led by Chief Judge J. Edward Lumbard, resolved they would ignore the order and asked that it be repealed. The ninth circuit on the west coast also voted against it. Judge Robert A. Ainsworth, Jr., of the Fifth Circuit Court of Appeals, one of the more respected jurists in the nation, said many of his colleagues felt it "demeaning" to have to ask permission to teach, write or lecture. He said the Judicial Conference "acted in haste and without mature consideration."

The general public, however, sided with the Judicial Conference. A Harris Poll published July 31, 1969, found that Americans felt it wrong for judges to receive outside money in addition to their salaries by a margin of 55 to 34 percent. Editorial support was strong, with some newspapers urging even tougher rules; the *Washington Post,* for example, called the rule "more of a beginning than an end."

But the judges, not the public or newspaper editors, were in a position to decide the fate of the Warren reform rules. And by the time the Judicial Conference convened for its November 1969 meeting, the Warren rules were in deep trouble. Warren Burger, who had become chief justice soon after the June resolution was approved, had private reservations about it. Burger recognized that the opponents were numerous enough, and mad enough, to make the rule unenforceable. Widespread flouting of the voluntary rule would put the judiciary in a worse public position than if no rule existed at all, Burger reasoned. Too, Burger had some ideas about reforms in judicial administration, the success depended upon their acceptance by the district and circuit judges. So Burger was willing to let the Warren resolution be scuttled as a sop to its opponents. And, finally, the American Bar Association told Burger it was somewhat upset that the Judicial Conference had acted without waiting for an ABA task force to finish revising the canons of judicial ethics.

So the Warren resolution was scrapped, by Judicial Conference members meeting in the private sanctum of the Supreme Court Building. In its place the judges adopted another resolution with markedly softer requirements. The new rules dropped the ban on compensation for outside activities, and the requirement that a judge ask permission before undertaking them. The only reporting required would be of payments of more than $100 for non-judicial services (but not of investment income). The conference abandoned the earlier requirement for reporting of assets and all income. One new positive step was creation of an "interim advisory committee on judicial activities" to give judges opinions on the propriety of off-bench activities upon request.

As justification for the turnaround the conference cited the lack of any codified standards to guide the circuit councils; the pending ABA study; and a lack of statutory authority to enforce the rules. Regardless of the validity of these reasons, the new set of rules was widely viewed as a setback for judicial reform. The *Washington Post* called the new rules a "retreat from the bold stand taken under the prodding of former Chief Justice Warren." Senator Joseph Tydings said the action reflected a "myopia characterized by an inability to perceive the threat to the institutional integrity of the judicial system." And, incredibly, the judges acted in the face of episodes that had blackened even darker the public image of the judiciary. During the summer and fall the nation heard much public testimony about supposed financial improprieties of Judge Haynsworth, but two other isolated episodes are indicative of the interest being paid to judges' extra-judicial activities:

● Chief Judge John R. Brown and Judge Warren L. Jones were on a three-man Fifth Circuit Court panel hearing the appeal of a Federal Power Commission ruling that cut rates on Louisiana natural gas. The case meant $80 million a year to gas consumers in northeastern states, and companies that extract gas fought the order. During oral arguments, Jones casually mentioned that his wife owned stock in some of the companies but gave no details. He asked lawyers whether they objected. None did. Four days later, Judges Brown and Jones had the court clerk send letters to lawyers detailing their holdings. They turned out to be far more substantial than hinted. Brown had $35,000 in stocks in Gulf Oil, Getty Oil, and Tenneco; he was also trustee for five separate trusts with oil and gas holdings. Jones put no valuation on the stock but listed holdings in Phillips Petroleum and the Texas Company, as well as in trusts. The letter asked lawyers whether they "desire to make comment one way or the other"; if none were heard within a week, "the court will assume that no one has any objection" to Brown and Jones continuing in the case. The proposed procedure put the lawyers in what some of them considered an "untenable situation." As one told *The New York Times'* Eileen Shanahan, "the burden of deciding" whether a conflict of interest existed was put on the lawyers, not faced by the judges. The lawyers, if they objected, risked offending the judges (and their colleagues) in future cases in the fifth circuit. When the anonymous criticisms were published, Brown and Jones disqualified themselves—claiming, as they did so, that there was no "legal disqualification" but not citing a reason either.

● Judge William E. Miller of Nashville was revealed to have purchased 1,000 shares of stock in Minnie Pearl's Chicken, a Tennessee-based franchise enterprise, at an insider's price of 50 cents a share, from two lawyer/politicians who practiced regularly in his court. A day after the shares went on public sale Miller sold some of them for $39 each, reaping a profit of almost 2,000 percent. The Minnie Pearl's stock was highly volatile; it soared to $57 at one point, but was down to $9 when Miller's dealings were revealed at a Senate Judiciary Subcommittee hearing on his appointment to the Sixth Circuit Court of Appeals. A Nashville attorney opposing Miller's promotion charged him with lending his name and official prestige to a stock promotion scheme. The Senate confirmed Miller anyway.

By the spring of 1970 Senator Tydings was convinced that the Judicial Conference would do nothing concrete on reform in the absence of legislation giving the force of law to its resolutions. The judges' internal "advisory committee" on specific ethical questions he suspected to be little more than public relations window dressing. In its first five opinions (the only ones ever published) the committee approved a judge teaching two weekend hours weekly in a law school for $1,750 a semester, a judge serving on the board of the Salvation Army and Red Cross in his home city, a judge teaching in a two-week seminar on "humanistic studies" without compensation, a judge serving on an arbitration board of his church, and a judge accepting fees as a testamentary trustee for his uncle's estate.* Each case was so clear-cut under accepted

---

* The internal committee paralleled work of the ABA's Committee on Ethics and Professional Responsibility. The ABA group's opinions show the scope of ethical decisions a judge must make. Should he be a guest of honor at a testimonial dinner where funds will be solicited for the sponsoring charitable organization, even if he makes no appeal for money himself? Should he accept a free ticket to a $50 per plate dinner intended to raise funds for the 1966 reelection of a United States senator, at which former Vice President Nixon was to be speaker? Should he accept a Christmas gift from lawyers who practice in his Court? The ABA's answer in each instance was no.

ethical canons that they smacked of make-work. So once again Tydings tried for a judicial reform act, and once again he was beaten down. Opposing judges (and Senate conservatives, especially Senator Sam Ervin) simply would not accept his proposals for a disability commission, and for financial disclosure. A resolution presented to the Ninth Circuit Judicial Council (written by the redoubtable A. Andrew Hauk of Los Angeles was especially vehement about the reporting requirements. Listing assets, Hauk said, could possibly result "in such valuations being used against [judges] in income, estate and inheritance tax inquiries, audits and assessments." Further, unauthorized disclosure of the statements could subject judges "to needless harassment, public ridicule and invasion of privacy."

Unwilling to act on its own, and lacking congressional guidance (other than the negative mandate to do nothing) the Judicial Conference settled back to await the conclusion of the ABA judicial ethics study, which finally came in August 1972. The following April the Judicial Conference adopted a somewhat tighter version of the code—yet one that still did not possess the force of law, nor apply to Supreme Court justices. The salient features:

- A semi-annual report of gifts of more than $100 and any income from outside work. The old Warren rule about disclosure of assets, indebtedness and income from investment or stock earnings was ignored. The reports are filed with a review committee of the Judicial Conference, the judicial council of the circuit where the judges served, and with the clerk of his own court. Only the latter is for public inspection. There is no central location where an interested citizen can view reports from all the nation's federal judges; he must visit the clerks of each of the 92 district courts.
- Automatic disqualification when a judge had a financial interest, however small, in a case. If both parties insisted, however, the judge could still sit.

But any discussion on whether disqualification should be waived would be outside his presence.*

- In borderline areas of disqualification (where remote relatives or friends are parties) "regard for the appearance of propriety" should induce judges to withdraw from a case. Under earlier practice many judges maintained they had a "duty" to sit unless clearly disqualified for statutory reasons.

- A prohibition on judges serving as an executor or trustee except for the estate of a member of their families. The ABA code contained a "grandfather clause" permitting judges already serving as executors to continue; only future judges would be barred. The Judicial Conference went a step further: its rule gave current executors one year to wind up their business; thereafter they could not serve, except in instances of "special hardship," and then without compensation.

So how has the code worked? Given the limitations of the public reports, the finances of a federal judge remain essentially a private affair. Real estate and dividend income are not reported, which means that two prime sources of extra-judicial income are a secret. The only instance in which stock holdings are revealed publicly is when a judge withdraws from a case because of a conflict of interest. Random samplings of the report forms show that such withdrawals are rare; of the 20 judges in the Eastern District of Pennsylvania who filed reports in a reporting period, for example, only one showed a voluntary disqualification. Judge C. William Kraft withdrew from a case involving General Motors because he owned $6,650 of GM stock, even though lawyers asked him to continue. Reports in other cities are generally equally sparse. Judge Miles Lord of Minneapolis found a logical solution to a conflict of interest in a 1973 case.

---

* Federal law at the time permitted a judge to sit unless his interest was "substantial," a word subject to broad interpretation. In late 1973 Congress changed the law to conform with the ABA code: a judge is now required to bow out of a case if he owns only one share of stock in one of the parties.

He was presiding at a hearing on a suit against Northern States Power Company when he recollected that his wife owned stocks in the company. Because time was important to the parties, they did not wish for him to reassign the case. So Lord càlled a brief recess, telephoned his broker, and directed him to sell the stock at the going price. "I hope my wife will forgive me," Lord told the attorneys, and the case went on.

Reports of outside earnings are similarly slim: a thousand bucks or so for teaching a Saturday morning law course; an occasional honorarium for speaking to a legal institute. Judge George H. Barlow of Newark, New Jersey, once listed a gift of a $375 set of golf clubs from the Mercer County Bar Association. Judge Robert Shaw of Camden, New Jersey, dutifully reported complimentary subscriptions to the *Congressional Record*, the Federal Reporter Service, and the Internal Revenue Code.

As stated previously, the Judicial Conference reporting rule does not carry the force of law. The only "enforcement" is peer pressure, supposedly achieved through publication of the names of non-reporters in the biennial proceedings of the Judicial Conference. The holdouts usually number less than twenty, and the proceedings dutifully mark with an asterisk those who refuse to file as a matter of principle.*

By all indications Chief Justice Burger, a majority of Judicial Conference members, and those Congressmen who are interested in judicial reform are satisfied with the current code. Tydings' old subcommittee has passed on to Senator Quentin Burdick, a pleasant but nonaggressive Democrat from North Dakota, who has displayed no enthusiasm for exploring how well

---

* The September 1973 report listed these non-filers: second circuit, Edmund L. Palmieri, Sylvester J. Ryan, Edward Weinfeld and Inzer B. Wyatt; fifth circuit, Gerald B. Tjoflat; sixth circuit, Don J. Young and Frank J. Battisti; ninth circuit, Roger T. Foley, Robert F. Peckham, William M. Byrne, Walter E. Craig, Warren J. Ferguson, Peirson M. Hall, William D. Murray, Harry Pregerson and Manuel L. Real; and tenth circuit, Stephen S. Chandler. Everyone on the list is "of principle" except Ryan, Tjoflat, Foley, Peckham and Chandler.

the code works in practice. The judiciary committees of both houses never even bother to gather the judges' financial reports. "Judicial reform is a dead issue in Congress," said a staff member of the Senate Judiciary Committee. "Unless, of course, we have another Fortas thing blow up on us." The lack of mandatory reporting bothers a handful of people who work around the judiciary. Because these persons answer to the judges and understandably do not wish to rile their feelings, they speak from anonymity. But as one man states: "The reporting form is essentially worthless. It doesn't get to the core of a judge's income. Further, if a judge has taken money that is forbidden under the code, he certainly isn't going to turn himself in by reporting it to the Judicial Conference." What would this person require? "A full net worth statement, with specific assets and liabilities, and a certified copy of the income tax return for each year. But that's not going to happen."

The man thought a moment. "The only benefit of the Fortas thing, if you could call it a benefit, is that it scared the hell out of a lot of judges. So financial conflicts of interest aren't going to be a problem, say, for the rest of this decade. Further reform right now is a dead issue, no one cares about it any more."

Epilogue

Thus some of the personalities and the peculiarities of the federal judiciary, for better or for worse. One overriding fact about the system is that it works—usually. Fortunately for the American citizenry, each Stephen Chandler and James Parsons is offset, by a factor of ten, by a David Edelstein or a Peirson Hall. Nonetheless, the question must be asked: What could be done to make the federal judiciary an even better mechanism for delivering justice to Americans?

Justice is not a concept that can always be equated with efficiency. The judicial bureaucrats do much fussing over court calendars and juror utilization and wider use of magistrates and bankruptcy judges. Yet this tinkering does not get to the heart of an even more important question: Given the judges' method of selection, their guaranteed tenure in office, and their freedom of personal and professional action, do we wish to permit the judges to continue their exalted position in our society? Or again, should we increase even further their existing authority?

Candidly, I began *The Benchwarmers* with misgivings about the federal judges, for my instinctive reaction to unbridled power is mistrust. I am wary of government, corporations, the big-rich, foundations, labor federations, and any other institution or individual that purports to know what is best for me and attempts to shove me in that direction, regardless of my own feelings. And in the last 18 months I was subjected to enough rudeness and disdain by judges, court bailiffs and law clerks to reinforce my opinion that so

397

much of the judiciary is run by outright bastards. At midpoint my attitude was that the entire arrogant crowd should be tugged down from the clouds and be forced to pay more attention to the rest of us.

Perhaps they should. But after witnessing numerous instances where the system worked—where a semblance of justice was achieved, either through talent or blind, dumb luck—I began taking a more charitable view of the judges. And I eventually came to agree with something Senator Sam J. Ervin (D., N.C.) said during the spring of 1970, when Congress was hearing ideas on improving the "discipline" of federal judges. Ervin remarked that "one of the most overriding purposes" of the constitution was to establish an independent judiciary. The goal, Ervin said, was to "guarantee that no outside influence can invade a judge's chambers or determine how he decides a case." Ervin is old enough, and wise enough, to reason that the federal judiciary has its quota of boobs and incompetents. Nonetheless, he is willing to take his chances with the Constitution: "If we are going to have freedom, we are going to have to let people act foolishly as well as wisely; otherwise, we are not going to have any freedom." Ervin felt it "better at times to put up with a little senility and things like that as the price of maintaining the independence of the judiciary."

Independence. In the context of colonial America, judicial independence equated with nonaccountability to the sovereign. In a modern sense, independence means that a judge is expected to act without regard to the fortune of the president or the political figure responsible for his appointment. An example: before the trial of former Nixon cabinet officers John Mitchell and Maurice Stans in the Vesco case, several judges in the Southern District of New York suggested that the case be heard by someone other than Judge Lee Gagliardi, who had gone on the bench while Mitchell was attorney general, and who had been assigned the trial under the court's routine selection system. Because Mitchell had given tacit approval to Gagliardi's appointment, these judges felt the public might infer he was biased. They did not prevail. A solid majority of the judges said that if Gagliardi were to step aside, the judiciary would be admitting that politics and personalities, not the law, determined what happened in a federal court.

Independence was even more acutely illustrated in a 1970 decision by Judge Damon Keith, a black Democrat appointed in 1967 under sponsorship of Senator Philip Hart (D., Mich). Keith was assigned to hear the case of Lawrence Robert Plamadon and two other white radical activists accused of bombing the Ann Arbor office of the Central Intelligence Agency. In answer to a pretrial motion the Justice Department admitted that Plamadon had been overheard "by government agents who were monitoring wiretaps which were being employed to gather intelligence information deemed necessary to protect the nation from attempts of domestic organizations to attack and subvert the existing government of the United States." The Justice Department did not name the "domestic organizations" subject to the wiretaps; at the time of the CIA bombing, however, Plamadon had been a leader of the White Panthers organization. The government admitted the taps had not been authorized by a court. When Plamadon's lawyers demanded that the logs be produced for inspection, the Justice Department, through Attorney General Mitchell, replied that the President had ordered the wiretaps as an exercise of "the historical power of the sovereign to preserve itself." Mitchell maintained that in national security cases the President could order taps without a court order, and that the fruits did not have to be disclosed to anyone—not even the defendants in a case arising from the eavesdropping.

Keith, in a ruling in January 1971, said Mitchell's argument was so much nonsense. Quite simply, he wrote, the law requires that a judge authorize wiretaps: "It is the procedure of obtaining a warrant that inserts the impartial judgement of the court between the citizen and the government." He ordered the Justice Department to hand over logs and transcripts, and added, "An idea which seems to permeate much of the government's argument is th.. a dissident domestic organization is akin to an unfriendly foreign power and must be dealt with in the same fashion."

When the government appealed to the Sixth Circuit Court of Appeals, it suffered an even more stinging rebuke. The court tartly quoted the administration's description of itself as a "sovereign," and noted, "We find in the government's brief no suggestion of limitation on such power, nor, indeed, any recognition that the sovereign power of this nation is by constitution distributed among three coordinate branches of government." The court continued:

It is the historic role of the judiciary to see that in periods of crisis, when the challenge to constitutional freedom is greatest, the constitution of the United States remains the supreme law of the land. . . . Strange, indeed . . . that the traditional power of sovereigns like King George III should be invoked on behalf of an American President to defeat one of the fundamental freedoms for which the founders of this country overthrew King George's reign. [The government's argument for unrestricted wiretapping] in an argument *in terrorem*.

When the Supreme Court upheld both Keith and the circuit court the Justice Department dismissed all charges against Plamadon rather than disclose the contents of the wiretaps.

Keith's action is recounted at length because it is a prime example of an independent federal judge interposing his authority between an executive action and the general citizenry. As the public now knows through the various Watergate-related disclosures, the Nixon Administration had grandiose schemes for surveillance of domestic "enemies," political and otherwise; warrantless wiretapping of the sort used against Plamadon was a key weapon. But Judge Damon Keith, a jurist not answerable to a presidency which likened itself to a "sovereign," had the courage to say "no," thereby halting an illegal activity. In the words of Chesterfield Smith, the outspoken Florida lawyer who served as ABA president in 1973–74, "Every American knows that the courts are our first line of defense against governmental tyranny and arbitrary power."

The strength of the judiciary is rooted in just such independence as that displayed by Keith. Once a judge begins responding to the shouts of a mob— or to the nudges of the White House, or any politician —he is unfit to hold office. Lifetime tenure supplies the extra psychological courage some judges need when they make unpopular decisions. Several Senate conservatives, notably Harry S. Byrd, Jr. (D., Va.), feel federal judges should be subject to reconfirmation after eight or ten years service.* I share Byrd's sentiment that this Republic would be a better place to live if in fact a number of judges *were* clubbed from the bench—but for entirely different reasons. As stated previously, a few rogues and scoundrels are the price one must pay for an independent judiciary; Byrd and his ilk should be prepared to tolerate the southern judges who take a civilized attitude towards civil rights, for the Kennedy and Nixon Administration more than balanced the scales with appointees who were totally unenthusiastic about the lot of blacks. To command that a judge should be "answerable" to the public as is a congressman or a justice of the peace runs contrary to reality.

Nevertheless I do offer a parallel idea: that the federal judges cease posturing as demigods, and accept the notion that the public deserves to know more about them as humans. Judicial pomp might put a protective shield around judicial authority; at the same time it makes many egalitarian Americans distinctly

---

* Although Byrd introduced a constitutional amendment to this effect, and littered the *Congressional Record* with supporting resolutions from the Virginia General Assembly, whether he should be taken seriously is doubtful. Many of his constituents wanted the hide of Judge Robert Merhige, of Richmond, because of a controversial school busing order, and Byrd's windy attacks on lifetime tenure harmlessly vented much of the conservative anger. At any rate, Byrd's amendment has absolutely no chance of passage.

uneasy. Perhaps the mystique of the judiciary *does* give it a reverence essential to public acceptance. Perhaps Americans, as a nation of "constitution worshippers," in the delightfully sarcastic phrase of Washington law professor Arthur S. Miller, should regard the law as a "sacred covenant," with the judiciary as its guardian and keeper. Perhaps. But as a citizen (and a journalist), I find the notion preposterous. Institutions thrive, and survive, only when they are trusted by the general public, and understood. The time has come for the judges to realize that, while they occupy the judiciary, they do not own it.

Appendix

Criteria used by the American Bar Association's Standing Committee on the Federal Judiciary for evaluating judicial nominees.

The following are the ratings used by the Committee in its reports:

1. "Exceptionally Well Qualified"—To be so rated, an individual must stand at the top of his profession; he must rank among the very best qualified judges or lawyers available for judicial service. He must have not only outstanding legal ability and background, and wide experience in the Federal court system, but also other exceptional qualities. The Committee employs the classification of "Exceptionally Well Qualified" very sparingly. In short, the prospective nominee should be a person whose preeminence in the law and as a citizen is widely acknowledged and whose qualifications for the position are virtually unanimously hailed by judges and lawyers.

2. "Well Qualified"—This rating is also regarded by the Committee as a very high one. It indicates the Committee's strong affirmative endorsement of a prospective nominee and that the Committee believes the prospective nominee to be one of the best available.

3. "Qualified"—This rating indicates that the investigation has not disclosed significant adverse reports and that, on the basis of experience and ability, the prospective nominee should be able to

satisfactorily perform the duties of a Federal Judge.

4. "Not Qualified"—A person so classified has been found unsatisfactory as to either professional ability, experience, temperament or integrity.

5. "Not Qualified by Reason of Age"—This classification applies to persons over the age of 60 who, but for their age, might otherwise have been found qualified.

With respect to the age of prospective candidates (other than those already serving as Federal judges), the Committee believes that an individual 60 years of age or over should not receive an initial appointment to a lifetime judgeship in a Federal court unless he merits a rating of "Well Qualified" or "Exceptionally Well Qualified" and is in excellent health and, in no event should he be eligible for such appointment after he has reached his 64th birthday.

In the case of a Federal Judge being considered for appointment to the United States Court of Appeals, the Committee believes that a judge 60 years of age or over should not receive such an appointment, unless he merits the rating of "Well Qualified" and is in excellent health. It is the view of the Committee that ordinarily it is preferable not to appoint to the Court of Appeals judges who are already eligible for retirement or who will be eligible for retirement within two years because such an appointment, or the hope of such an appointment, is likely to defer the transfer of older judges to senior judge status.

A Federal District judge who has reached his 68th birthday should not receive an appointment to the United States Court of Appeals under any circumstances.

The point at which the age of the candidate is determined for the purpose of applying the foregoing rules is the date of the letter from the Deputy Attorney General to the Chairman of the Committee requesting an Informal Report on that candidate.

The Committee believes that ordinarily a prospective appointee to the Federal bench should have been admitted to the Bar for at least 15 years and that he should have had a substantial amount of trial experience.

The Committee believes that trial experience is important in the case of appointees for the United States Court of Appeals as well as appointees to the District Court. In exceptional cases candidates for the Court of Appeals might be approved without trial experience. However, we cannot conceive approving a candidate for the District Court who has not had adequate trial experience.

With respect to the question raised as to political activity on the part of a prospective candidate, the Committee is of the view that such activity is a point in his favor. The Committee, however, does not regard political activity as a substitute for experience in the practice of law and the other necessary qualifications.

CHAPTER NOTES
AND ACKNOWLEDGMENTS

Chapter Notes and Acknowledgments

The vast majority of the lawyers interviewed for *The Benchwarmers*—and many of the judges as well—spoke to me only after I swore with my hand raised on high that I would never reveal their names. Hence any listing of persons who were "helpful" would either be misleadingly abbreviated or foolishly revelatory, so none is offered. But *The Benchwarmers* was possible only because more than one hundred lawyers and judges and other court buffs set aside time for interviews with me over an 18-month period, and supplied me with case citations, briefs and other documentary matter. In so doing they benefitted not only a journalist but, hopefully, the federal courts as well. My thanks also to four charming ladies: Jody Goulden, researcher, editor and wife; Irene King, typist; Catherine Wilson, copy editor; and Laurie Rockett. Finally, my appreciation to M. J. Rossant, who suggested through publisher Truman M. Talley that the federal trial judiciary warranted journalistic scrutiny, and who was right.

Prologue

Page 4. " '. . . custodians of a special body of knowledge, . . .' " Rifkind to the subcommittee on separation of powers of the Senate Judiciary Committee, hearings, "Nonjudicial Activities of Supreme Court Justices and Other Federal Judges," July and September 1969.

Page 5. " '. . . further above mere local influence. . . .' " *Congressional Globe*, 42d Congress, 1st Session 460 (1871); quoted in "Judicial Expansion of Federal Jurisdiction," by

Ruggero J. Aldisert, *Arizona State University Law Journal*, No. 3 (1973).

Page 9. "'Judges should be clothed in robes. . . .'" Quoted in *William Howard Taft, Chief Justice,* by Alpheus Thomas Mason, Simon & Schuster, New York, 1965.

Page 11. ". . .'the most remarkable and original. . . .'" The Fiske quotations are from his *The Critical Period of American History,* Houghton Mifflin Company, Boston, 1897.

Page 12. ". . . 'are incapable of doing a first-rate job. . . .'" From *Federal Judges: The Appointing Process,* by Harold W. Chase, University of Minnesota Press, Minneapolis, 1973.

Page 13. "'A great many practicing lawyers. . . .'" Voorhees to the subcommittee on improvements in judicial machinery of the Senate Judiciary Committee, hearings, "Judicial Reform Act," November 1969 and April 1970.

Page 17. "'You pick your lawyer. . . .'" Weinman to the House Appropriations Committee hearings, "Departments of State, Justice, and Commerce, the Judiciary and Related Agencies, Appropriations for 1974," March 1973.

Page 22. "'. . . was universally understood. . . .'" Lewis, "A Court That Rules on Its Own Motions Has a Fool for a Judge," *Chicago Journalism Review* (April 1972).

CHAPTER ONE

Getting There: The Politics of Judicial Selection

General background on the ABA's role in judicial selection is contained in the annual reports of its committee on the federal judiciary. The major shortcoming of these reports is their avoidance of controversy: even if the ABA is in a bloody confrontation with an administration, seldom does more than a hint of the argument sneak into the reports. A valuable study of the politics of the judiciary is *Federal Judges: The Appointing Process,* by Harold W. Chase, University of Minnesota Press, Minneapolis, 1973. A solid book on the ABA's role is *Lawyers and Judges,* by Joel Grossman, Wiley, New York, 1965.

Page 28. "'. . . routinely promote United States attorneys to the federal bench. . . .'" "Justice Without Politics," by Arthur S. Miller, *The Progressive,* April 1974.

Page 32. ". . . the, scent of a political quid pro quo. . . ." The Sharples letters were put into the record of Van Dusen's confirmation hearing before the Senate Judiciary Committee in 1954.

Page 34. "'. . . drunk half the time. . . .'" Truman tells of the Clark appointment in *Plain Speaking,* by Merle Miller, Berkley/Putnam, New York, 1974.

Pages 35–36. Judge Perry's speech to the Chicago Bar Association on November 20, 1951, is quoted in *Courts, Politics, and Judges,* edited by Walter F. Murphy and C. Herman Pritchett, Random House, New York, 1961.

Page 37. The Devitt talk is quoted in *Proceedings of the Seminars for Newly Appointed United States District Judges,* published by the Judicial Conference of the United States, undated.

Page 38. "'. . . existing practices diminish. . . .'" Richardson at New York University law school, quoted in the *Miami Herald,* November 18, 1973.

Page 39. "'Appointments by Mr. Truman . . . include. . . .'" 45 *American Bar Association Journal* 446, 1959.

Page 39. "'We Deem Him Qualified.'" Quoted in *The Role of the Bar in Electing the Bench in Chicago,* by Edward M. Martin, University of Chicago Press, Chicago, 1936.

Page 44, footnote. "'Fuck the ABA.'" "The ABA and the Supreme Court," talk by John P. MacKenzie at the Nader-sponsored ABA counterconvention, at George Washington University, Washington, August 1973 (mimeographed).

Pages 46–47. Biographical data on the ABA committee members is from the 1973 edition of *Martindale-Hubbell,* the legal directory.

Page 58. ". . .'disquietening allegations. . . .'" The two Chase anecdotes are from his *Federal Judges: The Appointing Process.*

Page 60. The Grossman book is *Lawyers and Judges.* The succeeding historical paragraphs draw heavily from Grossman.

Page 64. The Segal anecdote is in hearings, "Judicial Reform Act," subcommittee on improvements in judicial machinery of the Senate Judiciary Committee, November 1969 and April 1970.

Page 67. "'When you deal with the ABA. . . .'" From *To the Victor,* by Martin and Susan Tolchin, Random House, New York, 1971.

Page 80. "'If judges don't have the intestinal fortitude. . . .'" Conti to the *San Francisco Examiner,* April 14, 1971.

CHAPTER TWO

When the System Works I: Watching Wall Street

The basic source on the main IBM case is the official court file —69 Civ 200—in the Southern District of New York. Background on the IBM suits in Minnesota, Oklahoma, and Arizona came from daily press coverage, chiefly by the *Wall Street Journal* and from hearings, "Industrial Reorganization Act," Part 1, before the antitrust and monopoly, subcommittee of the Senate Judiciary Committee, March and May 1973. An invaluable compendium of business and trade press coverage of the IBM actions is "The United States vs. International Business Machines: The First Nine Months," published by the Computer Industry Association, 16255 Ventura Boulevard, Encino, California 91316.

Page 88. ". . .'the largest and most complex. . . .'" *Business Week*, November 11, 1972.

Page 94 ff. Neville's consolidation activities are recounted in his testimony in hearings, "Industrial Reorganization Act."

Page 101, ". . . 'a note of impatience. . . .'" *Electronic News*, February 26, 1973.

Page 102, footnote. "Although, oddly, the Cravath firm. . . ." *The New York Times* and the *Wall Street Journal* stories were on March 7, 1973.

Page 108. "Edelstein's colleagues in the Southern District. . . ." Biographical data on the other New York judges is from the files of the *New York Law Journal*, the official court publication for the New York courts and legal community.

Page 111. ". . .'quite descriptive of high judicial conscientiousness. . . .'" Quoted in the *New York Law Journal* March 6, 1973.

Page 115 ff. the Dioguardi case is discussed in *U.S. v. Dioguardi and Ostrer*, 361 Fed Supp 954.

CHAPTER THREE

When the System Flops I: The Shame of Chicago

Pages 131–133. The Chicago Council of Lawyers study is formally titled "Results of a Survey of Lawyers Concerning the Performance of Judicial Officers in the Federal District Court," 1972 (mimeographed).

Page 136. ". . .'should have been quickily terminated. . . .'" *Chicago Sun-Times*, April 28, 1973.

Page 138. Warren's dissent and Campbell's attack on the chief justice are in the *Chicago Tribune*, January 15, 1963.

Page 138. "Quick as he was to criticize. . . ." The *Chicago Tribune*, November 13, 1965.

Page 139. "Christmas Spirits." The *Chicago Tribune*, December 21, 1969.

Page 139. ". . .'rebellion against authority. . . .'" The *Chicago Tribune*, April 23, 1969.

Page 139. ". . .'often reaches a point. . . .'" The *Chicago Tribune*, April 27, 1967.

Page 140. ". . .'manage to enhance himself. . . .'" *The Great Conspiracy Trial*, by Jason Epstein, Random House, New York, 1970.

Pages 141–143. A good summary of Campbell's real estate dealings was done by Max Sonderby of the *Chicago Sun-Times*, September 5, 1972.

Page 148. ". . .'the only significant politics. . . .'" Much biographical data on Marovitz is contained in a somewhat peculiar five-part profile by Wayne Thomis in the *Chicago Tribune* beginning May 21, 1967. The articles are pantingly effusive and portray Marovitz as a latter-day Horatio Alger. Just why the Republican *Tribune* chose to honor a creature of the Democratic machine is a question the Chicago journalism community could not answer.

Page 161. ". . . a lissome 49-year-old divorcee. . . ." The *Chicago Tribune*, February 8, 1972.

Page 162. "Attention to ethnic background. . . ." The *Chicago Tribune*, August 31, 1960.

Page 163. "'I expected the voice. . . .'" *Chicago Magazine*, charter issue, 1964 (no month specified).

Page 163. ". . . any black who joined was 'enslaved'. . . ." The *Chicago Tribune*, January 20, 1963; Malcolm X's retort, The *Chicago Tribune*, January, 21, 1963.

Page 163. "'I am not in agreement. . . .'" The *Chicago Tribune*, January 25, 1966.

Page 164. "'Let them desert. . . .'" The *Chicago Tribune*, 1967.

Page 164. ". . .'relentless and effective prosecution.' . . ." The *Chicago Tribune*, October 20, 1965.

Page 164. "Parsons interrupted the trial. . . ." The *Chicago Tribune*, September 9, 1965.

Page 165. ". . . threatened to call out military forces. . . ." The *Chicago Tribune*, October 29, 1971.

Page 165. ". . . a bearded man pleaded guilty. . . ." The *Chicago Tribune*, November 21, 1962.

Page 166. "'not the easiest of jobs. . . .'" *Chicago Today*, May 3, 1969.

Page 167. "'You're facing five judges, . . .'" The dispute over the chief judgeship was covered by all four major Chicago dailies in the last ten days of January 1972.

Pages 168–169. Austin's relations with Daley and his courtroom demeanor are discussed in The *Chicago Tribune*, October 10, 1971.

Page 171. ". . .'one of the cleverest of the parliamentary tactics. . . .'" The *Chicago Tribune*, March 29, 1953.

Pages 172–177. Background on the Kerner case is from coverage by Chicago dailies in January and February 1973.

CHAPTER FOUR

When the System Works II: The Watergate Judge

Quotations from the various Watergate proceedings in this chapter are from trial transcripts on file in United States District Court and the United States Court of Appeals for the

District of Columbia Circuit. When I called an end to my own work the number of pages was beyond 10,000, with much much more to come. For a journalist living in Washington during the Watergate months much information about the case was absorbed as if by osmosis; hence, I have sought to keep chapter notes to a minimum. One document, however, deserves special mention. The analysis of Prosecutor Earl Silbert's trial conduct draws heavily upon "A Report to the Special Prosecutor on Certain Aspects of the Watergate Affair," prepared by Charles Morgan, Jr., director of the Washington National Office of the American Civil Liberties Union, and submitted on behalf of the ACLU and Association of State Democratic Chairmen. Silbert's reply was issued through the Senate Judiciary Committee—although without its imprimatur —during hearings on his nomination as United States attorney for the District of Columbia.

Secondary sources on Judge Sirica's life include a *Time* Magazine cover piece, January 7, 1974, and a profile, "A Man for This Season," by Howard Muson, *The New York Times Magazine*, November 4, 1973.

Page 180. "'We have absolutely no evidence. . . .'" The *Baltimore Sun*, September 16, 1972.

Page 180. ". . . the *'recently completed* federal investigation. . . .'" *The New York Times*, October 6, 1972.

Page 186. ". . .'a symbol of the American judiciary's insistence. . . .'" *Time*, November 4, 1973.

Page 187. ". . . a judge of 'singular cruelty.'" Buckley in the *Washington Star-News* November 27, 1973.

Page 187. "'It seems ironic. . . .'" Rauh in the *Washington Post*, June 2, 1973.

Page 191. "'It's like a man who sits on the bench. . . .'" *Washington Post*, September 9, 1973.

Pages 192–193. The Winchell-Patterson dispute is told in *Cissy*, by Paul Healy, Doubleday, New York, 1966.

Page 195. The Katz quotations are from his "Some Call It Justice," *Washingtonian*, September 1973.

Page 196. "'Don't you think these companies. . . .'" *The Corrupted Land*, by Fred J. Cook, Macmillan, New York, 1966.

Page 200, footnote. ". . .'to blow the White House out of the water. . . .'" McCord memo given to federal prosecutors May 7, 1973.

Page 212. "'A clubby atmosphere has prevailed. . . .'" *Los Angeles Times*, January 28, 1973.

Page 222. ". . .'a constitutional apocalypse. . . .'" "The Story Continued," by J. Anthony Lukas, *The New York Times Magazine*, January 13, 1974.

Page 224. " . . .'has saved his skin. . . .' " Reston in *The New York Times,* October 24, 1973.

Pages 228–229. Ehrlichman's account of his meetings with Judge Byrne are in "Presidential Campaign Activities of 1972," hearings before the Select Committee on Presidential Campaign Activities [the Watergate Committee], Book 6, page 2617, *supra.*

Page 231, footnote. " 'I wish you wouldn't ask. . . .' " The *Washington Post,* August 12, 1972.

Page 231. " 'I think there is . . . a suggestion. . . ' " The *Washington Star-News,* August 24, 1972.

Page 232. The Dean testimony about the approaches to Judge Richey is in the Watergate hearings, Book 3, page 958 *supra.*

CHAPTER FIVE

When the System Flops II: The Tiger Who Drinks Wild Turkey

"The Chandler Case," the umbrella term for the multiple woes of the Oklahoma jurist, consists of so many component pieces of litigation that a simple listing would require several pages. Hence, these notes will be as concise as is practical. Any scholar interested in tracking the O'Bryan matter through the courts is advised to start with a 1971 opinion of the Tenth Circuit Court of Appeals (*Chandler v. O'Bryan,* 445 F2d 1045), which lays out the disputed facts of O'Bryan's disbarment and prosecution and Chandler's claimed abuse of judicial power in straightforward fashion. For bibliographical purposes, this opinion is valuable in that it contains case citations for earlier phases of the dispute. Post-1971 developments are to be found in various briefs filed with the tenth circuit court in Case No. 73-1466, the major case still pending as of this writing.

The major cases and briefs in Chandler's dispute with the Tenth Circuit Judicial Council are contained in hearings, "The Independence of Federal Judges," subcommittee on separation of powers of the Senate Judiciary Committee, April and May 1970. For scholars who would prefer to trace the dispute through case reports, a good starting point is the United States Supreme Court file in Misc. Order No. 1111, 382 U.S. 1003.

Page 235. ". . .'a long existing criminal conspiracy. . . .' " Chandler to a meeting of the Tenth Circuit Judicial Council, April 25, 1962. (A transcript of the statement is in United States Supreme Court files in the case of *Chandler v. Judicial Council,* No. 563, October term 1962.) (Hereafter, Chandler Statement.)

Page 236. " 'I finally got to the point. . . .' " *Ibid.*

Page 237. ". . . 'questionable' and 'inconsistent.' . . ." "Report of Investigation of Judicial Behavior in the Tenth Circuit United States Court of Appeals," House Judiciary Committee, April 30, 1968. This report, marked confidential, has never been released by the committee. (Hereafter, House Report.)

Page 238. " 'Even among the judiciary,' . . ." Pence letter to Chandler, June 22, 1973.

Page 239. "Political and personal hatreds. . . ." House Report. Much of the historical background of Chandler's varied feuds is drawn from this report.

Page 240. ". . .'more than anyone else,' . . ." *Oklahoma City Times,* September 27, 1941.

Page 241. ". . . serious charges were developed. . . ." House Report.

Page 241. "Mr. Bohanon came over. . . .' " Chandler Statement.

Page 243. "To a Senate subcommittee in 1970, . . ." Chandler to the subcommittee on separation of powers, Senate Judiciary Committee, "The Independence of Federal Judges," hearings, April and May 1970.

Page 248. "Chandler dealt with FNBTCO in two capacities." House Report. The subsequent discussion of Chandler's finances is drawn from the same source.

Pages 254–261. The material on the Occidental Petroleum Case is drawn from various pleadings and affidavits in the United States Supreme Court file on *Chandler v. Occidental,* 303 F2d 55; cert. den. 372 U.S. 915; rehearing den., 373 U.S. 906.

Page 255. "Luther Bohanon, meanwhile, had some good fortune." House Report.

Page 261. ". . . in the privacy of a circuit court conference room, . . ." Chandler Statement.

Page 266. ". . .'in excess of $2 million. . . .' " *Oklahoma Journal,* July 14, 1967.

Page 268. "CHANDLER CHARGED WITH FRAUD." Both Oklahoma City daily newspapers devoted copious space to the Chandler prosecution from August through November, 1965. The criminal case was No. 31299, *State of Oklahoma v. Chandler and Kessler,* Oklahoma District Court for the Seventh Judicial District, 1965.

Page 269. ". . .'special treatment accorded . . . Chandler. . . .' " *Oklahoma Journal,* November 11, 1965.

Page 271. " 'It is my sincere conviction. . . .' " The Bohanon letter is in House Report.

Page 271. " 'their corrupt designs. . . .' " *Ibid.*

Page 281. ". . . reprints of two Battisti speeches. . . ." "The Independence of the Federal Judiciary," *Boston College Industrial and Commercial Law Review,* February 1972; and

"The Independence of the Federal Judiciary: An Argument Against the American Bar Association Section of the United States Courts," dedication of the Roscoe Pound Library at the Harvard law school, 1973 (mimeographed).

CHAPTER SIX

The D.C. Court of Appeals:
The Mini Supreme Court

Page 286. "A Washington psychiatrist named Henry Stack Sullivan, . . ." "Radical in Judicial .Robes," by Julius Duscha, *Washingtonian,* September 1973.

Page 286. The Durham case is reported as *94 US App DC 228* (1954).

Page 287. The Mallory case is reported as *354 US 449.*

Page 289. " 'The court of appeals has said the Secret Service. . . .' " *Washington Post,* November 9, 1971.

Page 290. " 'This is the most outrageous thing. . . .' " *Washington Post,* October 16, 1971.

Page 290. ". . .'believes the bridge should not be built. . . .' " *Washington Post,* November 9, 1971.

Page 292. " 'I told the story of the old boatrigger. . . .' " Acheson to the subcommittee on separation of powers of the Senate Judiciary Committee, hearings, "Nonjudicial Activities of Supreme Court Justices and Other Federal Judges," July and September 1969.

Pages 292–296. A good account of Fahey's career is in "Charles Fahey and the Criminal Law," by A. Kenneth Pye, *Georgetown Law Journal,* Summer 1966.

Page 293. "Critics charged the office. . . ." *How to Get Rich in Washington,* by Blair Bolles, W. W. Norton & Company, New York, 1952.

Page 298. " 'I had hoped that. . . .' " From "Radical in Judicial Robes," by Julius Duscha, *Washingtonian,* September 1973.

Page 299. "By requiring a psychiatric witness to describe. . . ." *U.S. v. Leazer,* 460 F2d 864 (1974).

Pages 300–301. The Gesell exchanges are in *U.S. v. McNeil,* 434 F2d 502 (1970).

Page 303. The Nixon quotes are from "Nixon on the Issues," published by the Nixon–Agnew Campaign Committee in 1968.

Page 304. The controversy over MacKinnon's appointment is outlined in *The New York Times,* July 31, 1969.

Page 304. "MacKinnon promptly picked up. . . ." *U.S. v. Walker,* circa September 1971 citation.

Page 305. " 'The feeling is that Robb cannot now be nominated. . . .' " The *Washington Post,* July 4, 1958.

Page 306. The Allen charge was disallowed in *U.S. v. Thomas,* 449 F2d 1177.

Pages 306–307. " 'We do not believe that convictions for drunkenness. . . .' " *U.S. v. Wooden,* 420 F2d 251.

Page 312. The *Washington Star* editorial attacking Wright was October 9, 1966.

Page 312. " '. . . a law may be consistently and evenly applied, . . .' " "Courts Have Failed the Poor," by Judge Skelly Wright, *The New York Times Magazine,* March 9, 1969. Wright describes the two succeeding cases in the same article.

Page 314. The Burger quotations are from his annual report for 1974 entitled, "The Federal Courts: The Year in Review," January 1974, issued by the Administrative Office of the United States Courts.

Page 317. The *Washington Times-Herald* editorial denouncing Youngdahl was July 7, 1951.

Page 317, footnote. " 'I can do 50 situps. . . .' " *Washington Evening Star,* May 29, 1966.

Page 318. "A man charged with robbery. . . ." *U.S. v. Thomas,* 450 F2d 1355.

Page 318. "A man was charged with carnal knowledge. . . ." *U.S. vs. Ashe,* 427 F2d 626.

Page 318. "A robbery victim told. . . ." *U.S. v. Vereen,* 429 F2d 713.

Page 319. " 'We find that the instructions. . . .' " *U.S. v. Wharton,* 433 F2d 451.

Page 319. The Katz quotations are from "Some Call It Justice," by Harvey Katz, *Washingtonian,* September 1970. The Skeens case is reported as *U.S. v. Skeens,* 449 F2d 1066.

Page 324. " 'I guess I just got frustrated. . . .' " The *Washington Post,* Nov. 15, 1964.

Pages 326–327. The Mallory case is reported as *Mallory v. U.S.,* 354 US 449.

CHAPTER SEVEN

Judging the Judges

Page 332. " 'Get rid of the aged judges. . . .' " Hearings, "The Judicial Reform Act," subcommittee on improvements in judicial machinery of the Senate Judiciary Committee, June 1969.

Page 333. " '. . . far less culpable than others. . . .' " *Ibid.*

Page 334. The *Wall Street Journal* exposé was published May 2, 1963.

Page 335. " '. . . appearance of impropriety. . . .' " From *In His Own Image,* by James F. Simon, David McKay Company, New York, 1973.

Page 337. Judge Edwards' position on disqualification is told in his article, "Commentary on Judicial Ethics," *Fordham Law Review*, December 1969.

Page 337. The Rifkind comments are in hearings, "Non-judicial Activities of Supreme Court Justices and Other Federal Judges," subcommittee on separation of powers of the Senate Judiciary Committee, July and September 1969.

Page 338. The Woodrough anecdote is in the *Congressional Record,* September 20, 1973, p. S-17139.

Page 338. " 'He was blind and could not read. . . .' " Hearings, "The Judicial Reform Act."

Page 340. A good overview of Judge Ritter's handling of the El Paso Natural Gas Case is in "The Closed Enterprise System," edited by Mark J. Green, published by the Center for the Study of Responsive Law, June 1971 (preliminary draft).

Page 341. "In a 1971 drug trial. . . ." *U.S. v. Davis,* 442 F2d 1971.

Page 341. "In another case. . . ." *U.S. v. Peterson,* 456 F2d 1135.

Page 342. "For sheer judicial whiffleness, . . ." *U.S. et al v. Bill Hathaley et al,* 257 F2d 920.

Pages 343–344. The Segal anecdote is in hearings, "The Judicial Reform Act," before the subcommittee on improvements in judicial machinery of the Senate Judiciary Committee, April through July 1968.

Page 344. The Biggs anecdote on "involuntary retirement," *Ibid.*

Pages 348–349. The Hall testimony is in hearings, "The Independence of Federal Judges," subcommittee on separation of powers of the Senate Judiciary Committee, April and May 1970.

Page 349. " 'They have no authority to remove me. . . .' " Quoted in "The Case for Judicial Disciplinary Measures," by Marvin Frankel, 49 *Journal of the American Judiciature Society* 218, 1966.

Page 350. ". . .'inclined to abuse the use of alcohol. . . .' " "The Independence of Federal Judges."

Page 350. " '. . . suffered a drastic heart attack. . . .' " *Ibid.*

Page 352. " '. . . not in the glowing language. . . .' " *Ibid.*

Page 352. " 'The discomfort of being about. . . .' " *Ibid.*

Pages 354–355. The Tydings-Chambers exchanges are from hearings, "Federal Judges and Courts," subcommittee on improvements in judicial machinery of the Senate Judiciary Committee, April and May 1969.

Pages 355–361. Travels of the various judges are discussed in hearings, "The Omnibus Judgeship Bill," subcommittee on improvements of judicial machinery of the Senate Judiciary Committee, January through May 1973.

Page 358. " 'He complained about sitting. . . .' " "The Independence of Federal Judges."

Page 372. " 'They were cantankerous, . . .' " "The Place of the Federal Judicial Councils in the Administration of the Courts," by Judge J. Edward Lumbard, *American Bar Association Journal*, May 1961.

Page 374. Katz's comments on Judge Lewis are in his "Some Call It Justice," *Washingtonian*, September 1970.

Pages 377–378. The Garbus suit is described in *Ready for the Defense*, by Martin Garbus, Farrar, Straus & Giroux, New York, 1971.

Pages 379–380. Shaw's observations of Carr are in the *Los Angeles Times*, December 4, 1972.

Page 383. "The case involved the conviction of a securities dealer. . . ." *U.S. v. Carroll*, 326 F2d 72.

Page 384. "But listen to Carr ten years later, . . ." *U.S. v. Carrion*, 403 F2d 704.

Pages 387–389. A superb discussion of the Warren-Tydings attempts at judicial reform, including many of the draft proposals discussed in this chapter, along with judicial reaction, is in hearings, "The Judicial Reform Act," subcommittee on improvements in judicial machinery of the Senate Judiciary Committee, November 1969 and April 1970.

Page 388. " '. . . more of a beginning than an end." The *Washington Post*, June 13, 1969.

Page 389. " '. . . retreat from the bold stand. . . .' " The *Washington Post*, November 4, 1969.

Page 389. " '. . . myopia characterized by an inability. . . .' " The *Washington Post*, November 8, 1969.

Pages 390–391. The Brown-Jones disqualification is discussed in *The New York Times*, October 14 and 21, 1969.

Page 391. The Miller transaction is in *The New York Times*, March 19, 1970.

Page 392. ". . .'needless harassment, . . .' " Hearings, "The Independence of Federal Judges."

Pages 392–393. The Judicial Conference's varying approaches to a judicial ethics code are contained in proceedings for April 6–7 and October 26–27, 1972, and April 5–6 and September 13–14, 1973 (printed by the House Judiciary Committee, to which they were submitted).

Page 393. ". . . a logical solution. . . ." The *Minneapolis Tribune*, March 19, 1973.

Epilogue

Page 398. " '. . . guarantee that no outside influence. . . .' " Ervin testifying to the subcommittee on separation of powers,

Senate Judiciary Committee, hearings, "The Independence of Federal Judges," April and May 1970.

Pages 399–400. The Plamadon wiretap case is reported as *U.S. v. United States District Court, Eastern District of Michigan*, 321 F.Supp. 1074 and 444 F.2d 651.

Page 402. " '. . . constitution worshippers." "Secrecy and the Supreme Court," by Arthur S. Miller and D. S. Sastri, 22 *Buffalo Law Review* 799.

INDEX

Index